ADVANCE PRAISE FOR THE PSYCHOLOGY OF WORLD RELIGIONS AND SPIRITUALITIES

"If you want to understand major world religions, you have to read this indispensable volume. It takes a humble and indigenous approach to explaining the worldview of religions, embodying humble and culturally insider views. In this way it complements and, in many ways, surpasses an important but often limited scientific approach to understanding religions. Anyone interested in any religion should read and digest this germinal work."

—**ADAM COHEN, PHD,** professor of psychology, Arizona State University

"A book well worth having. Psychology of religion researchers have long recognized that scientific yields are limited unless more indigenous approaches are adopted. With this book, those words are now put into practice. Need to learn more psychology through Chinese or African traditional religions, or Hinduism, or North American Indigenous spirituality? How about Islam, Buddhism, Judaism, or Christianity? Get taught here by the insights of psychological researchers and scholars who themselves are religious insiders within the tradition presented. This one stays on my bookshelf within arm's reach."

—**PETER C. HILL, PHD,** Rosemead School of Psychology, Biola University

"After reading these descriptions by believers and sympathetic insiders of diverse indigenous religious traditions, any open-minded psychologist will recognize that a paradigm shift is imminent. Students and researchers alike will find that a genuine conversation with, and sharing of, other worldviews does not threaten but rather enriches us all."

—**RALPH W. HOOD JR., PHD,** professor of psychology and LeRoy A. Martin Distinguished Professor of Religious Studies, University of Tennessee at Chattanooga

"This is a tremendously important book. The editors have done an excellent job of addressing the most significant unresolved issue in the field of modern psychology—that of its antagonistic relationship with religion and spirituality. They provide a thoughtful analysis, make recommendations for conceptual and applied ways forward, and present what a variety of religious and spiritual psychologies look like in today's world. This should be mandatory reading in every single psychology class everywhere. An absolute must-have text for anyone interested in any subfield of psychology or the intersection of psychology and religion."

—**CARRIE YORK AL-KARAM, PHD,** president, Alkaram Institute

"Increasingly, mental health workers are treating clients whose backgrounds span the world's faith traditions. To successfully address such diversity, practitioners must have a comprehensive and respectful understanding of the belief systems that animate religious observers from all walks of life. This indispensable text is the resource they need. Wise, thorough, and compassionate, it is a major contribution to the psychological study of religion."

—**HAROLD G. KOENIG, MD,** professor of psychiatry and behavioral sciences, Duke University Health Systems, and director of Duke's Center for Spirituality, Theology and Health

"This book is fascinating. By covering a range of assumptive frameworks, it gives insider perspectives on mental health and healing from different faith traditions. It also encourages us to examine some of our own Western assumptions and understand the prominence of spirituality in nearly all indigenous psychologies."

—**KATE LOEWENTHAL, PHD,** Emeritus Professor of Psychology, Royal Holloway University of London, and visiting professor at Glyndwr University, Wales, and New York University in London

"An amazing and timely work providing an emic perspective on religious and spiritual psychology. The authors have challenged the limitations of methodology and provided a psychological perspective on each religion from the 'inside,' while acknowledging that it is but one of many perspectives within the religion. The authors must be lauded for their expertise and the humility with which they have presented their material. A true masterpiece which will help advance dialogue not just in the psychology of religion and spirituality but in the field of psychology and its applications."

—**SONIA SUCHDAY, PHD,** Professor and Chair, Psychology Department, Pace University

"Such a timely resource that incorporates world religion into understanding human psychology. The various chapters provide profound insights and understanding of the psychology of different faiths from insiders' perspectives, which makes *The Psychology of World Religions and Spiritualities* an excellent resource for researchers, clinicians, and students! A wonderful book for readers to understand, digest, and contrast the rich diversity of world religions."

—**KENNETH T. WANG, PHD,** professor and PhD Program Chair, Clinical Psychology, Fuller Theological Seminary

THE PSYCHOLOGY
OF WORLD RELIGIONS AND
SPIRITUALITIES

THE PSYCHOLOGY
OF WORLD RELIGIONS AND
SPIRITUALITIES

AN INDIGENOUS PERSPECTIVE

Edited by Timothy A. Sisemore

and Joshua J. Knabb

TEMPLETON PRESS

Templeton Press
300 Conshohocken State Road, Suite 500
West Conshohocken, PA 19428
www.templetonpress.org

Set in Athelas and Mr. Eaves Sans by Kachergis Book Design

Library of Congress Control Number: 2020937028
ISBN: 978-1-59947-576-9 (cloth: alk. paper)
ISBN: 978-59947-595-0 (pbk: alk. paper)
ISBN: 978-1-59947-577-6 (ebook)

This paper meets the requirements of ANSI/NISO Z39.48-1992
(Permanence of Paper).

A catalog record for this book is available from the Library of Congress.

21 22 23 24 25   10 9 8 7 6 5 4 3 2 1

Printed in the United States of America.

To the memory of P. J. "Paul" Watson: professor, scholar, psychologist of religion, mentor, friend, and role model. You embodied the best of being human.—*TAS*

———————

This book is dedicated to my wife, Adrienne, who regularly lends me her ear to talk about all things transcendent.—*JJK*

CONTENTS

Foreword   ix

LOUISE SUNDARARAJAN

Part 1
Conceptualizing Religions
for Western Psychology

Seeing Religions and Spiritualities from the Inside:
Problems for Western Psychology That Can Be
Addressed with an Indigenous Psychological Perspective   3

TIMOTHY A. SISEMORE AND JOSHUA J. KNABB

Indigenous Psychologies of Spirituality: Remembering,
Excavating, and Individuating   29

AL DUECK

Part 2
Religious and Spiritual Psychologies
through an Indigenous Lens

I Created the Evil Inclination and I Created Torah Its
Antidote: An Indigenous Jewish Psychology   59

STEVEN PIRUTINSKY

Walking Home with God: Toward an Indigenous
Christian Psychology   85

JOSHUA J. KNABB AND M. TODD BATES

An Overview of an Islam-Based Psychology   117

SAYYED MOHSEN FATEMI

An Indigenous Perspective on Buddhism   137

KIN CHEUNG (GEORGE) LEE AND CHUN FAI (JEFFREY) NG

Psychology of Hinduism from the Inside Out   165
DOUG OMAN AND ANAND C. PARANJPE

Psychology of North American Indigenous Spirituality   197
JACQUELINE S. GRAY

Chinese Traditional Religions and Mental Health:
An Indigenous Psychology Perspective   237
RACHEL SING-KIAT TING, SIEW-CHUNG MAH,
AND KEJIA ZHANG

African Traditional Religion and Psychology
of Religion   263
INNOCENT F. OKOZI

Conclusion   285
JOSHUA J. KNABB AND TIMOTHY A. SISEMORE

Acknowledgments   303

About the Editors   305

About the Contributors   307

Index   311

FOREWORD

With this edited volume on the indigenous psychology of religions, Timothy Sisemore and Joshua Knabb are breaking new ground in the field. In contrast to the scene of indigenous psychology (IP), in which the IP status of Western mainstream psychology is still being debated, the psychologies of Christianity and Judaism—religious traditions that constitute the building blocks of Western culture—have joined the ranks of the indigenous psychologies of world religions. This is a big step forward toward a more equalitarian community of global psychology (see Pe-Pua, in press).

The contributors generally agree that mainstream psychology of religion impedes the development of a psychology that aspires to capture more fully the religious scene of humankind. The permission granted in this volume for free expression of religiosity does much to foster the delightfully unique styles and panache with which each contributor presents a particular religious tradition. The result is a rich tapestry of religious diversity, a mosaic of religious traditions based on the insider's experience. Before I go over the insider's unique contributions to psychology of religion, I would like to start with a few caveats.

DEMYSTIFYING THE INSIDER'S PERSPECTIVE

The insider does not necessarily know best (see Sundararajan, 2019). Depending on the depth of insight and breadth of knowledge, some insiders may know better than other insiders, but the insider's role or identity itself is no guarantee of quality or validity of knowledge. It is safe to say that the insider and the outsider point to each other's lacunae in knowledge, such that neither is sufficient in and of itself.

Another caveat of the insider's perspective is homogenization. The insider tends to give a homogenized account of her religious traditions, which are intrinsically heterogeneous. Along this line, the believer's perspective constitutes only one of the possibilities of being an insider of a tradition. This has practical implications for the clinician. Do not assume that the client in front of you subscribes to everything you have read about her tradition, since the insider has a full range of possibilities, as adumbrated by the anthropologist Edward Sapir (1924):

Those ... of us who take their culture neither as knowledge nor as manner, but as life, will ask of the past not so much "what?" and "when?" and "where?" as "how?" and the accent of their "how" will be modulated in accordance with the needs of the spirit of each, a spirit that is free to glorify, to transform, and to reject. (p. 423)

UNIQUE CONTRIBUTIONS OF THE
BELIEVER'S PERSPECTIVE

Mostly authored by adherents of religious traditions, this edited volume is a treasure trove of local, that is, indigenous, categories. This constitutes a major contribution to psychology of religion in many ways. First, local categories of religion can be used to test the universality of conventional psychological concepts (Sundararajan, 2015). For instance, the standard notion of religion in terms of a trajectory marked by points of entry (conversion) and exit (deconversion) is not universally applicable. For many non-Western traditions, religion is a way of life, a tradition that one is born into, and from which there is normally no exit. This has implications for theory and research. Most of the standard measures in the field are based on the notion of religion as a matter of choice, thereby obliterating the distinction between institutionalized and diffused religions (see Ting et al., this volume)—only the former, not the latter, factors in choice.

The contributors have made it amply clear that religious categories in general do not readily fit the secular, scientific framework in psychology of religion. Take for instance the possibility that a person is not atomic but rather composed of layers of being, or that life in the present body is only one of the many permutations of a soul that spans multiple lifetimes. Asking someone with this type of orientation to focus on the here and now as the only reality of consequence is akin to forcing an astronomer to abandon her interest in the galaxies to become an accountant. Such a shift of framework entails a drastic reduction in dimension and scale of the human as *homo religious*, yet this is routinely done in psychology of religion. For instance, when we measure the health "benefits" of faith, we have cast the spiritual yearnings of the believer in the framework of instrumental rationality. Similarly when we reduce love for God to attachment styles, we fail to address the question of why humans have such passion for the transcendent in the first place.

In the final analysis, the insider's story broadens the horizon of the psychology of religion by posing the more fundamental question: What makes us human? Consider the following dialogue between the first human and the Raven, according to the creation myth of the Yup'ik People (Dalton, 1999):

"What am I doing here?"
"You are here to be," Raven said.

The story goes on to show that one of the hallmarks of being human is to question the ground of one's being. Put another way, the being of a human being is never taken for granted. Furthermore, there seems to be a need to ground our being in something beyond what is readily available in the world of facticity. This point is best articulated by an Islamic analogy, in the words of Fatemi: "beings operate as prepositional modes: A preposition loses its sense of being the moment it is placed outside a sentence" (this volume).

This analogy sheds some light on the power of a religious tradition in which believers may feel at home like prepositions functioning properly in a well-constructed sentence. Conversely, people who are displaced in a foreign context—for instance, migrants—may feel useless, like prepositions without a sentence. In sum, the hallmark of our being human lies in the question we raise about the ground of our being. The world's religions constitute answers from various cultures to this fundamental question. By taking an inventory of these answers, this volume opens up multiple new possibilities in the psychology of religion.

First, when we take an inventory of world religions, we see more clearly the questions and concerns that reverberate throughout the ages across cultures and populations. This invites investigation of the social-cultural consequences of the answers to these universal questions. For instance, where does life come from? Many creation myths are attempts to tackle this question, with answers ranging from ancestors and mythical animals to the creator God. What are the social-historical consequences of these answers? For another example, is God singular or plural? Now that we have a well-conducted study of the far-reaching social and cultural consequences of monotheism (Norenzayan, 2013), a comparable study of the consequences of polytheism would be an imperative next step for the psychology of religion.

Second, answers from religious traditions are among the most useful tools we have in meeting the challenges posed by the twenty-first century. For instance, throughout history different religions have advocated for the supremacy of the heart (Islam), of awareness (Hinduism, Buddhism), of kinship-based relations (reverence for the ancestor), or of cosmic unity (animism), but the supremacy claim of the intellect has prevailed in the secular age of modernity. The unbridled cognitive supremacy has given us unprecedented advances in science and technology, and also an escalating global crisis in the destruction of the biosphere, the loss of bio- and cultural diversity, and the widening gap between the haves and have-nots. As we teeter on the edge of this global crisis, we may need to regain our balance by keeping open other dimensions of being human above and beyond the dazzling purchase of the intellect.

On a less grand and more practical level, this volume is a valuable resource for clinicians in their endeavor to restore a culturally displaced client to her rightful site of being. It can also be a source of inspiration for anyone interested in the possibility of a genuine world peace. To get a glimpse of this possibility, let us go back to the dialogue between the first human and the Raven, as told in the creation myth of the Yup'ik People (Dalton, 1999):

The Raven told the inquisitive creature (the first human): "You are here to be."
    "Be what?" the creature asked.
    "To be yourself," Raven replied.
    "Who am I?" the creature asked.

Now we are on familiar ground: This is the question we ask ourselves all the time. We also know the conventional answers to this question: I am a lawyer, doctor, parent, student, Chinese, Baptist, and so on. But Raven's answer is different—it takes us beyond all identities of ethnicity, culture, and religion:

You are a human being. Human is your form, the part of you which looks the way it does and moves in the way it moves. It is the physical part of who you are, but it is not all of you. By asking who you were, you showed that you know you are more than your form, more than just the physical. This something more is the being. It is your beingness that makes you different, makes you special. (see Gray, pp. 226–227, this volume)

Religious discourse such as this may open up the possibility of grounding world peace on something that all religions share in common, namely the question: What makes us human?

Enough said. Wherever you are heading as you journey through the twenty-first century, I think you will be glad to have packed this book with you.

Louise Sundararajan
Rochester, New York

REFERENCES

Dalton, J. (1999). The creation legend of the Yup'ik People: When Raven met the first human being. http://www.angelfire.com/bc/yupik/create.html (accessed March 12, 2020).

Norenzayan, A. (2013). *Big gods: How religion transformed cooperation and conflict.* Princeton, NJ: Princeton University Press.

Pe-Pua, R. (in press). "From indigenous psychologies to cross-indigenous psychology—Prospects for a 'genuine, global human psychology.'" In L. Sundararajan, K. Hwang, & K. Yeh (eds.), *Global psychology from indigenous perspectives: Visions inspired by K. S. Yang.* Palgrave Studies in Indigenous Psychology Series. New York: Springer Nature.

Sapir, E. (1924). Culture, genuine and spurious. *American Journal of Sociology, 29,* 401–429.

Sundararajan, L. (2015). Indigenous psychology: Grounding science in culture, why and how? *Journal for the Theory of Social Behavior,* special issue on indigenous psychology, *45,* 64–81. DOI: 10.1111/jtsb.12054

Sundararajan, L. (2019). Whither indigenous psychology? *Journal of Theoretical and Philosophical Psychology, 39,* 81–89.

PART 1

CONCEPTUALIZING RELIGIONS FOR WESTERN PSYCHOLOGY

TIMOTHY A. SISEMORE AND
JOSHUA J. KNABB

SEEING RELIGIONS AND SPIRITUALITIES FROM THE INSIDE

Problems for Western Psychology That Can Be Addressed with an Indigenous Psychological Perspective

Modern technology is wonderful. Having just moved to a new part of the United States, I am frequently trying to find new places. (First-person singular references ["I," "me"] in this chapter are to Timothy Sisemore.) Modern science makes this easier than ever as I simply dictate my destination to my trusty phone, and it tells me how to get there. While not infallible, the technology is accurate and dependable. In its place, science is a boon to contemporary society.

But my phone has limits. While it will navigate me from place to place based on detailed maps and access to satellites, it is quite useless when it comes to telling me where I want to go. Even more so, it is useless in telling me *why* I want to get there. If I ask my phone to tell me where I should go, what I should do, or the meaning of the places to which I travel, I ask in vain. These questions are beyond the responses of what a navigation system is designed to offer.

Psychology as a science faces similar limitations. As a discipline it has helped us gain considerable insight into human behavior, from methods designed to peek into the unseen recesses of our minds to a better ability to understand and predict behavior. Science has even given us considerable insight into religious and spiritual behavior and thinking.[1] But the science of psychology is limited when it interprets what is it like to be a person of faith, or to act within a specific cultural context, and can lose perspective on its limitations and overreach its area of competence.

This is seen, as beautifully explained by Dueck in the chapter that follows, when psychology tries to study other cultures scientifically. It can lose its sense of boundaries and actually colonize other cultures when it strives to pursue a global understanding of local psychological functioning. After all, science is a Western way of knowing, and Western psychology views others through its methods shaped by efforts to be objective and agnostic. Indigenous psychology (IP) arose in response to this, arguing that people and people groups should be viewed from within their categories and concepts and not squeezed into the categorical boxes of Western psychology. To state it differently, psychologists have often utilized an *etic*, outsider, "top-down" approach to studying psychological phenomena, employing purely secular theories that are divorced from the very populations they strive to empirically investigate (Kim, Park, & Park, 2000, p. 66).[2]

This Western strategy becomes even more problematic when we try to look at religions and spiritualities. If science struggles to understand human cultures, it will have an even more difficult time grasping the nature of beliefs in the transcendent that mark most cultures. When psychologists encounter groups that believe something other than science provides an epistemology, be it a divine being, spirit, ancestors, or tradition, they tend to colonize these "backward" beliefs; a solid indigenous approach seeks to learn and understand from these. For example, Christianity values humility and meekness, yet psychology has pathologized that at times to assert that Christians lack "self-esteem," for that is the Western value at present (Watson et al., 2003). With this approach, "indigenous knowledge" is viewed as a legitimate foundation for conceptualizing religion and spirituality, rather than merely "auxiliary" to the secular assumptions of Western psychological theories (Kim et al., 2000, p. 65; Kim, Yang, & Hwang, 2006).

INTENTION FOR THIS BOOK

An indigenous approach to understanding all peoples is at the heart of this volume. We have compiled this collection to be a one-stop resource for a thorough orientation to religious and spiritual diversity, covering the major religions and spiritualities as presented from within the cultural framework of such faiths by persons who also are familiar with scientific psychology. The reader thus receives these summaries from a perspective that can be understood by a student of Western psychology, yet spoken in a way amenable to these indigenous faiths. It is an exploration of the psychology of religions and spiritualities that is broken down by religion (not topics) and intentionally gives equal voice to the various faiths (whereas most psychology of religion books built solely on research are imbalanced in favor of Christianity, which has received by far the most scholarly attention—itself a reflection of the Western bias in science). This book also summarizes the available psychological science for each faith system while giving the indigenous context to fill in the areas lacking current research.

Moreover, this book also offers Western psychological scientists ways to better understand the "ideological surround" (Watson et al., 2003) of religious groups and individuals so that Western constructs are not inappropriately forced, like square pegs into round holes, onto indigenous groups. This sets the stage for a more accurate understanding of the groups and better approaches to research these groups while also making a case for the inadequacies of scientism (the overreaching of scientific methods) as a way of understanding them.

Overall, we offer an introduction to the psychologies of religion and spirituality for specific groups, spoken from an inside perspective, and incorporate the current research while opening doors for further and more appropriate research. Here, it is important to mention that the authors or coauthors writing from within each faith system offer one of many possible interpretations. Given that there is no way to fully capture the lived experience of billions of people from around the world, no one indigenous perspective exists for each world religion or spirituality. Rather, our hope is that these insider discussions will serve as a catalyst for subsequent theory building and research from an *emic* perspective, recognizing that the vast array of diverse indigenous perspectives from around the world can deepen our understanding of the psychology of the human experience.

We wrote this book with three audiences in mind. The primary audience is psychologists and other mental health professionals seeking to gain a working multicultural knowledge of the psychology of the major world religions. These include psychologists and others in practice and in training, as well as the broader group of psychologists in nonclinical settings desiring to be more competent in this field. This volume is also for graduate students to receive a scientifically founded yet culturally sophisticated perspective on persons of faith and thus gain more knowledge in this area. Even undergraduate students can benefit from this work as a cultural resource. Third, this book is written for researchers who may be drawn to a fresh perspective on ways to study faith groups and believing individuals. Finally, this book should find an audience in students of religion in seminaries and other religiously oriented schools, hopefully springboarding a discussion on viewing religions with more care.

PROBLEMS, SOLUTIONS, AND LOOKING AHEAD

For this initial chapter, we examine some of the problems science—particularly psychological science—must address. Like a car's navigation system, science must concede its limitations but, moving beyond that metaphor, also learn to adapt to better understand the majority of humans who believe in some sense of the transcendent. We briefly trace a history of how science supplanted religious ways of knowing, then consider in detail the limitations of Western psychological science as a way of knowing. Then we survey some approaches to IP that may help bridge this gap and lead psychology to a better understanding of the beliefs, thoughts, actions, and cultures shaped by shared views of the transcendent. We conclude with some clinical implications of this shift in method, framing the following chapters that detail how this applies to some of the world's major religious and spiritual groups.

A BRIEF HISTORY OF THE RISE OF SCIENCE

Western science is a relative newcomer as a way of knowing. For most of history up until some 500 years ago, the world was "enchanted" (Taylor, 2007). A realm of the spiritual crossed the boundary into our everyday lives and influenced us. Most people assumed that this enchanted dimension had to be reckoned with if we were to truly understand the way the world really was, and many assumed that the transcendent not only existed but interacted with the material in a variety of ways, such as by revealing itself into the world. Thus, the three major monotheisms—Judaism, Christianity, and Islam—are built on the belief that a transcendent God has spoken into our world, and these faiths draw knowledge from the supernatural. Other faiths and spiritualties have other views on how the transcendent enters the mundane.

In the West, Christianity dominated culture for centuries. Its authoritative text, the Bible, was seen as the primary source of truth and knowledge, with the study of it, theology, being coined the "queen of the sciences" due to its examining God's revelation to humanity. *Science* itself was a term used consistently with its original meaning of "knowledge" until the nineteenth century, being applied to any area of knowing. It then came to refer to natural science, or the knowledge of nature, and then to mean science as specifically empirical science (Hutchinson, 2011).

As has been well documented (particularly in the work of Taylor, 2007), the Enlightenment effectively dethroned knowledge as in any sense determined by anything outside ourselves, at least in most of the West, and operated on the idea that we do not need "enchantment" to understand and master the universe. Science arose in the humanistic environment of the Enlightenment, donning a methodology that was committed only to the observable and measurable in an effort to objectify knowledge apart from a belief in enchantment. This new naturalistic methodology would bring about unprecedented progress in technology and multiply knowledge in the physical sciences, revolutionizing industry and even health care.

The areas of science's impact were largely physical—understanding how the elements of the world act and interact. Emboldened by this success, proponents of the new, empirical, and agnostic methodology set their sights on other areas. Psychology came into view around the turn of the twentieth century (Lamiell, 2018). No less a psychologist than Wilhelm Wundt (2013) expressed concern with the shift of psychology away from philosophy and toward science as it would divorce the empirical from the metaphysical. To borrow again from Taylor (2007), psychology became disenchanted. This became a move into what Lamiell (2018) has called "statisticism," the effort to explain human experience and psychological functioning by numbers, based on the assumption of science that human psychology can be known in the same way that we know how water boils. The drive for psychology to be deemed an objective science and thus earn respect meant that other approaches to knowing how persons think, feel, and act were essentially abandoned in service to empiricism. Over the past century, statistics have become more and more sophisticated, while it seems we languish in the genuine understanding of human nature. Yet only a few (e.g., Gantt & Williams, 2018; Polanyi, 1962) have challenged its orthodoxy and authority.

A position of holding science as essentially *the* way of knowing has led to a place where the method itself supplants religion. While those of the enchanted world had religions that were the source of knowledge, science became its own religion in a sense, one that has been called "scientism" (Williams & Gantt, 2018, p. 6). Scientism is the pushing of Enlightenment science beyond its bounds, with the intent of revealing our own humanity to ourselves and the hope of this understanding leading to a solution to our problems as a species. "The key aspect of religious conviction that scientism shares with most organized religions is that it offers a comprehensive principle or belief, which itself cannot be proved (certainly not scientifically proved) but which serves to organize our understanding and guide our actions (Hutchison, 2011, loc. 113).

The survey of this problem in Gantt and Williams (2018) is summarized by Wertz (2018). Scientism excludes mental life from the scope of science, as it is ultimately not observable or measurable (despite attempts to infer mental life from data). Moving beyond scientism will require seeing science as its own project having "teleology, meaning, emotions, values, and communal practices," which embraces "humility, egalitarian openness, and accountability rather than assumed superiority in relationship to humanities, the arts, professional expertise, and personal experience" (Wertz, 2018, p. 110). We touch on several of these points again later in this chapter.

We would add to this that science's Western heritage also leaves it ill equipped to consider other cultures of people who do not share its presuppositions and values, points that we see in Dueck's comments in Chapter 2.

The key issue of science's role in how we understand the transcendent is that the disenchanted scientist is required to understand the enchanted realm with only the tools of disenchantment available. While important information has come from the psychological study of religion, this fundamental disconnect is prohibitive of genuinely understanding human spiritual life and its encounter with the transcendent.

THE CHALLENGE OF SCIENCE IN CONSIDERING RELIGION AND SPIRITUALITY: EPISTEMOLOGY

Science operates on the assumptions that only the observable and measurable can be studied, given its presumption that only objective knowledge that can be corroborated is permitted into the discussion of what is real. Science peels back the subjective aspects of humans attending to nature as best it can, leaving the (virtually) raw data of nature to be comprehended, and in so doing, rendered more useful for human thriving. Ultimately, science prioritizes empiricism above all other epistemologies.

This method of objective observation has been applied to religion since early in the history of psychology. William James (1902/1985) produced what was in many ways the seminal work in the field as he attempted to describe and explain some of the more colorful types of religious experience. Despite his being somewhat sympathetic, his survey was largely lacking in grasping what the experience was like *for the person*, given the etic perspective of science that he used. While he brings us some insight into these experiences, what we learn is not from within the person's experience, but as an outside observer not privy to the nonempirical facets of the experience.

In the ensuing years, the psychology of religion has continued the trend of trying to understand human religious and spiritual experience, but largely from the outside in, consistent with an empirical approach.

In my (Sisemore, 2015) extensive review of this literature, an impressive amount of information is helpful. The important distinction between intrinsic and extrinsic religiosity is an example, as is the insight into spiritual struggle. But the research ultimately falls short of grasping the lived experience of persons of faith. The situation is further complicated when one considers how some of the scholars who have studied religion have had the ulterior motive of dismissing it, proudly looking down at persons who believe from the new faith of scientism that "knows better." Yet others have approached the study of religion to prove religion true, and while much is covered in my review about the positive aspects of believing, this still falls short of apprehending the nature of faith in the lives of humans.

Science is incredibly important and useful, yet it is not equipped to give us direction for our lives—a *telos* toward which we move—though many draw this from their faith in an enchanted world. We turn now to consider some of the challenges science faces in studying religion and spirituality.

FOUR PROBLEMS

We focus here on four problems with empirical science, and psychological science in particular, that impair its ability as an epistemology to provide accurate and truly useful information about religious and spiritual persons and groups.

SOCIAL ISOLATION. Empirical science is a product of Western philosophy via the Enlightenment yet purports to be universal in reach and application. That works well in the physical sciences, for oxygen is oxygen wherever you go. Granite is granite. A pancreas is a pancreas. An electron is an electron. People are not all the same psychologically, however, and people in the West are not like people in other parts of the world. The people who dominate the academy in the West are shaped by the agnosticism (if not atheism) of the scientific method. That assumption shapes a common worldview for scientists but may not jive with the perspectives and beliefs of many peoples of the world.

These suppositions in turn isolate science to the West. Many indigenous ways of knowing do not fit the scientific approach, and these are not easily studied from Western science. Thus we risk being deceived by science's universality in the physical world to believe it is an adequate method to study all the world's people as though they are the same. Clearly people are different, and as Western psychological science attempts to broaden its horizons past its preoccupation with American college freshmen, it must concede there need to be adaptions and accommodations to its methodology when examining those outside its social milieu, and even more so when attempting to address the transcendent.

PERSONAL KNOWLEDGE. Leaving aside for the moment the challenges science faces in moving beyond its cultural context, science qua science is not as objective as it might want to believe. We are indebted to Michal Polanyi (1962; this discussion follows the comparable section in Sisemore, 2018a), who boldly asserts his intention is "to show that complete objectivity as usually attributed to the exact sciences is a delusion and is in fact a false ideal" (Polanyi, 1962, p 18). Notice he takes aim at the "exact sciences," so his critique is even more applicable to the "less exact" science of the psychology of religion and spirituality. For example, emotion moves us to choose topics of study and even impacts how we frame the questions that we ask. The study of religion is rife with this problem, with prejudices of those seeking to use science to prove religion and, very often, those who endeavor to use science to disprove religionists. Either way, the study can be far from neutral.

Scientific explanation has to break down information into bits and then impose an interpretation on it post hoc, which creates more problems. For example, one can observe a person riding a bicycle and describe their efforts and actions as they move. The observer can survey them on how they felt while riding the bicycle. But whatever the observer concludes will still fall short of understanding the full experience of riding a bicycle and thus be subject to that person's own "take" on the data. One's personal inclinations supplant the actual experience of riding a bicycle.

Part of the problem of interpretation is in its dependence on language to describe experience. All of us know that words often fail us, particularly in those most ineffable moments of life. Yet religion and spirituality are plentiful with appeals to the mystical nature of experience that cannot be expressed in words. Language fails us as we try to explain such experiences.

Polanyi (1962) used three "*I*"s to summarize the language problem in science. First, language is inherently *interpersonal* and so must resonate with the person for whom it is intended. As I write this, I assume the reader speaks English even as I am conscious of the fact that English lacks nuances found in other languages. The study of ancient spiritual texts scuffles with this issue: How do we differentiate how certain words were used in the original context versus how we use them today? Nuance is lost. How, then, do we study religions intelligently if we have no regard for their language and constructs?

Second, science is *impassioned*. As observed earlier, science begins with a curiosity about its subject and often a motive to prove something that has emotional value to the scientist, commonly being a drive to reduce anxiety associated with not understanding something. This can be key in the scientific study of religion—going back to William James (1902/1985), who was fascinated by unusual religious experiences as he sought to find explanations for them.

Third, language is *imprecise*. The first two "*I*"s ensure that what we know will never be precise. Especially in studies in psychology, we aim for the $p < .05$ outcome, but that is a probability and by no means precise. Even if it were, it is shaped by the subjectivities of the experimenters.

The role of personal knowledge in science leads scientists to explore "a vision of reality, to which our sense of scientific beauty responds" and thus suggests "to us the kind of questions that it should be reasonable and interesting to explore" (Polanyi, 1962, p. 135). What is beautiful from this scientific perspective may miss the beauty as perceived by other subjects. For example, James's (1902/1985) fascination with religious experiences seeks a beauty in explaining them, often a far cry from the beauty of those who experienced them in the context of their religious meaning system.

THEORY CONSTRUCTION AND THE HYPOTHETICO-DEDUCTIVE METHOD. Somewhat related to the previous problem, much of scientific psychology relies on a hypothetico-deductive approach to research, starting with a theoretical understanding of the psychological phenomenon of interest, followed by the generation of study hypotheses and collection of data via empirical observation (Haig, 2018). These theories within the psychological sciences, to be sure, are meant to explain the world, offering a "blueprint" for understanding and testing the relationship between variables (Rosenthal & Rosnow, 2008). Therefore, prior to observing a psychological phenomenon, we must have some sort of theoretical understanding of what we are going to examine (Farrell, 2014). Yet this very theoretical knowledge is supposed to come from observation, leading to the problem of circularity—theory comes from observation and observation comes from theory.

Interestingly, many of the most popular theories in personality psychology seem to (at least in part) come from the lived experiences of the supposedly neutral theorists. For example, in *Faces in a Cloud*, the psychoanalytic authors George Atwood and Robert Stolorow (1993) argued the following:

The ultimate aim of personality theory is to arrive at comprehensive principles to account for human experience and human conduct. But the empirical phenomena of the human world present themselves differently according to the perspective of the observer. The particularity of the psychological context from which the personality theorist views reality guarantees that his [sic] interpretations will be focused on selected features of the empirical field, and that the specific dimensions of human conduct bearing a correspondence to his [sic] own pretheoretical vision of man [sic] will be magnified in his [sic] eventual theoretical constructions. (p. 10)

In this important work, the authors explored the ways in which personality theorists' subjective life experiences shaped the grand theories they attempted to build and project onto the world. The highly subjective nature of theory building, then, seems to beg a fundamental question—if secular psychologists can start with their own lived psychological experience to build a theoretical understanding of the human condition and use the scientific method to empirically confirm a set of operationalized variables within such a theoretical understanding, why cannot indigenous religious groups do the same by drawing upon their own lived experiences (and sacred texts) as a starting point for subsequent empirical observation (Pankalla & Kosnik, 2018)?

A PRIVILEGED EPISTEMOLOGY. Concurrent with the rise of science in the Enlightenment and an overreliance on the hypothetico-deductive method to the current day, there has been an increased secularization of Western society and the loss of enchantment mentioned above. Postmodernism, with its skepticism about the very possibility of objective knowledge, has only served to move science into a more entrenched posture regarding epistemology. In an unenchanted world, if we give up science, we run the risk of having no basis for knowing other than our own subjectivity.

Science is thus the sole hope for knowledge in the West. As it touts its successes in many areas, it expands its reach. In so doing, science becomes the privileged epistemology, with empiricism being the way of knowing accepted as the only one in the secularized West. It expects all people to submit to its models and methods, and for others to be seen only in the light of its worldview.

Here is common ground for religious and spiritual persons in the West and similar persons and groups around the world. They share the notion that there are ways of knowing outside of science and naturalism. These ways of knowing permeate their views of the world and shape their understanding and their very psychology. This exposes the point of tension in the psychology of religion and spirituality: believers studied by a methodological atheism (Watson, 2019).

The privileged epistemology of science also shows up in the efforts to find a scientific basis for morality. Hunter and Nedelisky (2018) traced the quest of science to address morality and determine right and wrong. This also is a field historically populated by theology and philosophy, but recently infiltrated by a variety of scientists, evolutionary and others, who have sought out the roots of morality and even to determine what the moral is. In other words, science then tries to move from describing what is to what ought to be. Their careful critique concludes the following:

It seems fair to say that much of the current science of morality is no longer really a science of *morality*. Instead, part and parcel with the metaphysics of philosophical naturalism, the bulk of the new moral scientists do not think there is any such phenomenon as morality, as traditionally conceived. (p. 196; emphasis in original)

Here again science confronts indigenous ways of knowing. Most cultures have determined morality from other sources, be it divine revelation, guidance of the spirits, or tradition. Science is clearly out of its element in claiming it can derive the "ought" of life based on its methodologies.

This overreach leads it to attempt to colonize spiritually minded peoples into its methodological atheism. This is already a tense area for people of faith in communities in the West with a shift in morality based on spiritual traditions to one based on humanism. Science tries to give authority to the latter, but fails because it is trying to do what it is not intended to do. To retrieve our opening metaphor, science now tries to tell us where to go, not just the most efficient route to get us there.

This need not be. Science can inform us of the ways of religious and spiritual groups by adapting its methods and empathizing with the adherents. Hood (summarized in Hood & Williamson, 2008) has spent much of his long career learning of serpent-handling groups, religiously motivated communities who act on faith to fulfill a promise they attribute to Jesus, who stated they could safely pick up serpents by faith.[3] In his work, Hood earned the trust of these often-reclusive groups and was welcomed into their rituals even as he sought to adapt scientific methodology to understand them. He did not go to judge or change them. If anything, he went to better understand and give them a voice through his research. Here is a model for an indigenous psychology of religion, honoring those studied, taking an emic approach, and adapting empirical methods to do so.

Reiterating a vital point, science is of great value, and nothing in this chapter intends to deny that or diminish its importance. Yet it easily oversteps its bounds and takes on the characteristics of a religion, impairing its ability to provide accurate and useful knowledge about many topics, including the psychology of religion and spirituality.

CONSEQUENCES OF THE OVERREACH OF SCIENCE

Science's failure to stay within its purview and to acknowledge its imperfections and limitations has consequences when it attempts to study religious and spiritual groups. We consider a few here.

"RELIGIOUS GLOSS." In other areas of diversity, *gloss* refers to a stereotyping of all people of a certain type into a specific category, oblivious to subtle differences. In the psychology of religion, this is the erroneous assumption that all faiths are essentially the same and that constructs that apply to one will apply to others (based in part on the notion that the spiritual is not real, they are merely various manifestations of the same psychological construct). I encountered this when my colleagues and I (Bufford, Sisemore, & Blackburn, 2017) developed a scale to assess the nature and import of the Christian construct of the grace of God. One reviewer of the article suggested it was of value only if it applied to other religions and not just Christianity. This is an example of religious gloss. If only constructs true across all religions can be published, we will miss out on much we need to know.

COLONIZATION. This term, of course, comes from the notion of moving in among an indigenous people and establishing control over them. This might involve imposing language and customs. Colonization is an apt description of what science, if left unchecked, will do to indigenous religious groups. Here again scientism can act like a religion, with scientists as missionaries going to religious peoples with the intent to explain away their beliefs and customs and to replace them with a superior scientific worldview. For example, prayer does not serve to approach the divine so much as to produce positive psychological effects in the pray-er. Scholars who study religion do well to assess themselves as to hidden motives, agendas, and biases when applying science to religious groups. Polanyi (1962) acknowledged we have our motives when we scientifically study something; yet minimally we should be self-aware and be good enough scientists as to endeavor not to be biased, nor to seek to colonize the groups we explore.

HUBRIS. Science, when it becomes scientism, becomes too proud of itself. As helpful as empiricism is as a way of knowing, when applied to understanding the psychology of persons, it provides knowledge that at best is asymptotic. That is, carefully conducted, science can get closer and closer to an accurate understanding of spiritualities, but it will never reach a perfect understanding. Given that, science does well to approach others humbly with an openness to the value of other ways of knowing and of forming morality and community.

One can appreciate the scientific humility of the popular science book *We Have No Idea* (Chan & Whiteson, 2017), wherein the authors admitted that we know something about only 5 percent of the universe, leaving 95 percent to mystery. To be honest, as psychologists of religion, we probably do not know more than 5 percent about the peoples we study. How much better would our efforts be if we approached these groups with due humility and openness to learn.

BIASES AND MICROAGGRESSIONS. All of this adds up to science often being biased when it studies persons of faith, possibly even displaying microaggressions (e.g., microinsults and microinvalidations; Sue et al. 2007) toward religion and spirituality in the psychology literature. For example, some authors may engage in (a) microinsults when they generate study hypotheses that religion and spirituality will be linked to psychopathology and express surprise when their results do not confirm their expectations, or (b) microinvalidations when they either develop theories that suggest the purpose (or *teleology*) of religion is to merely function as a stepping-stone toward mental health (Slife & Reber, 2012) or solely pursue an etic understanding of the psychology of religion with global measures that combine all religious groups together. With the former, a "subtle snub, frequently unknown to the perpetrator, but clearly convey[ing] a hidden insulting message to the recipient" (Sue et al., 2017, p. 274) may arise, reminiscent of someone saying with surprise, "You are so articulate for your race," to another with a different racial identity. For the latter, authors may "exclude, negate, or nullify the psychological thoughts, feelings, or experiential reality of a [religious] person," similar to comments like, "I don't see color" or "We are all human beings" concerning race (p. 274). These biases and microaggressions contradict the basic principle of science that it is objective. Objective means it is open to the results and will adapt theory to them, not impose the theory on the methods and interpretations of results. This is particularly the case when we look at groups with which we are most likely to disagree. As long-time researcher in the psychology of religion Peter Hill (2018) observed, at times, "fundamentalists are being studied not in terms of what they believe, but in terms of what we as psychologists believe about them." How, then, will we ever understand fundamentalist groups? We risk bias with such etic approaches to religious and spiritual groups and are compelled—if we are to be consistent with the objectivity required of good science—to move to more emic approaches.

Given the limitations of science in general, and the psychology of religion and spirituality in particular, as we try to understand the myriad faith traditions of our diverse world, science can own its weaknesses and adapt. Indigenous psychology has afforded a more emic approach that still provides scientific knowledge that may be less pure empirically but more accurate as a reflection of reality. We consider now some of the ways indigenous psychology can resolve the problems we have considered and lead us to better ways to understand the psychology of religion and spirituality.

SOLUTIONS FROM AN INDIGENOUS PSYCHOLOGY OF RELIGION

The concerns about applying empirical science to understand the psychology of religious and spiritual persons and groups that we have covered call for a fresh approach to our efforts to understand the nearly ubiquitous aspect of human life and society: the transcendent. Here is a summary of a few ways an indigenous approach addresses the challenges we have presented.

CULTURAL HUMILITY

The notion of cultural humility comes out of clinical work and the effort to develop multicultural competencies (Hook et al., 2013), building from the American Psychological Association's (2003) guidelines. Hook et al. (2013) summarize these nicely:

APA MCCs guidelines encourage psychologists to (a) develop an understanding of their own cultural background and the ways that their cultural background influences their personal attitudes, values, and beliefs (i.e., attitudes/beliefs); (b) develop understanding and knowledge of the worldviews of individuals from diverse cultural backgrounds (i.e., knowledge); and (c) use culturally appropriate interventions (i.e., skills). (p. 253)

These apply well as part of the remedy to the biases of science we have been discussing, though we might alter the third to use culturally appropriate research methodologies. Those authors define cultural humility as "the ability to maintain an interpersonal stance that is other-oriented (or open to the other) in relation to aspects of cultural identity that are most important to the client" (Hook et al., 2013, p. 355), though again we might adapt that to be the subject of our research rather than the client. We mention clinical application later.

To apply these directly, such an approach sees Western psychology as the culture of the researcher (and only one of many psychologies in a pluralistic literature base) who then needs to see how that culture impacts their approaches to populations who do not share its agnostic, empirical epistemology. Rather, the researcher needs to adapt to understanding the worldview of those of other religious faiths under scrutiny, and adapt methods to provide the best chances of understanding the groups from within (an emic approach). The shift is to be other-oriented and seeing research as a service to the group being studied more than promoting a conflicting agenda being pursued by the researcher.

OPENNESS TO OTHER EPISTEMOLOGIES

Openness to other epistemologies can certainly be viewed with suspicion in the psychology literature, but those who study religion and spirituality do well to be open to these groups' epistemologies as genuine sources of insider knowledge that shape their worldviews, cultures, and psychological functioning (Pankalla & Kosnik, 2018). This openness entails not trying to frame these within the agnosticism (or even atheism) of science in an effort to explain them away within the Western framework. Doing so will be a challenge when one considers that none of the major religious and spiritual groups that are presented in this book arose in the Western philosophical mind-set and culture of science, which has alienated the major religions of the West (Christianity and Judaism) and had a distant relationship to all of the groups we consider.

Yet, if we approach the task with cultural humility, we will not assume Western empirical science is the road to all knowledge, but more realistically see it as a vital tool to many aspects of knowing the physical world and affording some insight into the psychology of those who live in a more enchanted world. We might even place more of an emphasis on exploring the influence of other epistemologies on these religious groups.

WORKING FROM AN IDEOLOGICAL SURROUND MODEL (ISM)

An exemplary project in trying to accommodate the scientific method to those who have differing worldviews was the Ideological Surround Model (ISM) of the late P. J. Watson (Watson, 2019). Watson shared the asymptotic metaphor described earlier, saying that the way to come closest to "truth" and "objectivity" when two competing social rationalities encounter one another is through a never ending dialogue aimed at understanding one another more than merely observing the subject. We all know in relationships we can study another person's attire, features, demeanor, and behavior, but to truly understand that person, dialogue has to occur. I found my wife attractive when we first met, but only in spending time with her and talking with her have I come closer to understanding her. Scientists might take a similar tack in approaching persons who differ in how they see the world. (This, of course, approaches the realm of qualitative research.)

The core of the ISM is to consider that science is a social rationality, and as such, it emerges from a set of ultimate standards that cannot rationalize themselves by any higher logical standard (Watson, 2019). It is thus an ideology at heart and its assumptions surround its understanding and interpretation of the world. Science then encounters a religious group that has a different ideological surround built on different assumptions and standards that are incommensurable with science (MacIntyre, 1988). So, Watson explains, science sees nature as the ultimate standard while religionists see God as the ultimate standard. For these to be commensurable, one or the other would have to subject their standard to that of the other group—something not likely to occur on either side. The ISM posits a methodological theism that gives space for both from a meta-perspective (Watson notes that an atheist version might also be developed). Given this, dialogue can occur that moves toward understanding.

Watson's (2019) theory is difficult to summarize in brief, but adapting it to our context would entail science opening up the possibility of a theistic realm so as to create space for dialogue and subsequently for research, with a goal of understanding others within the context of their ideological surround while being mindful of our own.

MULTIPLE EPISTEMOLOGIES

The ISM is only one example of a way to work around this epistemological dilemma. Even scientists who are honest concede there is more than empiricism as an epistemology, for empiricism cannot be demonstrated empirically, and so we admit it as a source of knowledge based on a social rationality that lies outside of science itself. Stated bluntly, empiricism makes sense as a way of knowing. But now we have reason and science as ways to know. This reason aspect, however, is where the trouble of personal knowledge enters, about which Polanyi (1962) wrote. An indigenous psychology of religion and spirituality calls us to be aware of this epistemological problem and to be open to other social rationalities that allow for epistemologies that are not as bound to nature and embrace the transcendent.

FIRST-PERSON PERSPECTIVE

In the piece mentioned earlier, Hill (2018) argued for a "first-person" perspective, with psychologists of religion seeking to see the world from the eyes of the subjects we study rather than see them from our own eyes. In short, this is an emic, rather than etic, perspective. In a study of Pentecostalism (Sisemore, 2018b), I found that early research on this group stigmatized them as surveys showed they lacked self-esteem because of their religious views. Better research from a first-person perspective later clarified that what was being tapped was a sense of humility before God—quite a different conclusion.

INNOVATIVE RESEARCH METHODS

These indigenous approaches largely advocate for more creative methodologies when studying people whose faith is part of their identity and indigenous to their culture. The most obvious one not mentioned is the need for sensitive, careful qualitative research that could lead to mixed methods. We need to learn the constructs of faith groups and what they mean to the groups, then construct measures around these rather than forcing them into our categories like round pegs into square holes (see, e.g., Knabb & Wang, 2019).

Beyond that, Pe-Pua (2006) has outlined five principles for research in indigenous psychology that could be used for studying religious and spiritual groups indigenously. First, there needs to be a good relationship between the researchers and participants being studied if the data are to be useful. Also, "researchers should treat research participants as equal, if not superior" (p. 123). This will flow naturally from adapting cultural humility and becoming more open regarding epistemological differences. "We should give more importance to the welfare of the participants than to obtaining data from them" (p. 123). This third principle fits well with research ethics. Dismissive attitudes toward persons of faith have led to misunderstanding as we saw in the case of Pentecostals. Fourth, methods should be adapted to be appropriate to the population and suited to cultural norms. This may entail showing respect for traditions and sacred places and honoring practices that are unusual to Western scientists. Finally, "the language of the people should be the language of research at all times" (p. 124). We want to understand constructs from within their worldviews, not force them into ours.

One note to point out here is how many of the religious groups we examine in the remainder of the book are consistent with, if not definitive of, the culture surrounding them. For example, in many nations Islam frames the nature and laws of the government. However, this is not the case in the West, where Jews and Christians in particular often state they hold to a faith but may live and think more like the surrounding culture than different from it—even though the culture is increasingly secular. This contrasts with the Amish, for example, who have created and preserved their own culture in a largely coherent whole with their religious beliefs. Many persons who value faith, particularly in the West, may not hold it indigenously but actually be more in tune with the surrounding secular culture than their own religious faiths, unaware of the role that syncretism has played in shaping their view of the world. These are the exceptions to our argument in this book, given we are presenting an "insider" conceptualization of the psychology of each faith system.

CLINICAL APPLICATIONS

Most of this chapter has focused on research, but all of this has profound clinical implications. Psychologists are to respect religious and spiritual beliefs as part of their ethics (Principle E; American Psychological Association, 2017), treating persons of faith with respect as they do persons of any type of diversity. The disconnect between largely irreligious psychologists and a largely religious population has left many clinicians to take a "don't ask, don't tell" approach, where clinicians do not ask about faith, and clients, assuming faith is not a topic for the therapy office, do not speak of it. In response to this problem, some psychologists are moving to develop spiritual and religious competencies (Vieten et al., 2016). The attitudes of cultural humility, openness to dialogue, understanding multiple epistemologies, first-person perspective, and respecting the client over self that we have described apply quite directly to psychotherapists working with religious or spiritual persons.

Slife, Ghelfi, and Fox (2018) surveyed the problems of scientism when it comes to psychotherapy research, noting the problems with a single methodology for this important applied area of science. Particularly in the area of evidence-based treatments, overcommitment to these methods is less helpful than when used in developing medication. Psychotherapy does not lend itself as neatly to controlled methods of randomized trials given how humanness means each therapy session will have uniquenesses and inconsistencies far more than simply giving a medication to a subject or not. Slife et al. point to a need for methodological pluralism, including an openness to methodologies that may not even be known yet. The complex process of understanding psychotherapy may require more flexibility, such as with the use of qualitative studies. One could add the need to incorporate an indigenous understanding of those in therapy, including attention to their religion.

Many faiths offer a telos for life, a reason for living around which meaning is shaped. This serves as a motivation for action and an interpretive framework for events. For many persons of faith, this is *the* factor that shapes their actions and directions. Therapy has historically been more focused on fixing problems, but helping reorient persons of faith to their spiritual telos is another area where clinicians should be attentive, and researchers may need to see how this shapes not only symptoms, but interpretations and movement in therapy toward these spiritual ends— one might say a *teleology* for therapy. Recalling our opening metaphor, science struggles to provide a telos for life, the destination toward which we travel. Therapy, like our GPS, may help guide us, but we depend on the destinations of our clients, and for persons of faith, these are often rooted in their belief systems. Overall, balancing scientific psychology's "how-does-it-work" question with religion's "why-is-it-there" question (Cummins, 2002, p. 165) can only strengthen efforts to optimally respond to the unique needs of religious clients in psychotherapy.

There is also a place for specific faith traditions to develop their own indigenous clinical psychologies, working from a particular faith world-view to address clinical problems and their treatment. Examples of such are emerging, such as York Al-Karam's (2018) volume on Islamic psychology and Knabb, Johnson, Bates, and Sisemore's (2019) recent textbook on Christian psychology. The chapters that follow may open doors to further developing these across a range of religions and spiritualities.

As psychologists better understand their own attitudes and values regarding the transcendent and so enter the therapy office more self-aware, they are better equipped not only to invite the client to mention the client's spirituality in therapy, but to incorporate it as part of the process that attends to all the aspects that constitute that client's psychology. Much is being done in the area of how religion and spirituality impact psychological health and psychological therapy (e.g., Pargament, 2013), and as more psychologists and other therapists appropriate these approaches and insights, people of faith will be better served.

MOVING FORWARD

Having established the value of indigenous psychology, its applicability to the psychology of religion and spirituality, and the problems of science overreaching its area of expertise when indigenous factors are neglected, we now give voice to some of the world's major religions and groups of spiritualities. The following chapter provides a foundational history of the study of indigenous psychology, and each subsequent chapter provides an inside-out look at a specific faith tradition framed by six key issues: history and concepts of the faith, epistemology or how knowledge is acquired in the faith, views of the person or self, views of health and well-being, views of mental disorders, and clinical applications for those in the field. Moreover, each of the chapters on a specific world religion or spirituality is authored (or coauthored) by a psychologist who either practices or has roots in the designated faith system. None of these groups arose in the secular West, which gave rise to empirical science, so there is a tension between empirical science and these groups. We offer the following in an effort to enhance the understanding of people of faith and to promote collaboration and improved psychological understanding and treatment for them.

REFERENCES

American Psychological Association. (2003). Guidelines for multicultural education, training, research, practice, and organizational change for psychologists. *American Psychologist, 58,* 377–402. doi:10.1037/0003- 066X.58.5.377

American Psychological Association. (2017). *Ethical principles of psychologists and code of conduct.* Washington, DC: Author. Retrieved from https://www.apa.org/ethics/code/index

Atwood, G., & Stolorow, R. (1993). *Faces in a cloud: Intersubjectivity in personality theory.* Lanham, MD: Rowman & Littlefield.

Bufford, R. K., Sisemore, T. A., & Blackburn, A. M. (2017). Dimensions of grace: Factor analysis of three grace scales. *Psychology of Religion and Spirituality, 9,* 56–69. Supplemental materials at http:dx.doi.org/10.1037/rel0000064.supp

Chan, J., & Whiteson, D. (2017). *We have no idea: A guide to the unknown universe.* New York: Riverhead Books.

Cummins, R. (2002). Neo-teleology. In A. Rosenberg & R. Arp (Eds.), *Philosophy of biology* (pp. 164–174). Malden, MA: Wiley-Blackwell.

Enriquez, V. (1993). Developing a Filipino psychology. In U. Kim & J. Berry (Eds.), *Indigenous psychologies: Research and experience in cultural context* (pp. 152–169). Newbury Park, CA: Sage.

Farrell, M. (2014). *Historical and philosophical foundations of psychology.* Cambridge: Cambridge University Press.

Gantt, E. E., & Williams, R. N. (Eds.). (2018). *On hijacking science: Exploring the nature and consequences of overreach in psychology.* New York: Routledge.

Haig, B. (2018). *Method matters in psychology: Essays in applied philosophy of science.* Cham, Switzerland: Springer.

Hall, M., Shannonhouse, L., Aten, J., McMartin, J., & Silverman, E. (2018). Religion-specific resources for meaning-making from suffering: Defining the territory. *Mental Health, Religion & Culture, 21*, 77–92.

Hill, P. (2013). Measurement assessment and issues in the psychology of religion and spirituality. In R. Paloutzian & C. Park (Eds.), *Handbook of the psychology of religion and spirituality* (2nd ed.) (pp. 48–74). New York: The Guilford Press.

Hill. P. C. (2018, March 9). Pursuing a first-person perspective: The case of humility in conservative religious individuals. Keynote Address at the Annual Meeting of the Society for the Psychology of Religion and Spirituality in Riverside, CA.

Hood, R. W., Jr., & Williamson, W. P. (2008). *Them that believe: The power and meaning of the Christian serpent-handling tradition.* Berkeley: University of California Press.

Hook, J. N., Davis, D. E., Owen, J., Worthington, E. L., Jr., & Utsey, S. O. (2013). Cultural humility: Measuring openness to culturally diverse clients. *Journal of Counseling Psychology, 60*, 353–366. doi:10.1037/a0032595

Hunter, J. D., & Nedelisky, P. (2018). *Science and the good: The tragic quest for the foundations of morality.* New Haven, CT: Yale University Press.

Hutchinson, I. H. (2011). *Monopolizing knowledge: A scientist refutes religion-denying, reason-destroying scientism.* Belmont, MA: Fias Publishing. (Kindle edition)

James, W. (1902/1985). *The varieties of religious experience: A study in human nature.* Cambridge, MA: Harvard University Press.

Kim, U., Park, Y., & Park, D. (2000). The challenge of cross-cultural psychology: The role of indigenous psychologies. *Journal of Cross-Cultural Psychology, 31*, 63–75.

Kim, U., Yang, K., & Hwang, K. (2006). Contributions to indigenous and cultural psychology: Understanding people in context. In U. Kim, K. Yang, & K. Hwang (Eds.), *Indigenous and cultural psychology: Understanding people in context* (pp. 3–26). New York: Springer.

Knabb, J. J., Johnson, E. L., Bates, M. T., & Sisemore, T. A. (2019). *Christian psychotherapy in context: Theoretical and empirical explorations in faith-based mental health.* New York: Routledge.

Knabb, J., & Wang, K. (2019). The Communion with God Scale: Shifting from an etic to emic perspective to assess fellowshipping with the Triune God. *Psychology of Religion and Spirituality.* Advance online publication.

Lamiell, J. T. (2018). On scientism in psychology. In E. E. Gantt & R. N. Williams (Eds.), *On hijacking science: Exploring the nature and consequences of overreach in psychology* (pp. 27–41). New York: Routledge.

MacIntyre, A. (1988). *Whose justice? Which rationality?* Notre Dame, IN: University of Notre Dame Press.

Pankalla, A., & Kosnik, K. (2018). Religion as an invaluable source of psychological knowledge: Indigenous Slavic psychology of religion. *Journal of Theoretical and Philosophical Psychology, 38*, 154–164.

Pargament, K. I. (Ed. in Chief). (2013). *APA handbook of psychology, religion, and spirituality*: Vol. 2: *An applied psychology of religion and spirituality.* Washington, DC: American Psychological Association.

Pe-Pua, R. (2006). From decolonizing psychology to the development of a cross-indigenous perspective in methodology. In U. Kim, K.-S. Yang, & K.-K. Hwang (Eds.), *Indigenous and cultural psychology: Understanding people in context* (pp. 109–140). New York: Springer.

Polanyi, M. (1962). *Personal knowledge: Towards a post-critical philosophy.* Chicago: University of Chicago Press.

Rosenthal, R., & Rosnow, R. (2008). *Essentials of behavioral research: Methods and data analysis* (3rd ed.). Boston: McGraw Hill.

Sisemore, T. A. (2015). *The psychology of religion and spirituality: From the inside out.* New York: John Wiley & Sons.

Sisemore, T. A. (2018a). Christianity as diverse spirituality: Pentecostalism in the Southern Hemisphere. Part of symposium: Varieties of spirituality as indigenous ways of knowing (L. Sundararajan, chair). Presented at the annual meeting of the American Psychological Association.

Sisemore, T. A. (2018b, November). Explaining the psychology of religion and spirituality without explaining it away. *Society for the Psychology of Religion and Spirituality Newsletter.* https://www.apadivisions.org/division-36/publications/newsletters/religion/2018/11/explaining

Slife, B., & Reber, J. (2012). Conceptualizing religious practices in psychological research: Problems and prospects. *Pastoral Psychology, 61,* 735–746.

Slife, B. D., Ghelfi, E. A., & Fox, S. T. (2018). Psychotherapy and scientism. In E. E. Gantt & R. N. Williams (Eds.), *On hijacking science: Exploring the nature and consequences of overreach in psychology* (pp. 68–84). New York: Routledge.

Sue, D., Capodilupo, C., Torino, G., Bucceri, J., Holder, A., Nadal, K., ... Esquilin, M. (2007). Racial microaggressions in everyday life: Implications for clinical practice. *American Psychologist, 62,* 271–286.

Taylor, C. (2007). *A secular age.* Cambridge, MA: Belknap Press of Harvard University Press.

Vieten, C., Scammell, S., Pierce, A., Pilato, R., Ammondson, I., Pargament, K. I., & Lukoff, D. (2016). Competencies for psychologists in the domains of religion and spirituality. *Spirituality in Clinical Practice, 3,* 92–114. http://dx.doi.org/10.1037/scp0000078

Watson, P.J. (2019). *Psychology and religion within an ideological surround.* Boston, MA: Brill.

Watson, P. J., Sawyers, P., Morris, R. J., Carpenter, M. L., Jimenez, R. S., Jonas, K. A., & Robinson, D. L. (2003). Reanalysis from a Christian ideological surround: Relationships of intrinsic religious orientation with fundamentalism and right-wing authoritarianism. *Journal of Psychology and Theology, 31,* 315–328.

Wertz, F. J. (2018). Beyond scientism: Reaches in psychology toward a science of consciousness. In E. E. Gantt & R. N. Williams (Eds.), *On hijacking science: Exploring the nature and consequences of overreach in psychology* (pp. 107–119). New York: Routledge.

Williams, R. N., & Gantt, E. E. (2018). Introduction. In E. E. Gantt & R. N. Williams (Eds.), *On hijacking science: Exploring the nature and consequences of overreach in psychology* (pp. 1–12). New York: Routledge.

Wundt, W. (2013). Psychology's struggle for existence (J. T. Lamiell, trans.). *History of Psychology, 16,* 195–209.

York Al-Karam, C. (Ed.). (2018). *Islamically integrated psychotherapy: Uniting faith and professional practice.* West Conshohocken, PA: Templeton Press.

Zinnbauer, B., & Pargament, K. (2005). Religiousness and spirituality. In R. Paloutzian & C. Park (Eds.), *Handbook of the psychology of religion and spirituality* (pp. 21–42). New York: Guilford Press.

ENDNOTES

1. Summarized in Sisemore (2015).

2. Although some psychology of religion authors have recently advocated for a more balanced approach—that is, employing both etic and emic strategies (Hall, Shannonhouse, Aten, McMartin, & Silverman, 2018; Hill, 2013; Zinnbauer & Pargament, 2005)—additional work remains, given that the vast majority of peer-reviewed publications tend to simply import secular theories when studying the psychology of religion, then slightly adjust them to align with the religious culture of interest. When used excessively, this strategy, an "indigenization from without" (Enriquez, 1993; Kim et al., 2000, p. 65), can prevent scientists from fully understanding the unique daily experiences of those who identify with a specific faith tradition.

3. Mark 16:18, though literary critics note this is not likely part of the original manuscripts of Mark.

AL DUECK

INDIGENOUS PSYCHOLOGIES
OF SPIRITUALITY

Remembering, Excavating,
and Individuating

Millennia before the West developed the formal discipline of psychology, there were indigenous ethnoreligious communities that possessed what today would be called a "folk psychology." That folk psychology encompassed lay views of what it meant to be human, have relationships with one another, mature over time, interpret and interact with nature, acknowledge a deity (deities) or what is transcendent, address suffering and illness, develop modes of healing, encounter death, and so on. Over time these psychospiritual understandings were, in some communities and in varying degrees, rationally systematized, elaborated in stories, and incarnated in practices. These hunter-gatherer communities understood the significance of nurturing their young with touch, attending to their needs, and embedding the emerging adult in a close-knit community (Narvaez, 2014; Narvaez et al. 2019)—all psychological processes. In other words, they became what Geertz (2008) called a local culture. These societies and their spirituality have existed for most of human history and have accumulated psychological wisdom that is hidden in their spiritual practices.

Some of these communities emerged to become major, modern religions, whereas others did not. Though these communities with their emerging culture were at first local, as they encountered other communities, they refined their own convictions, developed a sense of identity, and garnered communal resources. In turn, these refinements created a sense of cohesion and differentiation from the cultures of other communities (Harvey, 2000). These communities developed over time a normative discourse to support and interpret their experiences, daily practices, and convictions. For example, Buddhist discourse encouraged letting go of desire (Cohen, 2010) and Pentecostal Christians' discourse valorized personal conversation with God (Luhrmann, 2012, 2017). Appalachian region serpent-handlers included in their discourse an explanation for their practice of handling poisonous snakes in their worship by pointing to God's promise of faithful protection (Hood & Williamson, 2008). The Amish engage in a spiritual practice that includes forgiving their enemies as enjoined by Jesus Christ. This was evident after the Nickel Mines incident when five Amish girls were raped and killed and the perpetrator was publicly forgiven by one of the Amish leaders (Kraybill, Johnson-Weiner, & Nolt, 2013; Kraybill, Nolt, & Weaver-Zercher, 2010). Like aboriginal peoples around the world, traditional Chinese Yi people have a nosology of spirit possession and consult with shamans for healing (Ting, Sundararajan, & Huang, 2017; Ting & Sundararajan, 2018). These ethnoreligious communities have implicit in their spirituality a unique folk psychology that undergirds their ethical practices and beliefs and are the focus of this chapter.

The question I ask is whether the Western paradigm of psychology of religion with its more than one hundred years of history is capable of understanding indigenous spirituality. It has formally viewed itself as embedded within mainstream psychology, with its criteria of scientific objectivity, operational definitions, and generalizability. However, the presumption of universality creates significant problems for appreciating the particularity of indigenous religious communities. And second, the hegemony of scientific psychological discourse may undermine local psychological and epistemological discourses (Gergen, Gulerce, Lock, & Misra, 1996; see also Teo, 2010, 2019 on "epistemic violence"). Gantt and Williams (2018) have pointed to the ways in which a scientific psychology has engaged in overreach when it presumes to be the only reliable source of knowledge about human nature.

This chapter honors the rich narrative of ancient and modern indigenous ethnoreligious communities by understanding their psychology emically rather than etically (Dueck & Reimer, 2009; Dueck, Ansloos, Johnson, & Fort, 2017). The chapter begins with the historical context that has stimulated the research in indigenous psychologies of spirituality. I then proceed with a brief history that remembers the critical players responsible for the emergence of indigenous psychologies of religion and spirituality (Chakkarath, 2013), such as Matteo Ricci (1985) and Bernardo de Sahagún (1970–1982). Third, I excavate psychologies implicit in indigenous culture-creating communities. Here I think of researchers like Dalal and Misra (2010) who unearthed a psychology in the Vedas and *Bhagavad-Gītā*. To answer the question regarding what indigenous psychology of spirituality actually looks like today, I point to the research of Hood and Williamson (2008) with the Appalachian serpent-handlers and Ting and Sundararajan's (2018) analysis of the cultural influences on psychological processes and subsequently spirituality. Finally, I discern how these aspirational communities reflect or are individuated from the dominant psychologies of their host culture.

THE HISTORICAL CONTEXT

What is the problematic that energizes indigenous research of spirituality? First, mainstream psychology tends to utilize psychological categories largely borrowed from Aristotle: mind-body, perception, motivation, memory, thinking, attitudes, and so on (Aristotle, 2010). These, however, may not be the categories used by Confucians, Buddhists, Christians, Daoists, Muslims, or animists for describing psychological processes correlative to their spiritual experiences. In fact, religious communities have their own implicit psychologies, as Cox (1973/2010) argued more than four decades ago.

The investigation of indigenous psychologies emerged, in part, in response to the disregard of the impact of local language on the understandings of the psyche and its relationship to spiritual maturity. The indigenous approach is less concerned about universal language than on what a religious community can teach us about psychological processes in its own language. This new information can then be added to the larger picture of what it means to be human.

Second, in the past half century, Western psychologists have become increasingly aware of their social location (Buss, 1975; Jacoby, 1975; Gergen, Gulerce, Lock, & Misra, 1996). The assumption that the psychology constructed in America is universal (Danziger, 2009) fails to understand that American psychology is indigenous to American society (Yang, 2012; Long, 2020). It is largely constructed on the data provided by North American participants with little input from research conducted elsewhere (Arnett, 2008). And, this "psychology" has been exported around the world as non-Westerners graduated from Occidental psychology programs and established facsimiles of Western psychological curricula in their home countries.

However, some of these psychology graduates changed their minds about the local relevance of the Western model. Virgilio Enriquez, a graduate of Northwestern University, returned to the Philippines to teach psychology in his native tongue, Tagalog, and created a psychology sensitive to the Filipino context (Enriquez, 1988). Ignatio Martín-Baró studied at the University of Chicago and then taught a form of psychology in El Salvador that was culturally sensitive but was also a political threat in the chaotic situation of his time. It resulted in his murder (Martín-Baró, 1994). K. S. Yang and K. K. Hwang, who graduated from the Universities of Illinois and Hawaii, respectively, returned to Taiwan to articulate a psychology with a Chinese face (Yang, 2012; Hwang, 2011). And the list of indigenous psychologists goes on: Nsamenang (1997) in Cameroon; Long (2013) in South Africa; Pankalla and Kośnic (2016) in Poland; Doi (2005) in Japan; Shweder et al. (1997), Ratner (2008), and Sundararajan (2015) in the United States; Ting & Sundararajan (2018) in Malaysia; Yeh (2019) in Taiwan; and Dudgeon & Walker (2015) in Australia.

Third, the rise of a culturally sensitive psychology around the world is a consequence, in part, of the lament of these indigenous psychologists for whom mainstream psychology does not recognize their particularity. Cultural psychology recognizes the impact of culture on the individual and the importance of honoring indigeneity. In the United States, Markus and Kitayama's (1991) review articles on the impact of culture on cognitions and emotions is still a key point of reference for the development of a culturally sensitive psychology. They argued that fundamental psychological processes such as one's self-concept, cognitions, emotions, and motivation are co-emergent with culture. The major publications by

Kim and associates were critical as well (Kim & Berry, 1993; Kim, Yang, & Hwang, 2006) in developing a cultural psychology. The two volumes of the *Handbook of Cultural Psychology* by Kitayama and Cohen (Kitayama & Cohen, 2010; Cohen & Kitayama, 2019) provided an overview of how culture shapes psychological processes, with topics such as attachment, personal identity, and subjective well-being. (For a recent summary of the history of cultural psychology, see Kashima [2019].)

Repeatedly, findings assumed to be universal have turned out to be local phenomena. The fundamental attribution error may hold in the United States but was not corroborated in Chinese families (Wu et al., 2008). Attachment research, with its focus on the parent-infant relationship, appears to be limited to Western settings (LeVine, 2014; Dueck & Xu, 2017). In his classic *The Geography of Thought,* Nisbett (2004) noted that context-sensitive thinking appeared to be more common in some cultures and communities than others. White (1994) and Sundararajan (2015) have reminded psychologists that emotions assumed to be personally generated also have a cultural origin. Jackson et al. (2019) contested the assumption that there are six universal emotions. His team discovered that some categories indeed are universal but there were significant variations between cultures in the number of words available for a particular emotion suggesting that the meaning of emotion shifts with culture.

An early example of an indigenous psychology is the classic research of Shweder and Bourne (1984) with the Oriya of India. They found that the Oriya use descriptions of actions when explaining the nature of a friend, whereas Americans use abstract labels or personality traits. Oriya, for example, would say, "She brings cakes to my family on festival days," but Americans would be more likely to say, "She is friendly"; "He shouts curses at his neighbors" versus "He is aggressive and hostile"; "He does not disclose secrets" versus "He is principled." The Oriya more frequently provided a context, whereas the Americans tended to give acontextual responses. In a another study, Shweder and D'Andrade (1980) found that Oriyan informants had the ability to recognize objects in terms of overarching categories. Shweder and Bourne (1984) proposed that what really differentiates the Oriya from Americans is that the former:

place so little *value* on differentiating (e.g., person from role), generalizing (e.g., "treat outsiders like insiders"), or abstracting (e.g., the concept of "humanity") and, the relativist is quick to point out, they show so little interest in such intellectual moves because Oriyas, Balinese, and other such folk live by [an organic] metaphor and subscribe to a world-premise that directs their attention and passions to particular systems, relationally conceived and contextually appraised. Indeed, a central tenet of a relativist interpretation of context-dependent person perception *is that the metaphors by which people live and the worldviews to which they subscribe mediate the relationships between what one thinks about and how one thinks.* (p. 189, italics in original)

This study illustrates the importance of privileging an emic approach rather than imposing Western categories. The focus of indigenous psychologies is not on the broader culture of a society but on smaller, isolated groups whose boundaries are thicker but still permeable. These communities appear to have greater communal coherence due to their unique rituals, language, convictions, values, and moral practices. Indigenous psychologists eschew the privileging of Western psychological categories external to the group and tend to work from the bottom up, favoring a local psychological vocabulary.

Methodologically, indigenous psychologists use a wide range of approaches sensitive to the spiritual norms and expressions of local culture: focus groups, interviews in the local language, text analysis, computational linguistic programs, and grounded theory analysis of text. The lack of generalizability of indigenous findings is usually considered a limitation by those committed to models of human nature that are universal. However, a view of the person as a mosaic of attributes, with some characteristics more pronounced in some subcultures or communities than others, decreases the value of universality. Carefully conducted research may isolate a local dimension of the psyche that can enrich our view of human potentialities.

DECOLONIZING NEOLIBERAL PSYCHOLOGIES
OF RELIGION/SPIRITUALITY

If one takes seriously these developments in understanding the relation of culture to psychology, what are the implications for our understanding of psychological processes embedded in the religious experiences of participants in various ethnoreligious communities? As research on how culture impacted psychological findings increased, there was a concurrent rise in awareness of the cultural implications for understanding religious expression. Religious/spiritual individuals in different communities utilized psychological processes in their experiences that were not universal in scope and function but molded by particular subcultures. Hence, the spirituality of a particular community that migrated from one culture to another may manifest very different expressions of their religious sentiments, convictions, and moral practices. One form of cultural colonization by the West is the neoliberal psychologization of life generally, and spirituality in particular. Neoliberalism is a sociopolitical and economic model of the individual and society (Harvey, 2000). Neoliberalism privileges free-market capitalism and holds the belief that continuous economic growth will bring about general human development, trusting the abilities of the autonomous individual, and endorsing a globalized free market. Sugarman (2015) wrote that in neoliberalism "the economy is optimized through the entrepreneurial activity of autonomous individuals and that human wellbeing is furthered if individuals are free to direct their lives as entrepreneurs" (p. 104). However, it is inconceivable that the members of indigenous communities view themselves as entrepreneurs in this sense.

Neoliberalism has shaped the moral norms and attitudes, thinking and feeling, and practices and rituals of every aspect of the psychological life of the individual, the structure of society, and cultures all over the world. It is considered one of the most invasive ideologies of the modern era, but it is hardly mentioned in the field of psychology (for exceptions, see Sugarman, 2015; Teo, 2018; Ratner, 2019). In the past, colonialists dominated by force; neoliberalism colonizes by permeating worldviews.

For example, an ancient religion such as Buddhism, which emerged originally as a monastic movement and stressed renunciation of worldly ways, has been, in neoliberalism, transmuted into psychological language with almost exclusive emphasis on mindfulness. Cohen (2010) stated that the fact that mindfulness has been so thoroughly embraced by Westerners is rather ironic for a religion that originally emphasized the absence of a "self" in the mature individual. Cohen noted, "A consistent feature in the earliest Buddhist scriptures contrasts the merits of

Pabbajja 'Going forth' into the 'homeless life' compared with the ordinary, spiritually limited, life of the householder" (2010, p. 98).

One can employ the methodologies of mainstream psychology to understand a local spirituality, but that imposition may only colonize the religion of the latter by psychologizing a more communal spirituality. If a globalized psychology is exported, what comes with the package? The tradition of neoliberalism. A neoliberal psychology may distort earlier indigenous folk psychologies and spirituality, subtly denigrate religion as superstition, assume an individualistic ideology, or dismiss tradition because its wisdom is irrelevant to the modern world (Narvaez, 2014). The researchers in the next section have explored folk psychologies prior to the influx of neoliberalism.

REMEMBERING THE PIONEERS OF AN INDIGENOUS PSYCHOLOGY OF SPIRITUALITY

Culture shapes how the language of moral development is constructed. In China, given the influence of Confucius, language to describe morality includes *golden mean, good will* (agree with nature), *ch'ing* (human affection), *jen* (love, benevolence), *sympathy, filial piety, group solidarity,* and *collectivism* (Ma, 1988, 1989). On the other hand, given the long shadow of the Enlightenment and Western liberalism, the American moral developmentalist Kohlberg (1971) construed morality in Enlightenment terms. It began with the lowest level being external morality, then levels based on reward, conformity to others, obedience to laws, and a social contract, before ending with a morality based on rational principles.

In contrast to global neoliberalism, the language of sacred texts uniquely influences the contours of different spiritualities expressed in a local language that is used to describe one's spiritual experiences. Maintaining those tradition-rich languages is a potent force in decolonizing religion and psychology. The Tao, the Qur'an, the *Bhagavad-Gītā*, and the Bible are sacred texts that each create a distinct ethos and community with a unique discourse that shapes the character of the individual rooted in that community.

One purpose in this book is to advance the field of the indigenous psychology of religion by remembering the pioneers of indigenous psychologies of religion. I seek to honor thick local psychologies and spiritualities by remembering those who originated the study of indigenous ethnoreligious groups (Dueck & Reimer, 2009).

PIONEERS

Jesuit priests Bernardo de Sahagún in Mexico and Mateo Ricci in China are pioneers of an indigenous psychology of religion (Chakkarath, 2013). The psychological community does well to claim them as indigenous psychologists because they were profoundly interested in the relationships between religion, local culture, and the human psyche. Only the work of Sahagún is briefly summarized here.

Upon arrival in Mexico, Bernardo de Sahagún (1499–1590), a sixteenth-century Catholic missionary, realized that the indigenous peoples still spoke their native tongue (Nahuatl) and held to their traditions and convictions. From his training at Salamanca, he understood that the meaning of words depended on the culture and its practices and so he set about gathering data (Leon-Portilla, 2002). He did so first with semi-structured interviews and then developed questionnaires. Three groups of Nahua experts from different regions examined his data and verified that the data collected were authentically Nahuatl. He gathered information on history, social life, physical environment, religious beliefs in the supernatural, the human sphere, and facts of nature. The result was a thirteen-volume bilingual (Nahuatl and Spanish) magnum opus titled the *Florentine Codex: General History of the Things of New Spain* (Sahagún, 1578–1579/1970–1982).

Sahagún concluded that the cognition, emotions, behavioral practices, and motivation among the indigenous peoples were different from those of his European counterparts. His European sponsors were less than enthused by Sahagún's attempt to reconcile Christian tenets with indigenous belief, and for his description of the high level of civilization of the Nahua people. Not surprisingly, his cultural psychological work was not published until the late twentieth century.

A second form of indigenous psychology of religion examines folk psychologies and mythic spiritualities. These have often been dismissed as superstition because they were contained in a religious tradition or folk psychological theory. Chakkarath's (2005) approach is to:

take a closer look at those indigenous psychological theories that were already formalized and had already integrated psychologically relevant concepts into a systematically elaborated theory before modern psychology was considered. In other words, I suggest focusing more attention on psychological frameworks and concepts that were indigenous right from the beginning and that provide systematic analyses and can therefore serve as a more adequate basis for comparison with concepts provided by academic western psychology. (p. 34)

An indigenous psychology of religion delineates how the culture and folk psychology of a local community dialectically shape the contours of indigenous religious experience and expression. This section reviews research projects that describe local psychologies implicit in local spiritual communities, that is, indigenous psychologies of spirituality. I explore several patterns in the way indigenous cultures constrain psychological processes and influence the expression of spirituality.

Indigenous psychology of religion research has a small but growing cadre of committed scholars, largely from Aboriginal and non-Western communities. This approach is illustrated in the research of Alfred and Corntassel (2005), Chakkarath (2005), Dalal and Misra (2010), Dudgeon and Walker (2015), Gone (2019), Grieves (2008), Pankalla and Kośnik (2016), Sundararajan (2015), and Ting and Sundararajan (2018). These researchers use local discourse to understand local religious forms of expression. Bringing forward an understanding of indigenous psychology and indigenous religions to a nascent indigenous psychology of religion means listening for the local understandings of the psyche embedded in the spirituality and myths of marginalized or colonized peoples.

This approach has been well demonstrated in the work of Chakkarath (2005) as he unearths a psychology in ancient Hinduism. Dalal and Misra (2010) found an implicit Buddhist psychology in the Vedas and *Bhagavad-*

Gītā. Pankalla and Kośnik (2016, 2018) uncovered a religious psychology among ancient Slavic people. These researchers are concerned about the psychology implicit in spiritualities before Western psychology emerged on the scene. They ask the question of what psychology nurtured ancient people when modern psychology had not yet emerged.

INDIAN HINDUISM. Chakkarath (2005) finds an indigenous psychology within ancient Hindu spirituality. Hinduism has for over three thousand years provided perspectives on relationships, human values, mind and body, introspection, personality, and therapeutic techniques for the purpose of well-being and fulfillment. An indigenous Hindu psychology takes as its point of departure human misery, and thus the therapeutic measures of meditation, restraint, indifference, and detachment are proposed. Theories on the origin of evil are clearly psychological in nature and call for cognitive reflection on the causes of suffering of humanity.

Chakkarath (2005) argues that in ancient Hinduism we have sophisticated views of human development of attachment, and selfhood that predate modern psychology. It is a psychology, he says, "that is constructed not only on observation but also on introspection that yields a view of motivation and self-regulation as social-cognitive mediators of personal adjustment and interpersonal relationships in a particular, ancient religious tradition—Hinduism" (p. 49). However, it is not a morally neutral psychology as it calls for proper personal conduct because it seeks to influence thoughts, feelings, and behavior so as to create a balance between individual and social needs. "Therefore, we may assume that the representation of psychological assumptions in the subjective theories of individuals is especially great in contexts in which indigenous psychologies are essential constituents of the cultural niche [namely, Hinduism]" (p. 49).

PRE-CHRISTIAN SLAVIC SPIRITUALITY. Pankalla and Kośnik (2016, 2018) explored the psychology of premodern Slavic spirituality. They too propose that in religious doctrine and practice psychological researchers have access to local forms of human mental life. Since mainstream psychology of religion has focused primarily on the great monotheistic religions, the small ethnoreligious traditions have been neglected and could be a source of new knowledge about human religiousness. Pankalla and Kośnik argue that religion should determine the subject matter and psychological discipline decides the research method. The result would be not a psychology of religion but a "religious psychology."

Following Wilhelm Wundt's model (2013) of a cultural-historical psychology (*Völkerpsychologie*), Pankalla and Kośnik (2016, 2018) focused on the social factors that shape the individual and his or her religion. The sources of data include the work of historians, linguists, ethnographers, or religious studies scholars. Traditions unique to a particular human community are analyzed in terms of speech patterns, practices, and myths. In so doing they hope to avoid methodological individualism that ignores factors beyond the individual.

The process of reconstructing former Slavic beliefs includes data from religious-historical findings and ethnographic observations (Pankalla & Kośnik, 2016, 2018). Slavic religion is polytheistic with a pantheon of gods: Perun—lightning and war; Swarog—fire and smiths; Weles—the dead. The indigenous rationality attributes intentional activities to supernatural beings (gods, ancestors' spirits, demons) and internal experiences as well. This is supplemented by a wide range of demons (the souls of ancestors) that served to explain unusual natural and social phenomena. Pankalla and Kośnik propose that the notion of soul and the practices of religious rites enable them to construct an understanding of Slavic human development.

A soul was believed to inhabit a person's head from where it governed cognitive processes—especially "the reason" (*rozum*—intelligence, abstract thinking, etc.) and "the memory" (*pamięć*—a sense of one's own existence, consciousness, etc.). Feelings were thought to exist mainly in the stomach. Pankalla and Kośnik (2018) commented:

The "multifunctionality" of the soul in Slavic religious beliefs leads to the conclusion that the soul was the essence of [the] human and their existence (whether in material or immaterial form) was in the shape of an individual being who is able to experience.... The uniqueness of the Slavic soul comes from its specific content connected with the local cultural context which is determined by social constructs about oneself and reality (e.g., Slavic personality traits like hospitality and pugnacity, family as a main value, local demons as an explanation of undesirable psychic phenomena). An indigenous psychology of religion which is built on the basis of Slavic culture requires (as is the case in many other faiths) the inclusion of the idea of the soul for organizing theoretical categories and presenting a direct subject of analysis. (p. 159)

In addition to the notion of soul, Pankalla and Kośnik focused on human development to illustrate the procedures for creating an indigenous psychology of religion. Religion provides the categories within which to organize the process of human development by marking movement across stages with a ritual that is linked to a myth. Indigenous psychology of religion emerges as the researcher identifies the religious rituals that focus on development and initiation and then analyzes/interprets the meaning of the associated myth. Pankalla and Kośnik (2016) reconstructed the Slavic understanding of human development in seven rites of passage. All of the rituals that mark a transition to a new state are religious in nature and reflect devotion to a particular Slavic god (e.g., to Weles, the god of the dead in the case of a funeral).

EXCAVATING INDIGENOUS PSYCHOLOGIES OF RELIGION

Few studies match the criteria we have set for research on indigenous psychologies of religion. We would suggest two studies as exemplary: the research by Hood and Williamson (2008) on serpent-handlers in the Appalachian region and the study by Ting and Sundararajan (2018) with the Yi people of Southwest China. I have reported on the former in another publication (Dueck & Johnson, 2016) and focus in detail on the latter study in this chapter.

The Ting and Sundararajan (2018) study asked the question I have focused on: How does culture influence the psychological processes in spiritual practices? Culture was operationally defined in regard to the kind of relational ties that existed between persons in each group. The two groups were from the Yi people in Southwest China. One group, the Yi-Bimo, came from the animist tradition, while the other group was originally Bimo but had a Christian history dating to the missionary efforts in the 1850s. Ting and Sundararajan theorized that these groups were culturally different in that communal coherence came for the Yi-Bimo as a result of bloodlines that reached back thousands of years, while the Yi-Christian community essentially comprised strangers bound together by their Christian tradition. The two groups differed in their cultural constitution. Rather than using the individualist/collectivist dichotomy (both groups had a collectivist history), the study relied on the model described by Granovetter (1978) of strong- and weak-ties communities. The Bimo were a strong-tie community in that they functioned as a clan with common bloodlines; the Christians were a 150-year-old community comprising (weak-tie) strangers who had converted to join a church.

A total of forty-seven individuals were interviewed from the Bimo and the Christian communities about their experiences of suffering: unemployment, AIDS, drug use, and the loss of the younger generation leaving for the city to find employment (Ting & Sundararajan, 2018). The interviews were conducted in the local dialect, translated, and coded based on the theory governing the study. Scales were developed from the coding of cognitive, emotional, and spiritual components.

The culturally sensitive psychological processes the researchers focused on were cognitive styles and emotional expression. Cognitively, Ting & Sundararajan theorized that the groups varied on several dimensions: concrete versus abstract and experience near or distant. Emotionality was assessed on the following dimensions: abstract description from a distance versus reporting immediate concrete experience, number of emotion words in the corpus of each group, implicit versus explicit reference to emotions, and internal versus external focus. The spiritual component was the mode of religious coping: seeking the assistance of a shaman, the Christian community, inner spiritual disciplines, and so on.

The authors predicted that the culturally formed psychological processes would influence indigenous spirituality. The researchers followed the model of ecological rationality developed by Todd, Gigerenzer, and the ABC Research Group (2012), which proposes that different cognitive styles coevolved with the ecological niches (e.g., strong- and weak-tie communities). Religions are also influenced cognitively by these cultural niches as well as influencing the cultural emergence of different cognitive styles. As a result, Ting and Sundararajan proposed that differences in cognitive styles and emotional focus would be due to specific cultural factors (strong-tie versus weak-tie) and religion (animist versus Christian). Concretely, they predicted that the Yi-Christians who functioned like a weak-tie culture would tend to think abstractly, be experience distant, be more explicit in emotional expression, and privilege an internal mental focus. Ting and Sundararajan proposed that the Yi-Bimo group, however, would lean toward concrete cognitive processing, be experience near, engage in more implicit emotional representation, and favor an external physical focus.

The results included the following findings on the impact of culture on psychological processes and religious expression. In terms of emotions, the Yi-Christians were more explicit in their expression of emotions (more emotion words and self-reported emotional expression ["I cried"]). The Yi-Bimo were more implicit in their expression of emotions in that they focused on bodily aches, physical discomfort, and observable (facial) reactions. In terms of cognition, the Yi-Christians more often had difficulty in articulation ("don't know how to say it"), while the Yi-Bimo were more concrete in their thinking. The Yi-Christians were more abstract in their cognition in terms of beliefs and suffering. Seeking help from family was not significantly different between Bimo and Christians, but Christians accessed their church community more than the Bimo accessed their local community. The Yi-Bimo significantly utilized more external help (e.g., shamans), but the Yi-Christians used more internal spirituality than the former (e.g., prayer). The Yi-Bimo group tended to rely on external supernatural causes to explain their suffering, whereas the Yi-Christian group made more use of internal attributions—such as that suffering may be related to God's plan.

Textual coding of these narratives and the resulting questionnaires provided the data for analysis. Data were analyzed via manual coding and three computational linguistic programs (Chinese-Linguistic Inquiry and Word Count, Topics, and the Sundararajan-Schubert Word Count). The programs all confirmed the hypotheses with much more clarity and focus than manual coding. The two religious groups, Yi-Bimo and Yi-Christian, differed on a number of dimensions consistent with the divide between strong-ties and weak-ties communities.

This study is a model for indigenous psychology of religion research. It focuses on indigenous people rather than large groups (e.g., the

Chinese versus Americans). It has a theory of culture (strong-tie and weak-tie, ecological rationality) that is testable. The dependent variable is help-seeking behavior rather than about religious beliefs. The model is clearly emic in approach, using the participants' own language to reveal their psychological processes and develop scales. It is a mixed-method study using both manual coding of text and computer linguistic programs. It honors local healing rituals whether by shamans or pastors.

The study challenges assumptions previously made about how to compare cultures. The dominant paradigm makes a distinction between collectivism-individualism, while this study does not find that model helpful. Both groups come from a collectivist culture but differ in religious orientation. This is a study of cognition and emotion directly connected to a specific culture (Yi) and specific religions (animism and Christianity). Second, this study does not examine cognition, emotion, and help-seeking behavior in general in China but among two indigenous groups. This approach avoids the problem of linguistic universalism in cross-cultural studies where meanings of words are assumed to be similar across cultures. Nor does this study compare large social bodies (e.g., East versus West), thus sidestepping the problem of essentialism.

INDIVIDUATION: CULTURAL CONTEXTS AND INDIGENOUS SPIRITUAL COMMUNITIES

Not only ecological niches shape spirituality; the larger culture also plays a significant role. Most ethnoreligious communities do not exist in complete social isolation. The extent to which the host culture influences these communities depends on how porous the boundaries, how pervasive the influence of the host culture, and a myriad of other variables. But that is not the focus here. My concern is to explore the ways in which the religious community absorbs the psychological model of the dominant culture in the expression of their indigenous spirituality. A religious tradition that takes root in two different host cultures may in fact develop into two religious communities with similar religious beliefs but different implicit psychologies depending on the cultural resources or affordances available. Family resemblances still persist in belief and practice (Wittgenstein & Anscombe, 1953). A host culture can augment psychologically some aspects of religious experience and mute other dimensions depending on the affordances. Those affordances include a rich or impoverished language for life experiences and aspects of freedom to explore nontraditional religious expression.

Over the past several decades, psychological research has shown how powerful a force culture is in shaping the discipline of psychology and the folk psychology of a society. We have discovered significant differences between cultures and communities in cognition (contextual versus abstract), privileged emotions, expressions of pathology, assumptions regarding the nature of the ideal self, theories of healing, and so on (Cohen, 2010; Cohen & Kitayama, 2019). And since culture seems to impact psychological processes and since religion is a human experience that employs various culturally shaped psychological processes, there may be differences between cultures and communities in the way they experience spirituality, transcendence, transformation, and religious health.

If the larger host culture privileges specific psychological processes, then the spirituality in the smaller indigenous community may be transformed, erased, or reinforced. Four ways in which the host culture, psychological processes, and spirituality intersect are language, individualism, collectivism, and neoliberalism.

LANGUAGE. Cassaniti and Luhrmann (2014) articulated one way the power of language provided by a culture shapes religiousness. If a culture does not provide a name for an experience, it may not be included in one's moral/spiritual vocabulary. Sleep paralysis, for example, is the experience of waking and being unable to move one's limbs. This was experienced by 33 percent of an American sample but virtually none of them framed it as an explicitly religious experience. However, 55 percent of Thai Buddhists had a name for this experience (*Phi Am*) and tended to talk about it as a spiritual event.

INDIVIDUALISM. Thousands of studies have used the distinction between individualistic and collectivistic cultures. In the psychology of religion research, well-being is usually associated with Western individualism. Perhaps this is the case because well-being is also defined individualistically. In a recent study by Krys et al. (2019), the researchers predicted, and then found, that individuals in more collective cultures seek a more communal/relational type of well-being. Here the reference to well-being is family health and relational harmony. It would not be surprising then that more individualistic cultures would encourage a spirituality that is more individual. The cultural context shapes the texture of indigenous religion (Dueck & Johnson, 2016). Hefner (1993) noted that an individualistic Christian message is less appealing to cultures or communities that see the individual as socially embedded.

COLLECTIVISM. How one hears the voice of God appears to depend on the host culture's emphasis on the individual, embodiedness, or communalism (Luhrmann, 2011). Charismatic religion has penetrated cultures as different as American, Ghanaian, and Indian. Pentecostalism is a Christian religion that is personal, emotional, and intense; worship services may include speaking in tongues, prophecies, and healings. Most notable is the report that Pentecostals may hear God speak to them personally.

Luhrmann (2017) has asked whether the way in which persons hear God's voice varies by culture. Indeed, it does. Luhrmann reported that American Pentecostals were more likely to report God's voice as private and an interior back-and-forth conversation where God might impart wisdom, give directives, and be playful and personal. The Chennai India participants said that God had spoken through the actions and feeling of other people. In Accra, Ghana, Christians heard God in their body. In the end, Luhrmann concludes the following: "The dominant way people experience God as speaking shifts across social worlds, even when people hold the same ideas about how God speaks" (2017, p. 128). Luhrmann summarized the three cognitive approaches as follows:

Thus, there are, one might say, different cultural invitations, different available ways of thinking about thinking: in the US, that the mind is private, bounded and supernaturally inert; in Chennai, that the mind involves a social process; in Accra, that the mind is supernaturally charged, more like a bodily process, and evil thoughts can harm. One could call these different invitations mind-mindedness, other-mindedness or body-mindedness. (p. 130)

NEOLIBERALISM. A shift from a traditional host culture to a neoliberal society creates correlative changes in moral commitments. This shift is evident in the relationships between Ghanaian culture, psychological relational processes, and spirituality. Salter and Adams (2012) used an African dilemma tale to explore this cultural context. "A man, his wife, his mother, and his mother-in-law were attacked by a marauding band. They fled to the river, but his canoe could take only the man and one passenger. Which did he take?" (Doke, 1947; cited in Bascom, 1975, p. 93). "Of course NOT his mother-in-law. His wife then? No, he can get another wife! But he could not get another mother" (Bascom, 1975, p. 93). To this day, West Africans tend to prioritize mother over wife in the dilemma described above, that is, kinship over nuclear family. When a WEIRD (Western, educated, industrial, rich, and democratic; Henrich, Heine, & Norenzayan, 2010) neoliberal culture informs Western mainstream folk psychology, the wife is privileged over mother—and the "romantic" relationship is the setting for "true love" (Wu, Zhang, & Lai, 2008).

Would ethical priorities change if the participants were urban or rural, lived in America or Ghana, or identified with a spirituality that is more independent or interdependent? The independent spirituality views salvation as rescue from poverty and the accumulation of wealth as a sign of God's blessing. Conversion is a personal experience with God based on an individual decision. Converts are encouraged to make a complete break with the past, non-Christian family members, and old traditions (offering food and drink to the ancestors). Traditional Ghanaian churches are, however, more conservative, interdependent, and connected to the past.

Salter and Adams (2012) created the following experimental situation: "Suppose there is a health emergency and several people request your help in paying for medical treatment. The requests are more than you can manage with your limited resources. Whom do you help?" (p. 236). They instructed participants to rank ten relationships in the order that they would provide treatment: best friend, brother, daughter, father, mother, neighbor, sister, self, son, and spouse.

Based on rankings of the participants (all Ghanaian), results showed that urban participants more so than rural tended to prioritize their nuclear family over kin relationships (i.e., spouses/children over parents/neighbors). This pattern was significantly reversed among Ghanaians living in Ghana over Ghanaians living in America. As predicted, more independent Pentecostals valued the nuclear family over kinship, and the reverse was the case in the traditional churches. Also, the more frequently that Ghanaian participants attended the Pentecostal church, the more they chose to support the nuclear family over the extended family. The results regarding church attendance and frequency of attendance suggest that the congregation played a critical role in moving church members toward a culture of independence and nuclearization of the family, and away from more traditional kinship commitments. In every setting in which one would expect greater influence of neoliberal folk psychology (urban, living in the United States, attending a more independent church, and attending it more frequently), the priority was on the nuclear family over kinship.

This study is a powerful example of how host cultures shape indigenous spiritual groups with modern neoliberal psychology as the moderating variable. The Pentecostal and traditional churches are two separate indigenous communities with their own history and relational structure. The more one attends a church shaped by neoliberalism, the more modern and individualistic become the ethical commitments of its members. What's more, geographical location (Kansas City or Accra) results in different levels of ideological socialization into neoliberalism.

Salter and Adams (2012) interpreted the results using "a cultural psychology perspective to explore the dynamic, mutual constitution of personal relationship tendencies and cultural-ecological affordances for neoliberal subjectivity and abstracted independence" (p. 232). In many West African communities, stable cultural ecologies or contexts encourage or call for embedded interdependence (eating together, communal co-residence, reduced choices, etc.). Prominent in WEIRD cultural settings is abstracted independence that affords a sense of insulation from others, tenuous relationships, and voluntary agreement between separate actors. The influence of globalization with its emphasis on the individual, increased circulation of capital, exchange of ideas, shift toward urbanization, increased mobility, nuclearizing the family unit, emphasizing relationships based on romantic love, and various psychological processes is synonymous with neoliberalism.

CONCLUSION

The pressing issue I have raised is whether Western psychological research empowers indigenous communities to access what they consider the best of their traditions. Our current reality is that the impact of neocolonialism on indigenous communities makes it difficult for these communities to maintain their values. Alfred and Corntassel (2005) state that concern well:

Current approaches to confronting the problem of contemporary colonialism ignore the wisdom of the teachings of our ancestors reflected in such concepts as Peoplehood and the Fourth World. They are, in a basic way, building not on a spiritual and cultural foundation provided to us as the heritage of our nations, but on the weakened and severely damaged cultural and spiritual and social results of colonialism. Purported decolonization and watered-down cultural restoration processes that accept the premises and realities of our colonized existences as their starting point are inherently flawed and doomed to fail. They attempt to reconstitute strong nations on the foundations of enervated, dispirited and decultured people. That is the honest and brutal reality; and that is the fundamental illogic of our contemporary struggle. (p. 612)

In response to this profound lament, the following suggestions and recommendations are addressed to Western psychologists of religion/spirituality.

1. When cultural psychologists colonized indigenous peoples in conversations about their life, suffering, and spirituality, they are engaging in an embodied act of moral witness, an act of care, and an act of love. Ullma (2006) commented that bearing witness is a social process that "exposes a disavowed reality of evil and suffering and witnessing as a distinct function of the therapist and as a curative element in psychoanalytic treatment" (p. 181). What has been said of therapy as an act of moral witness could be said of indigenous psychology of religion research as well. The Ting and Sundararajan (2018) study is a good example.

2. Psychologists need to understand the nature of neoliberalism that has captured Western imagination. Moreover, psychologists are encouraged to recognize the way Western psychology has been

colonized by this powerful tradition and the toxicity of this tradition for indigenous peoples' spirituality. Western psychologists can learn to bracket their colonized Western psychology when in conversation with non-Western psychologists.

3. We encourage psychologists to earn the right to interview participants in indigenous communities by building relationships for a lengthy period of time. Hood and Williamson (2008) have a twenty-five-year history with the serpent-handlers in the Appalachian region. They have defended their right to practice, commiserated with the families of individuals who died by a snakebite, and reported the community's beliefs and practices to the academic community with honor and respect.

4. A pressing issue is whether we can learn from indigenous moral and spiritual communities. Darcia Narvaez (2014) is clear; we can. Her confidence is based on her stellar research on processes of moral formation in hunter-gatherer communities with their profound attachment to their children, the inculcation of values, and the development of character. From these native communities she reported she has learned much about moral formation: kindness, generosity, respect, compassion, forgiveness, humility, and courage. Edward Sapir (1924/1956) suggested that culture is constituted by the desires of a people. In our understanding of culture, he suggested that we focus not on quotidian culture but on the refined emotions of high culture: art, literature, poetry, and so on. Culture is understood then in terms of what a community aspires to be and what gives them life.

In this chapter I reviewed a wide range of studies in the field of cultural and indigenous psychology, noting that the domination of the Western paradigm for psychology of religion research has muted and perhaps distorted the voice of indigenous spiritualities. In response I recommended that premodern folk psychologies be honored in understanding the then prevailing religious sentiments. Numerous studies were reported demonstrating the intimate relationship between local cultures and the expression of religiousness. Finally, I examined the impact of host cultures on the form and texture of local religion/spirituality.

REFERENCES

Alfred, T., & Corntassel, J. (2005). Being indigenous: Resurgences against contemporary colonialism. *Government and Opposition, 40*(4), 597–614.

Aristotle. (2010). *De anima: On the soul.* Newburyport, MA: Focus Publishing / R. Pullins Co.

Arnett, J. J. (2008). The neglected 95%: Why American psychology needs to become less American. *American Psychologist, 63*(7), 602–624.

Bascom, W. R. (1975). *African dilemma tales.* Paris: Mouton.

Buss, A. R. (1975). The emerging field of the sociology of psychological knowledge. *American Psychologist, 30*(10), 988–1002.

Cassaniti, J. L., & Luhrmann, T. M. (2014). The cultural kindling of spiritual experiences. *Current Anthropology, 55*(10), S333–S343.

Chakkarath, P. (2005). What can Western psychology learn from indigenous psychologies?—Lessons from Hindu psychology. In W. Friedlmeier, P. Chakkarath, & B. Schwarz (Eds.), *Culture and human development: The importance of cross-cultural research for the social sciences* (pp. 31–51). Hove, UK: Taylor and Francis.

Chakkarath, P. (2013). Bernardino de Sahagún and Matteo Ricci: Catholic missionaries as forerunners of a culture sensitive psychology. In A. Loretoni, J. Pauchard, & A. Pirni (Eds.), *Questioning universalism: Western and New Confucian conceptions and their implications* (pp. 185–198). Pisa, Italy: Edizioni ETS.

Cohen, D., & Kitayama, S. (Eds.). (2019). *Handbook of cultural psychology* (2nd ed.). New York: Guilford Press.

Cohen, E. (2010). From the Bodhi tree, to the analyst's couch, then into the MRI scanner: The psychologization of Buddhism. *Annual Review of Critical Psychology, 8,* 97–119.

Cox, R. H. (Ed.). (1973/2010). *Religious systems and psychotherapy.* Eugene, OR: Wipf & Stock.

Dalal, A. K., & Misra, G. (2010). The core and context of Indian psychology. *Psychology and Developing Societies, 22*(1), 121–155.

Danziger, K. (2009). The holy grail of universality. In T. Teo, P. Stenner, A. Rutherford, E., Park, & C. Baerveldt (Eds.), *Varieties of theoretical psychology—ISTP 2007* (pp. 2–11). Toronto: Captus.

de Sahagún, B. (1970–1982). *Florentine Codex: General history of the things of new Spain, from the Sequera manuscript of 1578–1579, rev. ed., Vols. 1–13.* Santa Fe, NM: School of American Research and the University of Utah.

Doi, T. (2005). *Understanding amae: The Japanese concept of need-love.* Leiden, the Netherlands: Global Oriental.

Doke, C.M. (1947). Bantu wisdom lore. *African Studies, 6*(3), 101–120

Dudgeon, P., & Walker, R. (2015). Decolonising Australian psychology: Discourses, strategies, and practice. *Journal of Social and Political Psychology, 3*(1), 276–297.

Dueck, A., Ansloos, J., Johnson, A., & Fort, C. (2017). Western cultural psychology of religion: Alternatives to ideology. *Pastoral Psychology, 66*(1), 397–425.

Dueck, A., & Johnson, A. (2016). Cultural psychology of religion: Spiritual transformation. *Pastoral Psychology 65*(3), 299–328. Doi: 10.1007/s11089-016-0690-8

Dueck, A., & Reimer, K. (2009). *A peaceable psychology.* Grand Rapids: Brazos Press.

Dueck, A., & Xu, H. (2017). Culture, attachment, and spirituality: Indigenous, ideological and international perspectives. *Research in the Social Scientific Study of Religion, 28,* 255–277. Doi: 10.1163_9789004348936_013

Enriquez, V. G. (1988). *From colonial to liberation psychology: The indigenous perspective in Philippine psychology.* Manila: De La Salle University Press.

Gantt, E. E., & Williams, R. N. (Eds.). (2018). *On hijacking science: Exploring the nature and consequences of overreach in psychology.* New York: Routledge.

Geertz, C. (2008). *Local knowledge: Further essays in interpretive anthropology.* New York: Basic Books.

Gergen, K. J., Gulerce, A., Lock, A., & Misra, G. (1996). Psychological science in cultural context. *American Psychologist, 51*(5), 496–523.

Gone, J. P. (2019). "The thing happened as he wished": Recovering an American Indian cultural psychology. *American Journal Community Psychology,* 1–13. DOI 10.1002/ajcp.12353

Granovetter, M. (1978). Threshold models of collective behavior. *American Journal of Sociology, 83*(6), 1420–1443. Doi:10.1086/226707.

Grieves, V. (2008). Aboriginal spirituality: A baseline for indigenous knowledges development in Australia. *Canadian Journal of Native Studies, 28*(2), 363–398.

Harvey, G. (Ed.). (2000). *Indigenous religions: A companion.* London: Cassell.

Hefner, R. W. (1993). Of faith and commitment: Christian conversion in Muslim Java. In R. W. Hefner (Ed.), *Conversion to Christianity: Historical and anthropological perspectives on a Great Transformation* (pp. 99–125). Berkeley: University of California Press.

Henrich, J., Heine, S. J., & Norenzayan, A. (2010). The weirdest people in the world? *Behavioral and Brain Sciences, 33,* 61–83.

Hood, R., & Williamson, W. P. (2008). *Them that believe: The power and meaning of the Christian serpent-handling tradition.* Berkeley: University of California Press.

Hwang, K. K. (2011). *Foundations of Chinese psychology: Confucian social relations.* Cham, Switzerland: Springer Science & Business Media.

Jacoby, R. (1975). *Social amnesia: Conformist psychology from Adler to Laing.* Boston: Beacon Press.

Jackson J. C., Watts, J., Henry, T. R., List, J. M., Forkel, R., Mucha, P. J., Greenhill, S. J., Gray, R. D., & Lindquist, K. A. (2019). Emotion semantics show both cultural variation and universal structure. *Science, 366,* 1517–1522.

Kashima, Y. (2019). A history of cultural psychology: Cultural psychology as a tradition and a movement. In D. Cohen & S. Kitayama (Eds.), *Handbook of cultural psychology* (pp. 53–78). New York: Guilford Press.

Kim, U., & Berry, J. (1993). *Indigenous psychologies: Experience and research in cultural context*. Newbury Park, CA: Sage.

Kim, U., Yang, K., & Hwang, K. (2006). Contributions to indigenous and cultural psychology: Understanding people in context. In U. Kim, K. Yang, & K. Hwang (Eds.), *Indigenous and cultural psychology: Understanding people in context* (pp. 3–26). New York: Springer.

Kitayama, S., & Cohen, D. (Eds.). (2010). *Handbook of cultural psychology*. New York: Guilford Press.

Kohlberg, L. (1971). From is to ought: How to commit the naturalistic fallacy and get away with it in the study of moral development. In N. Malcolm & T. S. Mischel (Eds.), *Cognitive development and epistemology* (pp. 151–235). Amsterdam, Netherlands: Elsevier.

Kraybill, D. B., Johnson-Weiner, K. M., & Nolt, S. M. (2013). *The Amish*. Baltimore, MD: Johns Hopkins University Press.

Kraybill, D. B., Nolt, S. M., & Weaver-Zercher, D. L. (Eds.). (2010). *Amish grace: How forgiveness transcended tragedy*. New York: John Wiley & Sons.

Krys, K., Zelenski, J. M., Capaldi, C. A., Park, J., van Tilburg, W., van Osch, Y., ... & Uchida, Y. (2019). Putting the "we" into well-being: Using collectivism-themed measures of well-being attenuates well-being's association with individualism. *Asian Journal of Social Psychology, 22*, 256–267. Doi: 10.1111/ajsp.12364

Leon-Portilla, C. (2002). *Bernardino de Sahagún: First anthropologist* (Trans. M. J. Mixco). Norman: University of Oklahoma Press.

LeVine, R. A. (2014). Attachment theory as cultural ideology. In H. Otto & H. Keller (Eds.), *Different faces of attachment: Cultural variations on a universal human need*. (pp. 50–65). Cambridge, MA: Cambridge University Press.

Long, W. (2013). Rethinking "relevance": South African psychology in context. *History of Psychology, 16*(1), 19–35. Doi: 10.1037/a0029675

Long, W. (2020). Psychology and oppression. In W. Pickgren (Ed.), *Oxford Encyclopedia of the History of Psychology*. New York: Oxford University Press.

Luhrmann, T. M. (2011). Toward an anthropological theory of mind. *Suomen Antropologi: Journal of the Finnish Anthropological Society, 36*(4), 5–69.

Luhrmann, T. M. (2012). *When God talks back: Understanding the American evangelical relationship with God*. New York: Vintage.

Luhrmann, T. (2017). Knowing God. *Cambridge Journal of Anthropology, 35*(2), 125–142. Doi:10.3167/cja.2017.350210

Ma, H. K. (1988). The Chinese perspectives on moral judgment development. *International Journal of Psychology, 23*, 201–227.

Ma, H. K. (1989). Moral orientation and moral judgment in adolescents in Hong Kong, Mainland China, and England. *Journal of Cross-Cultural Psychology, 20*(2), 152–177.

Markus, H. R., & Kitayama, S. (1991). Culture and the self: Implications for cognition, emotion, and motivation. *Psychological Review, 98*(2), 224–253.

Martín-Baró, I. (1994). *Writings for a liberation psychology*. Cambridge, MA: Harvard University Press.

Narvaez, D. (2014). *Neurobiology and the development of human morality: Evolution, culture and wisdom*. New York: W. W. Norton.

Narvaez, D., Arrows, F., Halton, E., Collier, B., & Enderle, G. (2019). *Indigenous sustainable wisdom: First-Nation know-how for global flourishing*. New York: Peter Lang.

Nisbett, R. (2004). *The geography of thought: How Asians and Westerners think different-ly ... and why*. New York: Simon and Schuster.

Nsamenang, B. (1997). Towards an Afrocentric perspective in developmental psy-chology. *IFE Psychologia: An International Journal, 5*(1), 127–137.

Pankalla, A., & Kośnik, K. (2016). Slavic indigenous psychology as a science about the Slavic soul. *Psychology and Personality, 2*(10), 21–31.

Pankalla, A., & Kośnik, K. (2018). Religion as an invaluable source of psychological knowledge: Indigenous Slavic psychology of religion. *Journal of Theoretical and Philosophical Psychology, 38*(3), 154–164.

Ratner, C. (2008). *Cultural psychology, cross-cultural psychology, and indigenous psychol-ogy*. Hauppauge, NY: Nova Publishers.

Ratner, C. (2019). Neoliberal psychology. In C. Ratner, *Neoliberal psychology* (pp. 145–174). Cham, Switzerland: Springer.

Ricci, M. (1985). *The true meaning of the lord of heaven* (Ed. D. Lancashire). St. Louis, MO: Institute of Jesuit Sources.

Salter, P. S., & Adams, G. (2012). Mother or wife? *Social Psychology, 43*(4), 232–242. Doi: 10.1027/1864-9335/a000124

Sapir, E. (1924/1956). Culture, genuine and spurious. In D. G. Mandelbaum & E. Sapir (Eds.), Culture, language and personality (pp. 78–119). Berkeley: University of California Press.

Shweder, R. A., & Bourne, E. J. (1984). Does the concept of the person vary cross-culturally? In R. A. Shweder & R. A. LeVine (Eds.), *Culture theory and essays on mind, self, and emotion* (pp. 158–199). New York: Cambridge University Press.

Shweder, R. A., & D'Andrade, R. G. (1980). The systematic distortion hypothe-sis. *New Directions for Methodology of Social and Behavioral Science, 4*, 37–58.

Shweder, R., Much, N., Mahapatra, M., & Park, L. (1997). Divinity and the "big three" explanations of suffering. *Morality and Health*, 119–169.

Sugarman, J. (2015). Neoliberalism and psychological ethics. *Journal of Theoretical and Philosophical Psychology, 35*(2), 103–116.

Sundararajan, L. (2015). *Understanding emotion in Chinese culture: Thinking through psychology*. Cham,Switzerland: Springer International Publishing.

Teo, T. (2010). What is epistemological violence in the empirical social sciences? *So-cial and Personality Psychology Compass, 4*(5), 295–303.

Teo, T. (2018). *Homo neoliberalus*: From personality to forms of subjectivity. *Theory & Psychology, 28*(5), 581–599.

Teo, T. (2019). Academic subjectivity, idols, and the vicissitudes of virtues in science: Epistemic modesty versus epistemic grandiosity. In K. O'Doherty, L. Osbeck, E. Schraube, & J. Yen (Eds.), *Psychological studies of science and technology* (pp. 31–43). Cham, Switzerland: Palgrave Macmillan. https://doi.org/10.1007/978-3-030-25308-0_2

Ting, R. S.-K., & Sundararajan, L. (2018). *Culture, cognition, and emotion in China's religious ethnic minorities: Voices of suffering among the Yi*. Cham, Switzerland: Palgrave Macmillan.

Ting, R. S.-K., Sundararajan, L., & Huang, Q. (2017). Narratives of suffering: A psycholinguistic analysis of two Yi religious communities in Southwest China. *Research in the Social Scientific Study of Religion, 28,* 231–254.

Todd, P. M., Gigerenzer, G., & the ABC Research Group. (2012). *Ecological rationality: Intelligence in the world*. New York: Oxford University Press.

Ullma, C. (2006). Bearing witness: Across the barriers in society and in the clinic. *Psychoanalytic Dialogues, 16*(2), 181–198.

White, G. M. (1994). Affecting culture: Emotion and morality in everyday life. In S. Kitayama & H. R. Markus (Eds.), *Emotion and culture: Empirical studies of mutual influence* (pp. 89–130). Washington, DC: American Psychological Association.

Wittgenstein, W., & Anscombe, G. E. M. (1953). *Philosophical investigations*. London: Basic Blackwell.

Wu, S.-T., Zhang, J.-X., & Lai, J.-W. (2008). Cross-cultural universality and variation of causal attribution: A comparative study of attribution of social events among Chinese, Korean and American. *International Journal of Psychology, 43,* S598–S604.

Wundt, W. (2013). *Elementary folk psychology*. New York: Routledge.

Yang, K.-S. (2012). Indigenous psychology, Westernized psychology, and indigenized psychology: A non-Western psychologist's view. *Chang Gung Journal of Humanities and Social Sciences, 5*(1): 1–32.

Yeh, K.-H. (2019). *Asian indigenous psychologies in the global context*. Palgrave Studies in Indigenous Psychology. Cham, Switzerland: Palgrave Macmillan.

PART 2

RELIGIOUS AND
SPIRITUAL PSYCHOLOGIES
THROUGH AN
INDIGENOUS LENS

STEVEN PIRUTINSKY

I CREATED THE EVIL INCLINATION AND I CREATED TORAH ITS ANTIDOTE

An Indigenous Jewish Psychology[1]

Jewish and *Judaism* are broad terms that describe a diverse ethnic-religious-cultural identity and a multifaceted ancient religious tradition that span over four thousand years of history, migrations across several continents, and interactions with innumerable cultural contexts (Wein, 1995). In terms of psychology, many of the Jewish ideas expressed throughout the centuries are psychological. Judaism, in fact, includes several organized systems of psychology, including Lurianic Kabbalah (Scholem, 2011), the ethical system of Rabbi Salanter (Etkes, 1993), the philosophical approach of Maimonides (Mizrahi, 2011), and modern systems such as those developed by Spero (Cohen, 2008). However, these frameworks, while respected and influential, are somewhat narrow in scope and were not widely adopted across time and place. Accordingly, describing an indigenous psychology of Judaism poses a significant challenge, as it cannot be fully defined by a set of specific principles. Rather it consists of numerous interwoven ideas that are highly contextual and at times contradictory. Nevertheless, it is possible to discern some central, broad, and common threads that run throughout the complex tapestry of Jewish psychological thought, and it is these threads that this chapter describes. Moreover, these keys ideas are compared with modern psychological theory, and clinical implications for working with Jewish clients are provided throughout this chapter.

HISTORICAL, CULTURAL, AND RELIGIOUS CONTEXT

JEWISH HISTORY

Although a complete discussion of Jewish history is well beyond the scope of this chapter, the traditional narrative has important psychological implications. Briefly, traditional Jewish history suggests that the Jewish people descend directly from the biblical patriarchs, were enslaved in Egypt, and were freed through divine intervention (Wein, 1995). G-d subsequently revealed his laws and knowledge to the Jewish people at Mount Sinai and led them into the land of Canaan. There they conquered land, established communities, built a central temple, founded dynastic kingdoms, and lived until the destruction of the First Temple around 600–500 BCE by the Assyrian Empire (Wein, 1995). Following this, the Jews spread out all over the Middle East and North Africa, and established communities most notably in Babylonia. While some returned to Jerusalem some seventy years later and built a Second Temple, many did not, and large Jewish communities continued to exist throughout the Near East (Wein, 1995). This Second Temple era lasted until Roman occupation of Israel and a series of subsequent rebellions that resulted in the destruction of the Second Temple and virtually all surrounding Jewish communities in 70 CE. This further scattered the Jews and initiated a series of migrations culminating in the formation of two somewhat distinct groups: Mizrachi Jews, who lived in the Middle East and Asia, and Ashkenazi Jews, who inhabited western and eastern Europe.

While there have been many intense and religious debates between and within these various communities, at times leading to formal schisms (e.g., the Karaites; Revel, 1913), most appeared to have largely adhered to coherent and similar sets of beliefs, laws, and traditions (Wein, 1993). These were preserved through a strong collectivist (Triandis, 2018) and "tight" culture (Gelfand, 2019) that included strict social norms, limited personal interactions with non-Jews, preservation of distinct languages, and a strong sense of social identity (Tajfel, 2010). Extensive anti-Semitism, ghettoization, and economic restriction, particularly in Europe, also enforced Jewish identity and limited both the desire and ability of Jews to assimilate into surrounding cultures (Wein, 1993). The current chapter focuses on this common religious culture, sometimes referred to as Rabbinic or Orthodox Judaism.

Because of these factors, traditional Jewish culture is moderately collectivist in that it emphasizes cohesive community, unifying rituals and laws, biologic descent, and the rights of the community over personal belief and individual religious experience. Recent empirical research corroborates these assertions, finding that Jews, traditional and nontraditional, residing in the United States express more collectivist attitudes (Cohen & Hill, 2007). In fact, communal responsibility is directly commanded in Leviticus (19:17)—"You should surely rebuke your friend"— and is enshrined in the Talmud dictum stating, "All of Israel are guarantors for each other" (Shavuos, 39a). It is also implicit in several Jewish religious laws, such as the obligation to honor parents, the elderly, and scholars; prohibitions against slandering others, harboring grudges, and taking revenge; the obligations to give charity, provide physical assistance to others, and comfort the sick; and the urging to greet others with a friendly face and judge them favorably (Lev, 2014). Accordingly, Jewish psychology includes a focus on harmonious interpersonal relationships, a strong sense of communal responsibility, and the valuing of this collective Jewish identity.

In recent centuries, adherence to traditional Judaism diminished, beginning with the cultural changes triggered by the European Enlightenment, emancipation of the ghettos, and growing economic and educational opportunities (Wein, 1990). This, in turn, led many to abandon traditional practices and generally weakened Jewish identity (Wein, 1990). The dramatic events of the mid-twentieth century rapidly accelerated this process, most notably through the total destruction of European Jewish communities in the Holocaust, the foundation of the largely secular state of Israel, and the subsequent expulsion of Mizrachi Jews from most Arab communities. Following these events, the vast majority of Jews relocated to Israel or the United States, and the religious nature of Jewish communities has declined steeply (Wein, 2001). Nevertheless, strong traditional communities, often identified as Orthodox or Haredi, exist in many countries, with the largest and most established communities in the United States and Israel (DellaPergola, 2016).

JUDAISM

In terms of religion, Judaism is an ancient monotheistic religion that encompasses the theology, religious ritual, civil law, and culture of the Jewish people. It is a textual religion centered on the Torah, which in the most general sense refers to the Pentateuch, various prophetic texts, and the oral interpretative tradition recorded in authoritative texts such as the Mishna (536 BCE–70 CE), Talmud (100–500 CE), and Midrash (400–1200 CE). While there are a variety of historical and modern variations of Judaism, the vast majority of traditional Jewish cultures believe that G-d gave the Torah and oral tradition directly to the Jewish people at Sinai (Cohn-Sherbok, 2003). These texts and traditions serve as the source of all religious, spiritual, moral, and ethical knowledge, and are also assumed to include all worldly knowledge. As the Mishna (Pirkei Avos, 5:6) states, "Turn in it, turn in it, because everything is in it." In fact, Midrashic (Genesis 3:5; 64:8) and Kabalistic traditions view the Torah as the basis for all creation: "G-d looked into the Torah and then created the world" (Zohar, Terumah, 161A).

In terms of theology, traditional Judaism views G-d as unitary, omnipotent, omnibenevolent, and actively engaged in human affairs. This engagement involves teaching ethical principles through the Torah and accompanying oral tradition, active involvement in world and personal affairs, judgment of individual actions, and the distribution of rewards and punishments (Birnbaum, 1975). Spirituality in Judaism focuses on prayer, observance of religious rituals and holidays, the development of a personal relationship with G-d, and most of all the study of Torah (e.g., "and the study of Torah is equal to all of them" [Mishnah, Peah, 1:1]). Ethical interpersonal conduct is also highly emphasized, as the Mishna (Pirkei Avos, 3:10) states: "Anyone with whom man is pleased, G-d is pleased." In fact, interpersonal conduct is often stressed even above Torah study: "The way of the land [referring to proper conduct that is pleasing to others] precedes Torah" (Midrash, Leviticus Rabbah, 9:3), and "if there is no way of the land, there is no Torah" (Mishna, Pirkei Avos, 3:17).

Judaism also includes a detailed set of religious laws that is codified in the Mishna, Talmud, and various compendiums written throughout the centuries (e.g., Karo, 1563/1992; Maimonides, 1170–1180/1990). These laws address all domains of personal and communal life, including rituals, prayer, purity, dietary law, family law, and civil law. They are based on the 613 biblical mitzvoth or commandments, and observing these laws embeds religious meaning and moral conduct within everyday life.

This tripartite focus on religious law, spirituality, and interpersonal relationships is illustrated by the classic aphorism quoted in the Mishna (Pirkei Avos, 1:1): "On three things the world stands, on Torah, service [prayer], and doing kindness." Finally, traditional Judaism also includes belief in the Messiah—a religious and political leader who will bring the Jews back to the land of Israel, rebuild the Temple in Jerusalem, and usher in an era of world peace that will unite mankind in a spiritual and moral way of life.

JEWISH KNOWLEDGE AND SCHOLARSHIP

Given this edited book's focus on an emic approach to the psychology of religion, I relied on indigenous methods of Jewish scholarship to develop the ideas discussed in this chapter. Accordingly, a brief introduction to traditional Jewish thought is required. While Jewish scholars have utilized various epistemologies, including empiricism, to understand humanity and the world around them, the primary and most authoritative sources were always the Sinaitic written and oral tradition. For example, a passage in Genesis (9:13)—"and my rainbow I have placed in the clouds, and it will serve as a sign of the treaty between me and the earth"—appears to imply that G-d created the rainbow specifically after the flood. Nachmanides (1194–1270) explains:

However, we are forced to agree with the Greeks that it [the rainbow] is born of the sun shining through the water in the air because in a vessel of water placed in the sun, you will observe the appearance of a rainbow. And when we look again at the text we will understand this as it says: "I have put my rainbow in the cloud" and not "I am putting." Also, the word "my rainbow" also shows that G-d already had a rainbow.

Thus, while Nachmanides utilizes empirical evidence to suggest an interpretation of this passage, in the final analysis he relies on the language of the passage itself. This process is characteristic such that the validity of ideas are judged by the degree to which they can be supported by the written and oral tradition. This has obvious psychological and clinical implications, as the adoption of any psychological ideas and clinical techniques may be predicated on supporting them through religious texts.

In addition to textual analysis, great weight is given to tradition and the opinions of previous generations, since they are viewed as closer to the initial revelation at Sinai, and their ideas are therefore more likely to resemble G-d's revealed truth (Kwall, 2015). Thus, while direct disagreement between Jewish scholars is encouraged and frequent, it is generally restricted to generational peers. For instance, it is rare to find a Talmudic author disagreeing with a ruling in the Mishna unless another sage of the Mishna era supports this position (Carmell, 1986). Accordingly, traditional Jewish culture encourages deference to the authority of Torah sages. As stated in Deuteronomy (17:8–11), "When something is obscured from you ... go to the priests, the Levites, and the judge.... And you shall do as they tell you.... Do not deviate from that which they tell you right or left." Adhering to rabbinic authority is in fact central to traditional Jewish belief, as each individual is enjoined to "make for himself a Rabbi" (Mishna, Pirkei Avos, 1:1) and to "make your house a meeting place for sages—sit in the dust of their feet and thirstily drink their words" (Mishna, Pirkei Avos, 1:4). This statement has important psychological and clinical implications, such as the need to respect authority and elders, seek rabbinic consultation and approval, and connect psychological and clinical ideas to tradition.

Finally, as described above, new Jewish knowledge is primarily generated by careful textual analysis of earlier textual and oral sources, interpretation and contextualization of those sources, deference to the sages of previous generations, and consultation with current rabbinic authorities. Accordingly, the current paper uses these traditional methods to develop several fundamental, broad, and widely accepted principles of indigenous Jewish psychology, as well as to discuss briefly their possible psychotherapeutic implications.

JEWISH PSYCHOLOGICAL PRINCIPLES OF THE SELF

THE GOOD AND EVIL INCLINATIONS

Judaism commonly acknowledges that the human mind is not a unitary integrated experience but rather that it consists of competing and divergent impulses, desires, beliefs, thoughts, and feelings—an idea that is present in many ancient and indigenous cultures (Haidt, 2006). As stated in the traditional liturgy for Rosh Hashanah and Yom Kippur, "It is true that you [G-d] created them and that you know their desires/inclinations" (*Machzor La'Yom Kippurim*, 2001, p. 310). These impulses are viewed as vexing and the source of immoral or sinful behavior. Jewish tradition describes them as the "*yetzer tov*" or good inclination and a "*yetzer hara*" or evil inclination. The idea of an evil inclination, however, can be misunderstood as similar to the doctrine of original sin, which suggests that humanity is a *massa damnata* (damned crowd) imbued with inherently sinful and unmanageable desires (Cross & Livingstone, 2005). Rather, the *yetzer hara* in traditional Jewish thought describes normative yet primitive biological and psychological impulses, which have helpful functions but need active management to maintain moral and adaptive behavior. This is illustrated by a Midrashic commentary (Genesis Rabba, 9:7) explaining that when G-d reflects on his creation, "And behold it was good" (i.e., Genesis 1:10), He refers to the good inclination. Yet when G-d states, "And behold it was very good" (Genesis 1:31), He refers to the "evil inclination … because without the evil inclination, man would not build houses, marry wives, have children, or engage in labor." While these drives are not inherently evil, they are referred to as the *yetzer hara* because they are viewed as naturally leading to evil without constant conscious stewardship. As stated in Genesis 8:21, "and G-d spoke in his heart no longer will I curse the earth because of man because the inclination of man's heart is evil from his youth."

Moreover, Judaism assumes that the evil inclination is more instinctual and biologically fundamental than the good inclination, and that it arises early in development. As stated in the Talmud (Avos de-Rabbi Nassan, 16:2), "The *Yetzer Hara* is 13 years older than the *Yetzer Tov*. From his mother's womb it grows and comes with him ... and after 13 years the *Yetzer Tov* is born ... and when he goes to commit a sin, it [the *Yetzer Tov*] rebukes him and says 'empty one!'" Finally, Judaism suggests that the *yetzer hara* has both conscious and unconscious elements. As stated in the Talmud (Sukkah, 52a), "The evil inclinations has seven names and Yoel (2:20) called it 'the Hidden One' ... because it is ready and hiding within the human heart." Accordingly, traditional Jews are likely to accept psychotherapeutic interventions that acknowledge conflicting impulses and thoughts, involve the acceptance of ambivalence, and may choose to frame maladaptive cognition, emotions, and behaviors as the work of the *yetzer hara*.

The force opposing this *yetzer hara* is the *yetzer tov* or good inclination. As described above, it is "born" at age thirteen for boys and twelve for girls when they begin to enter adulthood, and it continues to develop slowly throughout adolescence and adulthood through a variety of means. These include the recognition of G-d's presence—"Know before who you stand" (Talmud, Berakhos, 28b); the cultivation of religious and spiritual wisdom—"G-d says to Israel, my son, I created the evil inclination and I created Torah its antidote" (Talmud, Kiddushin, 30b); and by surrounding oneself with moral exemplars—"make your house a meeting place for sages, sit in the dust of their feet, and thirstily drink their words" (Pirkei Avos, 1:4). In addition, Judaism emphasizes that behavior plays a key role in building internal moral judgment, a point discussed at length below.

Finally, Judaism also suggests that relying only on internal mechanisms (i.e., the *yetzer tov*) to curb immoral or harmful behavior is insufficient, and Judaism therefore greatly emphasizes the need to cultivate a supportive environmental context. As stated in the Mishna, "Create a fence around the Torah" (Pirkei Avos, 1:1), and "Distance yourself from a bad neighbor; and don't befriend a wicked person" (Pirkei Avos, 1:7). This concept is codified in Talmudic law, which institutes many preventative measures—such as the laws of seclusion, which forbid the seclusion of unrelated males and females (e.g., Talmud, Kiddushin, 80b) and the limiting of otherwise permitted activities that can lead to violation of the Sabbath (e.g., Talmud, Shabbos, 123b).

The struggle between the *yetzer hara* and *yezter tov* is assumed to be monumental and lifelong, as stated in the Talmud: "It [the evil inclination] appears like a mountain" (Sukkah, 52a), and "The evil inclination renews itself every day" (Kiddushin, 30b), as well as in the Mishna (Pirkei Avos, 2:5): "Do not trust yourself until you die." Despite the difficulty, however, Judaism assumes that it is generally possible to willfully overcome these impulses and choose moral and adaptive behavior. As G-d tells Cain before he murders his brother, "Why are you angry and ashamed? ... At the entrance, sin is lying, and you are its desire—but you can rule over it" (Genesis 4:6–7). This concept, the human ability to consciously determine behavior in the presence of various impulses, is called *bechira* or choice.[2]

BECHIRA OR CHOICE

As described above, traditional Judaism views the human mind as a battleground of competing positive and negative impulses that interact with the environmental context to present human beings with difficult choices. G-d, however, gave humanity both the ability to make these choices and moral principles to guide them. As stated in Deuteronomy (30:17–18), "And behold I have placed before you good and evil, life and death. And you should choose life." This is further expanded on in various classical sources, including the widely studied ethical text *Mesilas Yesharim* [Path of Righteousness] (Luzzatto, 1738/1987): "Man is truly placed within a raging war, for all matters of the world whether good or bad are trials to man ... but if he is a warrior and victorious in this war on all fronts, he will become a complete person."

Reconciling this concept of human free will with the Jewish doctrine of G-d's omnipotence has been debated throughout the centuries (Manekin & Kellner, 1997). In fact, some Kabbalistic thinkers suggest that free will, like all other worldly phenomena, are "real" only from the human perspective and reflect illusions created by G-d's restriction of his presence. Accordingly, all human choices—even the evil and immoral— are expressions of G-d's will (Brill, 2002). This perspective, however, is controversial, and the vast majority of Torah sages presumed that human choices are volitional and not predetermined. As cryptically stated by Rabbi Akiva, a foremost authority of the late Second Temple period: "All is foreseen, but permission is granted" (Mishna, Pirkei Avos, 3:19). Similarly, Rashi in his classic commentary explains the Talmudic dictum, "Everything is in the hands of Heaven except fear of Heaven" (Berachos, 33b), by stating, "Whether one will be tall, short, poor, rich, wise, foolish, white, or black, is all in the hands of Heaven. However, whether one will be righteous or wicked is not in the hands of Heaven. This G-d placed in the hands of the human being."

Despite the primacy of *bechira*, however, it is widely acknowledged that there are some limits to free will and that not all thoughts, feelings, and behaviors are under conscious control. For example, Talmudic law includes the concepts of insanity and lack of capacity or competence, which absolves individuals of responsibility for their behaviors (Bleich, 1981). Moreover, the Talmud states that "a person is not held responsible at a time of pain" (Bava Basra, 16b), and the great Hasidic master Rav Tzadok haKohen of Lublin (haKohen, 1901/2012) wrote that "at times a person will face a challenge so great that it is impossible for him to not sin." In fact, some Jewish scholars have gone so far as to suggest that the majority of human behavior is predetermined by historical, contextual, and psychological factors—and that there is only a narrow "point of choice" on which the various factors are perfectly balanced, enabling free will (Dessler, 1955/1994). Despite these caveats, however, the concept of conscious control over behavior is foundational to Jewish psychology and is widely applied. Accordingly, traditional Jews are likely to prefer psychotherapeutic interventions that emphasize conscious control over behavior versus those that emphasize biological or unconscious factors.

MIDDOS OR CHARACTER TRAITS

As described above, traditional Jewish psychology understands the mind as a shifting battleground of contradictory impulses ruled to some degree by conscious decision making. These impulses are to some degree universal, yet it is also recognized that they included stable traits that differ between people. This is succinctly stated by the Talmud: "Just as no two faces are alike, no two minds are alike" (Berachos, 58a). These traits are called *middos* (literally measures), which refers to personality characteristics that yield stable patterns of thoughts, feelings, and behaviors.

As with many traditional ideas, the concept of *middos* is drawn from the Torah and in particular G-d's description of his own characteristics at Sinai (Exodus 20:2–6) and the thirteen attributes of mercy (Exodus 34:6–7). Midrashic and other sources accordingly suggest that the various names for G-d used throughout the Torah refer to the expression of these divergent characteristics (Nachmanides, Exodus 6:3). For example, the Torah uses the name *El-o-him*, which traditionally refers to G-d's attributes of justice, during the initial creation narrative, and then switches to the Tetragrammaton, which traditionally refers to His attributes of mercy, in later passages. Rashi (Genesis 1:1) explains, "In the beginning G-d intended to create the world with his attribute of justice but saw that it would not be sustained so he partnered his attribute of mercy with his attribute of justice."

Various Midrashic and Talmudic sources extend this concept to human experience, as the Torah commands Israel to "go in His ways" (Deuteronomy 28:9), which is widely understood as a commandment to cultivate personality traits that emulate G-d's *middos*. As stated in the Talmud (Shabbos, 133b), "Just like he is compassionate and merciful so too you should be compassionate and merciful." Consequently, personality patterns are understood to be somewhat mutable, such that they can change over time with repeated exertion of free will. Moreover, while G-d's traits are viewed as inherently morally good, even those such as "a jealous G-d who safeguards the sins of fathers and visits them on their children" (Exodus 20:5), human *middos* are conceptualized as tendencies that can lead to both moral and immoral ends.

This is powerfully illustrated by the Midrashic tradition that draws a parallel between Samuel's description of a young king David as "reddish" (1 Samuel 16:12) and the Torah's similar description of Esav [Esau] as "reddish" (Genesis 25:25). In this Midrashic account when Shmuel saw David's reddish coloring, he presumed that David, like Esav, had murderous tendencies, and he therefore hesitated to support his rule. G-d allays Samuel's fears by responding, "Esav kills as he wills, but this one [David] kills based on the decisions of the courts" (Genesis Rabba, 63:8), suggesting that while David and Esav had similarly passionate and murderous traits, David utilized his free will to channel those impulses toward justice, while Esav turned them to his own ends. In summary, traditional Jewish psychology understands that some aspects of the mind are indeed predetermined to tilt in one direction or another but that through the exercise of free will, they can be sublimated (e.g., Freud, 1930/1989) to positive ends.

THE PRIMACY OF BEHAVIOR

While thoughts and feelings are important in traditional Judaism and are indeed at the heart of many religious commandments, such as, "And you shall love the Lord, your G-d with all your heart" (Deuteronomy 6:5), traditional Judaism clearly prioritizes behavior over thoughts and feelings. As stated in the Talmud (Kiddushin, 40a), "Matters of the heart are not matters," which codifies the ruling that G-d does not judge or ascribe meaning to thoughts, feelings, and even intentions as long as they do not lead to behavior. In fact, recent empirical research suggests that Jews living in the United States weigh behavior over thoughts and feelings when judging moral character (Cohen & Rozin, 2001), suggesting that these traditional perspectives continue to exert psychological effects.

In addition, as described above, traditional Judaism includes a detailed set of biblically derived religious laws, generally referred to as the 613 *mitzvos* or commandments, which govern virtually all domains of behavior and are viewed as the primary religious expression and obligation (Eisenberg, 2005). This intense focus on fulfilling behavioral mitzvoth has led some to suggest that Judaism is primarily an orthopraxy, focused specifically on behavior and not belief (Grossberg, 2010). This assertion is highly debatable, however, as many traditional sources view the 613 mitzvoth and the accompanying body of religious law as behavioral methods for instilling moral and spiritual beliefs, values, and feelings. For example, the Midrash (Tanchuma, Shimini, 8:2) asks, "And what does G-d care if you properly slaughter an animal and eat it, or if you stab an animal and eat it? Will one help Him or the other hurt Him? … Only no. The commandments were given to refine G-d's creations, as it says, 'G-d's ways are perfect.… They are a shield for all those who take refuge in it' (Psalm 18:31)." The influential medieval Jewish philosopher Ibn Pakuda (1008/1996, Chapter 3:5) elaborated on these ideas:

Bodily pleasures come to man first ... and the attachment to them is ... strong, great and extremely urgent.... Man therefore needs external means, which aid him to resist his negative instincts.... These aids are the contents of the Torah, whereby G-d, through His messengers and prophets, taught His creatures.

Thus, it is clear that Judaism views moral and spiritual behavior as key to shaping further behavior. As stated in Pirkei Avos (4:2): "A good deed leads to another good deed, while an evil deed leads to further evil deeds." The Talmud (Arachin, 30b) expresses a similar idea regarding sinful behavior: "Once a person has sinned and repeated the sin, it becomes to him as if it is permitted." This concept, colloquially referred to as *hergel* or habituation, assumes that repeating a particular behavior leads to a degree of automatization (Twersky, 2003). In fact, habituation is a primary Jewish psychological and educational principle and is embedded within various religious laws. For example, the Mishna (Yoma, 8:4) states, "Young children are not afflicted on Yom Kippur [i.e., forcing them to fast]. However, we educate them for a year or two in order that they should be habituated to the commandments."

Moreover, traditional sources suggest that repeated behavior not only leads to automatization and habit but also induces cognitive and emotional changes—ideas that echo the theory of cognitive dissonance (Festinger, 1962). As stated by Maimonides (1170–1180/1990, Hilchos Dayos, 1:7): "How should a person habituate himself with these dispositions [i.e., positive character traits]? He should practice again and again ... until they become easy to him and no longer bothersome, then these dispositions will become established in his character." Similarly the Mishna (Pirkei Avos, 3:9) indicates that, "One whose deeds exceed his wisdom, his wisdom will be enduring, while one whose wisdom exceeds his deed, his wisdom will not endure," suggesting that thoughts and feelings unmatched by external behavior are ephemeral and will not persist.

Finally, even disingenuous behaviors are viewed as a gateway to genuine attitudes and feelings. This is vividly illustrated by the following Talmudic story (Bava Metzia, 85a): Rabbi Elazar died and left behind a son who was outrageously depraved. His colleague Reb Yehuda heard about this, found this son, ordained him as a rabbi, and placed him by his uncle to teach him. Every day the boy would say, "I'm going back," and his uncle would say to him, "You were made wise, and a golden cloak was spread on you, and they call you Rabbi—and you say I want to go back!" Eventually, he abandoned his desire to return and vowed to improve his ways. When he matured ... he became a righteous scholar in his own right. As the Talmud (Pesachim, 50b) states, "A man should always occupy himself with Torah and good deeds even if not for their own sake, because from out of [performing them with] an ulterior motive comes [performing them] for their own sake."

These ideas are expanded on in the introduction to the classical text Sefer HaChinuch ([Anonymous], 1300/1988, Mitzvah, 98), which enumerates all 613 commandments:

Why did G-d obligate us with so many commandments? Know that a man becomes who he is based on his actions. Thoughts of his heart and his intentions, always follow the lead of his actions whether for good or evil. Even a very wicked person, who decides to suddenly perform good actions, will transform quickly into a righteous individual. The same is true for a righteous person who carries out evil actions. He will become evil.

Thus, behavior is clearly central to Judaism, and thoughts, beliefs, and feelings are generally viewed as the inevitable result of moral and ethical behavior as opposed to merely the cause. This point has clinical relevance as traditional Jews are likely to quickly adopt to behavioral methods of treatment such behavioral activation, exposure, and behavioral analysis.

REWARD AND PUNISHMENT

Traditional Judaism includes a strong concept of divine reward and punishment for human behavior. This is reflected by the worldly rewards and punishments so vividly described in Leviticus (26:3–9) and Deuteronomy (11:13–15), as well as by Hillel's aphorism, "Because you drowned someone, you were drowned, and in the end, he who drowned you will be drowned" (Pirkei Avos, 2:7). These positive and negative consequences are viewed as perfectly just (e.g., "All His ways are just; He is a faithful

G-d, never unfair; righteous and moral is He" [Deuteronomy 32:4]; tempered with mercy (e.g., "He is merciful; pardons sin and does not destroy; turns His anger away and never arouses all His wrath" [Psalm 78:38]); and the result of wisdom (e.g., "Yet He is also wise and will bring evil" [Isaiah 31:2]). Moreover, Talmudic and Midrashic sources emphasize that these consequences are directly related to human behavior as illustrated by Hillel's aphorism and by the Mishna (Peah, 8:8), which states, "Anyone who takes charity when he has no need will not die until he become reliant on others." In fact, divine justice is generally viewed as the natural consequence of behavior, as stated in Proverbs 13:6: "Righteousness will guard the one who is upright in his ways, but wickedness overthrows the sinner," and in Isaiah 3:10–11: "Hail the just man because he do well, because the fruit of his labor he will eat. Woe to the wicked man because he will do poorly, because as his hands have done so will be done to him." A similar idea is advanced in the Talmud (Sanhedrin, 89b): "The liar's punishment is that even when he speaks the truth, no one believes him."

In addition to these worldly consequences, spiritual consequences are also mentioned in the Talmud and Midrash. For example, the Talmud remarks (Kiddushin, 39b) that "there is no reward for virtue in this world," and the Mishna states, "Know that the reward for righteousness is in the world to come" (Pirkei Avos, 2:16). While there is significant disagreement regarding the nature of these rewards and punishment, it is widely agreed that there are spiritual rewards and punishments, and that their purpose is to guide human behavior.

Accordingly, traditional Jewish psychology includes a strong concept of Skinnerian behaviorism (Skinner, 1953) in which contingences can shape behavior. This is most evident in parenting and education. For example, Maimonides (1168/1997) suggests that parents should incentivize children to learn with "nuts, honey, and dates" when young, and as they grow older continue to offer developmentally appropriate rewards such as fine clothes, money, and social approval with the goal of eventually motivating them to study "for its own sake." Thus, traditional Judaism supports the application of token economies and other contingency-based psychotherapeutic techniques.

MENTAL ILLNESS, MEANING, AND HAPPINESS

MENTAL ILLNESS AND EMOTIONAL HEALTH

Like many of the preceding topics, Jewish ideas regarding mental illness are diverse, and traditional sources frequently describe various states of mental distress and behavioral disturbance. While these sources provide few causal explanations, a clear distinction can be made between traditional notions of psychiatric illnesses and ideas regarding less severe forms of emotional distress and behavioral dysfunction. In terms of severe mental illness, traditional Judaism understands this to be outside of conscious control or *becheria* and attributable to divine punishment, developmental dysfunction, emotional trauma, or biological causes. For example, the Talmud defines insanity as "one who goes out alone at night, sleeps in a cemetery, and tears his clothes" (Talmud, Chagigah, 3b), suggesting a profound lack of judgment, adaptive skills, and social functioning. It groups insanity with developmental disability, childhood, and deaf-blindness and rules that anyone meeting criteria for one of these categories is exempt from religious obligations and cannot conduct business, get married, or bear witness (Shapiro, 1993). The Talmud also recognizes that mental illness is heterogeneous and describes distinct categories such as completely insane, someone who is at times sane and at times insane, and someone who is insane in only one domain (Shapiro, 1993). Various causes for these conditions are tangentially mentioned in the Talmud and include physical injury, developmental difficulties, effects of substances (e.g., new wine), and emotional trauma (Hankoff, 1972).

These ideas are present in the Torah as well. For example, biblical passages group mental illness with other biological diseases and suggest that it can be the result of divine punishment (e.g., "G-d will strike you with madness, blindness, and broken heartedness" [Deuteronomy 28:28]) or the consequence of trauma (e.g., "You will be engaged to a woman and another man will sleep with her ... your ox will be slaughtered before your eyes ... your sons and daughters will be given to another nation ... and you will be driven mad by the sights that your eyes see" [Deuteronomy 28:30–34]). Similarly, Saul is described as melancholic, jealous, and fearful of David as a result of divine punishment

(1 Samuel 18), and traditional commentaries link this with psychiatric disease. For example, the Abarbanel (fifteenth century) writes, "He [Saul] was surrounded by confusion and evil thoughts ... and he developed the melancholy disease.... The doctors have already written that in this disease, imagination and the power of thought are destroyed, pain and worry befell him, and he feared, trembled, and churned in depression." Finally, in the late Middle Ages, eastern European Jewish culture included the idea that demonic possession (i.e., a dyybuk [Meyerstein, 2004]) can lead to disturbed thought and behavior. However, belief in dybbukim was controversial at the time, is minimally supported by the broader Jewish tradition, and appears to have largely disappeared in modern times (Alexander et al., 2003).

Outside of severe mental illness, the traditional Jewish approach to behavioral dysfunction focuses on the expression of *middos* or character traits. As described above, every *middah*, including tendencies toward various negative emotions or behaviors, is assumed to have an adaptive function. However, when expressed in the extreme or channeled inappropriately, they are believed to result in distress or dysfunction. This idea is classically attributed to Maimonides, who writes (1:1–4):

There are many temperaments ... [and] the extremes of each temperament are not a good path.... The straight path is the middle midah which can be found in each and every temperament that a man can possess.... Therefore the sages commanded that a person should ... point himself towards the middle path to ensure that he will be whole in his body.... He should not be irritable and easily angered nor unfeeling like the dead.... He should not be tight fisted nor waste his money.... He should not be too playful and frivolous nor sad and mournful.

In summary, Jewish tradition includes a concept of severe mental illness resulting from biological, environmental, psychological, and perhaps spiritual causes that is beyond human choice or *becheria*, and also suggests that extreme variations of character traits can lead to distress and dysfunction, which is generally within human choice or *becheria*. Empirical research suggests that these traditional ideas are relevant to attitudes toward mental illness among Orthodox Jews living in the United States. For example, Pirutinsky, Rosmarin, and Pargament (2009) found that Orthodox Jews strongly endorsed causes such as "chemical imbalance," "genetic problems," "stressful circumstances," and "G-d's will" for a vignette describing mental illness. Moreover, recent research suggests that both biological and psychological explanations of mental illness are generally accepted even among traditional Orthodox Jews (Pirutinsky, Rosen, Safran, & Rosmarin, 2010) and that they view medical and psychological care as effective and appropriate treatments (Baruch, Kanter, Pirutinsky, Murphy, & Rosmain, 2014).

MEANING AND HAPPINESS

Traditional Judaism suggests that the meaning and purpose of human life are "to fear your Lord G-d, to walk in his ways, and to love him, and to serve your Lord G-d with all your heart and soul" (Deuteronomy 10:13). This is understood as utilizing the Torah and mitzvoth to imbue everyday life with spiritual and moral goodness, as the following verse states, "to keep G-d's commandments and laws that I am commanding you today, for your own good" (Deuteronomy 10:14). Moreover, traditional Judaism suggests that this goal does not require unusual or intense practices but rather is easily accessible in everyday life, as stated in Deuteronomy 30:11–14: "Surely, the commandments that I am commanding you today are not beyond you and not far from you. There are not in the heaven.... And they are not overseas.... But they are extremely close to you in your mouth and in your heart to perform them." As Luzzatto (1738/1987) writes, "Man was only created to delight in G-d and to enjoy the radiance of his presence."

Furthermore, Judaism views this moral life as "for your own good" (Deuteronomy 10:14) and rewarding to those living it. For example, Proverbs 3:17 states, "Her [the Torah] ways are pleasant and all her paths peaceful," and the Psalmist writes, "Serve G-d with happiness, come before him with joyful song" (100:2). The Talmud also emphasizes this in a lengthy discussion of various verses in Ecclesiastes that both point out the futility of happiness (e.g., "Of revelry, I said, it is mad; and of joy, what does it do?" [Ecclesiastes 2:2] and praise it (e.g., "I praised joy for there is nothing better for man under the sun" [Ecclesiastes 8:15]. It concludes (Talmud, Shabbos, 30b):

"I praised joy"—that is the joy of a commandant. And "of joy what does it do?" That is the joy that is not of a commandment. To teach you that the divine presence does not rest within sadness ... nor within frivolity ... but only through the joy of a commandment.

In fact, the Torah harshly reprimands and promises punishment for "not serving G-d with joy and with good heartedness" (Deuteronomy 28:47). As described above, serving G-d entails compliance with religious commandment as well as developing character traits or *middos* that emulate the loving and kind attributes of G-d. Developing these *middos* is believed to bring happiness, as the great medieval scholar Nachmanides (1194–1270) wrote: "Save yourself from anger, which is a bad middah ... and cultivate in your heart the middah of humility ... the middah of fear of G-d ... and with these middos, you will be happy with your lot in life." Thus, one strand of Jewish thought suggests that enduring human happiness is only possible through a life dedicated to the service of G-d and the perfection of *middos* or character traits. This is succinctly described in the Mishna (Perkei Avos, 4:2): "The reward of a mitzvah is the experience of the mitzvah itself."

On the other hand, traditional Judaism also acknowledges the importance to happiness of physical pleasure and social relationships. As the Talmud states, "There is no joy only in meat and wine" (Pesachim, 109a), and "any man with no wife lives without joy" (Yevamos, 62a). This is enshrined in religious law, as holidays are required to be dedicated "half to G-d and half to yourselves" (Talmud, Pesachim, 68b). Similarly, the Mishna (Brachos, 6–9) requires one to thank G-d for virtually all physical pleasures, including food, drink, fine clothing, and pleasant aromas. Finally, worldly pleasures are also viewed as a tool for enhancing mood, as it is written: "and David would take a lyre and play it, and Saul would feel relieved and it was good for him, and the evil spirit would leave him" (1 Samuel 16:23).

Thus, while there is some acceptance of asceticism in Jewish tradition (e.g., "eat bread with salt, drink water in small measure, and sleep on the ground" [Perkei Avos, 6:4]), disavowing physical pleasure is generally viewed as failing to accept G-d's generosity. For example, a *Nazir,* or one who accepts upon himself a biblically ordained ascetic lifestyle, must complete a ritual of repentance because "he denied himself wine" (Talmud, Taanis 11a). A similar sentiment is expressed in the Talmud Yerushalmi (Kiddushin, 4:14): "Man is destined to give an account for everything his eyes saw that he did not enjoy" [lit.: eat]. Traditional Judaism views physical pleasure as a gift provided by G-d that should be thankfully appreciated and shared with others. As Isaiah wrote (58:5–7), "Is such the fast I [G-d] desire, a day when men pain their bodies? ... No, this is the fast I choose ... to share your bread with the hungry and to take the wretched poor into your house." To synthesize, traditional Judaism suggests that enduring meaning and happiness results from an everyday awareness of G-d's presence, thankful acceptance of the gift of physical pleasure, and practicing spiritual and moral behavior.

TRUST IN G-D

Finally, Judaism includes a strong concept of an omnipresent ("Behold He does not slumber nor sleep" [Psalm 121:4]), omnipotent ("Who spoke and it was, unless G-d commanded it?" [Lamentations, 3:37]), and omnibenevolent ("G-d is good to all, and His mercies are on all His works" [Psalm 145:9]). Accordingly, the Torah is filled with exhortations to place trust exclusively in G-d as "A righteous man lives with his faith" (Habakkuk 2:4). This concept of *Bitachon* or trust in G-d encompasses both the belief that even apparently negative events are ultimately beneficial, as well as the recognition that the goodness of G-d's will is beyond human comprehension.

This concept is also enshrined in religious law (Mishna, Berachos, 9:5), which obligates one to bless G-d for "bad just as one blesses for good," which the Talmud (Berachos, 60b) interprets as referring to a similarly joyful attitude. The Talmud then relates a story regarding Rabbi Akiva who could not find lodging in a city and instead slept in a field where a gust of wind extinguished his candle, a cat ate his rooster, and a lion ate his donkey. Later that night, an army came and captured the city, and Rabbi Akiva survived because he was not in the city and had no light or noisy animals to reveal his location. "So he said to them, didn't I tell you that everything that G-d does is for the good?" (Berachos, 60b). A similar story is also told regarding Nachum Ish Gam Zu, who responded to negative events by stating, "gam zu le'tova" [this too is for the good] (Talmud, Taanis, 21a).

However, while these classic examples are of events in which G-d's benevolence is evident, Judaism also suggests that, in many instances, G-d's intent, while beneficial, is beyond human comprehension. As the Mishna (Pirkei Avos, 4:15) states, "it is not within our grasp—not the peace of the wicked nor the suffering of the righteous." This sentiment is widely acknowledged throughout the Torah, such as in Isaiah (55:8–9): "For my thoughts are not your thoughts, and neither are your ways my ways, says G-d"; and in Job (38:2–4): "Who is this who gives dark counsel, speaking without knowledge? ... Where were you when I established the earth to speak as if you have understanding?"

Accordingly, Jewish thought specifically emphasizes trust in G-d as a source of psychological strength in difficult times. As the Psalmist writes, "G-d is my light and my savior, from who shall I fear?" (27:1), and "Even when I travel in the valley of death, I do not fear evil because you [G-d] are with me" (Psalm 23:4). These ideas are elaborated on by Ibn Pakuda (1008/1996) in his classical work *Chovot HaLevavot* [*The Duties of the Heart*], *Shaar HaBitachon* [*Gate of Trust*], in which he describes the connection between trust in G-d's and emotional calm, as he states "One who trusts in G-d, has strong peace of mind that G-d will provide for him at any time and in any place He wishes, just like He sustains the fetus in its mother's womb." This idea is also vividly described by the prophet Jeremiah (17:5–8):

Cursed is the person who trusts man and makes flesh his source of strength and from G-d he turns his heart. He will be like a bush in the desert inhabiting the parched places of the desert, a salty, uninhabited land. Blessed is the person who trusts in G-d, and whose hope G-d is. He shall be like a tree planted by the waters sending its root to a stream. It will not fear when the heat comes, its leaf shall be radiant; and it shall not worry in a year of drought and will not cease from yielding fruit.

Consistently, empirical research suggests that trust in G-d serves as a primary psychological coping method for many traditional Jews and can be effective. For example, Rosmarin, Krumrei, and Andersson (2009) developed a scale measuring trust in G-d, including items such

as "G-d knows what is in my best interests" and "G-d is compassionate towards human suffering." Scores on this measure correlated with
lower anxiety and depression and higher happiness in several Jewish
samples (Rosmarin et al., 2009; Krumrei, Pirutinsky, & Rosmarin, 2013).
Similarly, a clinical intervention designed specifically to increase trust in
G-d demonstrated effectiveness comparable to progressive muscle relaxation (Rosmarin, Pargament, Pirutinsky, & Mahoney, 2010), and clinical
change over the course of this study was mediated by increased trust in
G-d (Rosmarin et al., 2011). Trust in G-d has also been found to relate to
improved psychiatric outcomes (Rosmarin et al., 2013) and appears to
protect against stress due to financial strain (Krause & Hayward, 2015).

CONCLUSION

Judaism, a diverse and multifaceted ancient religious tradition, includes
several central psychological concepts drawn from history, culture, biblical texts, and rabbinic oral traditions. These key points are summarized
in Table 3.1, and a fair amount of empirical research supports the relevance of these ideas for both Orthodox and non-Orthodox Jews, such
as Cohen and Hill's (2007) work on Jewish collectivism and moral judgments, Rosmarin et al.'s (2011) work on trust in G-d and mental health,
and Pirutinsky, Rosmarin, and Holt's (2012) work on religion and health.
These ideas echo prominent psychological theories such as Freud's
(1930/1989) tripartite theory of the mind, Festinger's (1962) theory of cognitive dissonance, Skinner's (1953) behaviorism, and Haidt's (2006) moral
psychology. Moreover, as discussed throughout this chapter, these ideas
have significant clinical and psychotherapeutic implications. Thus, it is
clear that any comprehensive human psychology should integrate ideas
from indigenous traditions as they provide fruitful avenues for research,
continue to exert psychological influence, and are directly relevant to
clinical care.

TABLE 1. PRINCIPLES OF AN INDIGENOUS JEWISH PSYCHOLOGY

Individuals are responsible for each other.

It is important to maintain harmonious relationships and comply with cultural norms.

All knowledge can be found in religious texts and tradition.

It is important to honor and respect religious authorities and elders.

The human mind is conflicted and subject to a variety of thoughts, feelings, and desires.

These desires are not inherently evil but must be actively managed and channeled to adaptive ends.

Humans are generally free to consciously choose their behavior.

Each person reacts to circumstances in characteristic ways.

Repeated behavior leads to automatization, habituation, and cognitive and emotional changes.

People are motivated to obtain rewards and avoid punishments, and this is an effective educational tool.

Mental illness is beyond conscious control, and these causes are multidetermined.

True happiness arises from a life imbued with spiritual meaning and conscious efforts to cultivate humility and kindness.

G-d is omnipresent, omnipotent, and omnibenevolent, and trusting his intentions is an effective tool for coping with difficult circumstances.

REFERENCES

Alexander, T., Alexander-Frizer, T., Bourguignon, E., Kallus, M., Dan, J., Faierstein, M. M., ... & Weinstein, R. (2003). *Spirit possession in Judaism: Cases and contexts from the Middle Ages to the present.* Detroit, MI: Wayne State University Press.

[Anonymous]. (1300/1988). *Sefer HaChinuch.* Jerusalem: Machon Yerushalayim.

Baruch, D. E., Kanter, J. W., Pirutinsky, S., Murphy, J., & Rosmain, D. H. (2014). Depression stigma and treatment preferences among Orthodox and non-Orthodox Jews. *Journal of Nervous and Mental Disease, 202,* 556–561.

Birnbaum, P. (1975). *Principles of faith: A book of Jewish concepts.* New York: Hebrew Publishing Company.

Bleich, J. D. (1981). Mental incompetence and its implications in Jewish law. *Journal of Halacha and Contemporary Society, 2,* 123–143.

Brill, A. (2002). *Thinking God: The mysticism of Rabbi Zadok of Lublin.* Jersey City, NJ: KTAV Publishing House.

Carmell, A. (1986). *Aiding Talmud study.* Jerusalem: Feldheim Publishers.

Cohen, A. B., & Hill, P. C. (2007). Religion as culture: Religious individualism and collectivism among American Catholics, Jews, and Protestants. *Journal of Personality, 75*(4), 709–742.

Cohen, A. B., & Rozin, P. (2001). Religion and the morality of mentality. *Journal of Personality and Social Psychology, 81*(4), 697.

Cohen, M. (2008). A dialogue between psychology and religion in the work of Moshe Halevi Spero, an Orthodox Jewish psychoanalyst. *Shofar, 26,* 13–41.

Cohn-Sherbok, D. (2003). *Judaism: History, belief, and practice.* London: Routledge, 2003.

Cross, F. L., & Livingstone, E. A. (2005). Original sin. In F. L. Cross and E. A. Livingstone (Eds.), *The Oxford Dictionary of the Christian Church* (3rd rev. ed.). Oxford: Oxford University Press.

DellaPergola, S. (2016). World Jewish population, 2015. In *American Jewish year book 2015* (pp. 273–364). New York: Springer.

Dessler, E. E. (1955/1994). *Michtav Me'eliyahu* (Kuntrus HaBechirah, Perek 2). Jerusalem: Sefrisi.

Eisenberg, R. L. (2005). *The 613 mitzvot: A contemporary guide to the commandments of Judaism.* Rockville, MD: Schreiber Publishing.

Etkes, I. (1993). *The mussar [ethics] system of Rabbi Yisrael Lipkin Salanter.* Philadelphia: Jewish Publication Society.

Festinger, L. (1962). *A theory of cognitive dissonance.* Vol. 2. Stanford, CA: Stanford University Press.

Freud, S. (1930/1989). *Civilization and its discontents.* New York: W. W. Norton & Company.

Gelfand, M. (2019). *Rule makers, rule breakers: Tight and loose cultures and the secret signals that direct our lives.* New York: Scribner.

Grossberg, D. M. (2010). Orthopraxy in Tannaitic literature. *Journal for the Study of Judaism, 41*(4–5), 517–561.

Haidt, J. (2006). *The happiness hypothesis: Finding modern truth in ancient wisdom.* New York: Basic Books.

haKohen, T. (1901/2012). *Tzidkas haTzaddik* (chapter 43). Jerusalem: Frank.

Hankoff, L. D. (1972). Ancient descriptions of organic brain syndrome: The "Kordiakos" of the Talmud. *American Journal of Psychiatry, 129,* 233–236.

Ibn Pakuda, B. (1008/1996). *Duties of the heart* (Trans. Y. Feldman). Northvale, NJ: Jason Aronson.

Johnson, P. (2013). *History of the Jews.* London: Hachette UK.

Karo, J. (1563/1992). *Shulchan Aruch.* Israel: Machon Yerushalayim.

Krause, N., & Hayward, R. D. (2015). Assessing whether trust in G-d offsets the effects of financial strain on health and well-being. *International Journal for the Psychology of Religion, 25*(4), 307–322.

Krumrei, E. J., Pirutinsky, S., & Rosmarin, D. H. (2013). Jewish spirituality, depression, and health: An empirical test of a conceptual framework. *International Journal of Behavioral Medicine, 20*(3), 327–336.

Kwall, R. R. (2015). *The myth of the cultural Jew: Culture and law in Jewish tradition.* Oxford: Oxford University Press.

Lev, D. (2014, June 29). *Practical Jewish law: Interpersonal responsibilities.* Retrieved from https://www.aish.com/jl/jewish-law/daily-living/

Luzzatto, M. H. (1738/1987). *Mesilas yesharim* [Path of righteousness]. Jerusalem: Feldheim.

Machzor La'Yom Kippurim. (2001). *Machzor La'Yom Kippurim, Seder Tefilasenu.* Jerusalem: Frank.

Maimonides. (1168/1997). *Perush Mishnah.* Jerusalem: Frank.

Maimonides. (1170–1180/1990). *Mishna Torah* (Hilchos Dayos, 1:7). Bnei Brak, Israel: Mishor.

Manekin, H., & Kellner, M. M. (Eds.). (1997). *Freedom and moral responsibility: General and Jewish perspectives.* College Park: University Press of Maryland.

Meyerstein, I. (2004). A Jewish spiritual perspective on psychopathology and psychotherapy: A clinician's view. *Journal of Religion and Health, 43,* 329–341.

Mizrahi, A. (2011). The soul and the body in the philosophy of the Rambam. *Rambam Maimonides Medical Journal, 2*(2), e0040.

Pirutinsky, S., Rosen, D. D., Safran, R. S., & Rosmarin, D. H. (2010). Do medical models of mental illness relate to increased or decreased stigmatization of mental illness among orthodox Jews? *Journal of Nervous and Mental Disease, 198,* 508–512.

Pirutinsky, S., Rosmarin, D. H., & Holt, C. L. (2012). Religious coping moderates the relationship between emotional functioning and obesity. *Health Psychology, 31*(3), 394.

Pirutinsky, S., Rosmarin, D. H., & Pargament, K. I. (2009). Community attitudes towards culture-influenced mental illness: Scrupulosity vs. nonreligious OCD among orthodox Jews. *Journal of Community Psychology, 37,* 949–958.

Revel, B. (1913). *The Karaite Halakhah and its relation to Sadducean, Samaritan and Philonian Halakhah.* Philadelphia: Cahan Printing Company.

Rosmarin, D. H., Bigda-Peyton, J. S., Kertz, S. J., Smith, N., Rauch, S. L., & Björgvinsson, T. (2013). A test of faith in G-d and treatment: The relationship of belief in G-d to psychiatric treatment outcomes. *Journal of Affective Disorders, 146*(3), 441–446.

Rosmarin, D. H., Krumrei, E. J., & Andersson, G. (2009). Religion as a predictor of psychological distress in two religious communities. *Cognitive Behaviour Therapy, 38*(1), 54–64.

Rosmarin, D. H., Pargament, K. I., Pirutinsky, S., & Mahoney, A. (2010). A randomized controlled evaluation of a spiritually integrated treatment for subclinical anxiety in the Jewish community, delivered via the Internet. *Journal of Anxiety Disorders, 24*(7), 799–808.

Rosmarin, D. H., Pirutinsky, S., Auerbach, R. P., Björgvinsson, T., Bigda-Peyton, J., Andersson, G., ... & Krumrei, E. J. (2011). Incorporating spiritual beliefs into a cognitive model of worry. *Journal of Clinical Psychology, 67*(7), 691–700.

Scholem, G. (2011). *Major trends in Jewish mysticism.* New York: Schocken.

Shapiro, Y. A. (1993). The status of the mentally ill in Jewish law. *Medicine and Law, 12*, 317–324.

Skinner, B. F. (1953). *Science and human behavior.* New York: Simon and Schuster.

Snyder, D. M. (1993). Judaism and Freud: The inclinations to do good and evil. *Psychoanalysis and Contemporary Thought, 16*, 103–122.

Tajfel, H. (Ed.). (2010). *Social identity and intergroup relations.* Vol. 7. Cambridge: Cambridge University Press.

Triandis, H. C. (2018). *Individualism and collectivism.* Abingdon, UK: Routledge.

Twersky, I. (2003). What must a Jew Study—and why? In S. Fox, I. Scheffler, & D. Marom (Eds.), *Visions of Jewish education* (pp. 47–76). Cambridge: Cambridge University Press.

Wein, B. (1990). *Triumph of survival: The story of the Jews in the modern era, 1650–1990.* Brooklyn, NY: Mesorah Publications.

Wein, B. (1993). *Herald of destiny: The story of the Jews in the medieval era, 750–1650.* Brooklyn, NY: Mesorah Publications.

Wein, B. (1995). *Echoes of glory: The story of the Jews in the classical era, 350 BCE–750 CE.* Brooklyn, NY: Mesorah Publications.

Wein, B. (2001). *Faith and fate: The story of the Jews in the twentieth century.* Brooklyn, NY: Mesorah Publications.

ENDNOTES

1. All quotations of classical Jewish texts were translated from the original Hebrew or Aramaic by the author, and transliterations follow Ashkenazi pronunciation. Following traditional Jewish custom, the names of G-d are abbreviated or hyphenated.

2. This tripartite psychological system (*yetzer tov, yetzer hara,* and *bechira*) clearly resembles Freud's description of the id, superego, and ego, and many indeed speculate that Freud's ideas were drawn in part from his Jewish cultural background (Snyder, 1993).

JOSHUA J. KNABB AND

M. TODD BATES

WALKING HOME WITH GOD

Toward an Indigenous Christian
Psychology

With a history that spans several thousand years, the Christian faith system offers a distinct perspective on epistemology and knowledge acquisition; the nature of the person (or self); the meaning of the human condition; health, well-being, and thriving; and psychological suffering and change. In fact, Christianity provides a well-developed *teleology*—or purpose, function, or "ultimate goal" (Johnson, Hill, & Cohen, 2011)—for those who are fully immersed in this system and faithfully follow the teachings of the Bible. This perspective shapes the Christian's embodied engagement with the world and, thus, provides a distinctive, holistic take on the meaning of human existence, often referred to as a "worldview" (Johnson et al., 2011). Christian psychology, then, is the salient epistemological expression of the interplay between empiricism and divine revelation (Lawson, Anderson, & Cepeda-Benito, 2018), offering a unique perspective within a local worldview community for making sense of the human condition. Put differently, the Christian faith system is its own indigenous psychology among a variety of other indigenous psychologies throughout the world, whether secular (e.g., Western psychology), cultural (e.g., Filipino psychology), or religious (e.g., Judaism, Islam, Buddhism). We believe the contributions of a Christian psychology dually enliven the living conversation on the similarities and differences between these indigenous psychologies and the pursuit of a more general, global psychology that attempts to capture the common psychological experiences that are threaded throughout the human life span.

Yet two additional points are worth making before we commence with a brief review of Christianity's history and concepts. First, if we only attempt to examine the mechanics (i.e., cause and effect) of a distinctly Christian psychology, without understanding its extrinsic or religious *teleology* (Perlman, 2004; Rychlak, 1994), the ultimate purpose may be overlooked, given the inherent limitations "in a physical-mechanical process" (Rychlak, 1994). In other words, "You cannot understand the Christian religion without seizing on its end-directed vision" (Ruse, 2018, p. 196). Scientific psychology, to be sure, has historically attempted to, like physics, focus on causality in the material world (King, Viney, & Woody, 2013), assuming there are "laws" that parallel those identified in the natural sciences (e.g., gravity, motion). This strategy, of course, was not always the case for science in general (Rychlak, 1994). Contemporary psychological science, moreover, often overemphasizes "experiment-based empiricism" and "materialism" as a sort of "scientism" (Marsella, 2009). In doing so, the teleology of Christianity as a religious worldview system can be glaringly missing, especially when researchers assume Christian beliefs and practices are merely instruments in the service of some other end, which may be inconsistent with the lived experience of Christians (Slife & Reber, 2012). Because of this, throughout this chapter, we consistently argue that a return to teleology, rather than continuing to overemphasize mechanics within the study of the psychology of Christianity, can provide a context and proper orientation for such empirical pursuits.

To offer an example of this teleology-mechanics distinction, if we only attempt to elucidate cause-effect relationships when examining the psychology of Christianity, we may end up overemphasizing its beliefs (e.g., views on God's sovereignty in the midst of suffering) and practices (e.g., Bible study, prayer, meditation) as merely predictors of *other* outcomes, such as mental health or symptom reduction. In such misguided pursuits, the entire faith system may be erroneously conceptualized as designed for the individual to meet his or her personal needs, and we might miss out on understanding the richness of the teleology of such beliefs and practices—a deeper relationship with God, regardless of how the individual ends up feeling in the pursuit of a devout life of faith, commitment, and conviction. Christianity is about prioritizing God, not self-interests, as the foundation of life (Davis, 2012).

Further, this return to teleology can help to recover a much-needed "internal point of view" (Howard, 1988; Kim, Yang, & Hwang, 2006), utilizing an emic strategy that also recognizes Christianity's sacred text as a vital source of knowledge for better understanding Christians' psychological functioning (Pankalla & Kośnik, 2018). Worded differently, Christians are goal directed and intentional, with agency, purposeful behavior, plans, and expectations (King et al., 2013), not mere objects (Rychlak, 1994). Just like "hearts are for pumping blood" and "eyes are for seeing" (Perlman, 2004), Christians have a function—to commune and fellowship with God and find contentment in depending on him[1] in the midst of a fallen, imperfect, suffering world. By engaging in daily Christian practices such as Bible study, prayer, meditation, and singing songs of praise, Christians are pursuing a more intimate, reciprocal connection with God and attempting to secure a more enduring psychological fulfillment and satisfaction in him, rather than overly relying on inner (e.g., pleasurable experiences) or outer (e.g., interacting with people, securing material possessions, achieving goals) events that are not fully reliable in an imperfect world.

Christian mental health, then, is a by-product of prioritizing fellowship with God, not something that is pursued unilaterally and on its own. Reminiscent of more relational, psychodynamic conceptualizations of human development and mental health suggesting that the self develops and optimally functions in safe, reliable relational systems (Mitchell, 1988; Wolf, 2002), Christians thrive when God is at the center, rather than on the periphery, of daily life. With God at the center, and worshipping and communing with God as a "life orientation" (Peterson, 1992, p. 18), Christians can confidently engage with a variety of other domains of life (e.g., family, work, community). Overall, understanding this local psychology can best occur when we take a "bottom-up" approach (Kim, Park, & Park, 2000) by further examining Christian functioning in its indigenous context.

Second, we believe that starting with an orthodox Christian foundation can protect against the problem of syncretism. Whether emanating from the surrounding culture, another religious tradition, or the untested assumptions of secular psychology, the integration of non-Christian influences can be problematic when attempting to capture an emic understanding of a Christian religious framework.[3] For example, secular psychology often employs a hypothetico-deductive approach to research, starting with a theory, then generating study hypotheses, before empirically observing the phenomenon of interest (Haig, 2018). Yet theorists are unable to fully separate themselves from their lived experience when attempting to develop and refine theory (Atwood & Stolorow, 1993), which means their own worldview may be intermingled with their supposedly objective scientific pursuits. When this is the case, some of what appears to be secular psychological "science" may in fact be an amalgam of untested assumptions and personal projections.

Therefore, in this chapter, we set out in broad strokes the key concepts of what we believe is an orthodox Christian psychology, as seen from *within* the faith, by relying on a biblically grounded worldview. We begin with a brief review of some of the central concepts in Christianity, including Christianity's view of ultimate reality, namely, the personal nature of God as the author of all reality and, thus, the source and goal of all knowledge. With God as the ultimate source of knowledge (i.e., epistemology), we discuss how God intentionally and personally reveals himself *to* and *through* his creation and gives to humankind the self-understanding and meaning by which psychological health, well-being, thriving, and disorder can be understood and, further, the means by which these experiences can be attained. We suggest that Christian mental health is thoroughly grounded in fellowshipping with God, with Christians developing a deeper contentment in God and the ability to endure suffering because of this foundational relationship. Stated differently, contentment and a more hopeful endurance in the face of psychological suffering in a fallen world are by-products of a more intimate communion with God. Prior to presenting the history of our faith tradition, though, we would like to briefly discuss both the "lens" through which we view our emic, "insider" conceptualization of Christian psychology and the ultimate purpose, or telos, of Christianity as a comprehensive faith system.

CHRISTIAN PSYCHOLOGY: A DISTINCTIVE "LENS"

As a faith system, there are several major Christian traditions throughout the world, including Catholic, Eastern Orthodox, and Protestant. In the United States, about 71 percent of adults identify with the Christian faith, with Protestants making up the majority of this group (Pew Research Center, 2015). Among US Christian adults, about 25 percent identify as Evangelical Protestant, 15 percent as Mainline Protestant, and 7 percent as Historically Black Protestant (Pew Research Center, 2015). In this chapter, we offer one of many possible Christian psychologies, writing from a Reformed, Evangelical Protestant perspective, because (a) the majority of US adults identify as Evangelical Protestant, and (b) both authors identify with this Christian background and can offer an "insider" perspective from this vantage point. In so doing, our hope is to provide readers with one possible example of how to conceptualize the psychology behind the Christian faith. Viewed through this lens, we also believe that the Christian tradition has a distinct telos, or end goal, which impacts our conceptualization of the psychology of Christianity throughout the chapter.

THE PURPOSE, OR TELOS, OF CHRISTIANITY

According to the Westminster Shorter Catechism, a widely cited Christian doctrine from the 1600s, the central goal of humankind is to "glorify God" and "enjoy him forever."[2] In other words, the purpose of life on earth is for Christians to commune with God, who offers his love from moment to moment, leading to a deeper and more stable contentment in him, regardless of the inner and outer experiences that fluctuate from day to day and year to year. In pursuing this reciprocal relationship, to "glorify" and "enjoy" God means to worship him. Worship, in the Christian tradition, is about a "life orientation or *total* relationship [and engagement] with the true and living God," rather than merely singing songs in a church service for a few minutes per week (Peterson, 1992, p. 18, italics added), and is pursued through a variety of practices that focus on God, not the self (e.g., Bible study, prayer, meditation, singing songs of praise, expressing gratitude to God, living a holy life, following biblical teachings) (Block, 2014). A distinctly Christian psychology, then, suggests that "Human life is to be centered in God, not the self; and human life finds its fulfillment not apart from God but in right relationship to God" (Davis, 2012, p. 86).

The end goal, from a teleological perspective, is to commune with God in heaven, where Christians will be free from all forms of physical, psychological, and other types of suffering that are experienced in this world (Sibbes, 2018). Embedded in a Christian psychological understanding of the human condition lies the notion that the purpose for followers of Jesus Christ is to eventually be in God's presence for eternity (Boersma, 2018), with God functioning as the perfect source of beauty, joy, goodness, and safety (Psalm 27). This hope of eventual life and communion with God, coupled with the current glimpses that Christians may get of God's glory in fellowshipping with him while walking together on the arduous roads of this life (1 Corinthians 13:12), can help Christians endure the time-limited nature of earthly psychological suffering. With the above distinctive lens and telos of Christianity in mind, what follows is a brief review of the history of Christianity, offered from a psychological perspective.

A BRIEF HISTORY OF CHRISTIANITY AND PSYCHOLOGY

Throughout the tradition, Christians have turned to the Bible for insights into the human condition, including an understanding of reality (ontology), knowledge (epistemology), the nature of the person (biblical anthropology), health, dysfunction, and healing/change, wherein they read of an overarching theme of existence—creation, fall, redemption, and restoration (Wolters, 2005). With creation, God made the world and everything in it, proclaiming that "all that he had made ... was very good" (Genesis 1:31). Included in God's creation, "Adam and his wife were both naked, and they felt no shame" (Genesis 2:25), given they were living in communion with God (Wolters, 2005). Yet, in the fall, Adam and Eve attempted to be like God, rather than dependent on God, turning away from him by eating from the tree of the knowledge of good and evil, which God had clearly forbidden; this act resulted in a deep sense of shame, banishment from the garden of Eden, and estrangement from God for both Adam and Eve and the rest of humanity (Genesis 3; Bonhoeffer, 1955; Wolters, 2005). Also because of the fall, suffering entered the world (Genesis 3), including psychological suffering. Although, at this point in the narrative, humankind has been separated from God and experiences widespread suffering, all hope is not lost. With Jesus Christ, the Son of God, entering the world roughly two thousand years ago, Christians believe that Jesus redeemed a broken world and restored humankind's communion with God for those who believe in him (Luke 4:18–19; John 3:16; Romans 6:1–11; 10:9) (Wolters, 2005).

This comprehensive and coherent motif reveals the inherent dignity and wonder of humankind, the resulting brokenness and fragmentation from the fall, and the loving in-breaking of God to mend human brokenness and bring redemptive healing through Jesus Christ, by which humankind can experience healing in the present in hope of future restoration by God. This motif frames the remaining discussion.

THE META-NARRATIVE OF THE BIBLE: A CHRISTIAN EPISTEMOLOGY

CREATION

GOD AS PERSONAL AND RELATIONAL ULTIMATE REALITY. While every religion rightly begins with the divine as ultimate reality, how such a notion is developed in each broader belief system differs significantly. Unique among monotheistic religions, Christianity views God as Tri-Unity, or, more commonly, as the Trinity. While the concept of the Trinity is complex, and many volumes have been written on this very topic over the last two millennia, the basic idea is that God is one in essence and three in persons (Father, Son, and Spirit): "Far from asserting themselves at the expense of the others, each of the divine persons manifests perfection whilst containing and manifesting the perfection of the others" (Bray, 1993, p. 242). This Trinitarian relationship creates a larger framework for understanding the unified nature of our relationships with God and others. For Christians, then, the inner life of the one God consists of Father,

Son, and Spirit, with each person identified in and by relation to the others in the oneness of the shared life. Stated differently, the inner life of God is a reciprocally determinative character of divine persons. The very identity of the Father is constituted in relation/communion with the Son. The relational nature of God (*ad intra*) shapes every work of God (*ad extra*)—creation. Thus, relationality and communion are at the heart of Christianity in the interpersonal nature of God.

CREATION AS AN EVENT OF COMMUNION. Because God is the source of all existential reality, Christians hold that there is a fullness to the world that reflects the fullness of God. Psalm 19 states that "The heavens declare the glory of God," and his wisdom and knowledge are seen in his handiwork. So, from an epistemological perspective, as human knowers approach the world, each created thing will always be fuller than any particular human or "conceptual framework" is equipped to perceive.

This relational nature of creation certainly deepens a Christian's understanding of the material world. Positively viewing the material world supports empirical discovery; but Christian discovery is without reductive, impersonal methods. As Christians care for the world, they can use the scientific method to better understand psychological functioning, but they do so with an awareness of God as the author of all of creation.

KNOWLEDGE AS AN ACT OF COMMUNION. The above Christian view of creation gives Christianity a particular view of knowledge acquisition, that is, a certain epistemology. Relational ontology establishes that wholeness and "normality" cannot rightly be considered separable from human relationality, namely, the Christian's relationship with God. This understanding, in turn, roots proper knowledge of God within an epistemological holism, which means that proper understanding requires knowing the parts and how they relate to the whole.

From a Christian perspective, then, it should not surprise us that the fullness of creation as a direct action of an eternal God would require multiple perspectives to even begin to understand the richness of reality. Indeed, "wisdom is found in a multitude of counselors" (Proverbs 11:14).

One implication from a Christian theory of knowledge is that skillful observation by multiple perspectives should yield common elements from such observations. Though the ideological stance and meaning drawn from it may differ from perspective to perspective, each perspective can yield truth that serves the whole. Christianity accounts for this through *general revelation*, which holds that God reveals himself and his truth through creation generally—the message of his reality is to and for everyone universally. Thus, from the perspective of Christianity, varying indigenous perspectives that study the world deeply and honestly will yield elements of truth. Because of general revelation, such truths can be received as truth and weaved into a Christian perspective.

Common factors in psychotherapy serve as one of many examples of this idea (Lambert, 2013). These factors are common because they are drawn from therapeutic practices proven effective from across the theoretical spectrum. Christian theologian Thomas Oden (1987) rightly suggested, "The work of Christian soul care has proceeded through many centuries in companionship with alternative views of human nature, varied psychologies, and therapeutic approaches" (p. 227). Viewed from a Christian viewpoint, each faith system observes the truth within God's general revelation and weaves the truth into varying indigenous theoretical perspectives. In other words, God has revealed himself through his creation, which means even secular scientific discoveries can help Christians to better understand the world God has created.

Continuing to view this discussion from a Christian framework, each indigenous perspective has parts of the truth, but none has the whole of truth. In the Christian tradition, this is entailed in the very fact of human creatureliness—humans were never meant to be complete in ourselves, but complete only in God, who knows fully and exhaustively. Indeed, in all our acts as human knowers standing in relation to the known, that is, the created world, we are actively communing with God. In Christianity, God is not only the source of all existent reality, but the context in which all the particulars are related to the whole and, thereby, have meaning. Thus, knowledge of the whole lies with God himself, and understanding truth and meaning, not in part but in whole, comes only through communing with God and his *special revelation* in the Christian Scriptures.

THE FALL

What has been explicit in the discussion thus far is the initial wholeness of creation and human interactions with creation; what has been implicit, however, is an assumed fragmentation of the wholeness. The assumed fragmentation becomes explicit in the Christian view of the fall of humankind from its state of grace and purity and the creational disorder that ensues. Because of the fall, humans now live in a broken world, which results in a loss of the whole. From this perspective, therefore, a purely secular scientific understanding of reality, knowledge, and the nature of the person will be limited and imperfect.

COMMUNION LOST. If we return to the concept of communion, we can see more clearly the profound impact of the fall. Consistent with the Christian view of creation in the first few pages of Genesis, the human person is incomplete in him- or herself. Initially, this was never a problem because of constant communion with God, in whom we have completion. In the Genesis account of creation, we were fully dependent on God, who was the center of our existence (Bonhoeffer, 1959). What is more, our being and knowing involved us in the relationality of the whole world, and daily life was a practice in communion—everything received was a gift and enjoyed in faithful gratitude. When humankind turned from God and sought "completion" elsewhere—in the self or other created things—our creaturely finitude and incompleteness became problematized. Stated differently, we sought to be "like God," rather than dependent on him, and we attempted to place ourselves, not God, at the center of existence (Bonhoeffer, 1955). In so doing, we have struggled with attempting to pursue our own limited understanding of reality, knowledge, and the nature of the person, at times autonomously striving to be "like God" in our efforts.

These results of broken communion invert the goodness of communion. Because of relational ontology, the world is an interconnected whole. When the human "part" turns away, existential alienation and displacement occur. In the aftermath, fragmentation is now a common human experience, rather than wholeness. Instead of communion, there is now alienation. The goodness of creation that served as the source of constant communion now consciously and unconsciously reminds us of our alienation from the source of all good and our completion.

Further, because human knowers are embedded and embodied and human knowing is limited, the effort toward order and meaning is frustrated. The world becomes a confusing place, fostering anxiety, isolation, depression, and a host of other human forms of suffering.

Though alienation and fragmentation are our common experience, the search for wholeness and meaning does not cease, but is a perpetual struggle. Understood from the Christian faith system, each indigenous perspective, whether secular (e.g., Western psychology), cultural (e.g., Filipino psychology), or religious (e.g., Judaism, Islam, Christianity), is an effort toward making meaning from the fragmentation. As an expression of God's goodness and "common grace" (Kuyper, 2011), there remains in humankind and creation sufficient truth in the parts (i.e., "earthly things") that can point us to the whole (i.e., "heavenly things") (Calvin, 2011). In the Christian tradition, however, the fragmentation and displacement do not have the last word.

REDEMPTION AND RESTORATION

God's goodness is displayed in the uniquely Christian view of redemption and restoration, expressed through the direct divine action of Jesus Christ, the Son of God, and explicated in the New Testament of the Bible. In this act, we are given the final components of the Christian meta-narrative of creation, fall, redemption, and restoration, which is a succinct summary of God's special revelation—God's specific message of salvation to humankind. Here, the Bible reveals a distinct teleology— God's unfolding work in human history—so that we might better understand a meta-perspective on reality, knowledge, the nature of the person, health, dysfunction, and healing. Aligning with creation, health originally involved perfect communion with God, which was broken with the fall. The fall brought about psychological change, leading to dysfunction, mental disorders, and suffering.

The existential displacement resulting from the fall, however, is overcome through restored communion with God. Because human finitude could not return the world to wholeness, God himself entered the human world as Jesus Christ to bring reconciliation and restore communion by offering his "special grace" (Kuyper, 2011). The work of God restoring the lost relationship starts humankind toward the completeness, which was lost through alienation. This leads to the seemingly counterintuitive claim that the only way to find life is to renounce the claim to it and for humankind to "once again accept and revel in its status as created, incomplete, not-God" (Canlis, 2010, p. 88).

Within the Christian tradition, this restored relationship with God is made possible through Christians' union with Christ. Based on this renewed ability to fellowship with God, Christians can have a personal relationship with God, pursuing a deeper connection to him through Bible study, prayer, meditation, participating in church life with other Christians, and so forth. In so doing, Christians are better able to function in daily life across a variety of domains (e.g., work, family, community), knowing God is with them each step of the way.[4]

With this atoning work of Jesus Christ, "redemption" has taken place, which leads to restored communion with God through union with Christ. On the way to God's eventual "restoration" of a broken world, optimal Christian mental health involves cultivating Christian contentment and a more hopeful endurance in each and every unfolding situation in life, which can be translated into clinical practice.

The process of restoration in Christianity is both instantaneous and ongoing, experienced and anticipated. The restored communion with God begins the healing process immediately, but the healing is ongoing. It involves relearning how to approach life as the practice of communion. It also anticipates a future complete healing and the hope of life everlasting in communion with God.

In this process of restoration, the life of the redeemed is not lifted from the brokenness of the world, but is lived fully engaged with it. This brokenness is still experienced by Christians—brokenness of the external world often revealing the brokenness of the internal world and their continued need for God's restoration in their union with Christ. Yet, in the midst of a fallen world, Christians are called to endure suffering with a sense of hope and contentment as they patiently wait for Jesus's return. To summarize the aforementioned relationship, Figure 1 offers a visual depiction of an indigenous Christian understanding of the relationship between God, ontology (reality), epistemology (knowledge), the biblical meta-narrative, and health, dysfunction, and healing.

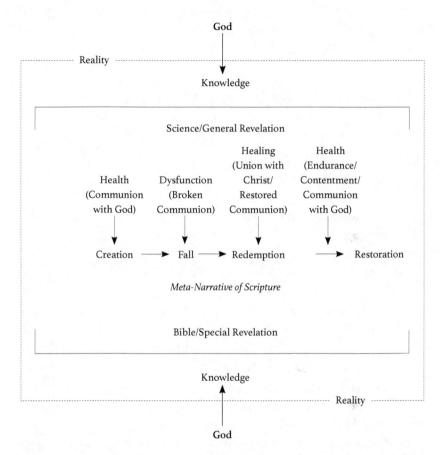

FIGURE 1. An indigenous Christian model for explaining the relationship between reality, knowledge, the meta-narrative of Scripture, and health, dysfunction, and healing.

Ultimately, for the Christian, we argue that psychological health in a fallen world involves dually cultivating a more hopeful endurance and contentment, with communion with God as the central aim, or teleology.

HEALTH, DYSFUNCTION, AND HEALING
IN THE CHRISTIAN TRADITION

Building on the above, we centrally argue that Christian psychological health involves communion with God—which is not always synonymous with personal pleasure, individual happiness, or self-fulfillment, as commonly understood—set against the backdrop of the meta-narrative of the Bible and God as the author of reality and ultimate source of knowledge. Christian mental health, to be sure, is conceptualized relationally, with Christians finding their very sense of self and purpose in a restored fellowship with God through union with Christ. Unfortunately, because of the fall, humans turned away from God, leading to widespread suffering. With the redemptive work of Jesus Christ, though, Christians can reexperience the ability to confidently walk with God on a daily basis. In doing so, suffering within a broken, fragmented world by no means miraculously ceases to exist. Rather, Christians improve their ability to endure suffering, given their increasing reliance upon a deeper communion with God. What is more, the temporary suffering in this world can be reframed as redemptive, not just random occurrences that are divorced from meaning and purpose. Because of God's infinite goodness, he uses suffering as a way to make Christians more like Jesus Christ. Thus, just like we need to persevere with strength training in spite of the pain so as to achieve a particular goal, Christians can endure the difficult seasons of life with hope, knowing that an ultimate purpose lies behind the ups and downs of this world.

To cultivate a deeper communion with God, Christians have historically relied upon a variety of daily Christian disciplines and practices, such as reading the Bible, praying, meditating, and listening for God's direction via solitude and quiet time (Calhoun, 2005). Certainly, pain and suffering continue to exist, but the corresponding loneliness and isolation are ameliorated, helping Christians to endure with a newfound sense of hope. Instead of merely walking with God, then, Christians are walking *home* with God, heading toward a specific destination with the path and practice of communion as they learn to shift from "earthly-mindedness" to "heavenly-mindedness" while on earth (Ball, 2016). In this process, Christians are growing more fully human—coming to understand the textures and nuances of being a whole being and learning to be patient, joyous, and long-suffering, all things that might lessen their humanity if they did not experience them.

What follows is a brief review of what we believe are some of the building blocks of Christian mental health, including communion with God, a hopeful endurance, and contentment. Then, with the remainder of the chapter, we offer a brief example of what psychological change might look like within an indigenous Christian model of psychotherapy, before concluding with a Christian hymn that we believe fittingly exemplifies mental health from within the Christian faith system.

COMMUNION WITH GOD: THE CORNERSTONE
OF CHRISTIAN MENTAL HEALTH

In the New Testament, the Greek word *koinonia* (i.e., fellowship) is often used to capture Christians' communion with God (see, e.g., 2 Corinthians 13:14). For the purposes of this chapter, based on a review of a range of classic theological Christian writings (Baxter, 2017; Beeke & Jones, 2012; Davis, 2012; Henry, 2011; Owen, 2007; Packer, 1990; Strong, 2015), we define *communion* with God as follows:

A mutual, intimate friendship with the Trinity, initiated by God and reciprocated by Christians through union with Christ, resulting in the psychological and spiritual benefits of being at peace with God, enjoying God's presence, feeling loved, accepted, and comforted by God, and communicating with God through prayer, meditation, and Bible study. (Knabb & Wang, 2019, p. 4)

In a recent psychometric study, the Communion with God Scale (CGS) was developed and validated with an online community sample of Christian adults, with results revealing that the scale has adequate internal consistency reliability and is positively correlated with daily spiritual experiences and mental well-being (Knabb & Wang, 2019).

But what, exactly, does communion with God look like in daily life, and what is so helpful about developing a deeper communion with God? Communion may involve a variety of practices, such as worshipping God by directly expressing gratitude to him, slowing down to sit in solitude and silence with God via contemplation, serving God by engaging in hospitality toward others, studying the Bible, and praying to God by way of formal and informal practices that are rooted in the Bible and classic Christian writings (Calhoun, 2005). With God at the center of existence, all of life becomes an act of worship before him (Peterson, 1992), given that Christians view each event (whether large or small or important or seemingly insignificant) through this relational lens. Moreover, in addition to the more obvious relational benefits, we suggest that "walking with God" allows Christians to psychologically shift from "earthly-mindedness" to "heavenly-mindedness" (Ball, 2016) in a fallen, broken world.

SHIFTING FROM "EARTHLY-MINDEDNESS" AND DYSFUNCTION TO "HEAVENLY-MINDEDNESS" AND HEALING

In conceptualizing a Christian understanding of dysfunction and healing, we believe that drawing a contrast between "earthly-mindedness" and "heavenly-mindedness" offers an important distinction in the Christian life. Based on a review of several classic theological writings in the Christian tradition (Burroughs, 2010, 2014; Owen, 2016; Rowe, 1672), we define *earthly-mindedness* as follows:

A past- to present-oriented, distracted mental state, preoccupied with the worries, uncertainties, and sufferings of the temporary physical world and struggling to maintain an awareness of a transcendent, spiritual reality, including heaven as an actual place and a real relationship with the Triune God.

On the other hand, *heavenly-mindedness*, also based on a review of several Christian authors (Burroughs, 2010, 2014; Owen, 2016; Rowe, 1672) is defined as:

A present- to future-oriented mental state of hope, prioritizing a moment-by-moment awareness of both a transcendent, spiritual reality and heaven as an eternal, permanent place, wherein Christians will find their true home, free from suffering, and experience a perfect, face-to-face communion with the infinitely good, wise, and powerful Triune God.

Notice the distinction between the two types of psychological "mindedness" among Christians. With the former, Christians are preoccupied with the inevitable psychological struggles emanating from a fallen world, planted solely in the here-and-now and disconnected from a more transcendent, spiritual reality, wherein God is at the center. With the latter, however, Christians are able to understand their psychological suffering in the context of a deeper communion with God and meta-perspective, recognizing that their main task is to slowly and steadily walk home with him toward heaven, given that this temporary, broken world is by no means a final destination. To offer a quick metaphor, in walking along the treacherous roads of life, regularly shifting the attention from the ground to the horizon is key in order to know where Christians are going and maintain a sense of hope that they will eventually get there— the proper "end" offers proper orientation. Likewise, Christian mental health involves focusing on heaven and a spiritual, transcendent reality, which can provide hope and constancy in a fallen, fragmented world and the proper meaning and context for Christians' current experiences.

HUPOMONE: CHRISTIANITY'S VERSION OF ACCEPTANCE

In the contemporary Western clinical psychology literature, acceptance-based models of therapy are currently quite popular, often embedded within a cognitive behavioral therapy (CBT) framework (Hayes, Follette, & Linehan, 2011). Typically influenced by Buddhist mindfulness, clients are taught to focus on a particular aspect of their present-moment experience, accepting a wide variety of symptoms with an attitude of nonjudgmental curiosity, rather than futilely striving to avoid psychological pain (Bishop et al., 2004). From this perspective, acceptance is cultivated for pragmatic reasons—letting go of the desire for psychological experiences to be somehow different and, thus, ameliorating suffering in the process.

Yet the New Testament concept of a hopeful endurance seems to offer a fitting Christian alternative, made up of a more active form of acceptance, coupled with perseverance and hope. Captured by the Greek word *hupomone*, a hopeful endurance is often translated as "patience" or "waiting" (Strong, 2001a, 2001b), pointing to the virtuous ability to calmly press on in the midst of persecution and suffering because the end goal is constantly in mind—future glory (Barclay, 1976). For Christians, the ability to dually endure adversities and hardships in the external world and psychological pain in the internal world comes from the hope of God's eventual restoration, a "heavenly-minded" frame of mind (Ball, 2016) that steadily focuses on the goal—faithfully and courageously continuing on with a joyful awareness that a greatness is just around the corner (Barclay, 1976). A hopeful endurance, then, is about yielding to God's will with a joyful hope, given that God's perfect plan is in view.

In the New Testament, the theme of *hupomone* seems to be threaded throughout the book of Revelation, given that the Christians to whom the letter was written were facing persecution as they patiently waited for Jesus's return (Barclay, 1976). Moreover, early Christian martyrs had to hold on to their faith in the midst of suffering and death. For example, in a letter written by Ignatius of Antioch roughly a century after Jesus's life, Ignatius anticipated a violent death by "wild animals awaiting [him] in the arena" (p. 48). Yet, in the conclusion of his famous letter, he declared, "May you stand strong to the end through the *endurance* provided by Jesus Christ" (cited in Liftin, 2014, p. 52, italics added). In another famous letter of the second century, Polycarp wrote,

We count as blessed and noble every martyrdom that happened according to God's will (for we who are truly reverent must consider God as sovereign over all that occurs). Who could fail to marvel at the martyrs' nobility and steadfast *endurance* and total devotion to their Lord? (cited in Liftin, 2014, p. 55, italics added)

Here we see a common theme of endurance among the early Christian martyrs, facing their inevitable death with courage and hope, given they believed that God was with them as they suffered and died for Jesus Christ and would eventually be in God's presence. In surrendering to the will of God, moreover, Christians throughout the ages appear to have been able to actively press forward in the midst of suffering with a sort of inner satisfaction. Thus, in addition to fellowshipping with God and enduring with a courageous hope, Christian contentment, from our perspective, is foundational to Christian mental health.

CONTENTMENT: INNER SATISFACTION REGARDLESS OF OUTER CIRCUMSTANCES

In recent years, the psychology literature has taken an interest in the construct of contentment, developing measures (Taylor, Medvedev, Owens, & Siegert, 2017) and offering an operationalized definition: "perceived completeness, [or] the perception that the present situation is enough and entire" (Cordaro, Bracket, Glass, & Anderson, 2016, p. 221). In fact, some authors have even suggested that contentment should be more closely examined as foundational to mental health (Cordaro et al., 2016; Gaskins, 1999).

From an indigenous Christian perspective, the *Holman Illustrated Bible Dictionary* (1998) succinctly defines *contentment* as "Internal satisfaction which does not demand changes in external circumstances" (p. 335). In addition, in one of the more famous passages in the New Testament, the Apostle Paul declared:

For I have learned to be *content* whatever the circumstances. I know what it is to be in need, and I know what it is to have plenty. I have learned the secret of being *content* in any and every situation, whether well fed or hungry, whether living in plenty or in want. I can do all this through him who gives me strength. (Philippians 4:10–13, italics added)

What is more, in Thomas à Kempis's (1983) widely read medieval classic *The Imitation of Christ*, he wrote the following fictional instructions from God: "If I am the cause and goal, you will be well *content*, whatever I do with you. But if anything of your own will remains in your heart, it is that which hinders you" (p. 88, italics added). As another example, in a Jesuit writing from the seventeenth century, *Trustful Surrender to Divine Providence* (Colombiere, 1983), the author explicated that Christian contentment is about "[remaining] indifferent to good fortune or to adversity by accepting it all from the hand of God without questioning, not to ask for things to be done as we would like them but as God wishes" (p. 31). Finally, the Puritan author Jeremiah Burroughs (2018) suggested that Christian contentment involves a "sweet, inward, quiet, grace-filled condition of spirit which freely submits to and delights in God's wise and fatherly management in every condition." Based on a review of a variety of Christian sources (Burroughs, 2018; Colombiere, 1983; Holman, 1998; Kempis, 1983; Watson, 2017), we define *Christian contentment* as follows:

An inner psychological state of enduring satisfaction, independent of outer circumstances, that is attributable to God's grace and involves freely and fully surrendering to God, finding pleasure in God, and thanking God in actively authoring every life event with perfect goodness and wisdom. (Knabb, Vazquez, & Wang, 2019, p. 8)

In recent research, Knabb, Vazquez, and Wang (2019) developed the Christian Contentment Scale (CCS), with results revealing that the scale has adequate internal consistency reliability and is correlated with daily spiritual experiences and general and life contentment.

Of course, Christian contentment may be one of the more difficult mental states to cultivate in a fallen, fragmented world. Yet, in surrendering to God's will, Christians throughout the ages seem to have been able to endure a wide variety of hardships and sufferings, recognizing that God is lovingly directing the world he created for good (Romans 8:28). This understanding of contentment is also related to a distinctly Christian teleology—Christians trust in God's purpose for daily living on both a global and individual level. Given the difficulty in developing this deeper contentment in the midst of human suffering, we offer the following example of what such arduous psychological change might look like within an indigenous Christian psychotherapy.

CLINICAL APPLICATIONS

In the last several decades, mindfulness meditation has had a significant impact on the clinical psychology literature, with meta-analyses suggesting it is efficacious for a range of psychological symptoms (Khoury et al., 2013). For Christians, though, there may be concerns that mindfulness's teleology is inconsistent with an indigenous Christian worldview, given mindfulness's Buddhist roots. To be sure, although some of the skills

developed in mindfulness meditation may overlap with Christian meditative practices—such as the cultivation of present-moment awareness;
focused, sustained attention; and an attitude of nonjudgmental, open
curiosity (Feldman, Hayes, Kumar, Greeson, & Laurenceau, 2007; Walsh
& Shapiro, 2006)—we argue that Christians should be able to draw
from their own indigenous religious heritage to impact psychological
change. Certainly, there is a growing literature base on the use of distinctly Christian forms of meditation for psychological problems (Knabb,
Frederick, & Cumming, 2017; Knabb & Vazquez, 2018; Knabb, Vazquez,
Garzon, et al., 2019), with the ultimate aim being a deeper communion
with God (Knabb & Wang, 2019) and more enduring contentment in him
(Knabb, Vazquez, & Wang, 2019).

Many of these distinctly Christian exercises help practitioners to
deepen their focus on God, his attributes, and his actions—as concentrative forms of meditation—rather than promote a more generic, fluid
awareness of whatever objects arise in the present moment (Walsh &
Shapiro, 2006). Theoretically, these indigenous Christian practices may
help followers of Jesus Christ to shift their focus from difficult psychological struggles to nonjudgmental acceptance of God's will in each
unfolding moment of life, yielding to God's providence and looking to
the future with hope and endurance, which may indirectly ameliorate
suffering (Ware, 2000). In other words, rather than aiming to change the
inner world, Christian meditation may help Christians to fill the mind
with God, focusing on a more positive experience, not ridding the mind
of unpleasant intrapsychic experiences (Walsh & Shapiro, 2006; Ware,
2000). Over time, an attitude of detachment may be cultivated (Knabb,
Vazquez, Wang, & Bates, 2018; Knabb, Vazquez, Garzon, et al., 2019), given
that Christian practitioners are repeatedly practicing this intentional
pivot, noticing unpleasant inner experiences with nonjudgmental acceptance, then shifting the attention to God with a more hopeful endurance
(Knabb, Vazquez, & Pate, 2019).

Upon examining a range of writings throughout Christian history
(Ball, 2016; Bangley, 2006; Gallagher, 2008; Lawrence, 2015; Ware, 2000;
Wilhoit & Howard, 2012), we offer the following definition of *Christian
meditation*:

A broad collection of mostly concentrative psychological and spiritual practices throughout historic Christianity, ranging from *apophatic* (emphasizing few to no words and no images) to *kataphatic* (emphasizing words and/or images), for shifting from earthly- to heavenly-mindedness and developing a deeper communion with God and enduring contentment in him in the midst of suffering.

Figure 2 offers a theoretical depiction of the role that Christian meditation may play in moving Christians from dysfunction to healing in a fallen world, helping Christian clients in psychotherapy to (a) notice difficult psychological symptoms, (b) shift toward "heavenly-mindedness," (c) accept difficult psychological symptoms with a more hopeful endurance, and (d) take behavioral action in life based on a deeper fellowship with God and enduring contentment in him.

To offer a more specific example that is grounded in a classic indigenous Christian writing from the Middle Ages, in *The Practice of the*

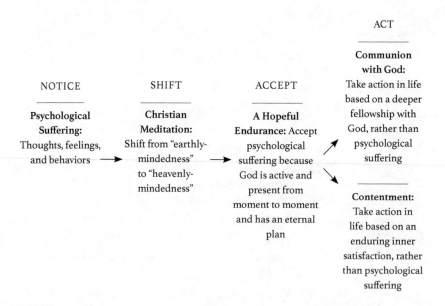

FIGURE 2. Theoretical model of Christian meditation. Adapted from Ball (2016); Bangley (2006); Bishop, et al. (2004); Hayes, Strosahl, and Wilson (2012); Knabb and Wang (2018); Knabb and Vazquez (2018); Knabb, Vazquez, and Pate (2019); Kristeller and Johnson (2005); Walsh and Shapiro (2006); and Ware (2000).

Presence of God, Brother Lawrence (2015) advocated for cultivating an awareness of God's presence from moment to moment, even in the seemingly mundane tasks of everyday life, which involves "[delighting] in and becoming accustomed to [God's] divine company, speaking humbly and conversing lovingly with him all the time, at every moment, without rule or measure, especially in times of temptation, suffering, aridity, weariness, even infidelity and sin." So, whether washing the dishes, folding the laundry, or speaking to a colleague at work, Christians can maintain a sense that God is with them by (a) slowly, gently, and deliberately performing the activity with focused, sustained attention, and (b) recognizing God's presence in the activity by silently repeating a simple phrase within the mind, such as "My God, I am completely yours" (Lawrence, 2015). In this practice, a healthy psychological process may start to unfold, with the Christian beginning to develop the skill of "[living] as if only he [or she] and God were in the world" (Lawrence, 2015).

Grounded in a loving awareness of God's presence, the Christian is practicing noticing unpleasant inner experiences, then shifting toward a more transcendent, "heavenly-minded" reality (Ball, 2016). Along the way, he or she is learning to fellowship with God and rest in a deeper contentment in him, given that even seemingly mundane daily activities—whether perceived to be pleasant or unpleasant—come to life because God is the author of all events. After all, according to Brother Lawrence, "All our thoughts, words and actions belong by right to him," and "Nothing is more pleasing to God than to turn away from all creatures many times throughout the day to withdraw and adore him present within."[5] As Christians deepen their fellowship with God and find a more enduring contentment in him, they are in a position to take behavioral action, making life decisions that are anchored to the teachings of the Bible, rather than impulsively reacting to psychological suffering.

Although additional research is certainly needed on indigenous Christian interventions, writings on Christian meditative practices have emerged in the psychology literature in recent years (see, e.g., Knabb, Johnson, Bates, & Sisemore, 2019). For example, Knabb and Vazquez (2018) recently conducted a randomized trial among Christian college students, employing the daily use of the Jesus Prayer (e.g., "Lord Jesus Christ, Son of God, have mercy on me") as an intervention for stress.

Results revealed a significant reduction in stress, over a two-week period of time, for the intervention group (a medium/large effect size), whereas no significant difference emerged for the wait-list group (Knabb & Vazquez, 2018). Also, Knabb, Vazquez, Garzon, and colleagues (2019) recently conducted a multisite randomized trial on the use of both *kataphatic* (using words/images) and *apophatic* (wordless/imageless) forms of Christian meditation for repetitive negative thinking (e.g., rumination, worry) among Christian college students. Results for the four-week study revealed a significant reduction in repetitive negative thinking for the intervention group (a large effect size), whereas no significant reduction was observed for the wait-list group (Knabb, Vazquez, Garzon, et al., 2019).

Consistent with these publications, Christian clients in psychotherapy should have the option of drawing from their own faith tradition, "[solving] their local problems through indigenous practices and applications" (Task Force on Indigenous Psychology, n.d.). In other words, rather than leaning on an overly mechanical understanding of psychological functioning, as is the case with much of the contemporary secular scientific literature, the Christian tradition offers a unique teleology of psychological health, dysfunction, and healing, embedded within a distinctly Christian worldview and meta-narrative that emanates from the Bible. As Western psychology rightly begins to embrace the notion that clients' culture should be central to effective psychotherapy (American Psychological Association [APA], 2006), an indigenous Christian psychology can only strengthen case conceptualization and treatment in the twenty-first century when working with Christian clients in clinical practice.

CONCLUSION

In this chapter we have attempted to present an indigenous Christian psychology, outlining a historical understanding of the Christian faith system—including epistemological considerations, a philosophy of science, and a perspective on the self, health, well-being, disordered functioning, and psychological change—and clinical applications. For Christians, life is about communing with God from moment to moment, walking home with him with a heavenly perspective, a hopeful endurance, and a deeper contentment in him as the author of all events. In walking home with God, there will certainly be psychological suffering on the roads of life. Still, because God is the author of all events, cultivating inner satisfaction in the midst of external adversities is paramount for Christian mental health. Although psychological suffering is inevitable, the promise of meeting God, face-to-face, helps Christians to repeatedly shift from earthly preoccupations to him, practicing the presence of God in each and every unfolding activity. Certainly, this practice is about living teleologically in day-to-day life by learning to "see" God in all of Christians' varying circumstances. Like a plant that continues to grow toward the sun, regardless of its surrounding environment (Barclay, 1976), Christian mental health and a stronger faith are dually realized in walking with God on the roads of life, steadily venturing home as devout Christians patiently wait for his eventual restoration of a shattered existence. Reminiscent of the early Christian martyrs awaiting an inevitable fate, facing psychological suffering with courage and hope is possible for twenty-first-century Christians, given a more transcendent awareness of reality placing everything into its proper context.

To conclude, we offer what we believe is a fitting example of Christian mental health, aptly captured by a popular Christian hymn, "This Is My Father's World," written in the late 1800s by the New York minister Maltbie Babcock:

> This is my Father's world,
> And to my listening ears
> All nature sings, and round me rings
> The music of the spheres.
> This is my Father's world:
> I rest me in the thought
> Of rocks and trees, of skies and seas;
> His hand the wonders wrought.
>
> This is my Father's world,
> The birds their carols raise,
> The morning light, the lily white,
> Declare their maker's praise.
> This is my Father's world,

He shines in all that's fair;
In the rustling grass I hear Him pass;
He speaks to me everywhere.

This is my Father's world.
O let me ne'er forget
That though the wrong seems oft so strong,
God is the Ruler yet.
This is my Father's world:
why should my heart be sad?
The Lord is King; let the heavens ring!
God reigns; let the earth be glad!

Above all else, a distinctly Christian psychology is a thoroughly relational psychology, with each moment in life offering the opportunity to engage in acts of worship before God. With such efforts, followers of Jesus Christ are gradually learning to recognize that God is the creator and sustainer of this world, who operates from the center, not the periphery. Whether Christians experience seasons of celebration or mourning, God is always present, walking with them as they learn to "glorify [him]" and "enjoy him forever."

REFERENCES

American Psychological Association (APA). (2006). Evidence-based practice in psychology. *American Psychologist, 61*, 271–285.

Atwood, G., & Stolorow, R. (1993). *Faces in a cloud: Intersubjectivity in personality theory.* Lanham, MD: Rowman & Littlefield.

Ball, J. (2016). *A treatise of divine meditation.* Crossville, TN: Puritan Publications.

Bangley, B. (Ed.). (2006). *The cloud of unknowing: Contemporary English edition.* Brewster, MA: Paraclete Press.

Barclay, W. (1976). *New Testament words.* Louisville, KY: Westminster/John Knox Press.

Baxter, R. (2017). *Walking with God.* Dallas: Gideon House Books.

Beeke, J., & Jones, M. (2012). *A Puritan theology: Doctrine for life.* (Kindle edition)

Bishop, S., Lau, M., Shapiro, S., Carlson, L., Anderson, N., Carmody, J., ... & Devins, G. (2004). Mindfulness: A proposed operational definition. *Clinical Psychology: Science and Practice, 11*, 230–241.

Block, D. (2014). *For the glory of God: Recovering a biblical theology of worship.* Grand Rapids: Baker Academic.

Boersma, H. (2018). *Seeing God: The beatific vision in Christian tradition.* Grand Rapids: William B. Eerdmans.

Bonhoeffer, D. (1955). *Ethics.* New York: Touchstone.

Bonhoeffer, D. (1959). *Creation and fall.* New York: Touchstone.

Bray, G. (1993). *The doctrine of God.* Downers Grove, IL: InterVarsity Press.

Burroughs, J. (2010). *Heavenly-mindedness recommended: In a discourse on Colossians 3:2.* Farmington Hills, MI: Gale ECCO.

Burroughs, J. (2014). *A treatise on earthly-mindedness.* Louisville, KY: GLH Publishing.

Burroughs, J. (2018). *The rare jewel of Christian contentment: Abridged and in modern English.* R. Summers (Trans. Rob Summers).

Calhoun, A. (2005). *Spiritual disciplines handbook: Practices that transform us.* Downers Grove, IL: InterVarsity Press.

Calvin, J. (2011). *Institutes of the Christian religion.* Peabody, MA: Hendrickson.

Canlis, J. (2010). *Calvin's ladder.* Grand Rapids: William B. Eerdmans.

Colombiere, C. (1983). *Trustful surrender to divine providence: The secret of peace and happiness.* Charlotte: TAN Books.

Cordaro, D., Brackett, M., Glass, L., & Anderson, C. (2016). Contentment: Perceived completeness across cultures and traditions. *Review of General Psychology, 20,* 221–235.

Davis, J. (2012). *Meditation and communion with God: Contemplating scripture in an age of distraction.* Downers Grove, IL: InterVarsity Press.

Feldman, G., Hayes, A., Kumar, S., Greeson, J., & Laurenceau, J. (2007). Mindfulness and emotion regulation: The development and initial validation of the Cognitive and Affective Mindfulness Scale-Revised (CAMS-R). *Journal of Psychopathology and Behavioral Assessment, 29,* 177–190.

Gallagher, T. (2008). *Meditation and contemplation: An Ignatian guide to praying with Scripture.* New York: Crossroad.

Gaskins, R. (1999). "Adding legs to a snake": A reanalysis of motivation and the pursuit of happiness from a Zen Buddhist perspective. *Journal of Educational Psychology, 91,* 204–215.

Haig, B. (2018). *Method matters in psychology: Essays in applied philosophy of science.* Cham, Switzerland: Springer.

Hayes, S., Follette, V., & Linehan, M. (Eds.). (2011). *Mindfulness and acceptance: Expanding the cognitive-behavioral tradition.* New York: Guilford.

Hayes, S., Strosahl, K., & Wilson, K. (2012). *Acceptance and commitment therapy: The process and practice of mindful change* (2nd ed.). New York: Guilford.

Henry, M. (2011). *Daily communion with God.* Westfield, IN: Digital Puritan Press.

Holman Illustrated Bible Dictionary. (1998). *Contentment.* Nashville: Holman Bible Publishers.

Howard, G. (1988). Science, values, and teleological explanations of human action. *Counseling and Values, 32,* 93–103.

Johnson, K., Hill, E., & Cohen, A. (2011). Integrating the study of culture and religion:

Toward a psychology of worldview. *Social and Personality Psychology Compass, 5,* 137–152.

Johnson, S. (2004). *The practice of emotionally focused couple therapy* (2nd ed.). New York: Routledge.

Kempis, T. (1983). *The imitation of Christ.* New York: Crown Publishing.

Khoury, B., Lecomte, T., Fortin, G., Masse, M., Therien, P., Bouchard, V., ... & Hofmann, S. (2013). Mindfulness-based therapy: A comprehensive meta-analysis. *Clinical Psychology Review, 33,* 763–771.

Kim, U., Park, Y., & Park, D. (2000). The challenge of cross-cultural psychology: The role of indigenous psychologies. *Journal of Cross-Cultural Psychology, 31,* 63–75.

Kim, U., Yang, K., & Hwang, K. (2006). Contributions to indigenous and cultural psychology: Understanding people in context. In U. Kim, K. Yang, & K. Hwang (Eds.), *Indigenous and cultural psychology: Understanding people in context* (pp. 3–25). New York: Springer.

King, D., Viney, W., & Woody, W. (2013). *A history of psychology: Ideas & context.* New York: Routledge.

Knabb, J., Frederick, T., & Cumming, G. (2017). Surrendering to God's providence: A three-part study on providence-focused therapy for recurrent worry (PFT-RW). *Psychology of Religion and Spirituality, 9,* 180–196.

Knabb, J., Johnson, E., Bates, T., & Sisemore, T. (2019). *Christian psychotherapy in context: Theoretical and empirical explorations in faith-based mental health.* New York: Routledge.

Knabb, J., & Vazquez, V. (2018). A randomized controlled trial of a two-week Internet-based contemplative prayer program for Christians with daily stress. *Spirituality in Clinical Practice, 5,* 37–53.

Knabb, J., Vazquez, V., Garzon, F., Ford, K., Wang, K., Conner, K., ... & Weston, D. (2019). Christian meditation for repetitive negative thinking: A multisite randomized trial examining the effects of a 4-week preventative program. *Spirituality in Clinical Practice.* Advance online publication.

Knabb, J., Vazquez, V., & Pate, R. (2019). "Set your minds on things above": Shifting from trauma-based ruminations to ruminating on God. *Mental Health, Religion & Culture, 22,* 384–399.

Knabb, J., Vazquez, V., & Wang, K. (2019). *The Christian Contentment Scale: An emic measure for assessing inner satisfaction within the Christian tradition.* Manuscript submitted for publication.

Knabb, J., & Wang, K. (2019). The Communion with God Scale: Shifting from an etic to emic perspective to assess fellowshipping with the Triune God. *Psychology of Religion and Spirituality.* Advance online publication.

Knabb, J., Vazquez, V., Wang, K., & Bates, T. (2018). "Unknowing" in the 21st century: Humble detachment for Christians with repetitive negative thinking. *Spirituality in Clinical Practice, 5,* 170–187.

Kristeller, J., & Johnson, T. (2005). Cultivating loving kindness: A two-stage model of the effects of meditation on empathy, compassion, and altruism. *Zygon, 40,* 391–407.

Kuyper, A. (2011). *Wisdom & wonder: Common grace in science & art.* Grand Rapids: Christian's Library Press.

Lambert, M. (2013). The efficacy and effectiveness of psychotherapy. In M. Lambert (Ed.), *Bergin and Garfield's handbook of psychotherapy and behavior change* (pp. 169–218). New York: John Wiley & Sons.

Lawrence, B. (2015). *The practice of the presence of God* (Trans. S. Sciurba). Washington, DC: ICS Publications.

Lawson, R. B., Anderson, E. D., & Cepeda-Benito, A. (2018). *A history of psychology: Globalization, ideas, and applications* (2nd ed.). New York: Routledge.

Liftin, B. (2014). *Early Christian martyr stories: An evangelical introduction with new translations.* Grand Rapids: Baker Academic.

Marsella, A. (2009). Some reflections on potential abuses of psychology's knowledge and practices. *Psychological Studies, 54,* 23–27.

Mitchell, S. (1988). *Relational concepts in psychoanalysis: An integration.* Cambridge, MA: Harvard University Press.

Oden, T. (1987). *Classical pastoral care.* Grand Rapids: Baker Books.

Owen, J. (2007). *Communion with the Triune God.* Wheaton, IL: Crossway Books.

Owen, J. (2016). *Spiritual mindedness.* Louisville, KY: GLH Publishing.

Packer, J. (1990). *A quest for Godliness: The Puritan vision of the Christian life.* Wheaton, IL: Crossway Books.

Pankalla, A., & Kośnik, K. (2018). Religion as an invaluable source of psychological knowledge: Indigenous Slavic psychology of religion. *Journal of Theoretical and Philosophical Psychology, 38,* 154–164.

Perlman, M. (2004). The modern philosophical resurrection of teleology. *The Monist, 87,* 3–51.

Peterson, D. (1992). *Engaging with God: A biblical theology of worship.* Downers Grove, IL: InterVarsity Press.

Pew Research Center. (2015). *Religious landscape study.* Retrieved https://www.pewforum.org/religious-landscape-study

Rowe, J. (1672). *Heavenly-mindedness and earthly-mindedness: In two parts.* London: Francis Tyton.

Ruse, M. (2018). *On purpose.* Princeton, NJ: Princeton University Press.

Rychlak, J. (1994). *Logical learning theory: A human teleology and its empirical support.* Lincoln: University of Nebraska Press.

Sibbes, R. (2018). *The Christian's desire to see God face to face.* Crossville, TN: Puritan Publications.

Slife, B., & Reber, J. (2012). Conceptualizing religious practices in psychological research: Problems and prospects. *Pastoral Psychology, 61,* 735–746.

Strong, J. (2001a). *The new Strong's expanded dictionary of the words in the Hebrew Bible.* Nashville: Thomas Nelson.

Strong, J. (2001b). *The new Strong's expanded dictionary of the words in the Greek New Testament.* Nashville: Thomas Nelson.

Strong, W. (2015). *The saint's communion with God.* Crossville, TN: Puritan Publications.

Task Force on Indigenous Psychology. (n.d.). *Division 32 (Society for Humanistic Psychology): American Psychological Association.* Retrieved from http://indigenouspsych.org/index.html

Taylor, T., Medvedev, O., Owens, R., & Siegert, R. (2017). Development and validation of the State Contentment Measure. *Personality and Individual Differences, 119,* 152–159.

Walsh, R., & Shapiro, S. (2006). The meeting of meditative disciplines and Western psychology: A mutually enriching dialogue. *American Psychologist, 61,* 227–239.

Ware, K. (2000). *The inner kingdom.* Crestwood, NY: St. Vladimir's Seminary Press.

Watson, P. (1993). Apologetics and ethnocentrism: Psychology and religion within an ideological surround. *International Journal for the Psychology of Religion, 3,* 1–20.

Watson, T. (2017). *The art of divine contentment* (Jason Roth, Trans.) (Kindle version). Retrieved from http://www.amazon.com

Wilhoit, J., & Howard, E. (2012). *Discovering lectio divina: Bringing Scripture into ordinary life.* Downers Grove, IL: InterVarsity Press.

Wolf, E. (2002). *Treating the self: Elements of clinical self psychology.* New York: Guilford.

Wolters, A. (2005). *Creation regained: Biblical basics for a reformational worldview.* Grand Rapids: William B. Eerdmans.

ENDNOTES

1. To preserve an emic perspective, we have elected to use masculine pronouns throughout the chapter, consistent with an orthodox reading of the Christian Bible and understanding of the Triune God as Father, Son, and Holy Spirit.

2. This quote is from the Westminster Shorter Catechism, published in 1648 by churches in Scotland, England, and Ireland, which summarizes a variety of teachings within Protestant Christianity.

3. Here, we wish to acknowledge that the Christian tradition generally allows for the integration of truths from outside influences that are consistent with biblical Christianity. For example, in *Institutes of the Christian Religion*, the sixteenth-century Protestant theologian John Calvin (2011) distinguished knowledge of "earthly things" and "heavenly things," suggesting that, despite the fall of humankind, non-Christians in scientific disciplines can still make some progress in elucidating "earthly" knowledge.

4. Consistent with emotionally focused couples therapy (EFT), which suggests that first creating safety and connection between couples in conflict can help them to more naturally problem solve and collaborate together (Johnson, 2004), we suggest that prioritizing communion with God can help Christians to more effectively respond to the demands of an uncertain world.

5. Here, though, we wish to acknowledge that this "turning away from all creatures" should be balanced with the discipline of coming to see God in/by/with/through all creatures and experiences. Part of contentment, in other words, is to endure in the midst of, rather than to depart from, all experiences.

SAYYED MOHSEN FATEMI

AN OVERVIEW OF AN ISLAM-BASED PSYCHOLOGY

A JOURNEY TOWARD PERFECTION: AN INTRODUCTION TO AN ISLAM-BASED PSYCHOLOGY

Is a human being summed up in the material realm and defined in physiological and neurological contexts with his attributes including geographical, ethnic, racial, and physical characteristics? Or is the realm of existence beyond what we have taken for granted in the material world? Is a human being merely a material being with no transcendental connection, or is there an immaterial component to human beings? These are some of the introductory questions that are addressed in an Islam-based psychology, and responses to them open up the realm of the immaterial and spiritual understanding of human beings.

An Islam-based psychology departs from the materialistic interpretation of human beings, affirms the spiritual component, and considers the path to spirituality as an essential element of growth and development. Humans are created to go beyond the material domain of life, to leap beyond the earthly and instinctual belongings and attachments. The physical and the material world is only a passage. An attachment to the material world and its manifestations is like falling in love with the rays of the sun. Its permanence takes place only until the sunset. An Islamic-based psychology begins with redefining humans—their mission and their responsibility.

Everything in this world, ontologically speaking, is composed of two elements: the physical, which is directly perceptible and tangible through our senses, and the heavenly (*Malakoot*), which moves in line with the divine direction. A piece of stone, for instance, is characterized as an object, but it also possesses a heavenly dimension. Beyond *Malakoot* or the heavenly realm, there also lies a higher realm (higher than the realm of heavenly) known as ARSH in Islamic terminology, which is not conceivable through our minds.

An Islam-based psychology argues that human beings are defined by a journey (an elevating and transcendental journey) toward perfection and elevation, and in that pursuit would embrace *Marefat* (a term beyond knowledge and wisdom and intelligence with two characteristics: tranquility and imperturbability)—and the more they attain *Marefat*, the more they experience their true heavenly truth. (The truth is individuated in accordance with one's ontological and epistemological capacity but is ultimately linked to the Higher Truth.) With more manifestation and crystallization of the heavenly truth, people get closer to God (not physically speaking) and experience *Qorb* (proximity toward God). *Qorb* is characterized through purification of the soul, where one mindfully, knowingly, and deliberately empties his or her heart from worldly attachments and belongings and attempts to enrich his or her soul by developing more connection to God. *Qorb* is also characterized through sincerity, authenticity and genuineness in action, and removing any signs of hypocrisy, pretentiousness, and ostentatiousness.

The more one's capacity for embracing the heavenly realm (*Malakoot*) grows, the more one acquires competencies toward psychological, spiritual, intellectual, and emotional empowerment. One's will becomes more empowered accordingly and finds a divine quiddity. In effect, many people may stand only in their own animalistic quiddity and they may not go up to reach the elevated status of becoming a divine nature. The body becomes weak not in the literal sense of the word, but in the spiritual, because without *Qorb*, one cannot transcend the body's limitations.

HEALTH AND WELL-BEING IN ISLAM

RIGHT RELATIONSHIP WITH POWER

Beyond the overarching theme of embracing *Malakoot*, Islam has other attributes and goals that lead toward well-being. One of these goals is to help people acquire a perspective that allows them not to misuse or abuse power. The world without power makes no sense, but the power conquered by egoism, egotism, arrogance, selfishness, hubris, utilitarianism, exploitation, and self-centeredness would bring havoc, destruction, annihilation, and despair. An Islam-based psychology elucidates the importance of self-management and self-regulation in giving direction to the use of power. One who feels needless and is saturated in hubris may set out to move in pursuit of power at any cost. One may feel powerful and yet in dire need of an obedience to the source of all powers, namely God, and one may feel needless of an attachment to such a source. An Islamic-based psychology considers one of the main causes of arrogance and its destructive implications in one's feeling of needlessness. When one feels groundless and needless, one does not feel it necessary to abide by any laws and hence considers himself or herself as entitled to do anything one wills.

Understanding one's need to be constantly and continuously connected to the authentic source of power, namely God, would help one observe the importance of self-management and self-regulation. Deep down, beneath human atrocities, human destructiveness, and human ferocities, there lies a relentless inattention toward the implications of selfishness, which takes place in an infatuation with one's feeling of needlessness and one's feeling of hubris in doing whatever one desires to do.

SPIRITUALITY AS AN INFINITE JOURNEY OF KINDNESS

The spiritual journey is infinite as it entails a journey toward God that has no point of ending. It constantly, incessantly, and continuously goes on. There is no single action where one can implement one's practical faith. Hazrat Zahra (Salamollah Alayha), in describing the available opportunities of spiritual growth in every single moment of life, indicates that true Muslims are characterized through their smiling faces, their kind and delicate hearts, and their compassion, kind words, and good deeds. The more one is in touch with one's spiritual performance and the more one is closely knitted to transcendental elevation, the more one becomes prepared for growth. One of the keys in putting this spiritual leap into effect is through doing and being good to others. Many Haidths and several Quranic verses emphasize displaying kindness, graciousness, benevolence, munificence, and friendliness to others to the extent that Prophet Muhammad (*Sallalah alayhe va alehee va sallam*) considers one of the easiest and closest ways to God is by the removal of sadness from the hearts of others.

MINDFULNESS

In line with an attempt toward doing good to others, an Islamic perspective explicates the need for increasing awareness prior to every single decision. Human perfection, the Islamic perspective argues, does not lie in the progression of automatic, instinctual, and habitual ways of living but in the enhancement and the enrichment of wise choices. One is mindfully responsible to monitor one's decisions, thoughts, feelings, and actions. In doing so, one is reminded of noticing the presence of God so that one is never alone.

ETERNAL LIFE

Death, in an Islamic-based psychology, is not meant to be the end of life but the commencement of an eternal life. One becomes the total sum of one's choices. The more one's choices intermingle with awareness, virtue, piety, morality, and wisdom, the more one's path to perfection opens up.

An Islam-based psychology highlights the importance of simultaneously taking care of the soul and the body. The nourishment for the body transpires through the body-oriented means, whereas the nourishment of the soul occurs through seeking connection to the source of all virtues and all of perfection, namely, God.

"HEART" AS A CENTRAL CONSTRUCT

Heart (*Qalb*) is not the physiological heart but the essence of human development and facilitates the path toward salvation, emancipation, growth, and transcendence. There are at least seventy meanings and ramifications for *Qalb*, including closed hearts, open hearts, locked hearts, contracted hearts, expanded hearts, and so on.

An important Quranic verse indicates that some people seemingly have hearts but are devoid of hearts:

They have hearts with which they do not understand, they have eyes with which they do not see, and they have ears with which they do not hear. Those are like livestock; rather, they are more astray. It is they who are the heedless. (Al-A'raf verse 179)

A Hadith from the leader of the faithful Imam Ali (Salavtollah Alayh) says:

People's hearts serve as capacities, the best of hearts are the ones with the most expansive capacities. (Haikimi, 1997, p. 69).

An authentic, genuine, and sincere journey toward God without any pretentiousness, hypocrisy, and deception enhances one's capacity. This is the nature of life for humans and a central aspect of what is termed "mental" health. One of the essential keys in enhancing and revitalizing one's capacity lies in one's compassion toward self and others. Again, a Hadith leader of the faithful Imam Ali (*Salavtollah Alayh*) indicates to "commit yourself with awareness and openness toward loving others, helping others, assisting others and solving their problems" (Haikimi, 1997, p. 70). In another Hadith from Prophet Muhammad (*Sallalaho alayhe va alehee va salaam*), the closest route to God is delineated through removing sadness from the other's heart, and this is done through compassion and mercy (Haikimi, 1997, p. 105).

COMPASSION AND MERCY

To demonstrate the essence of compassion and mercy in an Islamic psychological perspective, Jafari (2006), an Iranian contemporary philosopher and scholar of Islam, cites Imam Ali of Muslims with the following decrees on the rights of animals:

"Do not keep the animals and their children separate from one another."
"Make sure that you keep your nails short upon milking lest the animals may feel annoyed."
"If you happen to take the animals out for grazing, make sure that you walk them through the beautiful meadows if there are any."

"Rest assured that enough milk is left for the animal when milking."

"God will damn the one who uses profane language while addressing any animal."

"The governor can punish anyone who does not take care of his/her animal." (pp. 159–162)

Jafari (2006) then asks how a worldview that is so sensitive toward the rights of animals can be indifferent when dealing with human rights? He presents numerous examples from within the Islamic tradition to argue that Islam displays an essentially vital sensitivity toward the rights of any living creature with the maximum possible rights for any human being.

PEACE

There has been a misrepresentation of Islam's message in current culture that merits reconciling. In his book *The Clash of Civilizations and the Remaking of the World Order* (1996), Samuel P. Huntington discusses "Islamic civilization" and indicates that "Muslim bellicosity and violence are late twentieth-century facts which neither Muslims nor non-Muslims can deny" (p. 258). In discussing the comments and allegations, including those by Huntington and Payne, Spariosu (2004, p. 51) writes:

The traditional greeting among Muslims is "Peace be with you" (Al-Salam Aleikum) or that Sufi teachings do not condone violence and conflict any more than their Buddhist, Taoist, or Christian counterparts do. For example, the prophet Muhammad says: "If a man gives up quarreling when he is in the wrong, a house will be built for him in Paradise. But if a man gives up a conflict even when he is in the right, a house will be built for him in the loftiest of Paradise." (Frager & Fadiman 1997, p. 84)

If anything, Huntington's and Payne's arguments highlight the ignorance of even well-trained Westerners about other cultures and religions (not to mention their own) and the urgent need for educating the world's youth about each other's—and their own—cultural traditions.

Hakimi (2009), another Iranian philosopher and scholar of Islam, presents an in-depth analysis of the word *Islam* and the Prophet Muhammad and in light of Quranic verses and Haidths argues that the Prophet Muhammad serves as the source of mercy, peace, and compassion for the whole universe. In citing considerable evidence, he recounts the story of the Prophet Muhammad coming under the daily attack of an assailant, who even throws the bladder of a sheep at the prophet. Rather than retaliate, the prophet pays a visit to the man once he receives the news of his illness. Imam Reza, the eighth imam of Shias, also known as the Imam of Mercy (Al Iamam Ar Raoof), considered kindness toward others as half of wisdom. In a Hadith from Imam Hossein, the grandson of the Prophet Muhammad and the son of Imam Ali—namely, the fourth imam of Shias—sins are melted and dissipated as one practices being kind toward others (all cited in Hakimi, Hakimi, & Hakimi, 2005).

Referring to the ontological layers of the components of love, Nasr observed as follows:

Hence, the love of God and by God permeates the whole universe, and many Islamic mystics or Sufis over the ages have spoken of that love to which Dante refers at the end of the Divine Comedy when he speaks of "the love that moves the sun and the stars." (Nasr, 2007, p. 48)

In a famous Hadith, cited in Amali by Sadoogh (in Hakimi et al., 2005), Imam Ali of Shias reiterated to all Muslims, "Let the practice of mercy, forgiveness and kindness toward others be well embedded in your heart" (Hakimi et al., 2005, p. 102). In his government policies, Imam Ali told his governor-general, Malek Ashtar, he should "observe and practice kindness, mercy, compassion and respect to anyone in the world because people fall into two groups: They either belong to your Islamic viewpoint and thus they are your companions, or, even if not, they are equal to you in terms of being a human being" (Razee, 1993, p. 427).

LOVE

At the center of an Islam-based psychology lies the panacea of love. Many Hadiths from the prophet and his household promote the expansion and implementation of love in diverse points of human relationship—for example, "Half of wisdom lies in kindness and compassion toward people" (Imam Reza), and "Get yourself obliged toward loving all people" (Imam Ali, both cited in Hakimi et al., 2005).

Love constitutes the essence of interaction, and it is through love and its manifestations that human transformations occur. Rumi, the Persian poet, frequently discussed compassion, kindness, and love toward others as the keys of development, change, and transformation. He considered kindness toward others as the answer for human development when he indicated that "kindness changes thorns into flowers, kindness changes the prison into garden. Without kindness and love, garden changes into a place of thorn" (in Jafari, 1995, p. 146).

An Islam-oriented psychology begins with an in-depth understanding of the significance of peace and compassion and their implications. At the core of the Islamic ontological perspective, prevailing interpretations of a human being as a biological animal are nullified. Man is not confined within biological and evolutionary boundaries—a physiological machine that operates at the mercy of purely physiological and biological stimuli. Rather, according to Islam, the underlying spiritual ontology of humankind engenders etiological scopes that can define values beyond the utilitarian hegemony of the biologically driven mandates.

MENTAL DISORDER STEMS FROM
FRAGMENTATION OF THE SELF

As persons go about their tasks, they become so engaged in fragmentation and division that they can no longer experience unity and presence. Mainstream psychology, inspired by a utilitarian vision, cannot herald the promise of establishing sustainable human ties as it excludes an examination of human needs beyond the utilitarian domain. There is a need to relate to others for persons to flourish, which may mean valuing others (including the Divine Other) beyond one's own utilitarian and consumptive motives. An absence-centered philosophy—one that forsakes the experience of the immediate moment and rather falls to rumination and automatic thinking—cannot offer presence because it reduces the vitality of being to an indulgence in the frequency of multiplicities. With the loss of presence, people get trapped in mindlessness that impedes the process of their self-growth and self-enhancement.

Utilitarianism keeps one's attention away from one's values, one's spirituality, and one's transcendental journey. An Islam-based psychology advocates the necessity of presence through revisiting the reference points that have validated our habits of engaging utilitarian multiplicities. This would presuppose a shift—from a focus on possessiveness and focus on self to one on *Tasleem*, to letting go or releasing things. Power, wealth, paraphernalia, political games, parochialism, egoism, egotism, hubris, arrogance, and imperialism belong to the domain of possessiveness and encourage and foster multiplicities. *Tasleem*, however, promotes the principle of being as the fountain through which togetherness and belonging unfold themselves.

From a Quranic perspective, the sublimity of humans is found not through the possession of belongings but by virtue of piety and righteousness, or to use the exact Quranic term, *Taqwa*. *Taqwa* facilitates the process of becoming presence-oriented in that it allows one to comfortably and mindfully choose to disengage oneself from multiplicities, or indulgences in worldly tasks without attention to the spiritual. *Taqwa* serves as a preamble for going beyond time and place, breaking the boundaries of materialism and practicing the discipline of self, emotion, and relationship management. Piety, in the Islamic perspective, suggests that to transcend the constrictions of the body and supersede worldly longings, one must forsake the monolithic identification with materialism. This does not mean turning one's back on worldly demands and desires, but rather is a warning against a pure and blind indulgence in body-oriented discourse. Imam Hassan Mojtaba, the third imam of Shias, explained as follows how attention should be directed toward both realms: "Act toward your world as if you would live forever, and act toward your hereafter as though you would die tomorrow" (cited in Hakimi, 2004, p. 41).

Islam argues that human beings experience subjugation and entanglement in shadows and fragmentation, thereby distancing themselves from presence. Islam-based psychotherapy would then move the person away from these entanglements and toward the goals and values described above.

As people's exposure to multiplicities increases, their degrees of absence multiply and, through the heightened form of absence, they seek their manifestation in gaining possessiveness. Multiplicities, fragmentation, and mindlessness would impose a pseudo self. *Taqwa*, however, gives rise to a progressive and proactive form of being and becoming, as it nullifies any form of superiority based on worldly possessiveness, such as race, color, and even knowledge. Knowing, if not connected to the fountain of presence, turns out to be a cause of absence; it contributes to the accumulation of masks, disguises, and pretenses.

Deep within the ontological and epistemological perspective on Islamic psychology there lies an emphasis on the revelation-inspired intellect, which is in pursuit of unity, togetherness, oneness, and presence. Conversely, utilitarian-driven rationalism has its quest for multiplicity, materialism, consumerism, subjugation, exploitation, and absence. Focus on the earthly creates problems, and a return to the transcendent focus of Islam promotes health. It is developing the heart that brings health, not accumulating things of the world.

Thus, mental health is viewed quite differently than in a Western psychological view, with Islam seeing compassion and focus on others as healthy and self-indulgence as a form of slavery outside of our spiritual nature and thus demeaning to mental health. Slavery unfolds itself in attachments to the earthly and being devoid of any relatedness to the transcendental potentials of humans.

Mental health is also seen in good relationships, an area Western psychology has touched on in attachment theory, for example, but without Islam's understanding of the nonphysical world. A profound exploration of Quranic verses and Hadith along with the Sireh (behavior and communication) of the Prophet shows Islam's great emphasis on the significance of relationship, its management, and its implications.

Monotheism (*Tawhid*) as the first and foremost principle of Islam unfolds itself not only as a philosophical principle but also as a source of inspiration for relationship management in diverse human transactions. Monotheism teaches one to rely only on God as the source of all virtues. One's relationship to God brings tranquility and composure as God is the origin of all compassion, mercy, graciousness, perfection, and beauty. God never sleeps nor takes a nap. God is above all. Relatedness to God as the source of all virtues would bring comfort and peace. Monotheism (*Tawhid*) begins with understanding the nothingness of anything except God. This nothingness acknowledges that anything in the realm of existence is nothing except a connection to God. Once the connectedness of things is negated, their being is negated.

Analogically speaking, beings operate as prepositional modes: a preposition loses its sense of being the moment it is placed outside a sentence. Ontologically, beings are beings as long as they are connected to God, or Allah, to borrow the Arabic word. Monotheism enriches one's security as one's fear and anxiety are left behind through a transcendental process of self-exploration and the attainment of faith in God's oneness and that as a place to relate to others.

EPISTEMOLOGY

Muslim thought sometimes may misrepresent Islam when impacted by culture on subjective thinking. Although the ideas and perspectives of different Muslim scholars may provide information on the given topics of an Islam-based psychology, they may also be reflective and representative of the specific historical and cultural contexts to which they have been exposed. For example, the Muslim scholars who, through the translation of Greek peripatetic texts, were inspired to ponder the implications of these texts for the Islamic school of thought, were ultimately embedded within a domain that demonstrated their own intellectual creativity and not necessarily the Islamic viewpoints inherited from the Prophet Muhammad, the Qur'an, or the prophet's household.

This situation is even traceable in the citations of numerous Muslim scholars who have acknowledged the distinction between the creative discourses resulting from the interplay of their own cogitations and the pure Islam of Prophet Muhammad. To give just one example, one may cite the words from Ibn Sina, known as Avicenna (980–1037), when he questions the comprehensiveness and impeccability of the human-oriented intellect:

It is not in the capacity of human beings to apprehend the truth of things. We merely apprehend the accidental features and the formal characteristics of things without apprehending the true nature of things and their real distinguishing features. Our understanding provides us with the discernment that there are things in the world with their characteristics and features. Nonetheless, the true nature of the primordial source, the intellect, the soul, the fire, the celestial bodies, the water and the earth are unknown to us. We cannot even grasp the accidental (A'raz) features of the things. (Avicenna, Hijri 1404, pp. 34–35)

In other numerous works, including the Treatise on Definitions (*Resalate Alhodood*) and in the Book of Debates (*Almobahesat*), Avicenna ascertained the limitations of the human-made intellect and its circumscribing implications (Avicenna, Hijri 1404, pp. 34–35).

The same idea can be found in the works of other scholars such as Khaje Nasseereddine Toosee, who shows the inability and incompetency of the human intellect in apprehending the true nature of things, illustrating, at the same time, the urgent and striking need of the human intellect for divine revelation and revealed inspiration. He clearly indicated that "intellect cannot lead to what the prophets instruct" (Noorani, 1980, p. 53). Sheikh Alla Addin Toosee, in reiterating the feebleness of the human intellect, indicated that it alone "cannot grasp the truths behind the issues of theology, and the philosophical and intellectual ideas and doctrines cannot substantiate the consummate apprehension of these issues without the confirmation and support from the source of revelation namely God" (Azzakheere, as cited by Hakimi, 1997, p. 21).

In line with this principle, Shahabeddin Sohrevardee (1355, in Hakimi, 2013) also questioned the possibility of providing a comprehensively impeccable definition for anything, as argued by the peripatetic philosophers. Sadrolmotaaleheen, a great philosopher of Islam, propounded that "even the gifted scholars fail to apprehend the heavenly and earthly truths" (Asfar, as cited by Hakimi, 1997, p. 20). Such words and statements may vividly present the Muslim scholars' confirmation of the inability of the human intellect and the dangers behind what Hakimi (1997) calls the "overgeneralization of the domain of intellect" (p. 26). This is not to deny, however, that the very Muslim scholars who have declared the incompetency of the intellect have also rendered huge services through their own contemplative efforts, by virtue of the self-same feeble instrument of their scholarly activities, namely, their reasoning intellect. For example, in reiterating the significant share held by Muslim scholars in shaping the primordial pillars of modern science, Bernal (1954) indicated that "it is difficult to estimate the value of the actual contributions to this fund of learning that were provided by Islamic scholars themselves" (p. 196). Explicating the impact of Islam in new inventions and the creation of new modes of knowledge, Bernal added that "Islam became the focal point of Asian and European knowledge. As a result, there came into the common pool a new series of inventions quite unknown and inaccessible to Greek and Roman technology" (p. 195).

The point here is that many prominent Muslim scholars have often drawn a distinction between the reasoning human intellect and the revelation-oriented (*Vahy*) intellect, considering the former to be inferior to the latter. Therefore, although Muslim scholars have contributed to the advancement of knowledge and technology, one needs to make a distinction between the notions, ideas, doctrines, and perspectives presented within the scope of Muslim erudition, on the one hand, and the direct words, instructions, and Hadith of Prophet Muhammad, his household, and the Qur'an, on the other hand. Furthermore, Muslim scholars and philosophers themselves, including Mulla Sadra, Ibn Sina, Suhrawardi, and Khajenassereddin Toosee, have frequently acknowledged the necessity of going beyond the human intellect and searching for answers within the sources of revelation, thus questioning the sovereignty of human knowledge in providing comprehensive responses to everything, including the questions of psychology. To exemplify, Mulla Sadra cited a Hadith from the Prophet Muhammad and pinpointed that "my friend, explore this Hadith in order to grasp the substance of the knowing about the soul" (in Hakimi, 1997, p. 205).

CLINICAL IMPLICATIONS

Any form of therapy is embedded within a specific ontological and epistemological system where modes of knowing and the nature of existence are already defined and explicated. Therapists, albeit unbeknown to the systematic root analysis of their given therapy, may apply and move in line within what their already established system prescribes or proscribes. In this chapter I argue that Islamic-based psychology may be positioned within a distinct paradigm with its own productive implications. A spiritually integrated psychotherapy with Muslims may also be placed within the overall holistic Islamic-based psychology that operates based on the principles and premises that ultimately share common views and perspectives with the original structural reference points of Islamic schools of thought.

It may be worth mentioning here that spiritually integrated psychotherapy with Muslims requires a solid understanding of the Islamic culture and the Islamic perspective as a leading doctrine with significant prescriptive and proscriptive implications. This would suggest that the religious perspective of Islam, albeit independent, needs to be understood within the cultural situatedness of clients. This understanding may facilitate the process of accessing a great repertoire of knowledge within the Islamic perspective as a religion that can be reflected in the clients' mode of living.

For instance, clients who come from the Muslim world may incorporate *Duaa* (prayers) and *dhikr* (recitations of special holy words or verses) in their daily life as a strong source of emotional and spiritual support.

It may be very common to see Muslims in countries such as Iran, Iraq, Pakistan, and Bangladesh, and Muslim-populated regions in India engage in daily *dhikr* and *Duaa*. This is in addition to the daily prayers that are to be observed five times a day.

From an Islamic perspective, *Duaa* can have a great impact in improving and transforming one's life, so much so that a Hadith from Imam Baqer (*Salavattolah alayh*) indicates that *Duaa* or prayer can change one's firmly determined destination (Hakimi, 1997, p. 69).

The same imam was asked whether the virtue of reciting the holy Qur'an is more than the virtue of praying. The imam answered that reading prayers and praying are more preferable. In line with the same understanding, *Duaa* and prayers can be applied in psychotherapeutic contexts. This is contrary to the traditional psychoanalytic perspective in which spiritual, mystical, and religious experiences were considered as the signs of pathology—or in Freud's words, "regression to primary narcissism." Numerous studies within psychotherapy have confirmed the positive implications of prayer and contemplative acts in facilitating the process of well-being, or creating helpful psychological treatment interventions (see, for instance, Brelsford, 2011; Brelsford & Mahoney, 2008).

In doing spiritually integrated psychotherapy with Muslims, additional factors may be included. They are not limited to foundational components of an Islamic perspective as a general interconnected system. They consist of specific terminologies and their associated contextualization, such as *dhikr*, *Duaa*, *Maueza*, *Moraqebah*, *Nafs*, *towbe*, and so on. For instance, *Qalb* (heart) constitutes one of the essential components of Islamic-based psychotherapy, and it consists of so many divisions. *Qalb* is not just referring to the physiological heart but to something quite different. As the Qur'an says, there are people who have *Qalb* (physiological hearts) but are devoid of *Qalb* (the divine and spiritual heart). There are *Qalbs* that are locked, and there are enlivened ones. One of the core elements of doing psychotherapy in the Islamic context is to help the client enhance the level of their *Qalb's* receptiveness so that they get empowered to enhance their ontological way of living along with their existential expansion. The therapist helps the clients explore their *Qalb* status and expand their level of *Qalb's* elevation through strategies such as *dhikr*. *Dhikr* explicates an ongoing connectedness and remembrance of God. *Salavat* and *dhikr* open up *Qalb* and make it ready to experience the spiritual illumination. *Dhikr* can also be classified in several layers; one is the language-oriented *dhikr* followed by the *Qalb*-oriented *dhikr*. Islamic-based psychotherapists need to be well aware of the specific language of Islamic perspectives in dealing with psychological well-being.

All of this infers that psychotherapy within the Islamic tradition will move toward views of health that may be alien to many Western psychotherapists and involve techniques that are outside the standard repertoire of most psychologists. The prophet serves as inspiration for the process.

Through a shift from the external manifestations of security to the internal source of security, Muslims were inspired by the Prophet to overcome seemingly insurmountable difficulties and challenges: Monotheism became the panacea for managing both intrapersonal and interpersonal relationships. Monotheism teaches one that God is ubiquitous and omnipresent, and encourages adherents to liberate themselves from the different hogties and manacles of pretentiousness, arrogance, jealously, greed, selfishness, egoism, egotism, solipsism, deceptions, manipulation, and narrowmindedness.

Prayer is considered as the elevation and the ascension of man as it opens up a new chapter for relationships between the self and the creator, and thus can play a vital role in psychotherapy. Islamic relationship awareness may offer a turning point in understanding intercultural humanism within Islamic psychology because it introduces the connectedness of all human beings in a large cosmological project where all are linked to the creator.

The Prophet Muhammad introduced peace and mercy as the essence of relationship management. The Prophet is himself presented by the Qur'an and numerous Hadiths as the mercy for the world (*Rahmaton lel alameen*). The Qur'an describes the etiological mission of the Prophet and his ordainment as the completion and consummation of the best possible moral values. The emphasis on values within the context of the Islamic intercultural perspective suggests that there are unchangeable, universal, and unquestionably valid values that cannot be compromised. "We did not send you except as a mercy to the mankind and the world" (Anbeeya, verse 110). This goal for health may contradict many treatment approaches that stress self-justification and assertiveness.

The problem in our world today, according to Islam, lies in the degeneration of values as a result of egoism and egotism, ironically items promoted by much Western psychology. Values are no longer taken as ends but means, in a limited spectrum at that, with limited application. An Islam-based psychology propounds that for as long as we do not revive the shared human values through which humanity gains its decency, we will be merely pretending to elaborate emancipative discourses for humanity, which are in fact disconnected from the living reality.

It is in line with this understanding of the role of values in our being and becoming that Islam considers the revitalization of one human being as the revitalization of all human beings, and the killing of one human being as the killing of all human beings. The Qur'an explicitly makes this point (Ch. Ma'edde, verse 32). Furthermore, Quranic verses along with a wide array of Hadiths from the prophet and his household call for mindful and consistent implementation of these values in practice. The Qur'an reprimands those who instruct others to follow virtue and piety but who themselves do not practice what they preach. These ideas suggest Islamic psychotherapy helps all by helping one.

In a Hadith from Imam Sadegh of Shias (Hakimi et al., 2005), he pointed out that Muslims need to show the path to monotheism and virtue through their deeds and actions, and not through their words. Authentic human values, according to Islam, cannot be taken seriously and cannot be put into effect except through a quest for meaning and its connectedness to the Creator. If life is nothing except pleasure in the ephemeral earthly abode and its associated desires, then it cannot give rise to a genuine source of care for others. In Islam, the "other" is, in a materialist perspective, translated in the body of the earthly desires and its ramifications. "Others" make sense as long as they move in line with the manifestations of solipsism, egoism, egotism, and self-satisfying interests. Yes, attention to the "others" can also be meaningful if negligence toward them would hurt self-centered concentration. But there is no sense of togetherness, no true care for others.

An Islam-based psychology moves in the completely opposite direction: any extension, manifestation, and crystallization of being is revered and respected as they all unveil their being signs from God.

More formal efforts are under way to develop a more indigenous psychotherapy for Muslims. This would include the edited work (to which I contributed) of Al-Karam (2018a), who notes in her preface that there is also the challenge of overcoming the stigma for psychotherapy among many Muslims. Al-Karam (2018b) argues that psychotherapy may even be considered indigenous to the Islamic tradition as part of "purification of the self" (*tazkiyat al-nafs*) and as an effort to know oneself. She notes that "Prophet Muhammad said, 'Whosover knows himself knows his Lord'" (p. 18) and that psychotherapy may be a road toward self-knowledge. Much work remains to develop and disseminate an Islam-based psychotherapy built on an Islam-based psychology.

CONCLUSION

I have insisted on the distinction between intellectual reasoning and revelation-based intellect because it can help us excavate the ontological, epistemological, and etiological layers of an Islam-based psychology. Islam, etymologically speaking, comes from the word *Silm*, which means "peace." Islamic "peace" entails diverse human domains, from the intrapersonal relationship to interpersonal communication, international relations, and international negotiations. One of the main objectives of an Islam-based psychology is to develop peace in intrapersonal and interpersonal levels that would serve as the preamble for establishing peace in the international level. If one is arrogantly engaged in his or her needlessness to observe his or her dependency and need to the Creator, one gets drowned and lets others sink in their selfishness and absolute oriented desire of possessiveness. An Islam-based psychology posits that when one is devoid of securing a connection to the source of all good and the origin of all graces and compassion—namely, God—one is illusioned to see himself or herself in charge of both the inner and outer worlds.

Understanding an Islam-based psychology in the context of revelation-based intellect would espouse distinct features that need to be elaborated in their own place at another time. All systems of psychotherapy are essentially responding, albeit implicitly, to questions of existence and knowledge: Is existence epitomized in what we perceive through our five senses or are there sundry levels of existence? Is knowledge bound by what our scientific discourse, including empiricism and positivism, have created or are there infinite paths to knowledge? Likewise, any system of psychotherapy needs to be built upon a specific definition of human being: What is a human? What is the essence of being a human?

An Islam-based psychology offers a turning point as it broadens the scope of both epistemology and ontology beyond the mainstream psychology. It also offers a new definition of humanity and claims that the nature of being a human is way beyond what our psychological schools of thought have suggested so far. An Islam-based psychology moves within a new paradigm that needs to be explored and understood sufficiently enough to demonstrate its applications and implications. Regrettably enough, recent years have been drastically associated with Islamophobia and misrepresentations of Islam that may have impeded the process of implementing a rigorous exploration of an Islam-based psychology. Hopefully this chapter introduces the reader to an overview of an Islam-based psychology. These themes should be considered when doing psychological research with Muslims, and when working with Muslims in therapy.

REFERENCES

Al-Karam, C. Y. (Ed.). (2018a). *Islamically integrated psychotherapy: Uniting faith and practice.* West Conshohocken, PA: Templeton Press.

Al-Karam, C. Y. (2018b). Introduction. In C. Y. Al-Karam (Ed.), *Islamically integrated psychotherapy: Uniting faith and practice* (pp. 3–24). West Conshohocken, PA: Templeton Press.

Avicenna, Hijri 1404 Avicenna. (1993) Taaleeqaat. Published by Dr. Abdolrahman Badavee.

Bernal, J. D. (1954). Science in History. New York: Hawthorn Books.

Brelsford, G. M. (2011). Divine alliances to handle family conflict: Theistic meditation and triangulation in father-child relationships. *Psychology of Religion and Spirituality, 3,* 285–297.

Brelsford, G. M., & Mahoney, A. (2008). Spiritual disclosure between older adolescents and their mothers. *Journal of Family Psychology,* 22, 62–70.

Hakimi, M. R. (1997). *Ejtehad Va Taghleed dar falsafe. Ejtehad (Imitation in philosophy).* Qom, Iran: Daeele Ma Publications.

Hakimi, M. R. (2004). *Ijtehad va Taghleed dar Falsafe.* Qom, Iran: Daeele-Ma.

Hakimi, M. R. (2013). *Ejtehad va taqleed dar falsafe (Ijtihad and mimicry in philosophy).* Qom, Iran: Daleele Ma Publications.

Hakimi, M. R., Hakimi, A., & Hakimi, M. (2005). *Alhayat (Life).* Qom, Iran: Daleele Ma Publications.

Huntington, S. P. (1997). *The clash of civilizations and the remaking of the world order.* New York: Simon & Schuster.

Jafari, M. T. (1995). *Mathnavi Ma'navi: A critical interpretation.* Vol. 4. Tehran, Iran: Alame Jafari Publications.

Jafari, M. T. (2006). *Tarjomeh va tafseere nahjol balaghe.* Tehran, Iran: Daftare Nashre Farhange Islamee.

Nasr, S. H. (Ed.). (2007). *The essential Seyed Hossein Nasr.* Bloomington, IN: World Wisdom. Springer.

Razee, S. (Ed.), (1993). Najolbalaghe of Imam Alil (Alayhessalam). Qom, Iran: Hejrat Publications.

KIN CHEUNG (GEORGE) LEE AND
CHUN FAI (JEFFREY) NG

AN INDIGENOUS PERSPECTIVE
ON BUDDHISM

In the twenty-five hundred years of its dissemination since the historical Buddha, Buddhism has been interpreted and elaborated into many different forms and religious schools in response to cultural, political, and historical transformations. However, the origin of Buddhism is in a man who taught a comprehensive analysis of the human mind and an understanding of how to become completely liberated from suffering (the fundamental dissatisfaction of life). Instead of a godlike being who has the mystical power to govern and change human affairs by meting out rewards and punishments, the Buddha was a philosopher, a teacher, a religious leader, and a person capable of addressing psychological problems. In the early documentaries of the Buddha's life, the Buddha was depicted as an ordinary person devoted to teaching and sharing his realizations to help those who came to him to relieve or eliminate their mental suffering and attain sustainable happiness on their own. That depiction resonates with the role of psychologists in the modern world. To capture its most fundamental and original ideas and discuss the Buddhist teachings most common to all Buddhist schools, this chapter uses Early Buddhism—recorded in the Buddha's discourses in the Pali Nikayas—as the primary source of information and to present Buddhism as an ancient psychology.

BRIEF HISTORY OF BUDDHISM

During the fifth century BC, there was a republic called Shakya, which was located at the southern border of modern-day Nepal. According to legend, the leader of Shakya, Śuddhodana Gautama, learned from a prophet that his future son would become either a great king or, through renunciation, a great spiritual leader. In response to the prophecy, Śuddhodana decided to raise his son in the most luxurious and satisfying way that he could imagine, thereby sheltering his son from any reason to pursue a spiritual path. When Māyā Guatama, Śuddhodana's wife, died soon after giving birth to the young prince, her sister, Mahāpajāpatī Guatama, became the stepmother of the future Buddha, raising the prince through childhood. From the moment of his birth as the prince of Shakya, Siddhārtha Gautama was only exposed to a splendid life with abundant food, lavish clothes, and endless entertainment. He also received a royal education in preparation to become the future king, excelling in many branches of knowledge, including martial arts. As arranged by his father, Prince Siddhārtha was married at age sixteen and lived a fairy-tale life in the castle, until his curiosity grew beyond the walls of the palace.

At age twenty-nine, Siddhārtha decided to embark on the first adventure of his life to see the world outside his palace: the real world that his father had striven to hide from him. Immediately after his departure, he saw a world beyond imagination: one with aging people, incurable illnesses, death, poverty, and tears. Astonished and overwhelmed, Siddhārtha gradually realized that he was living in a world with unavoidable miseries, and compounding matters, no one had found a way to escape suffering. In spite of the devastation to his innocence brought about by this experience, Siddhārtha adamantly tried to search for an answer. Upon encountering an ascetic monk who seemed to be undisturbed by the miseries in life, the young prince started to wonder whether he might find his answer in renunciation. Siddhārtha left his palace, his wife, his infant son, and his family to start his life over again as a religious ascetic.

After first practicing extreme asceticism for six years, Siddhārtha, on the brink of starvation, discovered that severe renunciation only increased suffering and realized that only the Middle Way—a path of moderation beyond the extremes of sensual indulgence and self-mortification—led to peace of mind. Following this incident, at the age of thirty-five, after forty-nine days of meditation under a Bodhi tree,

Siddhārtha discovered the law of dependent origination, realized the Four Noble Truths, attained Enlightenment, and became known as the Buddha or the "Awakened One." For the remaining forty-five years of his life, he continuously taught these concepts in today's regions of India and Nepal. The teachings of the Buddha have since spread far from their geographic origins, mixing with various cultures across Asia, with the result that many schools of Buddhism developed. There are now three main branches of Buddhism: Theravāda, Mahāyāna, and Vajrayāna.

In spite of the differences in the theoretical orientations of the Buddhist schools, their primary concern, reflective of the reason for Siddhārtha's renunciation of worldly life, is the same—concern for human well-being and the desire to alleviate the suffering of oneself and others. As demonstrated by the failure of Siddhārtha to find the solution to suffering through renunciation, Buddhism does not consider rejection of worldly phenomena in their entirety as the way of liberation from suffering. Instead, Buddhism holds that all types of human suffering are mental, and therefore, the transformation of our minds is the only antidote to suffering. The Buddhist tradition has "concerned itself over the past 2,500 years with cultivating exceptional states of mental well-being as well as identifying and treating problems of the mind" (Smith as cited in Wallace & Shapiro, 2006, p. 690).

Buddhism has developed a complete and structured framework for the explanation and treatment of psychological problems based on the Four Noble Truths realized by the historical Buddha, which is still applicable to the present day. The Four Noble Truths—suffering, its origin, cessation, and path to the cessation—are the essence of the Buddha's teachings:

FOUR NOBLE TRUTHS

1. SUFFERING. To understand the Buddhist meaning of suffering, one needs to momentarily divorce from our assumption of suffering driven by Western psychology. In general, traditional Western psychology describes suffering as a psychological pain that is an abnormal state of body and mind. For example, the *Diagnostic and Statistical Manual of Mental Disorders,* Fifth Edition (*DSM-5*) defines suffering as a mental

health disorder, a label of psychopathology that describes clinical symptoms impairing a person's psychological well-being and functioning. In Buddhism, by contrast, suffering is a normal, inevitable, and multifaceted experience to life. Suffering, or *dukkha*, means dissatisfaction in Buddhism. The historical Buddha was the first person who eliminated this unavoidable and painful dissatisfaction through his insights gained from comprehensive mind analysis, and he used his own experiences to explicate suffering in many ways to help others see its nature and to liberate from it. We briefly mention three explanations in this section. First, suffering is a reality of existence while the extent and nature of suffering vary. Second, suffering can be mental or physical. Third, the human mind is "ignorant" in that it has an unskillful inclination to misinterpret experiences and aggravate the subjective experience of suffering. To liberate from suffering, one must first understand its nature and cause.

2. CAUSE OF SUFFERING. The etiology of suffering in Western psychology is usually explained by biological, psychological, environmental, social, spiritual, or other causes. Buddhism sees the ultimate cause of suffering as craving, or *tanha*, which is strong desire and lust for sensual pleasure, self-existence, or self-annihilation. To explain why craving is the cause of suffering, it is crucial to introduce the Buddhist assumption of reality. In short, the human mind has a powerful urge to continuously exist, so we try hard to convince ourselves of self-existence by building self-identities, personalizing belongings, developing relationships, and making every encounter in relation to a self. However, Buddhism makes a strong assertion that we do not exist the way we want to, which is a highly dissatisfying experience if we cannot accept this truth. According to the law of dependent origination, all phenomena, including consciousness, the concept of self, or the "I" who is typing and writing this chapter, arise through the amalgamation or co-arising of particular causes and conditions and cease when such causes and conditions change, thereby resulting in impermanence. In particular, the self is only viewed as the interactions of five interdependent sets of processes called the five aggregates (this is covered in more detail later). If an individual personalizes, identifies, and fabricates such ontological events to claim ownership of experiences and neglect the impermanent nature of phenomena, there will inevitably be dissatisfaction. Infantilizing a child to feel ownership

as a parent, using consistent cosmetic surgeries to resist aging, or taking responsibility for something that one has no control over would be some of the examples of denying reality.

3. CESSATION OF SUFFERING. While traditional Western psychotherapy aims for reduction of clinical symptoms as an alleviation of suffering, the ultimate goal of Buddhism is to achieve enlightenment, or *nibbāna* (*nirvāna* in Sanskrit), which is regarded as the highest psychological state in extinction of suffering. *Nibbāna* arises from realizations of the true nature of all phenomena to see things as they are or seeing the three marks of existence: knowing the nature of suffering, seeing phenomenon as dependently originated, and not craving a notion of self. The Third Noble Truth emphasizes that a path to this ultimate state of mind instills faith and provides for practitioners to start the path of liberation.

4. PATH TO THE CESSATION OF SUFFERING. The historical Buddha described a system to cultivate the cessation of suffering, namely the Noble Eightfold Path of eight practices in three pillars: (1) *wisdom*: right view and right intentions; (2) *discipline*: right speech, right action, and right livelihood; and (3) *concentration*: right effort, right mindfulness, and right concentration. Since the root of suffering is ignorance, the elixir to suffering in Buddhism is to raise awareness of the true nature of phenomenon through this three-pillar practice by self-governing behaviors to reduce choices resulting in suffering; cultivating a stable, clear, and discerning mind through meditation; and reflecting and contemplating on the true nature of all phenomena to see reality as it is.

Both modern Western psychology and Buddhism concern promotion of mental well-being and alleviation of psychological suffering. The dialogue between the two began in the beginning of the twentieth century (Aich, 2013), when scholars started finding commonalities between Buddhism and various psychology theories like phenomenological psychology, existential psychology, and psychoanalysis. One of the most significant contributions of Buddhism to psychotherapies is mindfulness, from which numerous prominent cognitive psychological treatments were derived, including mindfulness-based stress reduction (MBSR), mindfulness-based cognitive theory (MBCT), dialectical behavioral therapy (DBT), and acceptance and commitment therapy (ACT).

MAJOR THEORETICAL ASSUMPTIONS

Contemporary science emphasizes the advancement of knowledge based on observable, testable, and measurable evidence to understand phenomena. Significant scientific effort is devoted to the discovery and understanding of our outside world: biology, chemistry, physics, astrology, and cosmology. Early Buddhism, with its only goal to liberate human beings from suffering, emphasized an empiricism that involves the careful and comprehensive investigation and analysis of the mind in order to gain self-knowledge for the purpose of liberation. In fact, the Buddha's approach to life problems was pragmatic and experiential and did not encourage exerting effort to understand the outside world, such as learning about the cosmos or life after death, if such efforts would not facilitate liberation from suffering (MN 63). Therefore, contemporary science and early Buddhism are two different paradigms for seeking knowledge, with science striving to paint a full picture of all phenomena and Buddhism narrowing the empirical effort to a focus on gaining necessary knowledge for the liberation from suffering.

DEPENDENT ORIGINATION

A central teaching of Buddhism is the Buddhist theory of dependent origination (paṭiccasamuppāda). According to the Abhidhamma, the core book of Buddhist psychology, the principle of paṭiccasamuppāda book can be described in the following short formula:

> Whenever this is present, that is also present;
> From the arising of this, that arises;
> Whenever this is absent, that is also absent; and
> From the cessation of this, that ceases to be. (Karunadasa, 2013, p. 87)

In a general sense, dependent origination means that all phenomena arise only in relation to other phenomena (Bornaetxea, Morón, Gil, & Molloy, 2014). In other words, every phenomenon exists conditionally and interdependently because everything is mutually dependent on everything else for its existence. Before the moment a simple phenomenon occurs, numerous factors have collaboratively contributed to its existence, and the phenomenon will subside when all these interdependent factors that support it are no longer sustainable. The "phenomena" might be anything in the world, including people, relationships, space, places, or even thoughts, emotions, ideas, and beliefs.

A classic metaphor to explain dependent origination is the existence of a flame in an oil lamp, where the burning of the flame depends on the presence of oil and a wick. If either the oil or the wick is absent, the flame will cease to burn. Thus, we can describe the existence of the flame as being dependent on the existence of the oil and wick, which are its conditions. In this paradigm, everything is relative, interdependent, and conditioned. Our experience of a flower, a more complex example, has to be based on multiple conditions, including sunshine, oxygen, soil, water, and seeds. Moreover, each of those conditions has its own preceding conditions, such as how a particular plot of soil manifests as a combination of minerals, organic matter, air, water, microbes, and chemicals. Each one of these conditions, in turn, has numerous preceding conditions, and all the conditions aggregate at a certain time and space to become a phenomenon—in this case, a flower.

Dependent origination describes the process of life without the need to introduce any creator or created being that has a fixed identity. Instead, all phenomena are seen as created by a plurality of causes and conditions that co-originate and co-arise within and across lifetimes (Bornaetxea et al., 2014). Consequently, this view does not agree with the existence of a permanent self or with the nonexistence of self; instead, it describes the experience of a self as a phenomenon, and this phenomenal self is constantly susceptible to change. In other words, Buddhism posits that "self" is a concept without an objective reality because it is a logical abstraction or denomination, merely useful to label experiences as happening to an individually functioning entity. Stated differently, Buddhism assumes that cognitive events like thoughts do not arise in the mind; instead, the cognitive events themselves are the mind and there is not any "self" as a processor.

For example, one might think, "I am eating cheesecake and I love it!" From the viewpoint of dependent origination, however, when consciousness arises during the tongue's interaction with a cheesecake, there is a pleasant feeling and the mind starts to cling to this feeling by proliferating thoughts about it, such as, "It tastes so good," "It is so comforting and soothing for my soul," and "I have to have some cheesecake every Friday night or else I will be agitated for the whole week." Once the mind steps back and gains enough mental distance to observe how it engages in the phenomenon of eating cheesecake and understand that the experience of eating cheesecake is just the result of various conditions (e.g., the cheesecake, the restaurant, friends in the surroundings, tiredness from work, the sensation on the tongue, the feelings that arise, the mind's inner dialogue, the thirst, the heat in the chest, the release of tension in the shoulders), the mind will not find a solid entity called "I." These are all experiences of the consciousness that occur at the moment influenced by conditions and factors affecting the state of mind. With this realization, the mind can deliberatively choose whether to eat the cheesecake.

An important implication of the principle of dependent origination is that no life event can be attributed to a single cause or a limited number of conditions. Buddhism reckons that our mind has a tendency to attribute a single cause or several conditions to the occurrence of life events, but this is contrary to reality because any single event is actually caused by innumerable conditions. For example, the breakdown of a relationship might be due to a multitude of factors, but we are inclined to blame our partner for his or her faults, which helps us to protect our imaginary self-identities. After being abandoned by a partner who had sexual affairs, one may continuously ruminate on our partner's infidelity and furiously blame this person, thereby causing lots of emotional pain, anger, and restlessness in one's mind. That type of clinging to a specific set of conditions narrows our focus of awareness, confines our scope of experience, and incapacitates our ability to comprehend how life situations happen and see reality as it is.

But if we have the opportunity to view a life event without the interference of our usual fixation on our self-identities and as a phenomenon composed of numerous conditions, then our psychological suffering can be reduced. Taking the previous example, the phenomenon of "being abandoned by an unfaithful partner" can be a combination of various conditions, such as constant conflicts in the relationship, dissatisfied needs of both partners, lack of communication, existing anger and emotional wounds in the couple, and other factors. Buddhist teachings advise practitioners to detach from a fixated label of "being abandoned by an unfaithful partner" with a calm and clear mind and examine multiple causes and conditions within the phenomenon, especially our participation and contributions to the phenomenon from an objective and realistic perspective. For example, when one reflects on how one engages in the relationship, one may realize how he has been using the partner as a source of assurance of self-importance and a feeling of security to fend off fear of abandonment. However, he did not really listen and understand the needs of his partner, which planted a seed for her infidelity. When an attributed label to a phenomenon, or a mind's fantasy of how a phenomenon can satiate one's craving, becomes analyzable into different causes, conditions, and perspectives, one will find it easier to accept happenings and have realistic expectations, resulting in significantly less psychological suffering.

One of the most important implications of dependent origination for Western therapy to date is that therapeutic models based on Buddhist theories are present-focused. From a philosophical standpoint, long after the conditions that brought about the life situation to which a client is clinging have ceased to exist, the client's mind still strives to fabricate ownership of those conditions. For example, an insecure mother may ignore the emerging independence of her three-year-old son and strive to infantilize him, which serves to make her feel needed. From the perspective of dependent origination, conditions for the son are constantly changing in the areas of continuous physical, socioemotional, cognitive, and motor development, and her son today has grown to be different from her son yesterday. However, the mother may fixate on the previous concept of a "son" who is highly dependent on her, thereby ignoring the changes and grasping onto an unrealistic concept to fulfill her needs. Applying the dependent origination concept to an assessment of a client like this, a therapist might ask about, clarify, and explore details of the client's background to help the client raise his or her awareness of the multiple conditions that are contributing to the present moment of suffering, why the client is clinging to that particular set of conditions, and how traces of past events are hindering the client's ability to see external reality as it exists in the present. Once the client can ground the perturbed mind to the present moment, the therapist can reflect on how various factors in the past and current external environment have contributed to the client's suffering now and explore how factors like a child developing independence are beyond the control of the self. When the mother sees her desire to hold onto an image of her son, understands the objective development of him, and accepts conditions as the way they are, the mother will start to experience relief from suffering.

NATURE OF SELF IN BUDDHISM

Distinct from most philosophical assumptions about the existence of a permanent self or soul, Buddhism describes the self that, as a product of dependent origination, does not inherently exist. This position stands in critical opposition to theories that assume the existence of an eternal soul, a spirituality in connection with a higher power, or an intrinsic and authentic self. For new learners of Buddhism, a common question is, "If there is not a 'me,' then who is behind the consciousness of reading this chapter and thinking about these ideas?"

The short answer is the theory of non-self does not refer to an annihilation of self. Instead, it describes the mind's inclination to attribute neutral phenomena to a fantasized concrete identity. This inclination of the mind can be described as a habitual energy that leads consciousness to claim ownership of mental and bodily experiences, thereby fabricating an independent self-notion or self-identity. In other words, there is not any entity called "the self" that possesses a mind. Rather, consciousness, or the mental process itself, is the mind, and the mind becomes deluded and convinced of the notion that "this is my self." One of the most common Buddhist ways to describe such a concept of the self is through the notion of the five aggregates.

THE FIVE AGGREGATES

According to Early Buddhist scriptures, there are three systematic analyses of the human mind: (1) the five aggregates model, (2) the twelve-sense bases model, and (3) the eighteen cognitive elements model. Among the three models, the five aggregates (*khandhas*) is the most commonly used across Buddhist traditions to analyze the mind. Hence, this chapter will focus on the psychology of the five aggregates.

The five aggregates are five interdependent sets of processes that interact with the world, generate the idiosyncratic experiences for the human mind, and fuel our continued existence (Table 1). Suffering begins when an individual identifies wrongly the five aggregates as self, an independent and permanent entity. To illustrate, and to challenge the concept of the self, Buddhist scriptures use the metaphor of a chariot to describe a human being. For example, the Buddha expounded the question "What is a chariot?" One can answer by referring to the parts of a chariot, such as its axle, wheels, chariot body, flagstaff, yoke, reins, and goad-stick; but none of these is an entity called "chariot," and each can be reduced to smaller parts (AN 3.15). In essence, we label the combination of constituents a "chariot," but this is nothing more than a construct or logical abstraction based on a reification of the whole (SN 5.10; Miln 2). The analogy demonstrates that there is no separate "self" that can be found in any, or in any combination, of the five aggregates; instead, "self" is a denomination for the collective experiences of the five aggregates.

TABLE 1. THE FIVE AGGREGATES AS DESCRIBED IN EARLY BUDDHISM
(KARUNADASA, 2013)

Aggregate	Aggregate in Pāli	Description
Physical process (also translated as body/form)	*rūpa*	Sensory organs and objects
Sensation (also translated as feeling)	*vedanā*	Tone of sensational feelings
Perception	*saññā*	Recognition of objects based on previously learned concepts
Volition (also translated as mental formation)	*sankhara*	Mental construction, compounding and fabrications of ideas and concepts to form inclinations
Consciousness	*viññāna*	Bare awareness of objects

PHYSICAL PROCESS. For consciousness to arise, there needs to be presence of an object that passes through a sense organ to capture the attention of our mind, such as using our eyes (sense organ) to read (consciousness) this book (sense object). This contact between sense object, sense organ, and consciousness initiates physical processes that are direct, bare sensory input, and devoid of any subjective inclinations (Boisvert, 1997). External sense objects are not considered physical processes, but their mental imprints or records arising from the contact between sensory organs and sense objects are. This is because sense objects are *potentially* perceived while physical processes are *actually* perceived. For instance, when we are angry with somebody, we are often not mad at a person who is physically present in front of us; instead, we are mad at a mental impression of that person. Buddhism suggests the solution to such psychological issues should ultimately aim at the transformation of our own internal mental processes rather than at changing the external objects of perception.

SENSATION. Sensation, the internal response to sensory input, arises after the entrance of the initial sensory input. Sensation is a primitive response to sense contact manifest in three feeling tones: pleasant, unpleasant, and neutral. Sensation can be understood as a primitive and innate somatic feeling (Boisvert, 1997). Occurring without cognitive interpretation, it is our simplest form of direct response to sensory inputs. When we smell something pungent like a rotten egg or leaking gas, an unpleasant feeling instantly arises, and we do not need to undergo lengthy interpretations to determine that it is unpleasant.

PERCEPTION. Sensation serves as a condition for the arising of perception. Perception is a process of recognition, classification, and conceptualization of the incoming sensory data, followed by the naming and labeling of a perceived object based on past experiences. For example, when we recognize the redness of a shirt, we categorize this color as "red" by associating the color with our previous labels (Boisvert, 1997). As each individual has a unique system of concepts and knowledge, the same sensory inputs can generate different perceptions. Thus, the Buddhist understanding of perception appears to have some parallels to ideas in cognitive psychology with respect to the cognitive processing of sensory information.

VOLITION. Volition is a crucial concept in Buddhism because it is the core driving force of mind that determines consequences, as if the engine of a speedboat were deciding direction and destination. Volition is a subtle force of intentional physical, verbal, or mental action that has the capacity to generate an effect that will, in turn, become a new condition for producing a further effect. Volition is also analogous to a wheel that keeps rolling as far as the momentum that set it in motion allows (AN 3.15). In contemporary language, it can be understood as mental and behavioral choices, and the nature of these choices directly determines one's level of suffering. Volition has a tendency to establish a positive feedback loop. Every time we make a volitional decision, the energy fuels itself and fosters a stronger habit for similar decisions.

CONSCIOUSNESS. Consciousness is mere attention or pure "knowing" without any inherent content. Its content is derived from the other aggregates, and thus is responsible for our cognizance of the other aggregates. During a physical process, contact arises from the conjugation of the sense organs, the sense objects, and consciousness of the sense organs. This means that the five aggregates are part of an interdependent cyclical process—consciousness, the last element of the five aggregates, becomes the condition for the arising of the physical process of the next cycle. Consciousness can also be seen as a faculty required for the cognizance of pure sensation and for conceptualization. Buddhist scriptures explain that when one intends (i.e., volition) and obsesses about something, there is support for the establishment of consciousness, which then fuels the production of renewed existence (i.e., the next five-aggregate cycle [SN 12.38]). This is how the cycle of existence and human suffering repeats itself.

FIVE AGGREGATES IN EACH MOMENT OF EXPERIENCE. The five aggregates work together in each moment of our experiences; we use smoking as an example. When we come into contact with an external stimulus, we label the sensation pleasant and recognize its features, such as "freshness" in the mouth and taste of the tobacco; we label it as "smoking," which captures full awareness of the consciousness and brings us a pleasant feeling (if we like smoking). Naming and conceptualization performed by the first three aggregates do not necessarily lead to psychological problems, but our attachment to such names, labels, or pleasure does.

In other words, fully immersing and enjoying a cigarette is harmless from a Buddhist perspective, but the craving for the same pleasure and holding onto a concept that "I have to smoke to enjoy a break!" instantly creates distress and unease of mind. Through repeated volitional decisions to smoke and temporarily satiating the craving by having it, the volitional energy grows and becomes a habit. Since every conditioned phenomenon is subject to constant changes (when the conditions cease to exist, the pleasant phenomenon also ceases to exist)—such as if a heart condition starts to deteriorate due to smoking—discrepancies between our fixated expectation and reality arise, which creates deep inner dissatisfaction with the present moment. However, the strong volitional energy makes it difficult to stop the craving, and this state of mind tends to resist the changes in conditions. A mental volition of "Just one more cigarette will not kill me! Let's do it and I will quit once I have kids" emerges, and the person decides to have another cigarette regardless of his health condition, resulting in greater physical and mental suffering.

DUKKHA AS AN INNATE PSYCHOPATHOLOGICAL SYMPTOM

In Buddhism, *dukkha*, translated as "suffering" or "dissatisfaction," is the main target of "treatment." One major difference between Buddhism and clinical psychology is that Buddhism understands suffering as a universal phenomenon and a common human experience instead of as a psychopathology. In other words, psychological disorders are all part of *dukkha* and are an inevitable experience for every individual living in this world. Buddhism proposes that the factors that cause suffering—such as separation from loved ones, not getting what one wants, or association with people and things we dislike—are always present but that the subjective experience of suffering can be reduced, and even, in the case of enlightenment, completely eliminated. In a general sense, to be liberated from suffering is to understand the laws of all things (*Dhamma*) and to cultivate the mind through consistent, progressive practices of mindfulness.

In the Buddhist paradigm, the original root of suffering is ignorance. The idea of ignorance in Buddhism never refers to lack of knowledge or intelligence in worldly matters such as science, mathematics, or economics. Rather, it refers to a lack of understanding and acceptance of the universal laws of dependent origination. Under the law of dependent origination, Buddhism suggests, every phenomenon is signified by the three marks of existence: (1) impermanence (*anicca*), meaning that every phenomenon in the world is constantly arising and passing and our experience is constantly changing; (2) suffering (*dukkha*), meaning that every phenomenon is unsatisfactory and any object of attachment will inevitably change or cease to exist; and (3) non-self (*anatta*), referring to the fact that the existence of self is ultimately dependent on other things that are impermanent, such that the self is neither independent nor stable.

Buddhism holds that all forms of mental irregularity are derived from our strong identification of the five aggregates as our actual selves. The five aggregates, like masses of fire (SN 35.28), are also neutral conditioned phenomena—which arise, pass away, and change constantly, subject to the law of dependent origination and three marks of existence (SN 22.36) and give rise to the experiences of living—but they do not necessarily cause suffering. The cause of suffering, rather, is the mind's clinging to the five aggregates, which results in the mental creation of a stable, autonomous, and permanent sense of self through reification and conceptualization. It has been our deep-rooted habit to cling to the idea that these sets of ever-changing processes equal to "me" and to wrongly think that "I should always be under 'my' control." From this attachment to a fixated sense of self, we begin to erroneously believe that there is a separate, inherently existing personality, to define ourselves in relation to external objects, and to establish further clinging, such as clinging to a sense-pleasure and clinging to a wrong view (i.e., "this is mine" and "this is myself"). The problem that results from such beliefs is impaired functionality.

Human beings tend to personalize the five aggregates and take them too seriously without being aware of their nature. When we do this, we are unable to apprehend that all conditioned phenomena arise from external circumstances and internal mental actions that are subject to change. Constantly arising and ceasing thoughts and emotions are viewed as "my thoughts" and "my emotions" and grasped onto as real. Further, to protect the illusory existence of this self-identity, whenever the five aggregates change without our expecting them to, a habitual ego defense mechanism like a "fight-flight-freeze" reaction is automatically activated. As a result, the totality of our experience is confined to the limited perspective of ourselves, rendering us unable to accept reality as it is and present appropriate responses to the new sets of causes and conditions that meet us in the present moment. This is how suffering arises.

In particular, clinging, resulting from the attachment to the five aggregates, refers to the mental process of investing energy in pursuing and sustaining an experience. It is usually a continuous process that fuels specific mind actions and is reciprocally reinforced by existing habitual patterns. For example, when one witnesses the demise of his or her close ones, suffering results when the illusory self is disappointed by overestimating its own power to control inevitable and uncontrollable changes in life. Therefore, truly seeing, understanding, and accepting these three marks of existence would be a light against the darkness of ignorance as well as the remedy to suffering. However, attachment to the notion of a self makes apprehending reality difficult because our mind has a strong habitual energy to believe in its own inherent existence. Fortunately, the three marks of existence imply that making changes to psychological phenomena, and therefore the elimination of mental suffering, is possible.

PATH TO LIBERATION: PSYCHOLOGICAL CHANGES IN BUDDHISM

Since the root of suffering is ignorance, knowledge is the most direct therapeutic ingredient in the recipe for eradicating suffering. The first step to true knowledge is gaining awareness, which requires a continuous process of observing and noting how one's mind engages in actions that induce suffering. A lay understanding of Buddhism is that it requires letting go of things. However, no one can let go of anything without knowing what, or how, things are being held. Letting go does not require the denial or rejection of clinging. Letting go, instead, is a product of having the right view toward the arising and cessation of phenomena, understanding the reason for clinging, the multiple ways and processes through which the mind clings, and the suffering that such clinging brings about. When the mind sees and accepts the true nature of phenomena, it voluntarily and momentarily chooses to release it. This is the act of "letting go" of the object. It results from a continuous effort to observe one's mind and thereby cultivate a "higher mind" that can rest in a state of concentration and clarity. As a provisional understanding, the "higher mind" is a clear and stable mind state that can be trained through practicing self-cultivation to see the aggregate mind's unskillful actions and gain knowledge of which causes and conditions result in suffering. This helps people to make choices that result in less suffering.

IMPLICATIONS FOR MENTAL HEALTH PROFESSIONALS: THE EMERGENCE OF BUDDHIST COUNSELING

To increase multicultural sensitivity in working with Buddhist clients, we recommend several considerations for mental health professionals. First, it is important to gain fundamental knowledge of Early Buddhist teachings as described in this chapter. It is also key to be aware of the multiple schools, lineages, and interpretations of Buddhism and the idiosyncratic experiences of Buddhism in each Buddhist client. For example, a Buddhist client may be a Tibetan Buddhist who sees Buddhism as a religious practice, while another Buddhist client may see Buddhism as philosophical and a form of secular guidance to life. Good mental health professionals would possess a solid foundation of knowledge in a particular culture and learn from a client's subjective perspective of that culture to paint a full picture of a client's experiences. Second, every Buddhist client has his or her own practice of Buddhism. Mental health professionals can assess clients' type, nature, and reasons for their chosen practices in order to further understand the client's self-ascribed meaning of Buddhist. Third, many Buddhist clients have affiliations with Buddhist groups or temples, and mental health professionals can explore these affiliations as potential protective factors. Especially, many Buddhist clients have masters in their affiliated group who are influential figures to the community. Therefore, a client's masters may be an important area to explore. Fourth, when seeing monastic members, mental health professionals may need to be mindful of several customary Buddhist practices: Buddhists usually refer to monastic members as "venerables"; monastic members' temples are basically their home, with a master as a parental figure and fellow members as brothers and sisters; and some monastic members may maintain relationships with their immediate family but their primary roles are to serve in the temple, practice, or complete tasks assigned by their masters.

To foster strong multicultural competence in working with Buddhist clients, mental health professionals may need to familiarize themselves with the therapeutic process within the Buddhist framework. In fact, Buddhist counseling has emerged as one of the approaches to providing treatment based on the original Buddhist teachings to bring mindfulness back into its Buddhist context (see Lee et al., 2017, for more details). We believe that the most culturally congruent treatment approach is one developed from the client's own culture. For this reason, this section introduces a Buddhist counseling model, namely the Note, Know, Choose Model (Lee & Ong, 2019), developed from Early Buddhism to provide some recommendations for mental health professionals to work with Buddhist clients within a Buddhist framework.

Buddhist counseling is a holistic approach to helping clients use each encounter to open a gateway to the cultivation of the mind for the purpose of gaining an accurate understanding of reality. Congruent to the cultural understanding of Buddhism in many clients, the existence of the self is the result of a delusional grasping onto evanescent phenomena, and hence the goal of treatment in this model is to help clients clearly see through their delusion and increase their detachment from the concept of self, which is a deeper meaning of a common Buddhist slang term, "let go." Once clients gain a thorough insight into the mechanisms of the mind, they can gain the agency required to make deliberative life decisions that result in less suffering.

Buddhist counseling uses Buddhism as its theoretical orientation in the treatment process. In counseling, every micro skill used to enhance communication with clients should be driven by the practitioner's theoretical orientation; in Buddhist counseling, every micro skill is a technique targeted to understanding, developing, and liberating the mind. For example, when a client experiences strong anger due to her son's defiance, a Western counselor may reflect on and validate the client's emotions and help the client to find meanings of the anger. In the Buddhist framework, emotions are labels of body and mind states and the remedy for disturbing emotions is to deconstruct the label back into its conditions, such as bodily sensations, perceptions, and volitions, so that the person can become unbounded by the emotional label. To achieve this goal, a Buddhist counselor may reflect on the somatic sensations and mind activities involved in grief to help the client see the conditions contributing to suffering in the moment. For example, when the client reports a highly disturbing anger from being disrespected by her son, the Buddhist counselor will teach the client to breathe mindfully to momentarily cultivate some mental space from the "anger," scan bodily sensations during this angry state of mind, locate one spot of strong sensation, and observe how it changes when the client breathes in and out. Every moment of experience is understood as a discrete combination of causes and conditions, and gaining insight into how causes and conditions arise and cease can relieve the client's mind from clinging onto and ruminating on a strong experience of suffering.

SELF-CULTIVATION OF BUDDHIST COUNSELORS

A major distinction between psychotherapy and Buddhist counseling is that Buddhist counselors require their own personal contemplative practices for spiritual growth. There are two main reasons. First, self-cultivation is the spiritual nourishment required to drive and enhance the counselor's competency to practice. The level of self-cultivation of Buddhist counselors, or the skillful qualities of their minds, is central to the entire model, and the effectiveness of each component of an intervention is directly proportionate to the counselor's level of cultivation. Second, most Buddhist clients tend to have experiences with different forms of meditation, such as sitting meditation, chanting, or reciting mantra. A mental health professional with experiences in meditation may find it easier to understand clients' experiences and use meditation as an intervention. For example, chanting is a common Buddhist practice to pacify one's mind by sustaining attention consistently and repeatedly to the chanted words. A mental health professional with meditative experiences may relate to the client's experiences by drawing upon personal experiences in sitting meditation in which he consistently and repeatedly sustains focus on in-and-out breaths, thereby calming and soothing the body and mind. As chanting is a familiar cultural experience of this client, the mental health professional may collaborate with this client to use chanting as a self-soothing technique.

ATTUNEMENT

In Buddhist counseling, as in any form of counseling, attunement with clients to build a safe therapeutic environment is a crucial component of treatment. One item that mental health professionals might find useful is the Buddhist "non-knowing" mind, which reminds practitioners to avoid assumptions and stereotypes about their clients. In other words, Buddhist counselors should strive to let go of their own selves in order to see clients' perspectives. By noticing his or her own automatic judgment of clients, and by bringing back his or her own awareness to the here and now to become totally present with clients, a counselor, through embodiment of contemplative spiritual practices, automatically produces therapeutic effect, establishes connection with clients, and holds space for clients to express themselves throughout the counseling session. By deeply and attentively listening to clients, asking relevant questions to clarify and explore clients' worldviews, and reflecting on their own understandings with their clients to establish attunement, Buddhist counselors can foster a therapeutic relationship that allows their presence to soothe and calm their clients. This is especially important when counseling traumatized individuals, who are usually emotionally vulnerable.

INTERVENTIONS FOR BUILDING CONCENTRATION

Developing concentration and fostering wisdom are the two limbs of Buddhist meditation. Across previous studies and in the current findings (e.g., Lang et al. 2019; Shonin, Van Gordon, & Griffiths, 2014; Wu, Gao, Leung, & Sik, 2019), increasing clients' ability to pay attention and sustain that attention is a skill necessary to reducing suffering. To work effectively with Buddhist clients, it is advisable for mental health professionals to acquire training in mindfulness and commit to a personal practice. Practicing mindfulness by intentionally focusing on an object of concentration can teach clients to stay in the present moment and gain mental distance from negative thoughts and feelings. Regulated attention to breathing, which serves as a consistent practice of single-pointed mindfulness, can expand feelings of relief and thus become an anchor of the mind. A mind anchored in this way can more clearly see the physical sensations that arise from triggers—unpleasant thoughts about the trauma—and make a conscious decision not to focus and expand upon unpleasant thoughts. The mind can also switch focus to thoughts that are more positive, such as reminders of physical safety in the present moment, compassion for oneself, or associating new meanings with the trauma.

The goal of concentration practice is to help clients learn to gain more control over their minds by paying proper attention to the co-arising of their thought processes and their suffering. Buddhist counselors, or mental health professionals trained in mindfulness, can teach techniques such as guiding clients to practice mindful breathing, chanting, reciting mantras, reading Buddhist scriptures, *Nianfo* (reciting the names of the Buddha or other Bodhisattvas), calligraphy, painting, tea drinking, or other activities. Once clients start to pacify their minds, Buddhist counselors can deepen their awareness by guiding them to notice and observe their bodily sensations, feeling tones, and thought processes, which helps them to understand how their own minds work.

INTERVENTIONS FOR FOSTERING KNOWLEDGE

In Buddhism, wisdom is a direct cure for suffering, and mental health professionals hence need to understand the Buddhist meaning of wisdom. Ignorance implies an unskillful and mindless habit to pursue fantasized happiness using dysfunctional means that end with increasing levels of suffering. Wisdom, the contrast to ignorance, is a true understanding and acceptance of reality as it is, especially the discernment between mental and behavioral volitions resulting in suffering versus those resulting in reduction of suffering, thereby making more beneficial choices for self and others. This ability of making wise choices has to be supplemented by concentration. After clients are able to increase their ability to concentrate, Buddhist counselors can guide them to develop wisdom by acquiring an introspective knowledge of their minds.

Through meditative and contemplative practices, Buddhist counselors can help clients gain awareness of the body and mind, to shape their thoughts and behaviors by making positive changes and adjustments based on the insights they have gained; to release their desires and unrealistic expectations, freeing them from bondage to negative emotional states; and to develop skillful ways to maneuver through life's problems. For example, Buddhist counselors can teach anxious clients to focus on their internal processes and begin to realize the chain of experiences that lead to the arising of anxiety. A thought about work stress may induce stomach pain and expansion accompanied by a perception of physical discomfort that perpetrates feelings of anxiety; the person experiencing the anxiety then attempts to control it by ruminating about work, which leads to intensified anxiety and increased physical discomfort. Working with a client in a situation like that, a Buddhist counselor who is using meditation as an intervention may instruct the client to sit with those feelings, trace them back to the interpretation of bodily sensations, note the chain of mental activities that are interpreting those sensations, and pay close attention to how these processes arise and dissipate.

By teaching clients to reflect on and process introspective knowledge, Buddhist counselors can guide clients to notice the impermanence of their notions of "anxiety" and more mindfully choose their reactions when "anxiety" arises. Buddhist counselors can also deepen clients' understanding by teaching them to examine their attachment to a fabricated notion of self. For example, a Sri Lankan Buddhist male client growing up in a higher family socioeconomic status has received lots of high expectations from his family for outstanding achievement since he was born. These experiences created a notion of a "competent" man in him and he has clung onto this image to find his existence by earning validation from others through his achievements. This continuously volition-related decision to fuel a "competent" notion of self perpetrates a habitual pattern and consolidates the identity. When the external reality challenges his notion of competency by going through bankruptcy due to his investment decisions, a strong sense of dissatisfaction arises and his competent-self notion turns into an endless tirade of self-blame and self-criticism. His anxiety becomes significantly severe because he is very afraid of making another bad decision. By attuning with this client, counselors can lead him to see how he creates and clings onto a "competent" notion of self, how environmental conditions contributed to this fabrication, how he has suffered from sustaining this notion—and how to process his deeper yearnings and needs beneath the notion, cultivate self-compassion and understanding, and develop skillful ways to release himself from this attachment so that he can mindfully choose a new way to live.

BUDDHIST COUNSELING CASE EXAMPLE

Roy Cheung, our hypothetical case for this chapter, is a thirty-six-year-old Chinese male who works full-time as a marketing specialist. He self-referred to a counselor because of his anger problems. Roy reported that he has a conflicted relationship with his supervisor. He is highly devoted to his work and aspires to innovation and creativity, but his supervisor often criticizes and rejects his ideas no matter how hard Roy tries to please him. When his supervisor puts down his ideas, Roy's anger escalates momentarily, which makes him argue with his supervisor, shut down during meetings, or even sometimes run out of the office. He often ruminates over how his supervisor sabotages him, which causes irritability, stress, and insomnia. From a Buddhist psychological perspective, anger is rooted in a belief about the experience of an offense committed against oneself and the desire to retaliate. In this situation, Roy's sense of self is offended when his ideas are criticized and rejected. There is probably a sense of unfairness and injustice in Roy's mind that leads him to protest on behalf of his personal rights.

An analysis of Roy's reaction to criticism reveals that sensory contact with the supervisor appears to trigger several experiences. First, there are physiological reactions, such as a racing heartbeat, sweating, heat in the body, and other sensations (*First aggregate: physical processes*). Second, the feeling of that sensory contact is unpleasant and painful (*Second aggregate: sensations*). Third, his subliminal proclivity for aversion apparently creates interpretations of being offended or mistreated (*Third aggregate: perception*). Through these ruminations, his anger-provoking thoughts rapidly and uncontrollably proliferate and intensify. He has not trained and tamed his mind for meta-cognitive awareness of his thought processes and bodily changes, and hence his mind endlessly follows and chases unwholesome anger-provoking thoughts (*Fourth aggregate: volition*). At this moment, Roy has formed and held onto a story of being constantly attacked by an authority figure for no reason, thereby resulting in a great deal of anger and resentment (*Fifth aggregate: consciousness*). This story and associated negative emotions have dominated his mind and clouded his clarity and stability to see reality. Together with his motivational root of his strong desire for acknowledgment, his hatred and rejection of criticism, and his delusion of attachment to anger, he has formed a strong attempt to reject external reality by either fighting or fleeing. This sequence of experiences has resulted in a habitual and repetitive cycle in which Roy starts working hard and submits his work for approval, is dissatisfied with criticism, acts out based on his anger, and then restores his emotional stability in order to work again.

In the first step of attunement, any counseling relationship would require the genuine and therapeutic presence of counselors to be effective. To help Roy, the Buddhist counselor establishes rapport by attentively listening, understanding and validating his feelings, and building trust with Roy so that he can turn toward his anger without avoidance. Listening, in a Buddhist counselor's framework, requires counselors to understand that we can only listen through our five aggregates, which naturally filter and distort the clients' expressions. A strong self-awareness is necessary to keep track of the difference between what is actually being said, the mind's interpretation, and what assumptions, judgments, and postulations arise that hinder our understanding of a client. In our hypothetical case, the Buddhist counselor should refrain from judging Roy's anger and, instead, patiently engage him and attune with his feelings in the moment. For example, a counselor might say to Roy, "From what you have described, your supervisor did not just ban your proposal. He criticized your ideas in front of the whole team, which made you feel humiliated and unappreciated as a professional marketing specialist, regardless of how hard you have worked. No wonder you felt so angry!" With his complex feelings receiving acknowledgment and acceptance, Roy should be able to de-escalate his anger and open a cognitive space to practice mindfulness techniques.

Building on that foundation of rapport, the Buddhist counselor is then able to explore the causes of Roy's suffering in greater depth. One reason for Roy's anger may be his conceit that he is superior to others and, hence, that he should be treated with respect. This strong attachment to self, in turn, taints his perception and makes him prone to dissatisfaction. The first step in detaching from the delusion of self is to increase one's calmness and clarity of mind through the practice of concentration. With Roy's permission, the counselor might now teach Roy basic meditation skills, such as the sitting posture, the materials needed for practice, different physical breathing mechanisms, and focusing on the in- and out-breath. If Roy finds it difficult to concentrate on breathing, the counselor can provide another means of meditation, such as mindful walking, mindful eating, mindful movements, or mindful listening to sounds. These interventions can help Roy to tranquilize his mind so that he can develop a mental space between his thoughts and his sensations and gain awareness of how to relax his body in a moment of arising anger.

To counter anger, slow, steady, consistent, and rhythmical breathing is an effective remedy. In his experiences of mindful breathing, Roy begins to increase awareness of his bodily sensations and the interactions between his body and mind. When Roy is able to increase his ability to concentrate, the Buddhist counselor can prompt him to recollect the anger-provoking events, letting Roy notice his pattern of anger and examine the drawbacks of his actions. With a heightened awareness of his body and mind, Roy can begin to notice that there are many points of decision between the moments he senses criticism from his supervisor to the moment he runs out of the meeting room. After repeated meditation rituals and practicing the cultivation of a mindful state in daily life, Roy should gradually learn to step back from his mental formations and make a conscious decision about what actions may result in more beneficial outcomes.

Noticing that Roy is disturbed by hatred, the Buddhist counselor might next teach Roy to cultivate compassion for himself and others. Through loving-kindness meditation, Roy can learn to recollect feelings of gratitude and compassion, sustain those feelings with visualization and concentration, and radiate them toward others. When Roy is able to stabilize his feeling of compassion and visualize compassion for the people he dislikes, the counselor can further prompt him to try to radiate compassion toward his supervisor, which can result in the transformation of anger into loving-kindness. The counselor can guide Roy to practice his new skills consistently and, throughout the process of teaching those skills, address all of Roy's concerns and questions.

CONCLUSION

Buddhism provides a framework for the psychological study of the human mind and a comprehensive model to liberate clients from suffering. In the Buddhist understanding of the mind, suffering occurs when an individual identifies the five aggregates as self, which leads to a habitual thought pattern taking control of a mind and causing it to make decisions that result in suffering. Liberation occurs when awareness kicks in and carefully guides decisions that result in less suffering. Buddhism can be understood as a method of mind training or cultivation that provides a sequential way of gradually transforming the inclination and habits of the mind to foster positive qualities. A mind with high awareness and clarity notices and understands external events, bodily sensations, feelings, and thoughts in the moment, thereby responding wisely in daily encounters. The results of Buddhist mindfulness are usually mental flexibility to see events from multiple perspectives and deliberately choosing thoughts that lead to heightened emotions and behaviors that are beneficial to self and others (because a skillful mind knows which decisions are likely to result in less suffering for self and others). Applying Buddhism to counseling can help mental health professionals learn ways to cultivate clients' minds and help them reach these therapeutic goals.

REFERENCES

Aich, T. K. (2013). Buddha philosophy and Western psychology. *Indian Journal of Psychiatry, 55*(Suppl 2), S165–S170. Doi:10.4103/0019-5545.105517

AN 3.15. "Rathakara (Pacetana) Sutta: The chariot maker," translated from the Pali by T. Bhikkhu (2013, November 30). *Access to Insight (BCBS Edition)*. Retrieved January 5, 2020, from https://www.accesstoinsight.org/tipitaka/an/an03/an03.015 .than.html.

Boisvert, M. (1997). *The five aggregates: Understanding Theravāda psychology and soteriology* (1st Indian ed.), Bibliotheca Indo-Buddhica, no. 185. Delhi: Sri Satguru Publications.

Bornaetxea, F. R., Morón, D. A., Gil, A. A., & Molloy, A. A. H. (2014). Construction of reality or dependent origination? From scientific psychotherapy to responsible attention. *Contemporary Buddhism, 15*(2), 216–243. https://doi.org/10.1080/14639947.2014.934057

Karunadasa, Y. (2013). *Early Buddhist teachings: The middle position in theory and practice.* Hong Kong: Centre of Buddhist Studies, The University of Hong Kong.

Lang, A. J., Malaktaris, A. L., Casmar, P., Baca, S. A., Golshan, S., Harrison, T., & Negi, L. (2019). Compassion meditation for posttraumatic stress disorder in veterans: A randomized proof of concept study. *Journal of Traumatic Stress, 32*(2), 299–309. https://doi.org/10.1002/jts.22397

Lee, K. C., & Ong, C. K. (2019). The Satipaṭṭhāna Sutta: An application of Buddhist mindfulness for counsellors. *Journal of Contemporary Buddhism, 19*(2), 327–341. https://doi.org/10.1080/14639947.2018.1576292

Lee, K. C., Oh, A., Zhao, Q., Wu, F., Chen, S., Diaz, T., & Ong, C. K. (2017). Buddhist counseling: Implications for mental health professionals. *Spirituality in Clinical Practice, 4*(2), 113–128. doi:10.1037/scp0000124

Miln 2. "The Questions of King Milinda," translated from the Pali by T. W. R. Davids (1890). *The Questions of King Milinda.* Oxford: Clarendon.

MN 63. "Cula-Malunkyovada Sutta: The Shorter Instructions to Malunkya," translated from the Pali by T. Bhikkhu (2013, November 30). *Access to Insight (BCBS Edition).* Retrieved January 5, 2020, from http://www.accesstoinsight.org/tipitaka/mn/mn.063.than.html.

Shonin, E., Van Gordon, W., & Griffiths, M. (2014). Meditation Awareness Training (MAT) for improved psychological well-being: A qualitative examination of participant experiences. *Journal of Religion & Health, 53*(3), 849–863. https://doi.org/10.1007/s10943-013-9679-0

SN 5.10. "Vajira Sutta: Vajiram," translated from the Pali by B. Bhikkhu (2013, November 30). *Access to Insight (BCBS Edition).* Retrieved January 5, 2020, from http://www.accesstoinsight.org/tipitaka/sn/sn05/sn05.010.bodh.html.

SN 12.38. "Cetana Sutta: Intention," translated from the Pali by T. Bhikkhu (2013, November 30). *Access to Insight (BCBS Edition).* Retrieved January 5, 2020, from http://www.accesstoinsight.org/tipitaka/sn/sn12/sn12.038.than.html.

SN 22.36. "Bhikkhu Sutta: The Monk," translated from the Pali by T. Bhikkhu (2013, November 30). *Access to Insight (BCBS Edition).* Retrieved January 5, 2020, from http://www.accesstoinsight.org/tipitaka/sn/sn22/sn22.036.than.html.

SN 35.28. "Adittapariyaya Sutta: The Fire Sermon," translated from the Pali by T. Bhikkhu (2013, November 30). *Access to Insight (BCBS Edition).* Retrieved January 5, 2020, from http://www.accesstoinsight.org/tipitaka/sn/sn35/sn35.028.than.html.

Wallace, B. A., & Shapiro, S. L. (2006). Mental balance and well-being: Building bridges between Buddhism and Western psychology. *American Psychologist*, 61(7), 690.

Wu, B. W. Y., Gao, J., Leung, H. K., & Sik, H. H. (2019). A randomized controlled trial of awareness training program (ATP), a group-based Mahayana Buddhist intervention. *Mindfulness*. https://doi.org/10.1007/s12671-018-1082-1

DOUG OMAN AND ANAND C. PARANJPE

PSYCHOLOGY OF HINDUISM FROM
THE INSIDE OUT

Approximately one-seventh of humanity adheres to Hinduism, the world's oldest and third largest major religious tradition, and by far the largest indigenous Indian tradition. About 1 billion Hindus live worldwide, approximately 15 percent of the world's population. Among them, about 2.3 million live in North America (0.7 percent of its population), and 1.3 million live in Europe (0.2 percent of its population) (Pew Research Center, 2012).

Yet despite its age and size, Hinduism has been the focus of less empirical study in psychology than other major traditions, such as Christianity, Islam, and Buddhism (see Oman, 2019a, Figure 1). Although this comparative neglect appears to be gradually changing, the need remains for introductory materials to guide health and human service professionals in their interactions with Hindu clients.

A variety of excellent external resources offer general introductions for Western readers to how Hindus understand themselves and their tradition (e.g., Smith, 1991; also Fuller, 2004; Prabhavananda, 1963/1979). This chapter's "inside-out" presentation of Hindu perspectives on health is intended primarily as a focused resource for clinical work with Hindu clients. In addition, we hope this chapter serves as a resource for collaborative public health efforts involving Hindu communities (e.g., Oman, 2018). In what follows, we first describe several core features of Hindu tradition, noting similarities and differences with Abrahamic traditions. Then we examine in greater detail Hindu views of several key questions related to psychotherapy, including its views of science, human psychology, human nature, health, and suffering. We close by considering applications to psychotherapy, plus needed future directions. Indian and Sanskrit terms are included to aid further reading or conversation with religiously engaged clients, but are not essential for comprehending the chapter.

WHAT IS HINDU TRADITION?

When Hindus came west in substantial numbers to the United States and Europe in the mid- and late twentieth century, they brought with them Hinduism's most sacred scriptures, the *Vedas*, composed well over two thousand years ago, and only written down after many centuries of oral transmission. Over several thousand years, Indian civilization has been shaped by the *Vedas* in concert with derivative scriptures, philosophies, and culturally embedded practices such as respect for renunciates, pilgrimage, and adherence to various rituals and beliefs. Together, these inform the popular religion that ordinary Hindus in India and abroad practice every day in their homes, in temples, throughout the day and in personal relationships, and in practices such as pilgrimage.

Like other religious communities, Hindu communities build temples that serve as sites of collective ceremonial worship, called *pūjā* in Hinduism. Temple attendance and congregational worship exist everywhere in India, and are especially common in Hindu communities in the West, where they strengthen minority cultural identity (see, e.g., Baumann, 2009). Furthermore, the domestic Hindu home also serves as a major site of religious activity both in India and abroad, with worship typically centered on a household shrine (Mazumdar & Mazumdar, 2009).

Hindu worship, or *pūjā*, whether taking place in a temple, home, or other location such as a monastery or wayside shrine, typically focuses on one or more personifications of divine power, usually in English called gods. In temples *pūjā* is generally performed by priests, and in the home is often mainly the responsibility of women. When visiting a temple or shrine, merely gazing on a divine image (*mūrti*) for a "sight" or "vision" of the deity, called darshana (*darśana*), is an important activity, viewed as bringing good fortune, well-being, and grace. In addition, it is quite possible to adore and worship deities in imageless form; for the past few centuries, some Hindus have expressed opposition to worship involving images. Yet most commonly, formalized *pūjā* worship ceremonies involve a structured interaction with a divine image that proceeds through stages such as a chanting of *mantras*, bathing and decorating the image (*abhiṣeka, dīpārādhanā*), offering food (*naivedya*), and displaying lamps (*dīpārādhanā*) (see Fuller, 2004, pp. 57–82). Importantly, for Hindus, "the object of worship is not the image, but the deity whose power is inside it" (p. 60), after installation through a consecration ritual. *Pūjā* properly performed is "an act of respectful honoring whose objective is to please a deity in the hope or expectation—but not the certainty—that it will protect and favor human beings" (p. 71). Some worship, admittedly, "is motivated by a conscious intention to persuade or induce a deity to bestow [particular] reciprocal favors on the worshiper [but] many Hindus ... insist that it is always wrong to worship in such a spirit, as well as counter-productive, because the deities will be displeased by worship done with blatant ulterior motives" (p. 71).

Such *Pūjā* ceremonies operate in the context of a much broader set of teachings and practices transmitted for millennia through channels ranging from auxiliary scriptures to a variety of sanctified social roles, concepts, norms, and techniques. Sacred texts of special importance include the Upanishads (*Upaniṣads*), which report sages' experiences of elevated states of self-realized consciousness; many early Upanishads, dating from no later than the seventh century BCE, were incorporated within the *Vedas* (Radhakrishnan, 1953/1994). Somewhat later—perhaps in the second century BCE—many Upanishadic teachings about the nature and pathways to self-realization were synthesized, in only seven hundred verses, in the *Bhagavad-Gītā*, the most widely read and commented upon of all Hindu scriptures. A third influential group of Hindu sacred texts is the epics, especially the *Rāmāyaṇa* and *Mahābhārata*, which contain lengthy historical/mythological narratives roughly comparable to the Greek *Iliad* and *Odyssey*, supplying material for popular and devotional storytelling, music, drama, and other arts that for millennia have nurtured popular devotion and learning of spiritual discernment.

GOALS AND PATHWAYS

Hinduism recognizes four major classes of legitimate human goals (*puruṣārthas*), roughly translatable as duty (*dharma*), success (*artha*), gratification (*kāma*), and the attainment of self-realization or liberation/salvation through a spiritually elevated and transformed state of consciousness (Rao & Paranjpe, 2016). Self-realization/liberation is viewed as the ultimate goal of human life—the highest so-called religious "destination" (Oman & Paranjpe, 2018, p. 142)—and has been designated by numerous names, such as *mokṣa, apavarga, niḥśreyasa, kaivalya,* and *nirvāṇa* (Rao & Paranjpe, 2016). Through such self-realization, individual personal suffering comes to an end (*duḥkhāntaṃ, Bhagavad-Gītā* 18:36).

For attaining such self-realization/liberation, Indian tradition since ancient times has recognized several different pathways or *yogas*, especially the four so-called classical *yogas* that emphasize meditation (*dhyāna yoga*), love and devotion (*bhakti yoga*), work (*karma yoga*), and knowledge (*jñāna yoga*). Note that these classic yogas do *not* include the sets of physical exercises known in the West as "yoga" (see appendix to this chapter). Corresponding to each classic yoga are frequent or prototypical practices, such as selfless action (*niṣkāma karma*) in the yoga of action, discrimination between the changing and the changeless (*nitya-anitya viveka*) in the yoga of knowledge, and earnest-hearted calling of God's name (*nāma-japa, nāma-kīrtana*) in the yoga of love and devotion. Postclassical and contemporary approaches to yoga often emphasize an integrated combination of practices associated with many or all of the major classical yogas (Oman & Bormann, 2018; Rao & Paranjpe, 2016; Smith, 1991). This yoga-based pathway/destination structure renders many features of Hinduism coherently understandable with reference to Pargament's influential framework for conceptualizing religion and spirituality as involving a "search for the sacred" (Oman & Paranjpe, 2018, p. 142).

These *yoga* pathways are viewed as alternative ways through which an individual person may attain self-realization, by whatever name it is designated. In Hindu tradition, the ordinary individual is often called a *jīva*, meaning an individual "person," "embodied consciousness," or "individual spirit" (Rao & Paranjpe, 2016, p. 343). Hinduism teaches that most people have been "conditioned" to identify with their body and mental habits, so that their "thought, passion, and action are biased and distorted by the conditions of the body" (p. 7). However, the persistent practice of yoga can enable the *jīva* to become "deconditioned" (p. 7) so that an individual's consciousness can become aligned with the highest reality (i.e., God, also called *Brahman*), ultimately resulting in an abiding state of self-realization. This state of self-realization parallels the "awakened" states that are identified by the meditative and mystical traditions within other major religious traditions (Oman, 2019b), and is understood to involve an ongoing awareness of divine realities (God/*Brahman*), as well as ongoing understanding/awareness of the individual's deepest, most abiding self, often in Hinduism called the *ātman*.

The attainability of salvation/liberation through nonidentical and diverse pathways is perhaps more pronounced and well-recognized in Hinduism, but Abrahamic parallels range from the affirmation of individual vocations to the existence of diverse Roman Catholic religious orders, such as Franciscans, Carmelites, and the Missionaries of Charity, each possessed of their own partly overlapping traditions.

BOTH PERSONAL AND IMPERSONAL

Yet some clear differences in emphasis do exist. Whereas Abrahamic religious figures have only rarely affirmed that divine realities may be approached and experienced as impersonal (e.g., the *via negativa* of Dionysius the Areopagite's "divine desert"), such affirmations are well established within Hinduism, alongside Hinduism's pervasive strong affirmations of *personal* divinity. For example, Hinduism teaches the realizability of *Nirguṇa Brahman*, an impersonal aspect of *Brahman* (e.g., see Maharaj, 2018; see also *Yoga Sūtras* 1:51). Such impersonal representations, although drawing disproportionate attention among Westerners and intellectuals, and perhaps other Hindu professionals living in the West, are neither the only representation, nor the most common in everyday Hinduism.

Hinduism's ongoing and diverse ways of recognizing personality in the higher powers of the universe—its affirmation of many "gods"—is often confusing to Westerners. Yet even here, as in most other facets of

Hindu tradition, partial parallels are evident in Abrahamic traditions. For example, Christianity recognizes a divine trinity of Father, Son, and Holy Spirit, understood as one God in three persons. Hinduism likewise affirms multiple divine persons that most prominently include Vishnu, Shiva, and several forms of the Divine Mother, as well as the capacity of divine persons—especially Vishnu—to become embodied as an incarnation (*avatār*). Like the single divine incarnation recognized in Christianity, a Hindu *avatār* serves to restore divine harmony and salvific energy on earth. Unlike Christianity, Hinduism affirms multiple avatars—including figures from nonindigenous religious traditions (e.g., Jesus the Christ).[1]

The diverse divine names, forms, and pathways are not viewed in Hinduism as inherently contradictory, as affirmed since ancient times in scriptures such as the *Ṛg Veda*'s (1:164:46) "Truth is One: sages call it by various names," and the *Bhagavad-Gītā*'s (4:11) "Whatever path men travel … it leads to me" (Prabhavananda, 1963/1979, pp. 355–356). Thus, local Hindu groups and communities may emphasize worship through one of these divine personalities, even as a Christian parish may emphasize a single patron saint. Yet Hindu temple complexes not uncommonly support multiple presiding deities, and members of individual families may harmoniously and uncontroversially direct their devotional energies to different cherished deities (*iṣṭa-devatā*). Consequently, from a social scientific perspective, whereas Indian society possesses a strong and largely collectivist family structure, Indian spirituality offers substantial support for individualization, with Indian identity arguably "dualist" in the sense that it "includes both collectivist and individualist values" (Suchday, Santoro, Ramanayake, Lewin, & Almeida, 2018, p. 148). Indeed, Hinduism's embrace of such diverse pathways renders virtually meaningless any attempt to use behavioral criteria to distinguish between "practicing" and "non-practicing" Hindus. No specific behavior or practice is enjoined on all Hindus. Conversely, Hinduism also affirms that non-Hindu religions, including not only other Dharmic traditions such as Buddhism and Jainism but also Abrahamic traditions, contain valid pathways to God—a perspective arguably reflected today in phenomena that include even "pluralistic" affirmations by Indian children that members of different religious groups should each adhere to their own sacred group norms[2] (Srinivasan, Kaplan, & Dahl, 2019, p. e799; see also Maharaj, 2018; Rao & Paranjpe, 2016, pp. 41–42).

As it embraces multiple gods and yet affirms that "Truth is One," outsiders may wonder whether Hinduism straddles or transcends the Western categorical distinction between monotheism and polytheism. Certainly if Hinduism is classified as polytheistic, it represents what anthropologist Christopher Fuller (2004) has called a very "fluid polytheism" (p. 31):

The dictionary defines polytheism as "belief in or worship of many gods." Although this definition broadly applies to Hinduism, all Hindus sometimes and some Hindus always insist that there is in reality only one God, of whom all the distinct gods and goddesses are but forms. To ask if Hindus do or do not believe in more than one god is therefore too simple, for they may say that there is one god and many in almost the same breath.... [Moreover,] a single deity with different names may be seen, in another context or from another perspective, as a set of distinct deities.... [Yet] the impression of inchoate abundance given by so many names [can] be mitigated once the main dimensions of the polytheistic pantheon have been grasped. (Fuller, 2004, pp. 30, 32)

Hinduism's affirmation of a multitude of divine personifications, names, and pathways is also helpful for clarifying the role of a man or woman who serves as a spiritual teacher, or *guru* (Pechilis, 2004). The guru "is a teacher, counselor, father-image [sic], mature ideal, hero, source of strength, even divinity integrated into one personality. Primarily, however, the guru is the personal teacher of spirituality, that is, of the basic, ultimate values perceived within the Hindu tradition. Further, the guru possesses experiential knowledge, not only intellectual knowledge, of these values" (Mlecko, 1982, p. 34). In Indian tradition, "the guru should be the one who has traveled the path before [and] serves as the reference point ... the 'caravan leader' who guides [the] pupil mindful of checkpoints and signposts in transit ... [to] the final self-certifying state of pure consciousness, playing an indispensable role of mediation" (Rao & Paranjpe, 2016, p. 30). Influential gurus may give rise to lineages (*paramparās*) or schools (*sampradāyas*) that teach specific spiritual practices or philosophical interpretations of tradition.

One major function of the guru—perhaps the guru's most important duty—is to prescribe individualized sets of spiritual practices (see Prabhavananda, 1963/1979, p. 67). Besides worship and ethical virtues, one commonly prescribed practice is frequent repetition of a mantram or divine name, a practice also known in Abrahamic traditions (Oman & Driskill, 2003). Sometimes sitting meditation may be prescribed. In contrast to some other traditions, traditional Hindu modes of meditation are concentrative, and apart from rare exceptions emphasize meditating on a name, symbol, or other representation of divinity. For example, the *Bhagavad-Gītā* 16:14 recommends meditating on God, and Patañjali's *Yoga Sūtras* recommend meditating upon the ancient mantram Om (1:28), or upon "the heart of an illumined soul" (1:37). Meditating on God in such a manner is believed to transform and sanctify character. Indeed, a long and authoritative stream of Hindu tradition, extending from the *Vedas*, teaches that "One becomes what one meditates on" (*Yajur Veda* 10:5:2:21; Oman & Bormann, 2018, p. 99).

PHILOSOPHICAL SYSTEMS

Since ancient times, Hindus have understood their practices and experiences through six orthodox systems of thought, often called philosophies. In Hindu tradition they are called *darśanas*, or "views"—the same word used to describe seeing a divine image in a temple—because the philosophies are viewed as "not merely metaphysical speculation [but as having] foundation in immediate perception" (Prabhavananda, 1963/1979, p. 15). Although these views or philosophies employ somewhat varying terminologies, unified understandings of them have existed at least since medieval times (Nicholson, 2010), and the six systems are generally understood as "not mutually contradictory.... [Rather,] [t]hey really represent ... a progressive development from truth to higher truth to the highest truth ... a perception of the same truth from different angles of vision" (Prabhavananda, 1963/1979, p. 200). Of the six systems, the two most important are Yoga and Vedānta. The Yoga system, represented by the *Yoga Sūtras* of Patañjali, gives special attention to the dynamics of meditation and related practices for spiritual growth. The Vedānta philosophical system offers comprehensive interpretations of the nature of divine reality, the universe, and the individual, with the nondualistic Advaita Vedānta philosophy being its best-known school (the remaining four philosophical systems, not as well known, are Sāṁkhya, Nyāya, Vaiśeṣika, and Mīmāṁsā).

Reincarnation—the idea that after death, a human being may be reborn in another body, perhaps in the same society—has been affirmed by Hindu and other indigenous Indian traditions since the time of the early Upanishads (e.g., *Bṛhadāraṇyaka* 4:4:3–4; *Kaṭha* 1:1:5–6). Such affirmation represents a significant difference from the nonendorsement or denial of reincarnation within most Abrahamic traditions, apart from rare exceptions (e.g., teachings on *gilgul* in Hasidic Judaism [Breslauer, 1983]). Nonetheless, the West, too, is no stranger to beliefs in reincarnation, which were common in the ancient Mediterranean world—having been taught by Plato—and although marginal, reincarnation belief has been "astonishingly persistent" in recent centuries in the West (MacGregor, 1978, p. 14). Recent findings from the World Values Survey show that between 20 percent and 40 percent of people believe in reincarnation in cultural zones as diverse as the United States, Western Europe, Eastern Europe, and Brazil (Peres, 2012).

Reincarnation provides a key context for the famous Hindu teaching known as the Law of Karma, arguably first affirmed in the Upanishads (*Bṛhadāraṇyaka* 4:4:5–6). "Karma" literally means "action," "work," or "the result of action" (Rao & Paranjpe, 2016, p. 343). In its simplest form, the Law of Karma holds that people eventually receive what they deserve, good or bad, based on their own good and bad actions, parallel to the Christian teaching that "whatsoever a man soweth, that shall he also reap" (Galatians 6:7 KJV). Belief in karma is widespread in India and correlates with belief in God and spirituality (White, Norenzayan, & Schaller, 2019). Importantly, since karma is viewed as carried over from one life to the next, one's present good or bad fortune may be the karmic result of actions in previous lives. Yet Hindu scriptures do not advance a single unified theory of karma, and both scriptural/philosophical and popular Hinduism offer many varied interpretations on issues such as dynamics of collective responsibility, under what circumstances one may become free from the law's effects, and the ways that people are called to actively resist evil (see Fuller, 2004, pp. 245–252; Maharaj, 2018, p. 263; *Bhagavad-Gītā* 3:31).

In the view of both Hinduism and Buddhism, good karma arises from adhering to *dharma*, sometimes understood as akin to "cosmic order," but also roughly and inadequately translatable as "duty; the righteous way of living, as enjoined by the sacred scriptures and spiritually illumined sages" (Rao & Paranjpe, 2016, p. 343). However, "*dharma* was not meant to provide an eternal and unchangeable set of rules carved in stone.... As a *living* tradition, it adapts to the historically changing environment" (p. 54). Thus, *dharma* is referenced at multiple levels, including the responsibilities that apply to all people (*sāmānya dharma*), as well as the responsibility or calling applying to a unique individual (*svadharma*), to people according to their stage of life or group (*varṇāśrama dharma*), and to the historical epoch in which a person is alive (*yugadharma*), as well as eternal universal human spiritual callings and responsibilities (*sanātana dharma*), with the latter a term sometimes used to designate the most essential and enduring features of Hinduism itself (Rao & Paranjpe, 2016).

Hinduism possesses an ambivalent relation to the caste system of birth-based occupational and social prescriptions and hierarchies that long dominated India. Even as biblical passages have been cited to justify various types of oppression and even slavery, various passages of Hindu sacred texts have been used to justify caste oppression (Oman, 2018; Sharma, 2001). Yet the most influential modern Hindu leaders such as Mahatma Gandhi, Swami Vivekananda, and Sri Aurobindo rejected the caste system. Since India's postindependence 1949 Constitution, caste discrimination has been prohibited as one of several "powerful" constitutional commitments toward the abolition of caste-related social inequalities (Grinsell, 2010, p. 206). Some scholars have argued that the caste system was not intrinsic even to classical phases of Hinduism (e.g., Nadkarni, 2003), and that "there is a theological vision at the heart of Hinduism that invalidates the assumptions of inequality, impurity, and indignity that are the foundations of caste belief and practice [resulting in] a chorus of Hindu prophetic voices, ancient and modern, protesting the practice of caste as a betrayal of Hinduism's highest teachings" (Rambachan, 2008, p. 59). Despite changed religious views and legal prohibitions, however, caste and caste-related injustice remain part of the experience of many

Hindus—even as ethnic and racial injustice remain an unfortunate part of human experience in many countries.

Less controversial than caste, and arguably more integral to the spiritual dimension of traditional Hinduism, is its teachings about roles and goals appropriate to four main stages of life (*āśramas*). In childhood and early youth, one is a student (*brahmacarya*) becoming oriented to one's culture and duties. Next, one becomes an adult householder (*gṛhastha*) expected to earn wealth and raise children, which is followed by the transitional stage of preretirement and gradual withdrawal from active life (*vānaprastha*), and finally a stage of renunciation and focus on spiritual growth and liberation (*sannyāsa*). Exceptions are made for "precocious individuals" who may skip earlier stages and enter renunciation at an earlier stage (often as a monk, or *svāmī*). This *āśrama* system represents "an ideal pattern ... more of a prescription ... rather than a description of what commonly happens" (Rao & Paranjpe, 2016, p. 61). Yet it continues as a frame of reference for Hindus, and has also stimulated reflection in the West (e.g., Savishinsky, 2004).

In the next five sections, we spotlight Hindu views on several universal issues of special relevance to psychotherapists and other health and human service professionals, including science, human psychology, human nature, health, and suffering. Emphasizing the main themes of scriptural/philosophical Hinduism, we occasionally cite relevant empirical research.

HINDU VIEWS OF KNOWLEDGE AND SCIENCE

Like Abrahamic traditions, Hinduism views some of its sacred scriptures—in particular, the *Vedas*—as divinely "revealed" and of "absolute authority" (Prabhavananda, 1963/1979, p. 17). Hinduism regards the *Vedas*—which include the Upanishads—as revealed, or *Śruti* (literally "heard"), whereas the epics and other scriptures are regarded as human-created derivations from them, referred to as *Smṛti* (literally "remembered"). The *Vedas* are viewed "as recording the transcendental experience of the first ... seers of India [that] cannot and should not contradict similar experience in any age or country"—nor should such experiences "contradict other truths [or] contradict reason" (Prabhavananda,

1963/1979, pp. 16, 18). Yet Hinduism's specific understanding of the nature of knowledge and of its revealed scriptures has helped minimize conflicts with many types of empirical investigation, both ancient and modern, especially in the natural sciences.

Beginning in the *Vedas* themselves, Hinduism has distinguished between two forms of knowing. Higher knowledge (*parā vidyā*), also referred to as wisdom (*jñāna*), is viewed as aiding and arising from self-realization (Misra, 2014; see also Rao & Paranjpe, 2016, p. 11). In contrast, empirical knowledge is derived from the senses and is known as lower knowledge (*aparā vidyā*). Similar distinctions between higher wisdom and lower knowledge are found in other major religious traditions (Walsh, 2015). As explained by Smith (2012, pp. 127, 129):

India recognizes … "lower knowledge"—knowledge that is gained by reason and the senses playing over objective, finite particulars. Higher knowledge (*paravidya*) … resembles "knowing how" more than "knowing that"; it is more like knowing how to swim or ride a bicycle than like recognizing that these activities require certain movements of arms and legs. Vedantic epistemology involves yoga. To know, one must be; to deepen one's knowledge of the kind in question, one must deepen one's being.

Of course, a map should not be confused with the territory that it represents, nor should a text on swimming be confused with actual skill in swimming. Similarly, the *Vedas* classify *themselves* as merely "lower knowledge." For example, the *Muṇḍaka Upaniṣad* 1:1:4–5, embedded within the *Atharva Veda*, states that "two kinds of knowledge are to be known.… The lower is the *Ṛg Veda*, the *Yajur Veda*, the *Sāma Veda*, the *Atharva Veda*, Phonetics, Ritual, Grammar, Etymology, Metrics and Astrology. And the higher is that by which the Undecaying is apprehended" (Radhakrishnan, 1953/1994, p. 672).

Perhaps in part because of their emphasis on higher knowledge, few if any *Vedic* teachings have generated significant ongoing conflicts with empirical investigations of the natural world, of which there have been many in India since ancient times, including discoveries in natural sciences, mathematics, and technology that have influenced other civilizations worldwide (Kumar, 2019). Subbarayappa (2006, p. 93) speculates that low levels of conflict between natural science and religion may also be related to Indian culture's general tendency toward "selective assimilation," consistent with *Vedic* injunctions to "Let noble thoughts come from anywhere, unhindered and overflowing" (*Ṛg Veda* 1:89:1). Moreover, scientific knowledge was embraced by several major Indian spiritual figures beginning in the late nineteenth century, and many Indian independence leaders sought to balance materialism and indigenous spirituality, "culminating in an integrated modernization ... modern and postmodern views of science seemed to be generally homologous with long-held Indian spiritual beliefs" (Dorman, 2011, p. 609).

Less easily reconciled with Vedic spiritual beliefs have been modern *human* sciences—or, more specifically, schools of their interpretation—that enunciate views of human nature denying the possibility of self-realization. A case in point is Darwinian theories of evolution, which span the natural and human sciences, and possess implications for human nature that are unclear and widely debated. Thus, as for many other world religions, controversies have arisen about the relationship between Hinduism and Darwinism, with some participants claiming irreconcilability and others describing possible reconciliations or syntheses (e.g., see the five-article special section in *Zygon*, Hinduism and Science: Contemporary Considerations, 2012). Nonetheless, a recent multinational survey of more than twenty thousand scientists found that 94 percent of Indian scientists identified with a religious tradition—nearly 20 percent higher than in the second-highest nation surveyed (Turkey)—and that "even though religion is everywhere, Indian scientists do not see it as a problem for the scientific enterprise" (Ecklund et al., 2019, p. 164).

HINDUISM'S INDIGENOUS
PSYCHOLOGICAL CONCEPTS

By the middle of the twentieth century, Indian psychologists had recognized that many ideas embedded in Hinduism were relevant to the new field of modern psychology (e.g., Akhilananda, 1951; Sinha, 1934). Yet apart from a few scattered publications, this awareness remained marginal until 2002, when more than 150 Indian psychologists gathered in Pondicherry and issued the *Manifesto on Indian Psychology* (Cornelissen, 2002). The *Manifesto* called for scholarly attention to psychological ideas embedded in indigenous Indian traditions, catalyzing what has become known as the *Indian Psychology Movement*, along with numerous conferences, books, and journal articles (e.g., Bhawuk, 2010; Misra, 2014; Rao & Paranjpe, 2016). The resulting scholarship can inform psychological practice in Hindu populations, and has also guided and informed empirical work, such as a recently published meta-analysis in *Psychological Bulletin* (Sedlmeier et al., 2012), as well as a special issue on spirituality that appeared in *Psychological Studies*, the official journal of the Indian National Academy of Psychology (Oman, Duggal, & Misra, 2018).

Rao and Paranjpe (2016, p. 16) argue that the indigenous development of psychological ideas can be found in each of the different systems (*darśanas*) of Indian philosophy, perhaps most prominently the Yoga system, whose basic concepts "are accepted by the other systems giving one the impression that Yoga psychology is Indian psychology ... [although] each of the major systems like Nyāya-Vaiśeṣika and Vedānta made significant contributions of their own for understanding human nature [as have] Buddhism and Jainism" (p. 16).

A long-term objective of the *Indian Psychology Movement* is to explore valid modes of *integrating* the best of modern psychology and traditional Indian psychology, an aspiration analogous to long-standing efforts to integrate psychology with Abrahamic traditions (e.g., Stevenson, Eck, & Hill, 2007). Work in that direction includes Rao's Body-Mind-Consciousness Trident model of the person, "implicit in the Indian tradition" and based on recurring themes in Indian psychology. Rao's Trident model distinguishes disturbances in the "mind-body nexus" from disturbances in the "interface between mind and consciousness," resulting in two different sets of practical problems in human living (Rao & Paranjpe, 2016, pp. 153, 209). A small number of measures have also been developed of distinctively Hindu psychological constructs (see Oman, 2019a).

The *Indian Psychology Movement* has generated reflection on epistemological and methodological compatibility (e.g., Bhawuk, 2010), perhaps most fully in Rao and Paranjpe's (2016) authored book. These authors reject behaviorist methodological limitations, affirming that Indian psychology should use a "methodological pluralism" (p. 32) that can embrace interviews, content analysis, phenomenology, participant observation, and case studies, as well as surveys and experiments. A similar stance now receives mainstream affirmation in the West, even if lapses often occur in practice (Patry, 2013). Less familiarly, Rao and Paranjpe (2016) also propose exploring whether psychology's methodological toolkit can be expanded by using meditation to reduce or eliminate "external noise and internal biases [enabling] subjective experience [to lose] its capricious variability and become objective in a significant sense," thereby striving toward an "objective phenomenology" (pp. 30, 34).

According to multiple Indian psychology contributors, a key conceptual difference between Western and Indian psychology concerns *consciousness*. In Western psychology, consciousness "is considered either identical with the mind or a species, a subcategory, of the mind" (Rao & Paranjpe, 2016, p. 33). In contrast, in the Indian conception, "the difference between mind and consciousness is fundamental [and] substantial.... Mind and consciousness are conceptually and functionally independent," yielding implications for the possibilities of altered states of consciousness as well as nonempirical modes of knowing (p. 121).

HINDU VIEWS OF HUMAN NATURE

Hindu views of the nature of the human being possess some distinctive emphases, but much is shared with other major religious traditions: Like other traditions, Hinduism does not identify the human being solely as a bundle of physically evolved impulses. Such views contrast with the scientism and materialism that pervade much of Western popular culture and retain influence in some schools of psychology. Hindu concepts about spiritual fulfillment were described earlier. This section further elaborates on key issues of how Hindus think about their own essential nature and self, and how the self is deeply inter-related with the divine.

Several major Indian psychological constructs are frequently translated as "self" (Rao & Paranjpe, 2016, pp. 12, 94, 133, 141), and were alluded to earlier:

1. The person in their individuality (*jīva*), possessed of individual opinions and traits, with connotations "closest to what is called 'person' in contemporary psychology" (2016, p. 130).

2. The principle of consciousness that resides at the deepest level of each individual (*ātman*, or related constructs such as *puruṣa* and *sākṣin*).

3. The supreme or cosmic principle of reality that as consciousness underlies all of reality as a "universal Self" (*Brahman*) (p. 342).

As noted earlier, Hinduism asserts that a human being's enduring and hence "true" self is his/her deeper consciousness (*ātman*) rather than his/her individual idiosyncrasies and particularities (*jīva*). Thus, Hindu teachings urge people to learn to identify themselves with this true self, paralleled in other traditions by teachings such as that one should "put away ... your old self.... Be renewed ... with the new self, created according to the likeness of God" (Ephesians 4:22–24 NRSV; see also Pennington, 2000).

Hinduism also teaches that one may experientially realize this deeper individual consciousness (*ātman/jīvasākṣin/puruṣa*) as *united* with the supreme divine reality (*Brahman*). As noted earlier, realizing such unity is seen as the primary goal of life. This view resonates with parallel teachings of mystics in many religious traditions, sometimes collectively called the perennial philosophy (Huxley, 1945/1970). Hinduism, like other major religious traditions, agrees that such unitive experiences are possible with the aid of divine grace (*deva-prasāda*, *Śvetāśvatara* 6:21; Radhakrishnan, 1953/1994, pp. 23, 749).

Importantly and distinctively, Hinduism offers varying narratives for the ontological bases of such experiences of unity, that is, varying narratives for *what* is merged during mystical unity experiences. One school of Vedānta conceptualizes realization as attained by "different selves among different individuals ... [each with] intrinsic resemblance to Brahman" (i.e., the Viśiṣṭādvaita Vedānta of Rāmānuja, Rao & Paranjpe, 2016, p. 142). Such views parallel the Abrahamic teachings about humans as created in the image of God (e.g., Genesis 1:27) that inform Western reports such as that of the Protestant Christian William Law (1750, Pryr-1.2–9), who wrote that:

Though God be everywhere present, yet He is only present to thee in the deepest and most central part of thy soul.... This depth is the unity, the eternity, I had almost said the infinity of thy soul; for it is so infinite that nothing can satisfy it or give it any rest but the infinity of God. (also quoted in Huxley, 1945/1970, p. 8)

In addition—or perhaps as a complement—other classical Hindu philosophies narrate experiences of unity through ontologies that affirm that the deepest individual self (ātman) is preexistently *identical* with the universal self (*Brahman*) (i.e., the Advaita Vedānta of Śaṅkara; Rao & Paranjpe, 2016, p. 142). In contrast, Abrahamic narratives are generally more restricted, and insist that "we can never be said to be 'one with God' in a univocal sense, because any affirmation of oneness with the divine nature is incorrect without the addition of some determination or qualification, like *unus 'spiritus'*" (McGinn, 1996, p. 66).

Perhaps due to Hinduism's emphasis on a transformational rather than doctrinal approach to such formulations, and its comfort with complementarities (Reich, 1991), major currents within Hinduism affirm that each form of narration—that evoking difference and that evoking preexisting identity—has an appropriate place, and each reflects different forms of valid spiritual experience (Maharaj, 2018). Moreover, even on the level of popular Hinduism, "identification with the deity, so that the human worshiper becomes divine, is a fundamental objective in Hindu worship (*pūjā*)" (Fuller, 2004, p. 31). Such a stance is consistent with Hinduism's broader tendency that:

unlike Jewish, Christian, and Islamic monotheism … Hinduism postulates no absolute distinction between deities and human beings. The idea that all deities are truly one is … easily extended to proclaim that all human beings are in reality also forms of one supreme deity … [although] in practice, this abstract monist doctrine rarely belongs to an ordinary Hindu's stated religious beliefs.... [Yet] examples of permeability between the divine and human can easily be found in popular Hinduism in many unremarkable contexts [such as the] idea that the bride and groom are divine on their wedding day … [or that] a priest … should carry out a ritual to make himself a form of the god during worship … [or that] a man or woman, or even a child, who becomes possessed by a deity is, while in this state, regarded as a bodily manifestation of the deity within.... A Hindu claiming to be divine is rarely saying anything extraordinary, let alone heretical, and human divine forms are no more and no less than a logical corollary of Hinduism's fluid polytheism. (Fuller, 2004, pp. 30–31)

HINDU VIEWS OF HEALTH, WELL-BEING, AND THRIVING FOR ADHERENTS

Hindu tradition sees mental and physical health as interconnected with each other and with spiritual engagement, which is seen as a support for both. For example, the *Śvetāśvatara Upaniṣad* 2:13 states that the first signs of progress in yoga are "health, a light body, freedom from cravings, a glowing skin, sonorous voice, fragrance of body" (*laghutvam ārogyam alolupatvam varṇaprasādaṁ svarasausṭhavaṁ ca gandhaḥ śubho*).

Moreover, Hindu tradition interprets health as involving a harmony between the various components of an individual. The *Bhagavad-Gītā* 6:16 offers the straightforward advice that success in *yoga* will not come to "those who eat too much or eat too little, who sleep too much or sleep too little." On another level, health represents a harmony between consciousness, mind, and body. Various traditional philosophical systems go into considerable detail in describing the operation of components that should be kept in proper balance, such as the mind, intellect, and ego (*manas, buddhi,* and *ahaṁkāra*), or temperamental tendencies (*guṇas*) such as purity, passion, and inertia (*sattva, rajas,* and *tamas*).

To a lesser but still significant degree, Hindu philosophy is also incorporated into the indigenous Indian healing system known as Āyurveda (Manohar, 2014). A primary emphasis of Āyurveda involves the balancing of bodily humors (*doṣas*) that roughly correspond to movement, heat, and heaviness (*vāta, pitta,* and *kapha*) (see Rao & Paranjpe, 2016, pp. 218–221 and pp. 157–159). Āyurveda views different individuals as possessing different balances (or imbalances) of the *doṣas*, and "each type has its own definition of healthy versus unhealthy functioning ... what promotes health for one personality type may cause illness for another type." For example, "Psychological problems such as anxiety, tension, and psychosomatic illness are associated with a *vāta* constitution and are treated accordingly ... [but] the pitta type ... needs to practice moderation in its relationships and lifestyle, whereas the kapha type needs to stimulate itself in its relationships and lifestyle" (Jaipal, 2004, p. 300).

Although Āyurveda is not the only indigenous Indian healing system—another is the Tamil-derived Siddha system—it demonstrates, according to Manohar (2014, p. 306), the "manner in which all knowledge systems in the Vedic tradition have been organized to serve the dual purpose of material prosperity (*abhyudayaḥ*) and spiritual uplift (*niśreyas*)." As aids to both lower levels of healing (*cikitsā*) and higher levels of healing on the spiritual level (*naiṣṭhikī cikitsā*), the Āyurvedic healer is expected to personally exemplify balance and awareness, and is trained to support and convey principles that include right parenting, right nutrition, right environment, right teacher, and right teaching (e.g., "a balance between acquisition of professional skills and personality development" [Manohar, 2014, p. 306]). Embodiment and individually sensitive support for such principles may be ways that psychotherapists can support Hindu as well as perhaps also non-Hindu clients. Finally, in common with other traditions worldwide, Hindu sacred texts, especially the epics, offer numerous portraits of saints, sages, and other persons who exemplify virtuous personal qualities that are deemed foundational for optimal mental and physical health (Oman, 2013). For example, the *Bhagavad-Gītā* 16:1–3 lists twenty qualities of virtuous persons, and elsewhere describes a self-realized person as manifesting qualities such as being friendly, compassionate, free from selfishness and egoism, firmly established in wisdom, and possessing equanimity (see *Bhagavad-Gītā* 2:54–76; 12:13–19; 14:21–25; and Rao & Paranjpe, 2016, p. 67).

HINDU VIEWS OF SUFFERING, CHANGE, AND MENTAL DISORDERS

Hinduism views the material world as a site of ceaseless change, and teaches that human desires directed to changeable objects can never lead to lasting joy or peace (e.g., *Mahābhārata* 1:75:50; *Manu Smṛti* 2:94). Rao and Paranjpe (2016, p. 59) paraphrase this common traditional theme as follows: "Human desires can never be completely sated by means of objects of pleasure; instead they get stronger like fire flared by fuel." In the Hindu view, only through self-realization/liberation will an individual's personal suffering come to an end, a teaching already present in the early Upanishads (e.g., *Chāndogya Upaniṣad* 7:26:2: "[He who sees life rightly] does not see death nor illness nor any sorrow; He who sees this sees everything and obtains everything everywhere" [Radhakrishnan, 1953/1994, p. 489]). Abrahamic parallels include Augustine of Hippo's theistically expressed observation in his *Confessions* (1.1) that "You have made us for yourself, O Lord, and our hearts are restless until they rest in you."

Within this framework, some of the orthodox Hindu philosophical systems have offered systematic analyses of the nature of suffering, although they avoid intricate diagnostic typologies akin to the *Diagnostic and Statistical Manual of Mental Disorders* or the *International Classification of Diseases*. The Sāṁkhya system, for example, distinguishes between several different internal and external sources of suffering, ranging from bodily imbalances and external falling objects to mental tensions. For overcoming suffering arising from mental tensions, the main remedies in the Sāṁkhya, Yoga, and Advaita approaches involve removing misconstrued notions of the self, and dispelling ignorance, what tradition calls *avidyā*. The main idea is that "a proper understanding of the one who suffers or enjoys would strike at the root of the problem" (Rao & Paranjpe, 2016, p. 60). In some philosophical systems, the domain for psychological intervention is "clearly delineated" from traditional medical approaches such as Āyurveda (Rao & Paranjpe, 2016, p. 58).

Notably, since ancient times, Hinduism has possessed conceptions of unconscious mind, including the well-known concept of *saṁskāra*, definable as "the impressions left behind by experiences and actions that are said to shape future experiences and behavior; cognitive schemas; innate tendencies," as well as "impressions in the mind from previous births" (Rao & Paranjpe, 2016, p. 346). Like habits, *saṁskāras* "predispose the person to behave in certain ways, often working below [the] threshold of one's awareness" (p. 206). A nuanced account of the operation of *saṁskāras* is provided in the Yoga philosophy, which classifies *saṁskāras* broadly into those that are generally helpful (*nirodha*) and those that are unhelpful and productive of suffering (*vyutthāna*). A parallel dual typology is offered for mental movements (*vṛttis*). Yoga practice aims to cultivate favorable *saṁskāras* and mental movements in order to supplant their unfavorable counterparts.

From this Yoga perspective, an underlying cause and contributing factor to addictive behaviors such as alcoholism or smoking, as noted above, is ignorance (*avidyā*). When afflicted with ignorance, people fail to identify with their deep abiding self (*ātman*), and identify instead obsessively with their body and mental habits (*jīva*), putting them at risk of identifying with addiction-related *sensory experience*: "With repetition [of the addictive experience], s/he eventually becomes identified with ... 'If I smoke I feel better'" (Brewer, Elwafi, & Davis, 2013, p. 369).[3] Conversely, by being supported to engage in appropriate spiritual, meditative, or other salutary practices, one may over time "dismantle the addictive loop through a dis-identification with the object or dismantling of [misconstrued] self- identity" (p. 373).

CLINICAL APPLICATIONS

A variety of guidance for working with Hindu psychotherapy clients has been offered in mental health literature (e.g., Durvasula & Mylvaganam, 1994; Juthani, 2004; Sekhsaria, 2019; Sharma & Tummala-Narra, 2014; see also the empirical and conceptual discussion in Hodge, 2004). Many suggestions may best be understood as cultural rather than religious, partly generalizing to Indians of other religious traditions. But the line between religion and other parts of culture can be fuzzy, as cultural practices may become sanctified over time (Oman & Paranjpe, 2018).

For Hindus and most other Indians, a foundational consideration is the importance and sanctity placed on the family. Durvasula and Mylvaganam (1994, p. 103) suggest that therapy with Asian Indians should aspire to achieve "a balance between the individualistic demands of Western culture and the interdependence of the Asian Indian family." Sharma and Tummala-Narra (2014) advise therapists to "Always assume the extended family is there, because they are certainly psychologically present in the client's mind.... A positive side ... is that the therapist can call on family members for support, if the client is willing.... The therapist's respect for the client's place within the family, and for the value that Hindus place on family ties, will accomplish much toward establishing trust and a therapeutic alliance" (pp. 334–335). US Hindus tend to be reluctant to access mental health services partly because they assume that the family should take care of its own (see Sharma & Tummala-Narra, 2014, for various implications).

Other important cultural concerns include the meaning of arranged marriages (and of divorce), divergence between experiences of immigrant parents and their more culturally assimilated children, and reluctance to discuss sensitive issues such as alcoholism or domestic violence outside of the family (Sharma & Tummala-Narra, 2014). Sharma and Tummala-Narra (2014) caution that in contrast to many contemporary ministers and rabbis, Hindu priests and other religious leaders are typically *not* utilized as counselors, and will likely *not* be well situated to refer clients to a psychotherapist—instead, referrals are more likely to come from heads of families, professionals, respected elders, or other community leaders, whose trust will be greatest if a health professional can communicate respect and understanding for the importance of family in Hindu communities. These authors also suggest that Hinduism's incorporation of developmental stages (student, householder, etc.) can make developmental approaches a natural fit for Hindu clients. "Which wants are they pursuing: pleasure, worldly success, or duty? The therapist can combine this information with her or his own knowledge of developmental psychology; then, the client and therapist can share a common language" (p. 339). Furthermore, when properly engaged, beliefs in karma possess an "empowering aspect" (p. 340) that may be used therapeutically by encouraging personal responsibility (for treatment suggestions regarding the rare instances of past-life memories, see Mills & Tucker, 2014).

Sacred and scriptural narratives may also be relevant to treatment. J. P. Balodhi has suggested that some Hindu clients may extensively employ a "nondirect" communication style involving traditional religious narratives ("religious mythology") in order to communicate underlying problems while safeguarding other community members (Balodhi, as described by Hodge, 2004, p. 34). For example, the *Bhagavad-Gītā* describes Prince Arjuna's anguished struggle with himself about engaging in an onerous duty that pits him against much of his extended family. A client who experiences conflicts about duty might potentially raise the topic of Arjuna's difficulties and responses to family conflicts, while remaining cautious about sharing details of his or her own family conflicts. More broadly, Hindu tradition and scripture are extremely rich in portraits of human situations and characters (Rukmani, 2005); asking clients to engage in role play based on a character chosen from the *Mahābhārata* has been found very useful in organizational development psychology (Raghu Ananthanarayanan, personal communication), but to our knowledge has not been tried in clinical psychology.

Like adherents to other religious traditions, Hindu clients stand to benefit when therapists implement general strategies and competencies suggested by Vieten et al. (2016), such as being aware of research on health effects from spiritual practices, and helping clients to "explore and access their spiritual and/or religious strengths and resources" (p. 100). Empirically supported practices drawn from Hindu tradition include frequent repetition of a holy name or mantram on many occasions throughout the day. An expanding empirical research base on this so-called portable practice, much of it involving randomized trials (e.g., Bormann et al., 2018), supports a variety of effects that include reduced depression, burnout, insomnia, and posttraumatic symptoms, and improved spiritual well-being, spiritual integrity, quality of life, leadership, and mindfulness (Oman & Bormann, 2018, p. 94).

Meditative practices are also increasingly studied and incorporated in psychotherapy, and much evidence supports their value (Sedlmeier et al., 2012). Yet many different methods of meditation exist, and evidence shows that different people prefer different methods, perhaps most often the more popular methods in their subculture (Oman, 2019b). For various reasons such diverse preferences should be respected. Science has only begun to study the ways that different components of meditative practices synergize with each other and with culture—using a well-matched method may quite plausibly support long-term maintenance of a meditative practice (Oman, 2019b). Similarly, Walsh and Shapiro (2006, pp. 227–228) provide a cautionary and forceful critique of the all-too-frequent scientific "recontextualization and revisioning of [meditation] practices within an exclusively Western psychological and philosophical framework ... adopting a purely etic (outsider) perspective rather than both etic and emic (insider or native) perspectives [leading to] an assimilative integration that feeds the global 'colonization of the mind' by Western psychology [and] overlooks much of the richness and uniqueness of the meditative disciplines and the valuable complementary perspectives they offer."

Thus, although secularly oriented methods of mindfulness meditation may be well received and indeed a good match for some Hindu clients, others may experience greater cultural affinity and additional benefits from spiritual and devotional forms of meditation that align with traditional Hindu methods and perspectives noted earlier (Lynch et al., 2018; Oman & Bormann, 2018). The acceptability of such approaches is further supported by empirical findings that methods of devotional concentrative meditation as well as mantram repetition can foster mindfulness gains comparable to those from highly promoted secular methods (Oman & Bormann, 2018; see also Xia, Hu, Seritan & Eisendrath, 2019). Yet choice of method is ultimately a matter for individual calling and discernment. Juthani (2004) recommends that therapists learn about local ashrams and monasteries as resources for meditation available to local Hindus.

On a related note, contemporary stretching exercises, popularly called "yoga," possess only a tenuous relationship to traditional Hinduism and to how many/most Hindus know and engage with their tradition. However, such exercises have drawn attention in India and may be a supportive fit for some Hindu clients, even as they may benefit adherents to other traditions. Appropriateness of fit should be handled as an individual matter (see appendix to this chapter).

More broadly, traditional Hindu views of the mind and healing are increasingly being incorporated into well-articulated approaches to psychotherapy. Research on spiritually oriented treatments, including meditation, has been under way at several sites in India, including SVYASA University near Bangalore, and the Krishnamacharya Yoga Institute in Chennai. Much of this research has focused on physiological outcomes, but psychological outcomes have also received attention (e.g., Tekur, Nagarathna, Chametcha, Hankey & Nagendra, 2012). Efforts are under way to integrate Indian psychology into graduate-level training in universities that include Sri Sri University in Cuttack, Odisha, MIT Pune in Maharashtra, and others. Furthermore, incorporation of coursework in Indian psychology nationwide has been recommended by the Indian government as a required topic in psychology training in Indian universities. In the long run, such developments stand to generate a wider spectrum of Hindu-oriented empirically supported psychotherapies available not only in India but worldwide and in the West.

Last but not least, psychotherapists who possess relevant skills may wish to follow Durvasula and Mylvaganam's (1994) recommendation to become familiar with community religious advisers as well as practitioners of traditional systems such as Āyurveda, and "introduce themselves as a referral for further treatment" (p. 106). Establishing cooperative referral networks has been found a feasible foundation for a health-care "pluralism [that] views all sectors as coexisting parts of a connected system in which clients concurrently or continuously use different types of care" (Shields et al., 2016, p. 386). Such models of care have been found especially helpful in rural India, where trained modern mental health professionals remain scarce, but may also potentially benefit Hindu communities in other locations where religiously and culturally sensitive mental health care may not be plentiful (Shields et al., 2016).

SUMMARY, FUTURE DIRECTIONS, AND CONCLUSION

To encourage better psychological understanding of Hindus, especially Hindu psychotherapy clients, this chapter began by summarizing a variety of beliefs and practices that are foundational to Hinduism, a tradition that is often misunderstood in the West. We pointed out similarities and differences with Abrahamic traditions, suggesting that one of the most distinctive features of Hinduism was its fluidity. In subsequent sections we looked more closely at several facets of Hinduism that are of particular relevance to psychotherapists and to implementing spiritual and religious psychotherapeutic competencies (e.g., Vieten et al., 2016). This deeper exploration of traditional views was intended to complement previous psychotherapeutic resources on Hindus that do not address recent developments, or that place greater emphasis on primarily cultural issues (Durvasula & Mylvaganam, 1994; Hodge, 2004; Juthani, 2004; Sharma & Tummala-Narra, 2014). Various sections of this chapter in turn explored traditional Hindu views of science, human psychology, human nature, health, suffering, and clinical applications. Each of these facets of Hinduism is relevant to building therapeutic alliances with Hindu clients, helping them gain insight about personal difficulties, and helping them draw upon resources from Hindu tradition as well as from mental health-care systems. Such information can also facilitate building collaborative public health partnerships with Hindu communities (Oman, 2018).

The growing literature on psychotherapy with Hindus represents a useful resource for Western psychotherapists, but additional information would support further expansion and strengthening of psychotherapeutic support for Hindu clients. One fundamental need is for more psychological study of Hindu populations and Hindu religiousness: compared to other major religious traditions, Hinduism has received comparatively little empirical psychological study. For example, relatively few measurement instruments have been validated in Hindu populations, and few instruments measure constructs specific to Hinduism (Oman, 2019a). Instrument development attempts are merited for diverse Hindu constructs ranging from views of stages of life (āśramas) to faith (śraddhā) in the human or personal possibility of self-realization. Of special relevance would be empirical studies from Indian psychology perspectives that explore and test, especially in Hindu populations, the validity and operation of Indian psychology principles and practices retrieved from Hindu tradition. For example, can we measure the multiple dimensions of how Hindus engage in the repetition of God's name (nāma-japa) in their daily lives? (See Oman & Singh [2018] for one agenda of potentially generative research questions.)

In addition, we need more understanding of Western immigrant Hindu populations and their help-seeking. Strength-based approaches can be valuable, and Sharma and Tummala-Narra (2014, p. 343) suggest studying how North American Hindus manage to "maintain Hindu family values ... cultivate the strong affection and care given to children and elderly people ... [and] shape their religious identity." Also needed is better understanding of how some North American Hindus, despite stigma and other obstacles, manage to effectively make use of professional support; of the incidence and prevalence of various problems; and of effective ways to train Western psychotherapists for working with Hindu clients (Durvasula & Mylvaganam, 1994). Of special practical interest will be understanding how therapy with Hindu populations may be informed by therapeutic findings and approaches emerging from the *Indian Psychology Movement* as well as research on spiritual practices especially congenial to or embedded in Hindu tradition (Lynch et al., 2018; Oman & Bormann, 2018; Rao & Paranjpe, 2016; Tekur et al., 2012). In the meantime, the authors hope that this chapter functions as a useful aid to informed and empathetic understanding of clients adhering to the world's oldest and one of its largest, most complex and inclusive, and increasingly global religious traditions: Hinduism.

APPENDIX: CLARIFYING THE WORD "YOGA"

For thousands of years in India, the word *yoga* as a cultural practice primarily referred to systematic spiritual practice for attaining self-realization (*mokṣa, kaivalya,* etc.). However, in the twentieth century, new primary connotations became widely dominant: In a sudden sea change over a few decades, "yoga" began to refer to various physical postures and stretching exercises disseminated widely in what Singleton (2013) has called "transnational anglophone yoga" (p. 38). If a Hindu client refers to "yoga," a human service professional would do well to seek clarity on whether a traditional or modern transnational meaning is intended.

Importantly, although most modern postural yoga instructors assert that their teachings can be traced to Patañjali's *Yoga Sūtras,* there is enormous heterogeneity in the attention given to spiritual goals in modern presentations of yoga stretching exercises. Many versions of modern postural yoga place almost exclusive emphasis on yoga as a physical exercise, rather than as an accompaniment and preparation for meditation and other components of the eight-limbed (*aṣṭāṅga*) yoga taught in the *Yoga Sūtras* as the classical yoga path of meditation (*dhyāna yoga*). In contrast, posture (*āsana*) is mentioned in only 2 of the *Yoga Sūtras'* 196 aphorisms (2:29 and 2:46), and was often omitted from early modern formulations of spiritual yoga (Singleton, 2013).

Much empirical research has linked "yoga" to favorable mental and physical health outcomes (Bussing et al., 2012). Yet whereas posture is a dominant component of such interventions, the role of spiritual goals in their content or impact remains far from clear. Among more than four hundred modern empirical intervention studies of "yoga" that had been conducted prior to mid-2012, Elwy et al. (2014) found that most (81 percent) included a posture component (*āsana*), with only much smaller proportions including other activities such as breathing practices/exercises (42 percent), meditation (23 percent), relaxation exercises (15 percent), mindfulness or awareness (5.6 percent), or various others (each less than 5 percent). "Devotional sessions/song or prayer" (p. 229) were a component of twenty studies (4.3 percent), all conducted in India. In view of such diversity, whether a Hindu client would experience any specific modern form of postural yoga practice as psychologically or spiritually beneficial or relevant must be handled as an individual issue.

REFERENCES

Akhilananda, S. (1951). *Mental health and Hindu psychology*. New York: Harper & Bros.

Baumann, M. (2009). Templeisation: Continuity and change of Hindu traditions in diaspora. *Journal of Religion in Europe, 2*, 149–179.

Bhawuk, D. P. S. (2010). A perspective on epistemology and ontology of Indian psychology: A synthesis of theory, method and practice. *Psychology and Developing Societies, 22*, 157–190.

Bormann, J. E., Thorp, S. R., Smith, E., Glickman, M., Beck, D., Plumb, D., Elwy, A. R. (2018). Individual treatment of posttraumatic stress disorder using mantram repetition: A randomized clinical trial. *American Journal of Psychiatry, 175*, 979–988.

Breslauer, S. D. (1983). The ethics of "gilgul." *Judaism, 32*, 230.

Brewer, J. A., Elwafi, H. M., & Davis, J. H. (2013). Craving to quit: Psychological models and neurobiological mechanisms of mindfulness training as treatment for addictions. *Psychology of Addictive Behaviors, 27*, 366–379.

Bussing, A., Michalsen, A., Khalsa, S. B. S., Telles, S., & Sherman, K. J. (2012). Effects of yoga on mental and physical health: A short summary of reviews. *Evidence-Based Complementary and Alternative Medicine, 2012*, 165410.

Cornelissen, M. (2002). Pondicherry Manifesto of Indian Psychology. *Psychological Studies, 47*, 168–169.

Dorman, E. R. (2011). Hinduism and science: The state of the South Asian science and religion discourse. *Zygon, 46*, 593–619.

Durvasula, R. S., & Mylvaganam, G. A. (1994). Mental health of Asian Indians: Relevant issues and community implications. *Journal of Community Psychology, 22*, 97–108.

Ecklund, E. H., Johnson, D. R., Vaidyanathan, B., Matthews, K. R. W., Lewis, S. W., Thomson, R. A., Jr., & Di, D. (2019). *Secularity and science: What scientists around the world really think about religion*. New York: Oxford University Press.

Elwy, A. R., Groessl, E. J., Eisen, S. V., Riley, K. E., Maiya, M., Lee, J. P., Park, C. L. (2014). A systematic scoping review of yoga intervention components and study quality. *American Journal of Preventive Medicine, 47*, 220–232.

Fuller, C. J. (2004). *The camphor flame: Popular Hinduism and society in India*. Rev. ed. Princeton, NJ: Princeton University Press.

Grinsell, S. (2010). Caste and the problem of social reform in Indian equality law. *Yale Journal of International Law, 35*, 199–236.

Hinduism and Science: Contemporary Considerations [special section]. (2012). *Zygon, 47*, 549–623.

Hodge, D. R. (2004). Working with Hindu clients in a spiritually sensitive manner. *Social Work, 49*, 27–38.

Huxley, A. (1945/1970). *The perennial philosophy*. New York: Harper & Row.

Jaipal, R. (2004). Indian conceptions of mental health, healing, and the individual. In U. P. Gielen, J. M. Fish, & J. G. Draguns (Eds.), *Handbook of culture, therapy, and healing* (pp. 293–308), Mahwah, NJ: Erlbaum.

Juthani, N. V. (2004). Hindus and Buddhists. In A. M. Josephson & J. R. Peteet (Eds.), *Handbook of spirituality and worldview in clinical practice* (pp. 125–137). Washington, DC: American Psychiatric Publishing.

Kumar, A. (2019). *Ancient Hindu science: Its transmission and impact on world cultures*. San Rafael, CA: Morgan & Claypool.

Law, W. (1750). *The spirit of prayer, or, the soul rising out of the vanity of time, into the riches of eternity*. 2nd ed. London: Printed for W. Innys.

Lynch, J., Prihodova, L., Dunne, P. J., Carroll, Á., Walsh, C., McMahon, G., & White, B. (2018). Mantra meditation for mental health in the general population: A systematic review. *European Journal of Integrative Medicine, 23*, 101–108.

MacGregor, G. (1978). *Reincarnation in Christianity: A new vision of the role of rebirth in Christian thought*. Wheaton, IL: Theosophical Publishing House.

Maharaj, A. (2018). *Infinite paths to infinite reality: Sri Ramakrishna and cross-cultural philosophy of religion*. New York: Oxford University Press.

Manohar, P. R. (2014). The blending of healing and pedagogy in Āyurveda. In M. Cornelissen, G. Misra, & S. Varma (Eds.), *Foundations and applications of Indian psychology* (pp. 303–313), Delhi: Pearson.

Mazumdar, S., & Mazumdar, S. (2009). Religion, immigration, and home making in diaspora: Hindu space in Southern California. *Journal of Environmental Psychology, 29*, 256–266.

McGinn, B. (1996). Love, knowledge, and *unio mystica* in the Western Christian tradition. In M. Idel & B. McGinn (Eds.), *Mystical union in Judaism, Christianity, and Islam: An ecumenical dialogue* (pp. 59–86), New York: Continuum.

Mills, A., & Tucker, J. B. (2014). Past-life experiences. In E. Cardeña, S. J. Lynn, & S. Krippner (Eds.), *Varieties of anomalous experience: Examining the scientific evidence* (pp. 303–332), Washington, DC: American Psychological Association.

Misra, G. (2014). Knowing in the Indian tradition. In M. Cornelissen, G. Misra, & S. Varma (Eds.), *Foundations and applications of Indian psychology* (pp. 119–133), Delhi: Pearson.

Mlecko, J. D. (1982). The guru in Hindu tradition. *Numen, 29*, 33–61.

Nadkarni, M. V. (2003). Is caste system intrinsic to Hinduism? Demolishing a myth. *Economic and Political Weekly, 38*, 4783–4793.

Nicholson, A. J. (2010). *Unifying Hinduism: Philosophy and identity in Indian intellectual history*. New York: Columbia University Press.

Oman, D. (2013). Spiritual modeling and the social learning of spirituality and religion. In K. I. Pargament, J. J. Exline, & J. W. Jones (Eds.), *APA handbook of psychology, religion, and spirituality*. Vol. 1: *Context, theory, and research* (pp. 187–204). Washington, DC: American Psychological Association.

Oman, D. (Ed.). (2018). *Why religion and spirituality matter for public health: Evidence, implications, and resources*. Cham, Switzerland: Springer International.

Oman, D. (2019a). Introduction to the special section: Psychology of Indian spirituality and religion, emerging perspectives. *Psychology of Religion and Spirituality, 11,* 87–90.

Oman, D. (2019b). Studying the effects of meditation: The first 50 years. In M. Farias, D. Brazier, & M. Lalljee (Eds.), *The Oxford handbook of meditation*. Oxford: Oxford University Press.

Oman, D., & Bormann, J. E. Eknath Easwaran's mantram and passage meditation as applied Indian psychology: Psycho-spiritual and health effects. *Psychological Studies, 63,* 94–108.

Oman, D., & Driskill, J. D. (2003). Holy name repetition as a spiritual exercise and therapeutic technique. *Journal of Psychology and Christianity, 22,* 5–19.

Oman, D., Duggal, C., & Misra, G. (Eds.). (2018). Spirituality and psychology: Emerging perspectives [special issue]. *Psychological Studies, 63*(2).

Oman, D., & Paranjpe, A. C. (2018). Indian spirituality: How relevant is Pargament's framework? *Psychological Studies, 63,* 140–152.

Oman, D., & Singh, N. N. (2018). Combining Indian and Western spiritual psychology: Applications to health and social renewal. *Psychological Studies, 63,* 172–180.

Patry, J.-L. (2013). Beyond multiple methods: Critical multiplism on all levels. *International Journal of Multiple Research Approaches, 7,* 50–65.

Pechilis, K. (Ed.). (2004). *The graceful guru: Hindu female gurus in India and the United States*. New York: Oxford University Press.

Pennington, M. B. O. (2000). *True self, false self: Unmasking the spirit within*. New York: Crossroad.

Peres, J. F. P. (2012). Should psychotherapy consider reincarnation? *Journal of Nervous and Mental Disease, 200,* 174–179.

Pew Research Center. (2012). The global religious landscape. Washington, DC: Pew Research Center. http://www.pewforum.org/global-religious-landscape.aspx.

Prabhavananda. (1963/1979). *The spiritual heritage of India*. Hollywood, CA: Vedanta Press.

Radhakrishnan, S. (1953/1994). *The principal Upaniṣads*. New Delhi: HarperCollins India.

Rambachan, A. (2008). "Is caste intrinsic to Hinduism?" *Tikkun, 23*(1), January/February, 59–61.

Rao, K. R., & Paranjpe, A. C. (2016). *Psychology in the Indian tradition*. New Delhi; Heidelberg: Springer.

Reich, K. H. (1991). The role of complementarity reasoning in religious development. *New Directions for Child Development, 52,* 77–89.

Rukmani, T. S. (2005). *The Mahābhārata: What is not here is nowhere else (Yannehāsti na Tadkvacit).* New Delhi: Munshiram Manoharlal Publishers.

Savishinsky, J. (2004). The volunteer and the sannyasin: Archetypes of retirement in America and India. *International Journal of Aging & Human Development, 59,* 25–41.

Schouten, J. P. (2008). *Jesus as guru: The image of Christ among Hindus and Christians in India.* Amsterdam: Brill.

Sedlmeier, P., Eberth, J., Schwarz, M., Zimmermann, D., Haarig, F., Jaeger, S., & Kunze, S. (2012). The psychological effects of meditation: A meta-analysis. *Psychological Bulletin, 138,* 1139–1171.

Sekhsaria, K. P. (2019). *Hindu Indian American conceptions of mental health.* Rutgers University. Psy.D. dissertation.

Sharma, A. (2001). *Classical Hindu thought: An introduction.* New Delhi; Oxford: Oxford University Press.

Sharma, A. R., & Tummala-Narra, P. (2014). Psychotherapy with Hindus. In P. S. Richards & A. E. Bergin (Eds.), *Handbook of psychotherapy and religious diversity* (pp. 321–345). Washington, DC: American Psychological Association.

Shields, L., Chauhan, A., Bakre, R., Hamlai, M., Lynch, D., & Bunders, J. (2016). How can mental health and faith-based practitioners work together? A case study of collaborative mental health in Gujarat, India. *Transcultural Psychiatry, 53,* 368–391.

Singleton, M. (2013). Transnational exchange and the genesis of modern postural yoga. In B. Hauser (Ed.), *Yoga traveling: Bodily practice in transcultural perspective* (pp. 37–56). Heidelberg: Springer International Publishing.

Sinha, J. (1934). *Indian psychology: perception.* London: Kegan Paul.

Smith, H. (1991). *The world's religions: Our great wisdom traditions.* San Francisco: HarperSanFrancisco.

Smith, H. (2012). *The Huston Smith reader.* Berkeley: University of California Press.

Srinivasan, M., Kaplan, E., & Dahl, A. (2019). Reasoning about the scope of religious norms: Evidence from Hindu and Muslim children in India. *Child Development, 90,* e783–e802.

Stevenson, D. H., Eck, B. E., & Hill, P. C. (Eds.). (2007), *Psychology & Christianity integration: Seminal works that shaped the movement.* Batavia, IL: Christian Association for Psychological Studies.

Subbarayappa, B. V. (2006). Science and Hinduism: Some reflections. In F. N. Watts & K. Dutton (Eds.), *Why the science and religion dialogue matters: Voices from the international society for science and religion* (pp. 91–100). Philadelphia: Templeton Foundation Press.

Suchday, S., Santoro, A. F., Ramanayake, N., Lewin, H., & Almeida, M. (2018).

Religion, spirituality, globalization reflected in life beliefs among urban Asian Indian youth. *Psychology of Religion and Spirituality, 10*, 146–156.

Tekur, P., Nagarathna, R., Chametcha, S., Hankey, A., & Nagendra, H. R. (2012). A comprehensive yoga program improves pain, anxiety and depression in chronic low back pain patients more than exercise: An RCT. *Complementary Therapies in Medicine, 20*, 107–118.

Vieten, C., Scammell, S., Pierce, A., Pilato, R., Ammondson, I., Pargament, K. I., & Lukoff, D. (2016). Competencies for psychologists in the domains of religion and spirituality. *Spirituality in Clinical Practice, 3*, 92–114.

Walsh, R. (2015). What is wisdom? Cross-cultural and cross-disciplinary syntheses. *Review of General Psychology, 19*, 278–293.

Walsh, R., & Shapiro, S. L. (2006). The meeting of meditative disciplines and Western psychology: A mutually enriching dialogue. *American Psychologist, 61*, 227–239.

White, C. J. M., Norenzayan, A., & Schaller, M. (2019). The content and correlates of belief in karma across cultures. *Personality & Social Psychology Bulletin, 45*, 1184–1201.

Xia, T., Hu, H., Seritan, A. L., & Eisendrath, S. (2019). The many roads to mindfulness: A review of nonmindfulness-based interventions that increase mindfulness. *Journal of Alternative and Complementary Medicine, 25*, 874–889.

ENDNOTES

1. Unlike the Buddha, who lived earlier and taught in India (circa fifth century BCE), Jesus does not appear in Hindu scriptural lists of avatars, although he has been viewed as such by a number of modern Hindu spiritual leaders. Similar affirmations are also widespread in popular culture (e.g., "In the very popular posters and calendar pictures sold in bazaars and at the temples, we invariably find illustrations of Christ next to the usual prints of Rama and Krishna.... Comic books with stories from Hindu mythology are especially loved by children in India [including] a volume devoted to Jesus Christ, which just like the others has undergone many reprints" [Schouten, 2008, p. 266]).

2. Srinivasan and colleagues (2019, p. 799) report findings suggesting "that children raised in a pluralistic society can not only be aware of the range of norms that exist within their society—including those they do not follow—but can flexibly differentiate between norms that apply only to their own group (e.g., Hindu norms for a Hindu child), norms that apply to other groups (e.g., Muslim norms for a Hindu child), and norms that apply to everyone (e.g., moral norms)."

3. Hinduism and Buddhism share many psychological understandings of addictions and other mental phenomena, and much of Brewer et al.'s (2013) mindfulness model applies equally well to the psychology of the *Yoga Sūtras*.

JACQUELINE S. GRAY

PSYCHOLOGY OF NORTH AMERICAN INDIGENOUS SPIRITUALITY

AN INTRODUCTION TO THE HISTORY OF
INDIGENOUS AMERICAN SPIRITUALITY

Trying to describe North American Indigenous spirituality of the original residents of Turtle Island is an enormous task. Turtle Island is the original name for the North American continent before colonizers came and renamed the Americas for the Italian explorer who sailed from Portugal, Amerigo Vespucci. The residents of these lands were called "Indians" because the explorers believed they reached the coast of India. The diversity of this land before colonization was vast. Even today the numbers are far beyond describing other organized religions throughout the world. Today, there are 574 federally recognized tribes[1] (Bureau of Indian Affairs, 2020), 63 state-recognized tribes[2] (Salazar, 2016), and about 400 unrecognized tribes (Mittal et al., 2012) in the United States. In Canada, there are 634 First Nations,[3] Métis,[4] and Inuit[5] (Parrott & Filice, 2019). During colonization, an estimated 10 million Indigenous people of North America were reduced to less than 250,000 remaining in 1900 from violence, biological warfare, and epidemics (Rensick, 2011). Many North American

Author's note: It is with great humility that I approach an effort that I feel very ill-equipped to complete. I am not a holy person from an Indigenous people, nor am I an expert or one to speak of the spirituality of Indigenous people of Turtle Island. I have asked for Creator's guidance as I attempt to describe Indigenous spirituality. I ask the forgiveness of my elders and the spiritual leaders and holy people who know far more than I can attempt to address in this one chapter. I apologize and mean no disrespect for any errors in that they are mine and mine alone and not representative of any tribal spiritual belief or ceremony.

Indigenous nations and spiritual beliefs were lost, but these numbers represent the ones who remain.

Before colonization, each North American Indigenous nation or village had its own spiritual beliefs and ceremonies that existed for thousands of years. Some may be similar within related tribal groups, such as the Ojibwe of the upper Midwest of the United States and Canada; the Pueblos of New Mexico; the Lakota, Dakota, Nakota (Assiniboine), Cheyenne, and Arapahoe of the Northern Plains; or the Iroquois Confederacy (Seneca, Cayugas, Onondagas, Oneidas, and Mohawks) along the border of New York and Canada. Alaska Natives[6] include seven distinct cultures: Athabascan; Evak; Hadia; Tlingit; Tsimshian; Eskimo, including Inuit, Yupik, and Sugpiaq; and Aleut or Unangan. The spirituality of each of these groups has a long history and was impacted by European colonization across the lower forty-eight states among American Indian[7] nations and by Russians and Europeans in Alaska.

Early colonization of North, South, and Central America included Christian missions from Spain, France, and other countries. This resulted in slavery, torture, murder, and genocide of the North American Indigenous residents of the area (Forbes, 1979; Methot, 2019; Tinker, 1993). The Spanish Inquisition that began in Europe came to the New World and was established in Mexico, where Catholic inquisitors tortured North American Indigenous people until they confessed their infractions or died (Vose, 2013). Mexico at the time stretched north through California in the west.

Another aspect of forced religious beliefs by colonizers is the concept of Thanksgiving. The stereotypical version of Thanksgiving where "Indians sat down with the Pilgrims who they saved by providing food and everyone became friends" is a concept still taught in schools today. The first "Thanksgiving Day," contrary to modern teachings, took place in 1637 when William Bradford, the governor of Massachusetts at the time, proclaimed "Thanksgiving Day" be celebrated "in honor of the bloody victory, thanking God that the battle had been won" where seven hundred Pequots were slaughtered (Estes, 2019). Subsequent "Thanksgiving Days" were commonly celebrated after massacres of Indigenous people along the eastern coast of Turtle Island.

Through most of US history, federal policy has outlawed North

American Indigenous spirituality (religion) and ceremonies. This was the antithesis of religious freedom guaranteed in the First Amendment to the US Constitution (Jefferson, 2019). The US policies that suppressed Indigenous traditions, practices, and religious freedoms through military force, imprisonment, and withholding of rations and starvation included the Indian Civilization Fund Act (1819), Rules for the Court of Indian Offenses (1882), the Indian Religious Crimes Code (1883), and Circular 1665 (1922).

In 1818, President James Monroe, encouraging the passage of the Indian Civilization Act of 1819, stated:

Experience has clearly demonstrated that independent savage communities cannot long exist within the limits of a civilized population. To civilize them, and even to prevent their extinction, it seems to be indispensable that their independence as communities should cease, and that the control of the United States over them should be complete and undisputed. (Monroe, 1818)

This act set up the process that established boarding schools. Indian Affairs Commissioner Thomas L. McKenney was to select people of "good moral character" to teach the Indians. McKenney's interpretation was to select missionaries to be the people of "good moral character" to establish the boarding schools that stripped North American Indigenous children of their identities, including their spirituality (Trafzer, Keller, & Sisquoc, 2006, p. 10).

The persistence of the commissioner of Indian Affairs lasted from 1878 until the secretary of the interior approved the "rules for the court of Indian offenses" that was established to repress the "heathenish dances" including the sun dance, scalp-dance, and Hopi snake-dance—basically, making spiritual gatherings and feasts illegal and punishable by imprisonment (Price, 1883; VanDevelder, 2009).

Once North American Indigenous people were relegated to reservation lands in the late nineteenth century, the children were taken and sent to residential schools, many run by religious orders, to "kill the Indian and save the man" as Captain Richard H. Pratt decreed (Churchill, 2004; Pratt, 1892; Zalcman, 2016). Children as young as five years were removed from their homes and transported with other children who did not speak their same language across hundreds of miles to schools where their hair was cut, their clothes were burned, and they were not allowed to speak their traditional language, pray in their traditional way, or eat the foods they were used to eating (Trafzer, Keller, & Sisquoc, 2006). Many died. Others were tortured, maimed, and abused by teachers, spiritual leaders, and caregivers.

The policies that helped to overturn these religious persecutions included the Wheeler Howard Act of 1934 (the Indian Reorganization Act) and the American Indian Religious Freedom Act of 1978 (O'Brien, 2008). The Indian Reorganization Act allowed North American Indigenous nations to reorganize for self-government. While this act, also known as the Indian New Deal, did not specifically address North American Indigenous religious freedom, it did provide more opportunities for self-determination(Deloria, 1969/1988). In 1978 Public Law No. 95-341, Stat. 469, the American Indian Religious Freedom Act (AIRFA), or US Code §1996, was enacted by the United States allowing for the protection and preservation of American Indians' inherent rights to "believe, express, and exercise the traditional religions of the American Indian, Eskimo, Aleut, and Native Hawaiians," including access to sites, use and possession of sacred objects, and the freedom to worship through ceremonies and traditional rituals (United States, 1978). AIRFA was amended in 1994 to allow for the religious use of peyote (United States, 1994).

By the time AIRFA passed, much traditional healing was erased from many North American Indigenous communities because of the persecution of their practices. Among those that retained their practices there is suspicion and secrecy because of previous oppression and misappropriation by "New Agers"[8] of anything that is shared (Gone, 2010; Trujillo, 2000). Because of persecution for their beliefs, North American Indigenous people became secretive about the practices and for many years did not speak outside clan and family circles about them. *Black Elk Speaks* and *The Sacred Pipe* are probably the most well-known accounts of Lakota spirituality from a Lakota holy man (Black Elk & Lyon, 1991; Brown, 1952/2012; Neihardt, 1932/1961/1996). The broadest description of North American Indigenous spirituality on Turtle Island comes from a project with over forty American Indian nations, Alaskan Native villages, and Canadian First Nations from *The Sacred Tree* (Bopp, Bopp, Brown, & Lane, 1988). Other broader North American Indigenous spirituality perspectives come from *A Native American Theology* (Kidwell, Noley, & Tinker, 2001) and *Native American Postcolonial Psychology* (Duran & Duran, 1995). Because of the forced assimilation of various forms of Christianity from Spanish missionaries, missionary boarding schools, and federal policies, much of North American Indigenous spirituality today is a mixture of those influences with the traditional spirituality of Western Christianity (Duran & Duran, 1995; Kidwell, Noley, & Tinker, 2001; Zimmerman, 2011). In some areas there may be a drum group and Indigenous singers and songs along with traditional gospel music, use of garments woven with Indigenous symbols, smudging with sage combined with the use of incense, and other meldings of Indigenous spirituality with Western Christianity.

CONCEPTS OF THE PSYCHOLOGY OF NORTH AMERICAN INDIGENOUS SPIRITUALITY

North American Indigenous forms of spirituality include and are characterized as animism, shamanism, and cosmology (Duran & Duran, 1995, p. 14; Tooker & Sturtevant, 1979). Animism is a worldview that recognizes the spirits of all things, including rocks, plants, water, animals, and people, and was first described by Christian theologians as primitive superstition and less enlightened than other religions from similar ages (Tylor, 1871). From creation and other stories of North American Indigenous people, animal, plant, and other spirit characters are anthropomorphized to communicate with each other and the people they interact with as a means of showing respect for everything that contributes to equilibrium in nature (Zimmerman, 2011, p. 146). These beliefs highlight the importance of maintaining environmental and life balance. An animal or plant taken for food is respected with ceremony and a prayer of thanks for sacrificing its life that the human may live. References in prayers and discussions may include terms that tend to be very inclusive of all creatures, such as two-legged, four-legged, winged, and fish people (see Table 1).

Shamanism, an ancient healing tradition and way of life, is considered a part of North American Indigenous spirituality. A shaman is chosen by the sacred spirits and tribal elders to act as an intermediary between the natural and supernatural worlds (Skyfire, 2019, p. 5). The

TABLE 1. TERMS FOR THE CREATURES OF THE EARTH FROM THE LAKOTA CULTURE

Name	Description
Creepy-crawlers	Those that live close to the ground or the Earth in holes, including snakes, lizards, ants, spiders, etc.
Fish people	Those beings that live in the water.
Four-leggeds	Quadrupeds, those beings with four legs.
Thunder Spirits or Thunder Beings	Those powerful beings that come from the West with either thunder or lightning.
Two-leggeds	Humans or those that come in the appearance of humans.
Winged people	All of those that fly in the air, whether bird, mammal, or insect.

Source: Black Elk & Lyon, 1991

shaman may share visions or prophecies that are important in guiding the people in a good way that respects tradition and spirit. Most North American Indigenous people dislike the term "shaman" because it comes from a foreign culture, the Tungus people of eastern Siberia, and prefer the term "holy people" instead (Zimmerman, 2011).

Holy people can be confused with medicine men, so it's helpful to differentiate. A holy person may be a medicine man, but a medicine man need not be a holy person. A holy person has visions and prophecies that are used to guide and help the people. Holy persons are looked to for their wisdom, vision, and guidance. The holy person may vary from someone who receives a powerful vision to a practitioner who is in touch with the spirits and attempts to impose his or her will upon the supernatural (Zimmerman, 2011). Medicine men are mentored and taught for years by other medicine men to learn all they must about healing before being fully accepted in their role. The training includes songs, prayers, ceremonies, herbal treatments, and other healing approaches. Medicine has to do with the power that is in the universe. As Black Elk said:

that I had the power to practice as a medicine man, curing sick people; and many I cured with the power that came through me. Of course, it was not I who cured.

It was the power from the outer world, and the visions and ceremonies had only made me like a hole through which the power could come to the two-leggeds. If I thought that I was doing it myself, the hole would close up and no power could come through. Then everything I could do would be foolish. (Neihardt, 1932/1961/1996, p. 127).

There are many types of medicine, not just prescribed drugs, but big (something major) versus little (something minor) medicine, good (something positive) versus bad (something bad or negative) medicine, medicine people (the plants used for healing), bear medicine (a ritual for healing), elk medicine (women's medicine), and many others (Black Elk & Lyon, 1991, p. 190; Skyfire, 2019).

Cosmology as related to a North American Indigenous worldview is process related, in relationship and in harmony with the wind, the seasons, and all of creation (Deloria, 1992/2003, pp. 15–16; Duran & Duran, 1995). The process includes what, how, and where something occurred instead of the outcome of the occurrence. It is important to understand the difference between the Western worldview that is dependent upon *when* an event took place and the North American Indigenous worldview that is based upon *where* an event took place. In helping differentiate a Western worldview from an Indigenous one, Duran and Duran (1995) describe the difference:

Western thought conceptualizes a history in a linear temporal sequence, whereas most Native American thinking conceptualizes history in a spatial fashion. Temporal thinking means that time is thought of as having a beginning and end; spatial thinking views events as a function of space or where the event actually took place. (p. 14)

Deloria describes the philosophical importance of American Indians as "their lands—places—having the highest possible meaning and any statements are in reference to that point in their mind" (Deloria, 1992/2003, p. 61). The frame of reference for Indigenous people is the land, especially the original homelands as places and landmarks are sacred. From the view of the eagle, the Black Hills looks like a beating heart over time and under changing weather conditions (Goodman, 1992/2017). The appearance comes from the treasure of minerals from the volcanic activity creating the Black Hills. The Lakota looks at this as the beating heart of the earth. The North American Indigenous view of the earth is that it belongs to all. In the Western European immigrant perspective of Manifest Destiny, the progression across Turtle Island is a steady movement of good experiences and events and placing history and time, in the best possible view. Manifest Destiny was a phrase from the mid- nineteenth century that professed the idea that God had destined the spread of the United States with its capitalism and democracy throughout the North American continent (Deloria, 1992/2003). This violated the North American Indigenous sacred sites that reflected the cosmos and damaged them with miners searching for precious metals (Goodman, 1992/2017). In addition, farmers tilling larger pieces of soil they claimed for their own and ranchers fencing off great areas for their grazing herds of cattle as they moved westward took a perspective of personal ownership of the land rather than a common respect for all it represents (Deloria, 1992/2003). The North American Indigenous worldview is one of process rather than the Western view of ownership and the end product.

COMMONALITIES OF NORTH AMERICAN INDIGENOUS SPIRITUALITY

Although there is great diversity among the North American Indigenous people of Turtle Island, there are some similarities in their beliefs. All have a belief or knowledge that unseen powers exist (Beck & Walters, 1977). God within North American Indigenous spirituality has many names, but significantly the experiences of "god" include a bi-gender representation such as Grandmother and Grandfather, Earth and Sky, Above and Below, Night and Day (Kidwell, Noley, & Tinker, 2001). Yet when North American Indigenous people pray in English, they use male gender pronouns. But in traditional North American Indigenous languages, the words carry the duality of the gender—both male and female (Petoskey, 2009). Another concept that crosses the many cultures and beliefs is the knowledge that all things in the universe are dependent upon each other and it is important to maintain balance and harmony (Beck & Walters, 1977).

The aspect of worship creates a bond between the individual, tribal members, and the great powers, although worship is a personal commitment to the source of life, Creator (Beck & Walters, 1977). To North American Indigenous people, "walking the red road" is a commitment to follow the beliefs and teachings of their ancestors (Petoskey, 2009). The Indigenous people of Turtle Island do not have a religion, but a sacred path that is the individual's unique spiritual journey. It encompasses a way of being, reverence, and compassion for all life, including one's own (Skyfire, 2019). Most North American Indigenous groups have a holy person who is responsible for specialized and secret sacred knowledge. They use the oral tradition to pass that sacred knowledge and ways and practices from generation to generation (Beck & Walters, 1977).

Symbolism is important in representing ideas and feelings that are important. Much like mathematics and writings, North American Indigenous symbols can carry many ideas, purposes, and understanding (Bopp, Bopp, Brown, & Lane, 1988). The eagle feather, medicine wheel, and sacred medicines such as cedar, sage, sweetgrass, and tobacco carry great symbolism and meaning (Bopp, Bopp, Brown, & Lane, 1988; Trujillo, 2000). An eagle crossing one's path is seen as a good sign and bringing "good medicine" to the path one is taking. Sage is looked upon as a means to bless, cleanse, and heal. The cedar is looked to for protection or to cleanse a new home, inviting the unwanted spirits to leave and protecting one from unwanted influences. Sweetgrass is holy grass, and the scent represents the blessing of the love of Mother Earth. The medicine wheel is looked upon as a sign of health, balance in life, and well-being or striving to reach those things. To be human is a necessary part of the sacred that acknowledges that humans make mistakes and are imperfect (Beck & Walters, 1977). The North American Indigenous lifestyle is directly related to their spirituality, the Sacred, and a way to express cultural values and beliefs (Trujillo, 2000).

NATURE OF THE PERSON/SELF AND
MEANING WITHIN THE SACRED

The North American Indigenous person describes oneself to others in relation to their relatives, their people or nation, rituals, spiritual relationships, and responsibilities that are all entwined with the land and nature or place they occupy in the universe (Morgan, Slade, & Morgan, 1997). When introducing oneself, the individual speaks not only their name but the names of parents and grandparents, and identifies their clan and tribal affiliation. They may also identify their spiritual relatives to identify their place in the society. For professionals, this may also come before where they went to school or what their position or profession may be.

For North American Indigenous people, their sense of self is tied to being removed from their ancestral lands because of how closely their identity is linked to that sense of place. The spirituality of each tribe is tied to local landmarks of the ancestral lands. For the Navajo (Diné) the five mountains of their lands are important to who they are as individuals, as a people, and spiritually. For the Lakota, that sense of who they are is related to the Black Hills of South Dakota. Additionally, removing children from their families and homes and sending them to boarding schools cut off the sense of identity with their responsibilities, family relationships, and spiritual relationships (Duran & Duran, 1995; O'Brien, 2008; Trujillo, 2000). The removal also took away their clothes, hair, language, food, ceremonies, and spiritual beliefs. It also disrupted ways of educating, parenting, and the roles each person filled in the community. This damage or "soul wound" frequently led to substance abuse and child abuse, broken relationships, and broken trust as part of the genocide of North American Indigenous people (Deloria, 1992/2003; Duran & Duran, 1995; O'Brien, 2008). North American Indigenous lands have diminished from all of Turtle Island to a total land mass about the size of the state of Idaho (Bureau of Indian Affairs, 2019). Some sacred lands were not given up. The Lakota still today have not accepted what the US government offered for the Black Hills, although the government took control of the land (Gulliford, 2003). All of these things that made the Indigenous persons who they were and linked to their spiritual selves were stripped away to "kill the Indian and save the man," according to Captain Richard Pratt's speech on educating American Indians (Pratt, 1892).

HEALTH AND WELL-BEING/THRIVING
FOR ADHERENTS

The values within North American Indigenous peoples are not identical but contain similar aspects and themes (see Table 2) such as respect, generosity, humility, wisdom, love, and bravery (BigFoot, 1999). These values promote the betterment of the person and preserve society.

TABLE 2. COMPARISON OF OJIBWE, LAKOTA, PUEBLO, AND INUIT VALUES

Ojibwe (Chippewa, Anishinaabe)— Teachings of the Seven Grandfathers	Twelve Lakota Virtues	Pueblo Values	Inuit Societal Values
Nibwaakawin Wisdom	*Woksape* Wisdom	Understanding	*Aajiiqatigiinniq* Decision making through discussion and consensus
Minwaadendamowin Respect	*Wawoohola* Respect	Respect	*Inuuqatigiitsiarniq* Respecting others, relationships, caring for people
	Waunsilap Caring and compassion	Compassion	*Tunnganarniq* Fostering good spirits by being open, welcoming, and inclusive
Miigwe'aadiziwin Generosity	*Canteyuke* Generosity and caring	Empathy	*Pijitsirniq* Serving and providing for family and/or community
Debwewin Truth	*Wowicake* Honesty and truth	Faith	*Pilimmaksarniq/ Pijariuqsarniq* Developing skills through observation, mentoring, practice, and effort

(*table continues*)

TABLE 2. (*continued*)

Ojibwe (Chippewa, Anishinaabe)— Teachings of the Seven Grandfathers	Twelve Lakota Virtues	Pueblo Values	Inuit Societal Values
Dibaadendiziwin Humility	Unsiiciyapi Humility	Balance	Piliriqatigiinniq/ Ikajuqtigiinniq Working together for a common cause
	Wowacintanka Perserverance	Spirituality	Qanuqtuurniq Being innovative and resourceful
Zaagidiwin Love	Cantognake Love	Love	Avatittinnik Kamatsiarniq Respect and care for the land, animals, and environment
Aakodewewin Bravery	Woohitike Bravery		
	Wayunonihan Honor	Peace	
	Icicupi Sacrifice		

Sources: Ojibwe.net (2019); White Wolf Pack (2019); Indian Pueblo Cultural Center (2019), Nunavut (2019)

Some tribes recognize the Sacred Tree as a central focus of their spirituality and a part of their creation stories while some others focus on the Medicine Wheel to give balance and direction for their spiritual growth and wellness. See Table 3 for characteristics of Indigenous creation stories.

THE SACRED TREE

The Sacred Tree, it is told, was planted by the Creator as a place under which all the people of the earth may gather to find healing, power, wisdom, and safety. Its roots spread deep into the body of Mother Earth, and

TABLE 3. CHARACTERISTICS OF NATIVE AMERICAN CREATION MYTHS (STORIES)

Explain the relationship between humans and nature or a natural event

Have ordinary human characteristics that may be good or evil, or animal characters that behave as humans

Have plots that present a problem to solve

Have repetition of phases or actions or the number four (a sacred number to Native Americans)

Contain supernatural elements or trickery

Source: Zimmerman, 2011

its branches reach up as praying hands to Father Sky. The fruits of the Sacred Tree contain the good things the Creator provides for the people: love, caring for others, generosity, patience, wisdom, fairness, courage, justice, respect, humility, and many other fine gifts (Bopp, Bopp, Brown, & Lane, 1988). The ancient ones taught that if the people move away from the protective shadow of the tree, if they fail to seek the nourishment of its fruit, or if they turn against the tree and try to destroy it, a great sorrow will come to the people. They will become sick in their hearts and lose their power. They will no longer dream dreams and see visions. They will quarrel among themselves over trifles and become unable to tell the truth and be honest with one another (Bopp, Bopp, Brown, & Lane, 1988). Some believe this great sickness is alcohol and drugs as it is referred to as "alcohol spirit" (Duran & Duran, 1995). Others believe the removal from ancestral lands (the long walk also known as the Trail of Tears, placement on reservations) and the continued destruction of sacred sites cause the "sickness of the soul" (Duran & Duran, 1995; Kidwell, Noley, & Tinker, 2001; Zimmerman, 2011).

THE MEDICINE WHEEL

The Medicine Wheel is utilized by many Indigenous peoples of Turtle Island (see Figure 1) and is found among societies around the world. Variations of the Medicine Wheel represent the seven directions or the four directions. (The numbers four and seven are particularly sacred

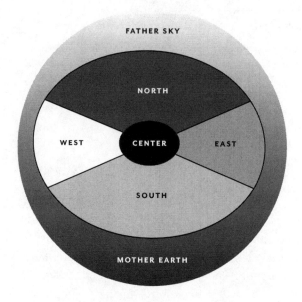

FIGURE 1. Medicine Wheel

among many North American Indigenous peoples.) The seven directions from the Ojibwe include east, south, west, north, up (Father Sky), down (Mother Earth), and inward (the Self or Spirit). This also addresses the Seven Teachings or Seven Grandfathers focused upon the seven teachings or values of the Ojibwe or Anishinaabe People (Ojibwe.net, 2019). The Seven Teachings are humility, bravery, honesty, wisdom, truth, respect, and love.

Among the Lakota, the Medicine Wheel has four directions (east, south, west, and north) (Black Elk & Lyon, 1991; Bopp, Bopp, Brown, & Lane, 1988; Brown, 1952/2012; Neihardt, 1932/1961/1996). Table 4 represents aspects of North American Indigenous beliefs that the four directions represent. The four directions include two crossbars of the Medicine Wheel, and thus those aspects opposite each other need to be in balance (mental-physical, emotional-spiritual) for the crossbars to remain in position and the person's life to be "in balance" or healthy (see Figure 1). (Black Elk & Lyon, 1991; Brown, 1952/2012; Neihardt, 1932/1961/1996).

TABLE 4. REPRESENTATIONS OF VARIOUS BELIEFS ENCOMPASSING THE FOUR
DIRECTIONS OF THE MEDICINE WHEEL

Aspect	East	South	West	North
Elements	Fire	Earth	Water	Air/Wind
Medicines	Tobacco	Sweet Grass	Sage	Cedar
Seasons	Spring	Summer	Autumn	Winter
Health	Mental	Physical	Emotional	Spiritual
Time of Life	Birth–Childhood	Youth–Adolescence	Adulthood –Parents	Elders–Grandparents
Peoples	Red (Indigenous)	Yellow (Asian)	Black (African)	White (European)

Source: Bopp, Bopp, Brown, & Lane, 1988

While the Lakota and Anishinaabe identified the Medicine Wheel as a mechanism demonstrating balance in life, today it is recognized across many North American Indigenous cultures because of the many interactions and cases of sharing between cultures or North American Indigenous religions, making certain aspects "Pan-Indian"[9] in perspective (Duran & Duran, 1995). Much of the Pan-Indian approach came about with the relocation of North American Indigenous people to urban areas in the 1950s and 1960s, which brought about a merging of various Indigenous ceremonies and spiritual beliefs into a collective spiritualism.

VIEW OF MENTAL DISORDERS, PSYCHOLOGICAL SUFFERING, AND PSYCHOLOGICAL CHANGE

While many in Western psychology do not include the spiritual when addressing psychological matters, the psychology of the Indigenous peoples of Turtle Island goes back to its beginnings; living daily a balanced life in concert with the community and acceptance of individuals for the gifts they bring and contributions they make to the community (Katz, 2017; Nebelkopf & Phillips, 2004). The North American Indigenous perspective is holistic and sees the physical, mental, emotional, and spiritual as being a part of the wholeness and health of the person. If all are in balance the person is healthy and becoming their best self. When people are out of balance, problems develop and physical or psychological pain ensues.

Several renowned Western psychologists spent time with North American Indigenous peoples to learn concepts that became "Western" principles of psychology. Abraham Maslow spent time with the Blackfeet Tribe or Blood Nation, taking away his understanding of what became the "hierarchy of needs"; however, clarification of the true North American Indigenous philosophy from the Blackfeet perspective paints a different interpretation that security comes from an understanding and growth within the cultural values and spiritual beliefs of the society (Brown, 2014). When Carl Jung wanted to know about dream interpretation, he traveled to the Southwest United States to learn from the Hopi; however, he too missed the point of North American Indigenous visions and dreams by looking at individual growth of self as opposed to how that growth could contribute to the betterment and direction of the community (Katz, 2017, pp. 188–189). Erickson focused his study of development with the Lakota, but he does not make the leap to the North American Indigenous perspective of the spiritual path as a way of life (Katz, 2017, p. 250). Although making substantial contributions to Western psychology, the interpretations of these North American Indigenous concepts were made from a Western perspective and not the holistic, integrated North American Indigenous perspective (Duran & Duran, 1995).

CLINICAL APPLICATIONS FOR THOSE WORKING
WITH PERSONS IN APPLIED SETTINGS

Some important aspects when counseling North American Indigenous people are addressed in the psychology literature. Some of those points include the following.

INITIAL CONTACT, THERAPEUTIC RELATIONSHIP, AND SOURCE OF PROBLEMS

Many North American Indigenous people do not return after the first counseling session. Thus, it is important to provide a place of cultural safety and trust (Williams, 1999). Cultural safety is "an environment which is safe for people: where there is no assault, challenge or denial of their identity, of who they are and what they need. It is about shared respect, shared meaning, shared knowledge and experience, of learning together with dignity and truly listening" (Williams, 1999, p. 213). This concept addresses developing a relationship between the counselor and the North American Indigenous person. Initially, the person should be welcomed warmly and offered a beverage or something to eat if it is available. This is common courtesy within Indigenous culture. No matter how poor, a person at least offers water to a visitor. The client is a visitor in the treatment setting. Intake paperwork should be minimized. The counselor should begin their introduction using self-disclosure and talking a little about his or her own background, where they come from, who they are, and who their family is. The client can then be asked to talk a little about who they are, their family, their tribe, and how they understand their problem (LaFromboise, Trimble, & Mohatt, 1990; Thomason, 2012). Counselors should listen respectfully, not interrupt, and avoid excessive emphasis on getting answers to standard intake questions. Indigenous North American clients may take a long time to answer and tell stories on the way to the answer that may seem to be off topic by Western counseling approaches. Counselors need to give clients plenty of time to answer and be tolerant of long silences. Indigenous North American clients tend to think and spend time forming their answers before responding. This may take several minutes more and requires a great deal of patience from the counselor. Counselors also need to be patient, genuine, and nondirective, and allow clients to determine the content of counseling sessions (LaFromboise, Trimble, & Mohatt, 1990; Thomason, 2012). Frequently, Western-trained counselors expect standard responses to questions rather than the storytelling approach of the oral tradition of Indigenous North American clients.

COUNSELING RELATIONSHIP ISSUES

The most important thing in working with North American Indigenous people is developing a mutually trusting relationship between the counselor and the client. The counselor should acknowledge that he or she does not know everything, but by working together they may find answers. Once the relationship is built, the North American Indigenous client may be willing to begin sharing information about physical complaints and alcohol, but still be hesitant to share mental health issues. This may be, according to Trujillo, because of the turnover of staff in mental health service units (Trujillo, 2000). A large number of Indian Health Service (IHS) providers go to a service area to qualify for student loan repayment, and once they have completed the two to five years to get that repayment, they leave. Today, more North American Indigenous psychologists are being trained, but there is still a shortage of Indigenous psychologists to fill all the openings in Indian country.

In a survey of mental health providers who worked with North American Indigenous people, 50 percent believed North American Indigenous counselors were more effective than nonindigenous providers; much of this comes from the initial meeting and understanding and respect between the two (Thomason, 2012).

ASSIMILATION INTO WESTERN CULTURE OR TRADITIONAL CULTURE (PRACTICING THE NORTH AMERICAN INDIGENOUS CULTURE)

This factor is always important to consider when working with North American Indigenous people (Garrett, 1996; Lowery, 1983; Rayle, Chee, & Sand, 2006; Zitgow & Estes, 1981). Thomason (2012) found that counselors working with North American Indigenous clients indicated that asking about the client's tribe and culture helps them to understand their tribal identification, acculturation, and how culture is a part of their lives. How knowledgeable and involved the client is with traditional values and practices makes a difference in counseling approaches. North American Indigenous clients who are more assimilated to the dominant culture may do fine with Western counseling practices, but those searching for their identity, even if assimilated, may need assistance in connecting with their North American Indigenous community and practices.

COUNSELING METHODS

More traditional clients view mental health as more holistic and spiritual than Western psychology and training would suggest. "Medicine" from a North American Indigenous perspective involves a system of healing where "forces of good and evil are interwoven in all aspects of the physical, social, psychological, and spiritual being and it is difficult to isolate one aspect for discussion" (Primeaux, 1977, p. 55). When North American Indigenous serving practitioners were asked about which Western counseling theoretical approaches worked best with North American Indigenous people, 24 percent indicated phenomenological approaches focused on relationship building, 12 percent recommended narrative therapy as it fit with the North American Indigenous teaching approach of storytelling, and 6 percent indicated each of the following: interpersonal therapy, family therapy, Jungian therapy, psychoanalytic therapy, and eclectic therapy (Thomason, 2012). Counseling techniques recommended by North American Indigenous serving providers included a client-centered approach (26 percent), narrative therapy (23 percent), cognitive behavioral therapy (23 percent), and motivational interviewing (13 percent), and 10 percent each recommended mindfulness-based approaches, dream analysis, and Gestalt (Thomason, 2012). LaFromboise et al. (1990) recommended "empowerment" of North American Indigenous clients to help them gain some control over issues in their lives by increasing their self-esteem, providing education concerning systemic oppression and its effects, organizing one's resources, developing and solidifying support systems, and advising North American Indigenous clients about tribal and traditional privileges and entitlements. The current focus includes a trauma-informed care perspective when addressing therapy with North American Indigenous people (Brave Heart, Chase, Elkins, & Altschul, 2011).

COUNSELING ISSUES

There are many counseling issues among North American Indigenous people, including historical trauma, depression, anxiety, substance abuse, suicide, anger, low self-esteem, and self-destructive behaviors (Gone, 2010).

HISTORICAL TRAUMA (HT)

In addition to personal traumatic events, North American Indigenous people are subject to adverse childhood experiences (ACEs). North American Indigenous children are two to three times more likely to have more ACEs than non-Hispanic white children of the same age; intergenerational trauma is also recognized as a factor (Brave Heart, 2003; Duran, 2006). Brave Heart (2003) describes historical trauma (HT) as "the cumulative emotional and psychological wounding over the lifespan and across generations, emanating from massive group trauma experiences," and the historical trauma response (HTR) includes "depression, self-destructive behavior, suicidal thoughts and gestures, anxiety, low self-esteem, anger, and difficulty recognizing and expressing emotions" (p. 7). As the number of ACEs increased, the rate of North American Indigenous children having them increased over non-Hispanic white children (Kenney & Singh, 2016).

ALCOHOLISM

This common issue needs exploration especially since the majority of American Indians do not drink or do so in moderation, but the few who do drink to excess usually binge drink (Substance Abuse and Mental Health Services Administration, Center for Behavioral Health Statistics and Quality, 2012).

SUICIDE

The rates of suicide among North American Indigenous populations are much higher among youth and young adults as compared to general populations. Since 2000, the suicide rate of North American Indigenous females has been three to four times that of non-Hispanic whites between the ages of ten and twenty-four (Gray & McCullagh, 2014). Male adolescents committing suicide from North American Indigenous populations did so at rates at 170 percent in 1999 to 264 percent in 2010 to 210 percent in 2016 the rate of Non-Hispanic white adolescents between ten and twenty-four (Gray & McCullagh, 2014). When all ages are considered, North American Indigenous populations have suicide rates 124 percent that of Non-Hispanic whites (Gray & McCullagh, 2014). Therefore, it is extremely important to assess for suicide and discuss the topic when counseling North American Indigenous populations.

TRIBAL-SPECIFIC TREATMENTS

More and more tribes are developing culturally specific treatments that include spiritual counseling, and some Indian Health Service (IHS) facilities have medicine men and medicine women who work with Western-trained providers to make the individual's care more culturally relevant (Rhoades, 2009). Duran (2006) presents his view of a traditional North American Indigenous approach to psychology, although he includes some Buddhism and "New Age" aspects into his integrated approach (Gone, 2010). The White Bison program provides a North American Indigenous approach to substance abuse and trauma healing from a resiliency perspective (Coyhis & White, 2006). One example from my practice was when an Indigenous woman came for counseling regarding a "bad medicine dream." After several sessions from a Western psychological approach, we were making little to no progress. She indicated a wish to go to a traditional sweat lodge ceremony and asked that I go with her. After the sweat that included songs and prayers, we returned to our regular therapy sessions drawing from the spiritual of the sweat lodge and made great progress.

The Society of Indian Psychologists created a commentary on the American Psychological Association's ethical principles and code of conduct to help address the clashes between North American Indigenous practice and Western perspectives. This document contains stories from actual North American Indigenous practices for each principle and standard in the ethics code to provide an understanding of how Western expectations do not fit within North American Indigenous culture and practice (Garcia & Society of Indian Psychologists, 2014). One story addresses a gift given to an Indigenous psychology intern after completing their therapy. The supervisor of the intern focused on the inappropriateness of the gift rather than the symbolism of what was accomplished (p. 47). Another common topic is multiple relationships. Multiple relationships occur when a psychologist who is treating a client is involved in other areas with the client as well, such as school activities, cultural events, commercial interactions, and other instances where they may interact. For example, when I was practicing within a county facility in a small rural community, my children attended the public school. I was part of the suicide assessment team for the school, traveled with the speech and debate team to tournaments, and attended events where my children were involved. I had clients who were on the speech and debate team, some of whom were concerned that I was checking up on them. I also had clients who were salespeople in the community from whom I purchased things. I reassured clients that I wasn't checking up on them and talked about the many roles I played in the community. It was also important to do business in the community to be seen as part of the community and not "too important to interact with community businesses." All of these relationships could be considered multiple relationships. While the American Psychiatric Association discourages such connections, these relationships are expected in Indigenous communities. So few Indigenous psychologists are available, and refusing to help someone who comes to you is considered offensive and can cause harm. The cultural competencies needed in these situations are to cause no harm, maintain boundaries, and most importantly, maintain confidentiality (American Psychiatric Association, 2013, p. 48).

CONCLUSION

Hopefully, this taste of the vastness of North American Indigenous spirituality and culturally safe psychology will help instruct readers on North American Indigenous culture and beliefs and offer an understanding of why North American Indigenous people may be hesitant to share the very personal and Sacred Great Mystery. Much of the cultural competence that is expected is impossible with the vast numbers of cultures represented among the Indigenous peoples of Turtle Island. Spirituality is extremely important and is best approached with cultural humility and a willingness to learn what is and is not appropriate to integrate Indigenous spirituality into the treatment of Indigenous clients. As the Lakota end their prayers and rituals, *Mitakuye Oyasin* (All my relations).

APPENDIX: CREATION STORIES

THE HAUDENOSAUNEE CREATION STORY

The Haudenosaunee (Oneida) People have always recognized that human people are complex, having both good and bad qualities. The creation story serves as a reminder: no human is flawless—the Great Spirit alone is perfect.

Keller George, Wolf Clan member of the Nation's Council, tells a story his maternal great-grandmother told him about the birth of the Evil Spirit and the Good Spirit.

"Long, long ago, the earth was deep beneath the water. There was a great darkness because no sun or moon or stars shone. The only creatures living in this dark world were water animals such as the beaver, muskrat, duck, and loon.

"Far above the water-covered earth was the Land of the Happy Spirits, where the Great Spirit dwelled. In the center of this upper realm was a giant apple tree with roots that sank deep into the ground.

"One day the Great Spirit pulled the tree up from its roots creating a pit in the ground. The Great Spirit called to his daughter, who lived in the Upper World. He commanded her to look into the pit. The woman did as she was told and peered through the hole. In the distance, she saw the Lower World covered by water and clouds.

"The Great Spirit spoke to his daughter, telling her to go into the world of darkness. He then tenderly picked her up and dropped her into the hole. The woman—who would be called Sky Woman by those watching her fall—began to slowly float downward.

"As Sky Woman continued her descent, the water animals looked up. Far above them they saw a great light that was Sky Woman. The animals were initially afraid because of the light emanating from her. In their fear, they dove deep beneath the water.

"The animals eventually conquered their fear and came back up to the surface. Now they were concerned about the woman, and what would happen to her when she reached the water.

"The beaver told the others that they must find a dry place for her to rest upon. The beaver plunged deep beneath the water in search of earth. He was unsuccessful. After a time, his dead body surfaced to the top of the water.

"The loon was the next creature to try to find some earth. He, too, was unsuccessful. Many others tried, but each animal failed. At last, the muskrat said he would try. When his dead body floated to the top, his little claws were clenched tight. The others opened his claws and found a little bit of earth.

"The water animals summoned a great turtle and patted the earth upon its back. At once the turtle grew and grew, as did the amount of earth. This earth became North America, a great island.

"During all this time, Sky Woman continued her gentle fall. The leader of the swans grew concerned as Sky Woman's approach grew imminent. He gathered a flock of swans that flew upward and allowed Sky Woman to rest upon their back. With great care, they placed her upon the newly formed earth.

"Soon after her arrival, Sky Woman gave birth to twins. The first born became known as the Good Spirit. The other twin caused his mother so much pain that she died during his birth. He was to be known as the Evil Spirit.

"The Good Spirit took his mother's head and hung it in the sky, and it became the sun. The Good Spirit also fashioned the stars and moon from his mother's body. He buried the remaining parts of Sky Woman under the earth. Thus, living things may always find nourishment from the soil for it springs from Mother Earth.

"While the Good Spirit provided light, the Evil Spirit created the darkness. The Good Spirit created many things, but each time his brother would attempt to undo his good work.

"The Good Spirit made the tall and beautiful trees, including the pines and hemlock. The Evil Spirit, to be contrary, stunted some trees or put gnarls and knots in their trunks. Other trees he covered in thorns or poisoned their fruit.

"The Good Spirit made bear and deer. The Evil Spirit made poisonous animals such as lizards and serpents to destroy the animals created by his brother.

"When the Good Spirit made springs and streams of pure crystal water, the Evil Spirit poisoned some and placed snakes in others. The Good Spirit made beautiful rivers. The Evil Spirit pushed rocks and dirt into the rivers creating swift and dangerous currents.

"Everything the Good Spirit made his wicked brother attempted to destroy.

"After the Good Spirit completed the earth, he created man out of red clay. Placing the man upon the earth, the Good Spirit instructed the man about how he should live. The Evil Spirit made a monkey from sea foam.

"Upon completion of his work, the Good Spirit bestowed a protecting spirit upon all of his creations. This done, he called his brother and told him he must cease making trouble. The Evil Spirit emphatically refused. The Good Spirit became enraged at his brother's wickedness. He challenged his evil twin to combat. The winner would become the ruler of the world.

"For their weapons they used the thorns of the giant apple tree. The battle raged for many days. The Good Spirit triumphed, overcoming his evil brother. The Good Spirit took his place as ruler of the earth and banished his brother to a dark cave under the ground. In this cave the Evil Spirit was to remain.

"The Evil Spirit, however, has wicked servants who do his bidding and roam upon the earth. The wicked spirits can take any form and cause men to do evil things.

"This is the reason that everyone has both a good heart and a bad heart. Regardless of how good a man is, he still possesses some evil. The reverse also is true. For however evil a man may be, he still has some good qualities. No man is perfect.

"The Good Spirit continues to create and protect mankind. It is the Good Spirit who controls the spirits of good men upon their death. His wicked brother takes possession of the souls of those who are evil like himself. And so, it remains" (George, 2016).

HOPI MIGRATION STORY

According to the Hopi, "The first people migrated upwards through three worlds, eventually emerging in this, the Fourth World. Másaw, their guardian spirit, told them to migrate in each direction until they reached the sea, and then to retrace their steps to find their common homeland. Not all the clans completed their journey. Those who returned symbolized their migrations by two types of spiral: Square, representing their turning back at the seas, and round, showing how they wandered ever closer to their home. The whole pattern traced by the people's journeys forms a great cross, Túwanasavi (Center of the Universe), whose center is in the present-day Hopi homeland" (Zimmerman, 2011).

LAKOTA CREATION STORY

In the beginning, prior to the creation of the Earth, the gods resided in an undifferentiated celestial domain and humans lived in an indescribably subterranean world devoid of culture.

Chief among the gods were Takushkanshkan ("something that moves"), the Sun, who is married to the Moon, with whom he has one daughter, Wohpe ("falling star").

Old Man and Old Woman have a daughter Ite ("face"), who is married to Wind, with whom she has four sons, the Four Winds.

Among numerous other spirits, the most important is Inktomi ("spider"), the devious trickster. Inktomi conspires with Old Man and Old Woman to increase their daughter's status by arranging an affair between the Sun and Ite.

The discovery of the affair by the Sun's wife leads to a number of punishments by Takushkanshkan, who gives the Moon her own domain, and by separating her from the Sun initiates the creation of time.

Old Man, Old Woman, and Ite are sent to Earth, but Ite is separated from the Wind, her husband, who, along with the Four Winds and a fifth wind presumed to be the child of the adulterous affair, establishes space.

The daughter of the Sun and the Moon, Wohpe, also falls to earth and later resides with the South Wind, the paragon of Lakota maleness, and the two adopt the fifth wind, called Wamniomni ("whirlwind").

Alone on the newly formed Earth, some of the gods become bored, and Ite prevails upon Inktomi to find her people, the Buffalo Nation. In the form of a wolf, Inktomi travels beneath the earth and discovers a village of humans. Inktomi tells them about the wonders of the Earth and convinces one man, Tokahe ("the first"), to accompany him to the surface.

Tokahe does so and upon reaching the surface through a cave (Wind Cave in the Black Hills), marvels at the green grass and blue sky. Inktomi and Ite introduce Tokahe to buffalo meat and soup and show him tipis, clothing, and hunting utensils.

Tokahe returns to the subterranean village and appeals to six other men and their families to travel with him to the Earth's surface.

When they arrive, they discover that Inktomi has deceived them: buffalo are scarce, the weather has turned bad, and they find themselves starving. Unable to return to their home, but armed with a new knowledge about the world, they survive to become the founders of the Seven Fireplaces.

Once there, Tokahe told the people about the wonders of the Earth's surface and showed them the pack on his back. One man took out the buck skin clothing and felt the soft leather. His wife tried on a dress and, when he looked at her, he thought the dress accentuated her beauty. Next, they took out the meat, tasted it, and passed it around among some of the people. The meat intrigued them. They'd never hunted before and had never tasted anything like meat. They wanted more.

The wolf told them if they followed him to the surface of the Earth, he'd show them where to find meat and all the other gifts he brought. The leader of the humans was a man named Tokahe—"The First One"— and he refused to go with the wolf. He objected, saying the Creator had instructed them to stay underground, and that's what he'd do. Most of the people stayed with Tokahe, but all those who tried the meat followed the wolf to the surface.

The journey to the surface was long and perilous. When they reached the hole, the first thing the people saw was a giant blue sky above them. The surface of the earth was bright, and it was summertime, so all the plants were in bloom. The people looked around and thought the earth's surface was the most gorgeous place they'd ever been before.

The wolf led the people to the lodge of Anog-Ite, who was in disguise; she had her sina—"shawl"—wrapped over her head, hiding her horrible face and revealing only her beautiful face. Anog-Ite invited the people inside, and they asked her about the clothes and the food. She promised to teach the people how to obtain those things, and soon she taught the people how to hunt and how to work and tan an animal hide.

This work was difficult, however. The people had never struggled like this in the spirit lodge. They grew tired easily and worked slowly. Time passed, and summer turned to fall, then to winter. The people knew nothing about the Earth's seasons and had worked so slowly that, by the time the first snow came, they didn't have enough clothes or food for everyone. They began to freeze and starve.

They returned to the lodge of Anog-Ite to beg for help, but it was then that she revealed her true intentions. She ripped the shawl from her head, revealing her horrible face, and with both faces—beautiful and horrible—laughed at the people.

The people recoiled in terror and ran away, so she sent her wolf after them to chase and snap at their heels. They ran back to the site of the hole from which they'd emerged, only to find that it had been covered, leaving them trapped on the surface.

The people didn't know what to do nor where to go, so they simply sat down on the ground and cried. At this time the Creator heard them and asked why they were there. They explained the story of the wolf and Anog-Ite, but the Creator was upset.

The Creator said, "You should not have disobeyed me; now I have to punish you." The way the Creator did that was by transforming them—turning them from people into these great, wild beasts. This was the first bison herd.

Time passed, and the earth was finally ready for people to live upon it. The Creator instructed Tokahe to lead the people through the passageway in the cave and onto the surface. On the way, they stopped to pray four times, stopping last at the entrance.

On the surface, the people saw the hoofprints of a bison. The Creator instructed them to follow that bison. From the bison, they could get food, tools, clothes, and shelter. The bison would lead them to water. Everything they needed to survive on the earth could come from the bison.

When they left the cave, the Creator shrunk the hole from the size of a man to the size it is now, too small for most people to enter, to serve as a reminder so the people would never forget from where they'd come (Cheyenne River Sioux Tribe, 2019).

THE CREATION LEGEND OF THE YUP'IK PEOPLE
BY JACK DALTON
(based on the legend passed down by the Paimiut people)

Raven flew over the water and wondered what he was going to eat next. It was very much like Raven to be thinking about what he was going to eat next. He had grown tired of fishing and decided it was time for something more interesting.

He flew to seal and cried, "Seal, do you not tire from swimming all the time? Wouldn't it be nice to lay on something solid and rest?"

Seal agreed.

"Try then," Raven continued, "to swim to the bottom of the sea and get some mud so that we can make land."

Seal swam down and down and down. But before he could reach the bottom, he knew he would run out of air and turned back. He apologized to Raven, who understood.

Next Raven went to muskrat. "Muskrat, would you try swimming to the bottom of the sea and bring some mud up? We are going to make some land."

Muskrat, too, swam down as far as he could, but was unable to make it even as far as seal. He returned and apologized to Raven, who understood.

He set out across the sea, looking for the animal who could make it to the bottom of the sea and bring up some mud. It appears it wasn't going to be possible until beaver dove swift, kicking with his great tail, down, down to the bottom of the sea. He scooped up the largest amount of mud he could manage and brought it to the surface.

"Oh, how wonderful!" Raven exclaimed.

Raven then asked turtle if he would let the mud on his back to become the land. Without hesitation, turtle agreed. As the island that turtle became grew, Raven flew about creating plants and mountains and rivers and streams. Seal rested on its beaches and muskrat and beaver moved to its rivers and streams.

One day, Raven was flying along the beach. There before him, he watched a strange pod wash upon the shore. It was quite large, much larger than Raven himself. He swooped down immediately to inspect it. And as he walked near to it, it broke, and a strange creature unfolded out onto the sand. Raven stared with intense interest at this creature. It was a very odd creature and didn't look like anything he had ever seen before.

Raven went closer as it began to move. The thing stretched this way and that before standing up on very long legs. Looking around, the creature asked, "What am I doing here?"

Raven was perplexed by this question. For as long as he could remember, all of the creatures knew what they were doing at this place. There was no need for question. But Raven was so enchanted by the creature, he decided to help it.

"You are here to be," Raven said.

"Be what?" the creature asked.

"To be yourself," Raven replied.

"Who am I?" the creature asked.

Raven cocked his head to the side in soft amazement. The question of the creature held him in a muted grip of awe. No animal had ever thought of itself as a "who" before. They had always identified themselves as "whats." Raven was not one to be mean, but he had to admit at being bored with most of the animals. They thought mostly of eating and of sleeping. Raven had many different thoughts, but no one to share them with, no one who was a who.

"Well," Raven thought briefly. "You are a human."

The creature, the human, seemed moderately impressed by this, but not overly. Raven knew this would not be good enough and continued thinking. He wanted the human to understand his difference from the other animals—the fact that it was something more than a "what," that it was a "who." But how to let the human know this?

Finally: "You are a human being. Human is your form, the part of you which looks the way it does and moves in the way it moves. It is the physical part of who you are, but it is not all of you. By asking who you were, you showed that you know you are more than your form, more than just the physical. This something more is the being. It is your beingness that makes you different, makes you special."

The human being smiled.

After a bit, the human being said the first important thing: "I am hungry."

Well, Raven thought, it was bound to happen sooner or later, this being hungry. Raven showed the human being about berries and the human being ate and ate. But Raven knew this would not do for very long. Something that is a being likes variety, like Raven. So Raven went to the stream and created a couple of small lumps in the mud. As the human being looked on, Raven swept his wing over the mud lumps and they came to life and scurried about. The human being became very excited.

"Catch them. You can eat them," Raven said.

And at that, the human being ran about, trying to catch the small creatures. He returned after some time to the stream, munching away on mice and shrews. But Raven could see that wouldn't even be enough. So he made some larger lumps in the mud and after sweeping his wing over them, kicked them into the water and they swam off.

"Catch them. You can eat them as well."

And again, the human being ran about, splashing around in the water this time.

"No, no," beckoned Raven. "To catch these, you must be patient. The fish are faster than you in the water. But if you wait patiently, if you wait still, they will forget you are there, and you can catch them when they swim close."

The human being thanked Raven and after a while was munching on the fish.

Before long, the human being said the second important thing: "I am cold."

Raven thought for a moment and went back to the stream. In the mud, he made a very large lump. Raven went to a willow and took four of its long, skinny branches, sticking them into the mud. After waving his wing over it, the lump turned into a caribou, jumping onto its long legs and bounding off.

"To catch this, you must be fast and strong. You must be smart. While [you] are fast and strong, you are not fast and strong enough to catch caribou on your own. You will need tools. And you must know how the caribou will move so you know where it will be when your weapon reaches it. It will be much work, but you can catch it. And when you do, you can take its skin and keep yourself warm."

The human being thanked Raven again, and after a while, he was warm.

Before long, the human being said to Raven, "I am lonely."

Raven was at first offended. Was he not interesting enough company? But Raven soon understood: The human did not have a companion as large as himself.

Raven went again to the stream and made another lump. He would look at the human being, trying to make some resemblance. He was about to wave his wing over it, but he knew this new human needed a beingness as well. He looked at the human being and noticed the twinkle in his eye.

Ah hah! Raven thought. And he flew up into the sky and plucked one of the stars. He put the star into the new human's forehead and waved his wing over it.

The new human being stood up and looked at the man. They looked at each other, noticing they were different. At first, Raven felt badly about not being able to make the new human being the same as the man, but the two human beings assured him this was OK. They liked the differences between them.

With this, Raven had an idea. He made it so the two had the power to create more of themselves. When the two humans were near each other, their beingness, the stars within them, grew stronger, brighter. Raven called this love, and when the love was strong enough, it made a new being and this grew in the woman until it had a body of its own.

The man and the woman thanked Raven, and after a while, there was a large family.

The family had no place to live, so Raven showed them how beaver and muskrat made houses. Soon there were dwellings and a small village. Raven made more caribou and fish.

But before long, the human beings were taking much more than they needed. He tried to talk to them, but they were unafraid. So Raven went back to the stream and made a very large lump of mud. He found shells and broke them into thin sharp pieces and put them on the lump in various places. He had made thick lumps for the legs instead of just willow branches, and a big mouth with more broken shells for teeth. The humans had come to see what Raven was making. But when Raven waved his wing over the lump, it jumped up, snarling, and ran after the humans. It caught one and killed it outright. When the bear left, the humans ran to the dead human and gathered around it in awe and fear. Raven flew down and took the star from it as the humans cried. He flew the star back to the sky.

When the Raven came back to the humans, he said, "You can be very happy. You can be as happy as you like. But you cannot forget that everything has the right to be happy as well. And besides, if you are not careful with how much you take, if you take more than you need, or make too many of yourselves, what is here will run out. And then you will all starve and die." The human beings shook with fear. "I do not say this to scare you. I say this so you will understand the way of things. If you live by this way, you will be very happy for as long as you want. When you are ready to die, I will take your stars as well back into the sky."

The human beings were comforted by this and lived with more reverence of that which was around them. They soon began to make kayaks to hunt the seals in the sea. And the women began to figure out how to use all the different parts of the animals for making clothes. They made baskets from the summer grasses. They taught the men how to use the parts of the animals for their boats. They made clothes that wouldn't let in water.

But before long, the human beings had forgotten about the way, because there was nothing to be feared in the sea, like the bear on land.

Again, Raven went back to the stream and this time made an even bigger lump. He found two big willow stumps, using his beak to make them sharp and only as long as the strongest part. He put these where the mouth would be. He waved his wing over the lump and it lived. It lumbered into the sea. When the first human being found it, the walrus tore apart his kayak and stabbed him many times. When the body washed up on the shore, the other human beings gathered around it and Raven took the human's star back to the sky.

"Remember the way," he said. Nothing more.

To this day, all human beings know about Raven and the way of the human beings. They revere Raven for all he did for the human beings, everything he taught, even when it meant hurting or scaring them. They always knew he was doing the best for them (Dalton, 1999).

CHOCTAW CREATION STORY

Choctaws are an ancient people, but by their own account, they were the last of earth's inhabitants to appear in this world.

According to Choctaw belief, the first people to appear upon the earth lived a great distance from what would become the Choctaw homeland. These people emerged from deep beneath the earth's surface through a cave near the sacred mound, *Nanih Waiya.* They draped themselves on bushes around the cave to dry themselves in the sunshine, and then went to their distant homes.

Many others followed the same pattern, finding homes closer and closer to the cave. Some of the last to emerge were the Cherokees, Creeks, Natchez, and others, who would become the Choctaws' closest neighbors. Finally, the Choctaws emerged and established their homeland around the sacred mound of *Nanih Waiya,* their mother.

Another Choctaw legend holds that they migrated to the site of *Nanih Waiya* after a great long journey from the northwest, led by a *hopaii* who carried a sacred pole that was planted in the ground each evening.

Every morning the people continued their journey toward the rising sun, according to the direction in which the pole leaned. Finally, they awoke one morning to find the pole standing upright. They built *Nanih Waiya* on that site and made their home there.

In another version of the migration story, two brothers, Chahta and Chicksa, led the migration. After arriving at the site of *Nanih Waiya,* the group following Chicksa became lost for many years and became the Chickasaws, the Choctaws' nearest northern neighbors.

Today, *Nanih Waiya* is a state park near the headwaters of the Pearl

River in the east-central portion of Mississippi. "Mississippi," from the Choctaw word *Misha sipokni,* means "older than time," the Choctaw name for the great river of the North American continent (Choctaw Creation Story, 2019).

REFERENCES

American Psychiatric Association. (2013). *Diagnostic and statistical manual of mental disorders* (5th ed.). Washington, DC: American Psychiatric Association.

Beck, V., & Walters, A. L. (1977). *The sacred ways of knowledge: Sources of life.* Tsaile (Navajo Nation), AZ: Navajo Community College Press.

BigFoot, D. S. (1999). *On the back of a turtle.* Oklahoma City, OK: Oklahoma Center on Child Abuse and Neglect.

Black Elk, W., & Lyon, W. S. (1991). *Black Elk: The sacred ways of the Lakota.* New York: Harper Collins.

Bopp, J., Bopp, M., Brown, L., & Lane, P. (1988). *The sacred tree.* Lethbridge, Alberta, Canada: University of Lethbridge.

Brave Heart, M. Y. (2003). The historical trauma response among natives and its relationship with substance abuse: A Lakota illustration. *Journal of Psychoactive Drugs, 35*(1), 7–13. doi:10.1080/02791072.2003.10399988

Brave Heart, M. Y., Chase, J., Elkins, J., & Altschul, D. B. (2011). Historical trauma among Indigenous peoples of the Americas: Concepts, research, and clinical considerations. *Journal of Psychoactive Drugs, 43*(4), 282–290.

Brown, J. E. (1952/2012). *The sacred pipe.* Norman: University of Oklahoma Press.

Brown, S. S. (2014). *Transformation beyond greed: Native self-actualization.* Gallup, NM: Sidney Stone Brown.

Bureau of Indian Affairs. (2019, November 21). About us. Retrieved from http://www .bia.gov/about-us

Bureau of Indian Affairs. (2020, January 30). *Federal Register.* Retrieved from https:// www.federalregister.gov/documents/2020/01/30/2020-01707/indian- entities-rec-ognized-by-and-eligible-to-receive-services-from-the-united-states-bureau-of

Cheyenne River Sioux Tribe. (2019). Lakota creation story. Retrieved from http:// www.sioux.org/lakota-creation-story.html. Accessed March 13, 2020.

Choctaw Creation Story. (2019). Retrieved from http://www.american-indians .org/142/choctaw-creation-story/. Accessed March 13, 2020.

Churchill, W. (2004). *Kill the Indian, save the man: The genocidal impact of American Indian residential schools.* San Francisco: City Lights.

Clements, F. (1932). Primitive concepts of disease. *University of California Publications in Archeology and Ethnography, 32,* pp. 85–252.

Coyhis, D., & White, W. L. (2006). *Alcohol problems in Native America: The untold story of resistance and recovery: "The truth about the lie."* Colorado Springs, CO: White Bison.

Dalton, J. (1999). The creation legend of the Yup'ik People: When raven met the first human being. Retrieved from http://www.angelfire.com/bc/yupik/create.html. Accessed March 13, 2020.

Deloria, V., Jr. (1969/1988). *Custer died for your sins: An Indian manifesto.* Norman: Uniersity of Oklahoma Press.

Deloria, V., Jr. (1992/2003). *God is red: A Native view of religion* (2nd ed.). Golden, CO: North American Press.

Duran, E. (2006). *Healing the soul wound.* New York: Teachers College, Columbia University.

Duran, E., & Duran, B. (1995). *Native American postcolonial psychology.* Albany: State University of New York Press.

Estes, N. (2019). *Our history is the future.* Brooklyn, NY: Verso.

Forbes, J. D. (1979). *Columbus and other cannibals.* New York: Seven Stories Press.

Garcia, M. A., & Society of Indian Psychologists. (2014). Commentary on the American Psychological Assocation's (APA) ethical principles of psychologists and code of conduct. Albuquerque, NM: Society of Indian Psychologists.

Garrett, M. T. (1996). "Two people": An American Indian narrative of bicultural identity. *Journal of American Indian Education, 36*(1), 1–21.

George, K. (2016). The Haudensaunee creation story of the Oneida Indian nation. Retrieved from http://www.oneidaindiannation.com/the-haudenosaunee-creation-story/. Accessed March 13, 2020.

Gone, J. P. (2010). Psychotherapy and traditional healing for American Indians: Exploring the prospects for therapeutic integration. *Counseling Psychologist, 38*(2), 166–235. doi: 10.1177/0011000008330831

Goodman, R. (1992/2017). *Lakota star knowledge.* Mission, SD: Sinte Gleska University Press.

Gray, J. S., & McCullagh, J. A. (2014). Suicide in Indian country: The continuing epidemic in rural Native American communities. *Journal of Rural Health, 38*(2), 79–86. doi:10.1037/rmh0000017

Gulliford, A. (2003, November 1). Sacred objects and sacred places: Preserving tribal traditions. Retrieved from https://sacredland.org/black-hills-united-states/

Indian Pueblo Cultural Center. (2019). About the Pueblos. Retrieved from https://www.indianpueblo.org/19-pueblos/. Accessed March 13, 2020.

Jefferson, T. (2019). Bill of Rights. Retrieved from https://www.archives.gov/founding-docs/bill-of-rights. Accessed March 13, 2020.

Katz, R. (2017). *Indigenous healing psychology: Honoring the wisdom of the First Peoples.* Toronto: Healing Arts Press.

Kenney, M. K., & Singh, G. K. (2016). Adverse childhood experiences among American Indian / Alaska Native children: The 2011–2012 National survey of children's health. *Scientifica, 14.* doi:10.1155/2016/7424239

Kidwell, C. S., Noley, H., & Tinker, G. E. (2001). *A Native American theology.* Maryknoll, NY: Orbis Books.

LaFromboise, T. D., Trimble, J. E., & Mohatt, G. V. (1990). Counseling intervention and American Indian tradition: An integrative approach. *Counseling Psychologist, 18*(4), 628–654.

Lexico. (2019). Pan-Indian. Retrieved from https://www.lexico.com/en/definition/pan-indian

Lowery, L. (1983). Bridging a culture in counseling. *Journal of Applied Rehabilitation Counseling, 14,* 69–73.

Methot, S. (2019). *Legacy: Trauma, story, and Indigenous healing.* Toronto: ECW Press.

Mish, F. C. (2014). *Merriam Webster's dictionary and thesarus.* Springfield, MA: Merriam-Webster, Inc. Retrieved January 13, 2020, from https://books.google.com/books?hl=en&lr=&id=TAnheeIPcAEC&oi=fnd&pg=PP12&dq=merriam+webster+dictionary&ots=3bZlB3_jX2&sig=P4sj_MaIorxmtlMjBtNJoxc-JhA#v=onepage&q=merriam%20webster%20dictionary&f=false

Mittal, A. K., Malcolm, J. D., Calderon, M., Candri, C., Cheung, J., Chu, E. W., … Soares, J. M. (2012). *Indian issues: Federal funding for non-federally recognized tribes.* Washington, DC: U.S. Government Accountability Office.

Monroe, J. (1818). State of the Union Address. Retrieved from http://www.stateoftheunionhistory.com/2017/04/1818-james-monroe-indian-civilization.html?view=timeslide. Accessed March 13, 2020.

Morgan, D. L., Slade, M. D., & Morgan, C. M. (1997). Aboriginal philosophy and its impact on health outcomes. *Australia and New Zealand Journal of Public Health, 21*(6), 597–601.

Nebelkopf, E., & Phillips, M. (2004). *Healing and mental health for Native Americans: Speaking in red.* Lanham, MD: Altamira Press.

Neihardt, J. (1932/1961.1996). *Black Elk speaks.* Lincoln: University of Nebraska Press.

Nunavut. (2019). Government of Nunavut. Innuit societal values. Retrieved from https://www.gov.nu.ca/information/inuit-societal-values. Accessed March 13, 2020.

O'Brien, S. J. (2008). *Religion and healing in Native America: Pathways for renewal.* Westport, CT: Praeger.

Ojibwe.net. (2019). The gifts of the seven grandfathers. Retrieved from https://ojibwe.net/projects/prayers-teachings/the-gifts-of-the-seven-grandfathers/. Accessed March 13, 2020.

Pape, N. (2019). Medicine Wheel Diagram. Center for Rural Health, University of North Dakota, Grand Forks, ND.

Parrott, Z., & Filice, M. (2018). *Indigenous peoples in Canada.* Retrieved April 1, 2019, from https://www.thecanadianencyclopedia.ca/en/article/aboriginal-people.

Petoskey, W. (2009). *Dancing my dream.* Greater Detroit: Front Edge Publishing.

Pratt, C. R. (1892). "Kill the Indian, and Save the Man": Capt. Richard H. Pratt on the education of Native Americans. Retrieved from http://carlisleindian.dickinson .edu/teach/kill-indian-and-save-man-capt-richard-h-pratt-education-native-americans. Accessed March 13, 2020.

Price, H. (1883, March 3). Rules governing the Court of Indian Offenses. Retrieved from https://rclinton.files.wordpress.com/2007/11/code-of-indian-offenses.pdf

Primeaux, M. (1977). American Indian health care practices: A cross-cultural perspective. *Nursing Clinics of North America, 12*, 55–65.

Rayle, A. D., Chee, C., & Sand, J. K. (2006). Honoring their way: Counseling American Indian women. *Journal of Multicultural Counseling and Development, 32*(2), 66–79.

Rensick, B. (2011). Genocide of Native Americans: Historical facts and histiographic debates. In S. Totten & R. Hitchcock (Eds.), *Genocide of Indigenous peoples: Genocide: A critical bibliographic review* (Vol. 8, pp. 15–36). New Brunswick, NJ: Transaction Publishers. Retrieved from Holocaust Museum of Houston Library Research: https://hmh.org/library/research/genocide-of-indigenous-peoples-guide/

Rhoades, E. R. (2009). The Indian Health Service and traditional Indian medicine. *American Medical Association Journal of Ethics, 11*(10), 793–798.

Salazar, M. (2016, October). State recognition of Amnerican Indian tribes. National Conference of State Legislatures. Retrieved from http://www.ncsl.org/research/ state-tribal-institute/state-recognition-of-american-indian-tribes.aspx

Skyfire, E. (2019). *Journeying between the worlds: Walking with the sacred spirits through Native American shamanic teachings & practices.* Woodbury, MN: Llewellyn Publications.

Substance Abuse and Mental Health Services Administration, Center for Behavioral Health Statistics and Quality. (2012). The NSDUH report: Need for and receipt of substance use treatment among American Indians or Alaska Natives. Washington, DC: SAMHSA.

Thomason, T. (2012). Recommendations for counseling Native Americans: Results of a study. *Journal of Indigenous Research, 1*(2). https://digitalcommons.usu.edu/ kicjir/vol1/iss2/4

Tinker, G. E. (1993). *Missionary conquest: The gospel and Native American cultural genocide.* Minneapolis: Fortress Press.

Tooker, E., & Sturtevant, W. C. (1979). *The eastern woodlands: Sacred myths, dreams, visions, speeches, healing formulas, rituals and ceremonials.* Classics of Western Spirituality. Mahwah, NJ: Paulist Press.

Trafzer, C. E., Keller, J. A., & Sisquoc, L. (2006). *Boarding school blues: Revisiting American Indian educational experiences.* Lincoln: University of Nebraska Press.

Trujillo, A. (2000). Psychtherapy with Native Americans: A view into the role of religion and spirituality. In P. Richards & A. Bergin (Eds.), *Handbook of psychotherapy and religious diversity* (pp. 445–466). Washington, DC: American Psychological Association. doi:10.1037/10347-018

Tylor, E. B. (1871). *Primitive culture: Researches into the development of mythology, philosophy, religion, art, and custom.* Vol. 2. London: John Murray.

United States. (1978, August 11). 42 U.S. Code §1996. Protection and preservation of traditional religions of Native Americans. Legal Information Institute. Retrieved from https://www.law.cornell.edu/uscode/text/42/1996. Accessed March 13, 2020.

United States. (1994, October 6). Public Law 103-344; American Indian Religious Freedom Act Amendments of 1994. Retrieved from https://www.fs.fed.us/spf/tribalrelations/documents/policy/statutes/American_Indian_Religous_Freedom_Act.pdf

VanDevelder, P. (2009). *Savages and scoundrels: The untold story of America's road to empire through Indian territory.* New Haven, CT: Yale University Press.

Vose, R. (2013). Beyond Spain: Inquisition history in a global context. *History Compass, 11*(4), 316–329. doi:10.1111/hic3.12045

White Wolf Pack. (2019). The 12 Lakota virtues. Essential to balance and happiness. Retrieved from http://www.whitewolfpack.com/2014/11/12-lakota-virtues-essential-to-balance.html. Accessed March 13, 2020.

Williams, R. (1999). Cultural safety: What does it mean for our work practice? *Australian and New Zealand Journal of Public Health, 23*(2), 213–214.

Zalcman, D. (2016). "Kill the Indian, Save the Man": On the painful legacy of Canada's residential schools. *World Policy Journal, 33*(3), 72–85.

Zimmerman, L. J. (2011). *The sacred wisdom of the Native Americans.* New York: Chartwell.

Zitgow, D., & Estes, G. (1981). The heritage consistency continuum in counseling Native American children. *American Indian issues in higher education: Contemporary American Indian Issues Series, No. 3.* (pp. 133–139). Los Angeles: UCLA American Indian Studies Center.

ENDNOTES

1. A *federally recognized tribe* is a policy term that refers to American Indian tribes (nations) and Alaska Native villages that have met specific criteria to be recognized by the federal government of the United States.

2. State-recognized tribes (nations) are those in the United States that have met state requirements for recognition, but not federal requirements. These are usually smaller branches of a larger indigenous nation that splintered off during periods of removal or annihilation.

3. First Nations is the term used to identify the Indigenous groups of Canada.

4. Métis is a term used to describe a person of Indigenous and European descent; in Canada it is usually French.

5. Inuit refers to a group of people Indigenous to northern Alaska and the Arctic of Canada.

6. *Alaska Native* will be used in this chapter to refer to the Indigenous peoples of the US state of Alaska.

7. *American Indian* will be used in this chapter to refer to Indigenous nations of the lower forty-eight states of the United States.

8. "New Agers" are a group that arose in the late twentieth century of Western culture that adapt and misappropriate beliefs, ceremonies, and experiences from other cultures outside the mainstream, and that advance alternative approaches to spirituality, right living, and health without necessarily understanding the spiritual meaning behind the ceremonies. It focuses more on the experience than the knowledge (Mish, 2014).

9. *Pan-Indian* is a term used to identify many or all of the Indigenous peoples of the Americas with a collective culture or system of religious beliefs (Lexico, 2019).

RACHEL SING-KIAT TING,

SIEW-CHUNG MAH, AND KEJIA ZHANG

CHINESE TRADITIONAL RELIGIONS AND MENTAL HEALTH

An Indigenous Psychology Perspective

The five major religions (Buddhism, Taoism, Protestant Christianity, Catholicism, and Islam) and various folk beliefs have influenced the daily life and customs of all Chinese populations (Jin, 2002, 2018; Zhang, 2016). Many psychological studies on Chinese religions have focused on world religions or institutionalized religion with origins from foreign lands (Dueck & Han, 2012). These world religions pay more attention to internal states of religiosity and spirituality—such as the relationship to a deity/universe, attachment issues, conversion experiences, religious identity formation, and so on (Dueck, Ansloos, Johnson, & Fort, 2017)—that are seldom a concern for traditional Chinese religions, which seem more externally oriented and instrumental. Traditional Chinese religions are often grounded and intertwined in people's daily lives and diffused within ethnic groups. They are often associated with certain social networks, customs, festivals, and regions, permeating lives from birth to death. Membership in traditional Chinese religions tends to be determined by bloodlines, geography, and ethnicity. Due to China's unique ecological and geographical environment, social and cultural traditions, and national identification (Han acculturation), the topographies of traditional religions are often different from that of the institutionalized religious systems studied in the West.

Yang (1961) proposed that two major types of religions are practiced in modern China—institutionalized and diffused religions. The former includes organized Han Buddhism, Confucianism (*ru jiao*), and Taoism (*dao jiao*) religious institutions, but the latter are rather diffused in their grassroots lifestyles characterized by a mixture of practices and beliefs drawing on Buddhism-Taoism-Confucianism (*ru-shi-dao*) and ancestor worship. Furthermore, we propose that among the latter "diffused religions" there are two subtypes—native religion and folk religions, which are practiced by different Chinese ethnic groups. Unfortunately, these two types of traditional religious practices are often deemed as "superstitious," "backward," "irrational," "materialistic," and "secular" under the scrutiny of scientism and positivism as embedded in modern psychology, being loosely referred to as "spirituality" or "shamanism" in the West (Laufer, 1917).

In this chapter, we aim to introduce briefly the above two types of Chinese traditional religions that are "diffused" and indigenous to Chinese societies and cultures. While we would mainly focus on diffused religious traditions (e.g., Confucianism and Taoism), we do not deny that many institutional religions (Buddhism, Christianity, Islam, etc.) have also been indigenized over the centuries by different ethnic groups, since China has such a long history of global exchange. Take the Miao (Hmong) ethnic group in China as an example. The Qing (green) Miao rejected Christianity, while the Hua (floral) Miao accepted it centuries ago. Similar diversity is observed among the Yi group. The Nuosu-Yi tribal group in Sichuan province practices the Bimo tradition and ancestral worship, but some Yi tribal groups (Luowu) in Yunnan province accepted Christianity since end of the nineteenth century. Another Yi group in Weishan practices a form of "Tuzhu worship" that combines ancestor worship with folk beliefs (Li & Cai, 2011). Therefore, in order to study Chinese traditional religions, we need to acknowledge first their within-group diversity and avoid adopting the cultural assumption of homogeneity by ethnicity.

To be inclusive of all Chinese populations, in this chapter we do not differentiate between Chinese from Mainland China, the United States, Malaysia, or elsewhere, as Chinese is known for its diasporic nature and migration (Ting, Foo, & Tan, in press). In fact, many folk religions are being contextualized and transmitted by different regions of migrants as time goes by; hence, it is really impossible to find a universal form of Chinese traditional religion. Even within China, the famous Chinese sociologist Fei (1999) summarized Chinese nationality as a form of "pluralistic integration" based on geographical settlements, religious affiliations, cultural traditions, and languages. There is no single unified definition of an ethnic Chinese group. Readers should be mindful of this precaution while reading this chapter.

After introducing the particular epistemology and philosophy of Chinese indigenous religion and folk religion, the second part of the chapter draws a parallel between them by using two scientific frameworks that analyze religious healing mechanisms on a micro level—Peircean semiotic analysis and the ecological rationality framework (Ting & Sundararajan, 2018). Both theories are being adopted to explain the healing rituals and power of social networks embedded in Chinese traditional religions and spiritualities. Only after mapping the universal psychological concepts of health/well-being, suffering/pathology, and help-seeking/strength within the traditional system do we then discuss the limitations of Western psychotherapy and the future expanded horizon of Chinese mental health practice.

THE MAJOR TYPES OF CHINESE TRADITIONAL RELIGIONS

In this section, we describe the complex characteristics of traditional religion among various Chinese groups. We differentiate between and define two major traditional religions practiced among Chinese—native religions and folk religions—from a population approach, whereas the former is widely practiced among Chinese ethnic minority groups and the latter among the Han majority. The very reason we include native religions and spirituality practiced by the minority of Chinese is to honor their existence as cultural heritage and give voice to often-forgotten groups in Chinese literature (Ting, Zhang, & Huang, 2019).

CHINESE FOLK RELIGION PRACTICED
BY HAN MAJORITIES

For thousands of years, Chinese folk religions have subtly constructed the Chinese way of being through fusion with people's psychosocial life (Cheng, 2010). Compared to institutionalized religion, folk religions display the following characteristics: no registered religious groups or social organizations, deity worship, and incense sacrifice in local small-scale temples. There are as many versions of folk religions as there are many versions of Chinese subcultures; hence there is a wide range of believers. Its worshipping practices are mainly bound to local participants in a certain region (Yang & Hu, 2012).

Chinese religion scholar Mou (2016) described the existence of a "traditional patriarchal religion" accepted by all strata of society uninterrupted for several thousand years in ancient Chinese history, which worships heavenly deities and ancestors, followed by the worship of deities of land and grain, the sun and the moon, spirits of mountains and rivers and other natural objects, and complemented by the worship of other supernatural beings. These modes of worship and sacrificial ceremonies became an important part of traditional customs and rituals of Chinese patriarchal society.

Alongside traditional patriarchal religion, which largely depended on imperial government and clan organizations, folk polytheism with obvious geographic and folk-custom characteristics was practiced by the middle and lower classes of the social stratum. For its believers, folk polytheism was a diverse set of customs that reflected the way the world was and was concerned primarily with efficacious response to immediate needs (Adler, 2005). The ecology of the traditional Chinese patriarchal socio-political system and hierarchical clan authorities has caused ancient folk polytheism to eventually be integrated into the daily lives of the grassroots Chinese and become the mainstream of modern Chinese folk religion, even after the fall of imperial China (He, 2012).

Modern-day Chinese folk religion consists of worship and veneration of (a) deities of ancient myths, such as various personifications of nature; (b) deities or exemplary figures from Buddhism, Taoism, and Confucianism—for example, Guanyin Bodhisatva (观音菩萨) and Jigong

(济公); (c) local deities and spirits such as Sanshanguowang (三山国王), originated from Guangdong; and (d) ancestors. Its beliefs are reflected in rites, rituals, and taboos associated with annual religious and cultural festivals, significant life and death events, and the practices of *feng shui* (风水) and divination (求神问卦) (Adler, 2005). For example, Goddess Mazu (妈祖) or Tianhou (天后) is a popular deity widely worshipped along the coast of southern Mainland China and in Taiwan, Macao, Hong Kong, and the Chinese diaspora in Southeast Asia. Through participation in religious activities during Mazu's festival, such as pilgrimage, divine inspirations reflected through worship rites and rituals are internalized as psychological resources and living guides (Cheng, 2010).

VIEW OF THE PERSON

In general, Chinese folk religion believes a person consists of a physical body from the parents, *qi* (气) or "energy" from the universe, and *ling hun* (灵魂) or "soul" from the "other world" (Yu, 2002). Body is the biological aspect of a person, but *qi* forms the person's second part. It is a form of energy or magnetic field that exists between the muscles and skin. It also runs around the body through the meridian system (经络, *jin luo*, is a somatic network mapped by traditional Chinese medicine) to coordinate various cells and organs of the body (Yu, 2002). The third part of a person is known as *ling hun*, commonly translated as "soul," which contains the important aspect of a person's personality that accounts for individual differences in temperament, abilities, likes, and dislikes (Harrell, 1979). Ancient Chinese texts posited different theories on the number of *ling hun*, varying from one to twelve. While the *san hun qi po* (three hun and seven po, 三魂七魄) is a common understanding of *ling hun* among the believers of Chinese folk religion, some communities subscribe to different theories of *ling hun*—for example, *shi er yuan shen* (twelve souls, 十二元神) (Lin, 2000). In fact, Harrell (1979) observed that lay believers treated the different *ling hun* as functionally one. A philosophical understanding of *ling hun* is not crucial to the practice of Chinese folk religion. The believers' emphasis is on the practice of rites and rituals such as what prayer is needed to restore their *ling hun* instead of how many *ling hun* have they lost.

VIEW ON HEALTH AND ILLNESS

Chinese folk religion derived its concept of health both from traditional Chinese medicines and a Daoist worldview. Traditional Chinese religion believes that heaven, earth, humans, and gods are one. The natural and supernatural exist relatively with humans, and supernatural beings such as ghosts and gods coexist with humans at any time and place (Cheng, 2008). Hence, traditional Chinese believers strive to maintain harmonious interactions with the natural and supernatural worlds. In contrast, illnesses or sufferings are perceived as the result of disharmony and disequibilirium among an individual's body, energy, and *ling hun*, and/or between an individual and the natural or supernatural worlds. Based on his observation of folklores and folk rituals, Li (1992, 1995) formulated a scheme of three systems of equilibrium and harmony that represents the traditional Chinese's ideal state of perfection for health and the universe. We would further distinguish these three systems from the folk religion perspectives:

THE EQUILIBRIUM OF THE TIAN (天) SYSTEM OR HEAVENLY ORDER. The harmony of natural order encompasses harmony and equilibrium in temporal and spatial relations. Traditional Chinese believe that one's fate, *ming* (命), is determined by an individual's horoscope, *ba zi* (八字). When an individual's horoscope combines with natural time at every point of one's life, one's opportunities, *yun* (运), are formed. Temporal harmony is achieved when the timing combination is coherent, leading to good opportunities, *hao yun* (好运). The harmony of spatial relation is achieved when there is a balance of energy exchange between the buildings and the natural environment according to Chinese geomancy, also known as *feng shui* (风水). Poor *feng shui* of ancestors' graves contributes to disharmony in the supernatural world, which in turn disrupts the equilibrium of individual organisms and causes illness (Lin, 2016).

The *Tian* (heaven) system also serves a purpose in regulating moral behaviors among the Chinese believers. Punishments from gods and ghosts due to individual or collective moral downfall or violation of taboos, troubles from malicious spirits that die unnaturally or lack of descendants' worship, and fierce deities (*xiong shen e sha*, 凶神恶煞) are perceived as common causes of physical and mental illnesses (Lin, 2016).

THE EQUILIBRIUM OF REN (人) SYSTEM OR INDIVIDUAL ORGANISMS. The harmony of an individual organism involves the harmony of its internal and external organisms. The harmony of the internal organism refers to a harmonious balance of the complementary forces of *yin and yang* in the body. The harmony of the external organism can be produced by being assigned a written name that balances one's *wu xing* (五行) or five elements (wood, fire, earth, metal, and water), depending on which element is lacking, as determined by the Daoist priest. Illnesses (both physical and mental) are the imbalance between the various forces and energies of *yin* (阴) and *yang* (阳), and five elements of the body (Cheng, 2008). The imbalance sometimes could be caused by an imbalance in dietary practices as well (Li, 1992; Cheng, 2008).

Besides internal balance, some Chinese folk religions commonly attribute many kinds of physical and mental diseases to the loss or frightening of the "soul" (*shi hun luo po*, 失魂落魄) (Harrell, 1979; Lin, 2016). For example, infantile colic is attributed to the frightening of the soul caused by exposure to loud noise or a dark shadow (Chang, 1996). Hence, the harmony between body and soul (*hun*, 魂) is also an important aspect of explaining the health and illnesses of Chinese believers.

THE EQUILIBRIUM OF THE SHE HUI (社会) SYSTEM OR SOCIETY. The harmony of society results from harmonious relationships in the world of the living and the world of the supernatural. The harmony of the world of the living consists of maintaining ethical interpersonal and intergenerational relationships based on the foundation virtue of filial piety, *xiao* (孝). The practice of filial piety is centered around family, *jia* (家), and extends to other interpersonal relationships. The harmony of the world of the supernatural is an extension of the harmony of the world of the living, where harmony with deceased ancestors, gods, and ghosts is maintained through the rites and rituals of worship, especially ancestor worship. For the Chinese diaspora, ancestor worship also helps to create and express Chinese ethnic identity as it involves the celebration of some form of relationship between the living and their deceased ancestors originating from China (Clarke, 2000). The rituals of ancestor worship prevent the deceased ancestors from becoming evil ghosts that would represent a threat to the psychological stability of the family and society (Li, 1988). In order to minimize harm from other homeless or vengeful ghosts that do not receive any worship from their descendants, some local Chinese try to harmonize the system by elevating those ghosts as gods for the local believers, such as Yiminye (义民爷) and Gaowangye of the Matsu Islands (马祖高王爷) (Lin & Chen, 2008; Cheng, 2010). A person who is in conflict with others (i.e., disharmony of the world of the living) may take revenge by disrupting the equilibrium of the spiritual world and therefore cast a charm on them. The interplay of the social and spiritual realms is also tightly knitted into the web of Chinese folk religions.

VIEW ON PSYCHOLOGICAL HELP AND TREATMENT

As to help-seeking, Cheng (2008) stated that Chinese folk religion and "folk treatments" have been intertwined for thousands of years and the latter often are a form of behavioral expression of the former. He categorizes folk treatments into five major categories:

* DIETARY TREATMENT. Traditional Chinese religion holds that diet has medicinal effects. An inappropriate diet can diminish the therapeutic effects of medicine, or even cause adverse effects to the body (*bing cong kou ru*, 病从口入).
* EXTERNAL FORCES (WAI GONG). External forces are techniques that exert force to relax the muscles and stimulate blood circulation— for example, massage, cupping therapy, and acupuncture.
* INTERNAL FORCES (NEI GONG). Internal forces include Chinese meditation and spiritual practices to regulate one's body, breathing, and mental state for the advancement of spiritual achievements, such as *dao yin* exercise (导引) and *tai ji* (太极). The practices are believed to have special preventive and therapeutic effects on physical and mental illnesses.
* WITCHCRAFT (WU SHU). Chinese witchcraft involves a witch doctor (*wu yi*) practicing specific rites and rituals to obtain sacred power from the deities to counter evil spirits that are the causal agents of illness. Treatment methods include prayer, divination, making offerings, casting spells, taking refuge in a deity through meditating or living in a temple, sleeping under the altar, drinking holy water, and becoming the deity's adopted child (Lin, 2016). The witch

doctor may also massage certain parts of the patient's body, or prescribe natural substances for oral intake that consist of plants, animals, or minerals. These natural substances are not prescribed for their nutritional or chemical properties but symbolically to represent the deities' suppression of evil spirits.

*DIVINATION/FORTUNE-TELLING. Divination is seen as a communication channel between the divine and human. It includes numerology, astrology, intepreting omens and dreams, and other practices that are related to the traditional Chinese understanding of the universe and its natural order. Divination can reveal the secret of one's fate (*ming*) and opportunities (*yun*), which then can be utilized to resolve misfortunes, treat various physical and mental illnesses, and maintain overall equilibrium of life. Divination is the primary popular treatment for many mental disturbances.

All of the above worldviews on person, illness, health, and treatments are quite common for Chinese folk religion believers as many researchers have documented (Chang, 1996; Cheng, 2010; Luo et al., 2017). In the following section we turn our attention to the less discussed type of Chinese religions, which are similarly diffused in daily life but mainly among ethnic minorities.

NATIVE RELIGIONS AND SPIRITUALITIES PRACTICED
BY CHINESE ETHNIC MINORITIES

Though there are different taxonomies for native religions (such as indigenous religion or tribal religion), in this chapter we use the definition of *native religion* as "a religious formation that originates in the unique ecological system of the particular ethnic group, which is rooted and co-evolves with the ethnic tradition, society, culture and customs, and is still actively practiced by the locals" (Zhang, 2015b, p. 16). Native religions and spiritualities usually have their own story of creation and heroic figures that are not widely recognized by the Han Chinese group. This form of religiosity is often found at the "bottom level" of the ethnic minority group's culture which consist of several main components—ancestor worship, nature worship, belief in a spiritual realm, and sacrificial rituals.

Often these types of religious traditions are represented by witch doctors or priests as the icons and core figures, who serve as mediums to the spiritual realm (ghost and spirits). Their religiosity is displayed through communal ceremonies and transmitted through family lineage.

All of the following could be categorized as indigenous religions:

* Shamanic tradition, Northern Mongolian groups
* Shibi (释比) tradition, Qiang ethnic group
* Badaixio (巴岱雄) tradition and Huqing (呼清) tradition, Miao ethnic group
* Heng-P (亨—批) tradition, Huayao Dai ethnic group
* Dongba (东巴) tradition, Naxi ethnic group
* Daba (达巴) tradition, Mosuo ethnic group
* Bonismo (本教), Tibetan group
* Dongsa (董萨) tradition, Jingpo ethnic group
* Bimo (毕摩) tradition, Yi people

These groups still take pride in the "purity" of their traditions by refusing to be assimilated into mainstream Han culture. Their ethnic identity is interconnected with their religious identity, and scholars also equate some indigenous religions to "ethno-religion" or "folk religion" (Wang, 2009; Jin, 2002). Unfortunately, due to lack of understanding, some Western scholars (e.g., Waley, 1955) have utilized a reductionist approach by simplifying the diverse and rich traditions of Chinese ethnic spirituality as "shamanism" or "animism." Some would describe indigenous people as possessing a "spirituality," yet "spirituality" itself is a Western concept that does not capture and honor local religion. In a recent literature review, Zhang, Ting, and Luo (2020) have identified that many Chinese ethnic minorities group still practice their indigenous religion as the core of their tradition and cultural identity.

VIEWS OF THE PERSON

Ethnic identity is a critical factor in forming the "self-concept" and "other-concept" for many native religions' practitioners. This type of ethno-religion helps to reinforce the bloodline boundary of "us versus them." Similar to the aforementioned folk religion, Chinese native religions regard "holism" (*yuan rong xing*, 圆融性) as their ultimate telos, which means the status of harmony between person, nature, and a spiritual realm. Since many native religions typically involve ancestor worship, the "attachment" with their ancestors' names and their ancestral lands is an essential part of personal identity. For example, among the Bimo-Yi tradition, bloodline lineage is significant and is reinforced by the elaborated religious practices of collective funerals (*ni mu cuo bi*). When orchestrating *ni mu cuo bi*, all of the relevant family clans have to attend the event, which can range from three to nine days. Everyone has to contribute, participating in the animal sacrifices and feasting procedure. A temporary altar of pine branches would be built for all the departed ancestors. The Bimo priest would carve the names of all the deceased family members on the bamboo stick that represents the souls who need to be sent off during the funeral. All ancestors are remembered by the family clan through ritual participation; at our field observation, some could recall their ancestors' name back through twenty-six generations. The significance of bloodline is further evident in the Bimo priesthood lineage, as the title of Bimo originally could only be transmitted from fathers to sons. "Personhood" is not defined individually, but collectively by the family clan. Family names are passed down only through sons, and the living mission of the traditional believers is to pass the torch of the family name to the next generations (Zhang, 2015a, 2015b). Therefore, many native religions' rituals focus on improving the "generativity" of persons and "breeding" of offspring, especially sons. Icons of productivity and harvest are deemed as "gods" or "goddesses" by many native religions. From birth until death, Chinese practitioners of native religions are on a pilgrimage or a journey to "return home" to be reunited with their ancestors. Only by finding the right path to their ancestors' lands can their souls find rest after death. If lost, they become the spirit form or ghost that seems restless, which is also why many native religions are bound to certain geographical regions.

Some native religions emphasize the household lineage rather than the bloodline lineage, such as the Jiarong-Tibetan group and the Mosuo group that worship the "mountain gods," which could help to reinforce the geographical-spatial constellation (Zhang, 2015). Another native reli-

gion practiced by the Huayao-Dai group is represented by their worshipping of the "god of fortress" (寨神 "布召社"), as the "fortress" is the most
important social unit among Dai people. In fact, being accepted by the
religious community is part of the "primordial ties" and psychological
resources of many Chinese ethnic minorities (Wang, 2006).

VIEW ON HEALTH AND ILLNESS

Similar to Chinese folk religion, native religions among many Chinese
minority groups also view health as "balance" and harmony with the
natural elements. However, the "natural elements" of native Chinese
religions are more than just the basic five elements or *qi* (energy), but
inclusive of all the living things on earth. The polytheistic nature of
native Chinese religions allows them to see spirits behind every stone,
and the reciprocal dynamic relationship with their environment grants
them a state of well-being. Evil spirits could come from dead persons or
they could be animistic spirits (e.g., toad, snake, mountain) that are being
offended. For example, Yi people who practice Bimo tradition believe
that it is important to sacrifice animals to the natural spirits in exchange
for a good harvest every year (Zhang, 2015b). In order to be free of plague,
native believers need to be mindful not to offend the spirits around them
or break social taboos.

Well-being is defined not by individuals but by the wealth and repu-
tation of the family clan. One of the personal characteristics of resilience
is to gain social recognition and be knowledgeable of one's cultural history (Ting, 2019).

There are no distinctive functions of mind, body, and spirits for native
religion, as these three interfaces are all being expressed through somatic
forms. Physical suffering is similar to psychological and spiritual suffering. In our recent study of Bimo-Yi (Ting & Sundararajan, 2018), their
emotions displayed in suffering events are often described in concrete
terms, such as how much they lost in cash or livestock. This expression
of suffering is seen in their concrete manipulation of religious rituals as
well. Native religious often explain natural disasters and calamities with
explicit reasons, including the breaking of social norms or taboos, an
inability to pass down the family bloodline, disturbance by uncleansed

spirits or lost souls, moral misbehaviors (lying, stealing), punishment from gods, broken social relationships, hauntings by evil ghost or uncleaned spirits, and spells cast by enemies. Biomedical explanations are seldom adopted by native religion believers, unlike Chinese folk religions, which still adhere to certain dietary restrictions.

VIEWS ON HELP AND TREATMENT

Similar to Chinese folk religion, many native religions also utilize rituals and traditional healers in treating mental health issues. However, rather than just labeling the healing ceremony as "witchcraft" or "divination," the native religions have their own specific hierarchies for different healers and various ceremonies named after their own dialects. Unlike folk religion, where Chinese believers only go to the witch doctor in times of distress, the indigenous healers for native religions usually are the center of the communal well-being. This is evident by the fact that many native religions are named after their religious priesthood. For example, the Shaman religion is actually named after the witch doctor among northern Chinese nomads (Bo & Xu, 2004).

Unlike mainstream Chinese, ethnic-minority Chinese express higher regard for their religious leaders and priesthood as they are usually deemed charismatic figures who possess special knowledge and compassion. The religious leaders are usually not paid for their treatment and services but are bestowed with gifts of appreciation (e.g., livestock or meals). The sophistication of native religion healings permeates the special calendar of tribal groups and different seasons of the years and life spans. For example, traditional Yi follows the ten-month solar calendar and celebrates three seasonal changes via rituals of blessings and exorcism every year. The practitioners are usually well versed with the elements of different festivals and ceremonies related to protection and healings (Zhang, 2015).

Another significant feature of indigenous healing traditions is their communal nature. The reciting of scriptures, spells, or poems is a common form of healing ceremony orchestrated by the native healers. Native religions have myriad scriptures or specific spells for different illnesses. Unlike folk religion, where rituals are usually practiced in an enclosed environment, native religion prefers an open space to allow the whole community or village to participate in the ceremony. For instance, Bimo-Yi normally invites the community to a feast after the animal-sacrifice ceremony (Zhang, 2015b). This kind of communal feast is also like the exchange of favors between different families where they help each other to kill animals in a more efficient way. The emotional support and social bonding between family members and relatives are formed naturally during the rituals and ceremonies. This could serve as a buffer against stressors such as the death of a family member or separation from the family. For example, Ting (2016) found that Tibetan earthquake survivors in Qinghai (China) adopted communal grieving in their unique sky-burial funeral ceremony. The burial ceremony involves extended family members' full participation by reciting prayers and scriptures, sculpting little pagodas, carrying the dead body to the funeral site, and performing full-body salutation around the holy temples together, as paying respect to the deceased and helping the latter to venture peacefully to the afterlife. The more people participating in the funeral, the more good karma is earned for the departed.

EPISTEMOLOGY: EXPLAINING THE HEALING MECHANISM
IN CHINESE TRADITIONAL RELIGIONS

Even though different Chinese ethnic groups tend to adopt different forms of traditional religions, most of the scholars agree that both folk religion and native religion in Chinese society are characterized by their high degrees of groundedness, embeddedness, diffusion, and communalism. Since the social boundary of traditional religions is very different from that of institutional religions, this section briefly introduces two different theories or epistemologies for an indigenous psychology of religion—the ecological rationality framework (Todd & Gigerenzer, 2012; Ting & Sundararajan, 2018), and Peircean semiotic analysis (Hoopes, 1991). They are chosen due to their sensitivity to the unique spirituality and communal ecology among native religions and could be extended to explain other similar indigenous religious ecology as well.

ECOLOGICAL RATIONALITY FRAMEWORK:
POWER OF STRONG TIES

Ecological rationality theory (Todd & Gigerenzer, 2012) is one framework that could be applied to study the psychology of religion and that may capture both institutional and diffused religions. With this framework, any religious or cultural system could be deemed as an ecological system that coevolves with a unique form of human cognition and emotion (Sundararajan, 2015).

In our framework of cultural analysis, we posit two evolutionarily ancient ecological niches—strong ties and weak ties (Granovetter, 1973)—each privileging the development of certain cognitive styles and not others. According to Granovettor (1973), a strong-ties society consists of the private sphere of families, close friends, and relatives (mostly blood-tie relationships), and the weak-ties society consists of the public sphere of strangers or acquaintances. We further posit that different religious traditions could be plotted on a continuum of weak ties to strong ties. Different cognitive orientations (attentional focus) and external focus on the physical space versus internal focus on the mental, could also be plotted on the other axis of cultural comparison (Figure 1, adapted from Ting & Sundararajan [2018]).

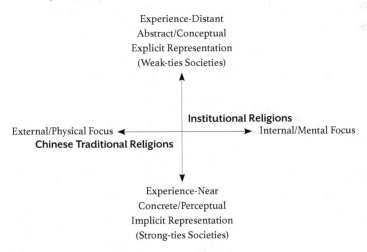

FIGURE 1. Mapping Cultures along the Axes of Cognition

Source: Adapted from Ting & Sundararajan, 2018

This theory also has been extended to explain the suffering of ethnic minorities of the Yi community in China (Ting & Sundararajan, 2018). Our earlier study showed that Yi-Bimo tradition revolved around bloodlines and the family clan (*jia zhi*) network, where family members organize religious rituals. Through a religious comparison study, we found that Yi-Bimo religious groups attribute the causes of their suffering more externally (e.g., sociopolitical discrimination and injustice, evil spirits disturbance, etc.) than do their Christian counterparts. Their emotional expressions are more somatic and concrete (e.g., describing the emotion-laden events) than the Yi-Christian group, who displayed more emotion lexicons. The Yi-Bimo group's help-seeking practices were also based on the strong-ties connection, namely, reliance on a Bimo priest for external orchestration of rituals, whereas the Christian group reported more internal religious resources and weak-ties relationships as help-seeking behavior (Ting, Sundararajan, & Huang, 2017).

Through the lens of ecological rationality, the view on personhood, illness and health, and healing resources are all informed by the difference of cognitive styles and coevolve with the religious ecology of many indigenous people, including traditional Chinese. For example, rather than seeing the externally focused religious healing rituals as "superstitious" or "materialistic" from the lens of weak-ties ecology, the healing ceremonies performed in the external space in Chinese traditional religion are adaptive to those people who reside in the strong-ties society.

SEMIOTIC ANALYSIS: HEALING MECHANISM EMBEDDED IN COMMUNAL RELIGIOUS RITUALS

Many psychologists have discussed the therapeutic nature of indigenous religious communities (Katz, 2017; Kirmayer et al., 2011) from anthropological and systemic perspectives. Aside from the macro-level (bird's-eye) analysis (such as the ecological rationality framework) of the healing mechanism, we would add micro-level (worm's-eye) analysis on the emotion and cognition changes embedded in the healing process. This semiotic analysis, originally developed by Charles Sanders Peirce (Hoopes, 1991), was applied by Sundararajan (2011) to interpret the spiritual transformation and healing practices of tribal peoples. According to semiotics theory, a sign is anything that represents something else, such as religion, and a fully developed sign consists of three modes of representation—icon, index, and symbol—each of which contributes uniquely to the overall efficiency of the sign as a system (Deacon, 1997).

An *icon* is a concrete expression of experience. It embodies a relationship of spatiotemporal contiguity between the sign and what it represents. This could be the goddess statues in the Chinese temple, the Black Stone in Mecca, and even the material possessions for the Yi-Bimo group (Ting & Sundararajan, 2018). For ethnic minorities who are more perceptual in cognition, animal sacrifices or food sharing would be a predominant sign of religious expression.

Index is also an implicit, experience-bound type of representation. The difference between icon and index is summed up by Parmentier (1994) as follows: whereas an icon provides some information about reality, such as the speaker's suffering and distress, an index "directs the mind to some aspect of [that] reality" (p. 7). An example would be a nonconscious automatic display of emotions, such as crying, blushing, dancing, or salutation in the religious ceremony. Another example is the gesture of pointing or chanting in the ceremony.

Symbol refers to linguistic expressions, which, unlike index and icon, have an arbitrary relationship with what they represent. For instance, blushing has a physical connection with the feeling of embarrassment, but the word "embarrassment" does not. The relationship between word and feeling is arbitrarily determined by culture. An example of using religious symbols would be scriptures, prayers or blessings, curses, or other verbal citations such as "hallelujah" or "amen."

According to Peirce (Hoopes, 1991), a fully developed sign system is capable of integrating its multiple functions of representation: subjective experience (foregrounded by the index), concrete expression (rendered visible by the icon), and abstract understanding (rendered explicit by the symbol). Historically, the folk religion and native tradition are able to keep a balance between their sensory-bound reality space, sustained by iconic and indexical sign use, on the one hand, and the virtual space of symbol use, sustained by a rich tradition of myths and rituals, on the other. Sundararajan (2011) points out that in the healing rituals of many indigenous cultures, the triadic structure of the sign is kept intact by a division of labor: the burden of symbolic representation by means of linguistic expression and interpretation is carried by the spiritual healer, while the client only has the responsibility of avowal ("yes, it hurts"), an indexical function that validates the representations presented by the healer. Through this division of labor, the healing ritual restores the integrity of the sign system and thereby the health of the sign user. Put another way, since the ritual expert can perform the symbolic function more than adequately, the limited capacity of the clients to express their emotions verbally (symbolically) becomes inconsequential.

Contributing to the accumulating evidence that suggests a buffering effect of religious coping (Pargament, Koenig, & Perez, 2000), the semiotic analysis sheds some light on the cognitive mechanism of such a buffering effect in the Chinese traditional religions as well (Ting & Sundararajan, 2018).

CLINICAL IMPLICATIONS FOR MENTAL HEALTH PROFESSIONALS

Chinese traditional religions have their unique biopsychosocial-spiritual understanding of health and illness based on the belief of harmony within an individual's personhood, and between an individual and the society, and natural and supernatural worlds. This understanding serves as foundation in its assessment, diagnosis, conceptualization, and treatment of both physical illnesses and mental illnesses. Therapists who have inadequate understanding and appreciation of traditional religions' unique worldviews may inadvertently impose their personal belief system and the ethnocentric model of health and illness on believers of Chinese traditional religions, and overlook their rich resources that can be utilized to promote health and recovery. Besides having some cultural awareness of their own cultural identities and projection, it is also an ethical mandate for the clinicians to expand their knowledge and skills to be culturally competent (Sue & Sue, 2003). We hereby propose the following guidelines and suggestions to mental health workers with potential clients from a Chinese traditional religions background.

AFFIRMING AND ASSESSING ETHNIC IDENTIFICATION

Differentiating whether the Chinese clients come from the Han ethnic group or other ethnic minority groups is the first step, as the latter have a stronger affiliation to their native religious belief system. Besides affirming the ethnic identity and boundary for the Chinese believers, we would encourage therapists to further explore the clients' degree of identification with their religious practice as many of them are afraid to be mislabeled or misunderstood for being "supertitious" or "backward thinking" for endorsing traditional practices that Western science could not explain. Normalizing their unique belief system would help to build rapport as well as to further assess the presented symptoms from a culturally sensitive lens.

REEXAMINING THE SUFFERING TAXONOMY AND CULTURAL DIAGNOSIS

As modern society is not especially friendly toward traditional religion or mysticism, Chinese practitioners of traditional beliefs could be expected to face cultural misfits in the urban setting or weak-ties society due to migration. Many of them might not be able to see the icons or symbols of their religious beliefs in a foreign land and hence lack the resources of emotional regulation and problem solving. Therapists need to hold their clinical judgment until a more holistic picture of symptoms formulation is confirmed. Therapists could start by eliciting clients' conceptualization of their presenting problems to formulate a culturally informed case conceptualization that may enhance culturally responsive clinical practice (Kilcullen & Day, 2018). If possible, incorporating the symbols and concepts of Chinese traditional religion can enhance clients' acceptance of their suffering without shame or confusion. For Chinese believers who come from a strong-ties society, nonverbal gestures or somatic expression should be equally weighted as verbal expression of emotion in the therapy process.

COLLABORATING WITH RELIGIOUS HEALERS

External attribution of an illness (such as being possessed by evil spirits) allows a less shameful way for Chinese believers to seek help from their indigenous healers. Therefore, a multidisciplinary approach would be helpful, including physicians, physiotherapists, social workers, psychiatrists, and even traditional healers. Some community outreach programs could also consider working with religious leaders to advocate for an integrated treatment method, so that some clients could benefit also from modern medication. We could encourage traditional Chinese believers to continue their healing rituals or diet, at the same time using professional mental health services as confidants. The concept of harmony (yin-yang) of individual organisms and society could be applied to explain the functions of a biopsychosocial treatment plan that can enhance clients' receptiveness to multidisciplinary interventions. Nevertheless, one caveat of referring clients to folk religious leaders is the risk of exploitation by fake healers or religious extremists (Connor, 2016). Hence, we would suggest that the therapist discuss with clients the general ethics of beneficence in their culture, and check with community authorities before suggesting clients to any indigenous healers.

ADDRESSING CONFLICTS IN BOTH INTERPERSONAL AND SPIRITUAL REALMS

Due to the belief in equilibrium between the heaven, person, and society, it is crucial for therapists to assess for conflicts in clients' interpersonal realm (e.g., family discords) and spiritual dimension (e.g., disapproval from the ancestors). For example, adherents of Chinese traditional religion may interpret the presence of mental illness in the family as the consequence of the wrong deeds of ancestors. Restoring harmony in those conflicts would then be the primary therapeutic goal. This could be achieved through inviting important family members to sessions or through home visits by social workers. A psychosocial treatment plan would be more effective as it tackles the complex interpersonal dynamic in traditional Chinese families. On the other hand, the strong social support in traditional Chinese families with well-defined roles for each family member may facilitate recovery.

The semiotic analysis suggests that one way to help the native religious group (e.g., Yi-Bimo) cope with the ravages of modernization is to promote their unique course of mentalization (mental heuristics) by restoring their symbolic communal space and empowering their ritual specialists to revive the myths and rituals that have given life meaning since ancient time (Ting & Sundararajan, 2018). In the case study conducted with Chinese in Malaysia, we also found that clients felt safe by imagining themselves in the temple of Guangyin (a Chinese folk goddess) during exposure therapy (Ting & Ng, 2012). Mental health practitioners could therefore mobilize the support system within the family clans by encouraging communal religious ceremonies. As many Chinese traditional religions could not "transport" their religious space from place to place, it is important to discuss with the migrant Chinese clients how to make their religious practice "portable" through religious icons. As previously mentioned, many Chinese traditional religions have their own richness in mind-body strategies to promote mental and physical health, similar to mindfulness or physical exercises. Therapists could explore these health-strengthening strategies within Chinese clients' religious ceremonies and cultural heritages.

For those mental health workers who choose to work with this community, such as in postdisaster areas or refugee camps, they could choose to build a temporary religious shelter for the affected Chinese believers, as it would restore the sense of control for victims to be able to visualize their religious space. Other creative communal activities that aim to bring the community together through religious rituals and festivals are highly encouraged.

CONCLUSION

The dualism of a mind-over-body telos has for decades influenced psychology discipline to the study of religion (Dueck, 1995). To many Chinese traditional communities in which the mind is embedded in the body, which in turn is embedded in the collective life of myths and rituals, a Western institutional approach for mental health services might not be applicable. Though after 1949, Han Chinese in mainland China have pledged themselves as "atheists" under the ideology of Marxism, many Chinese diaspora and traditional groups are still deeply rooted in their ancient cultural practices, spirituality, and healing rituals. Currently most of the religious studies on Chinese populations are of the Han tradition, which is mainly informed by a mixture of Confucian, Daoist, and Buddhist traditions. Hence our chapter concludes that both folk religion and native religion as espoused by different Chinese groups share similar characteristics as diffused religions, yet are different in organizational structure based on ethnic characteristics. In order to understand each of the folk and native religions in depth without reducing them to one unanimous taxonomy, we acknowledge the limit of the scope of this chapter but hope to spark interest in further in-depth study on each of the traditional religions in the near future.[1]

REFERENCES

CHINESE PUBLICATIONS

Bo, S., & Xu, J. (2004). *Heze shaman de paixi, zhonglei, mingcheng he zhineng* [Heze shaman's sects, categories, names, and functions]. *Heilongjiang National Series, 2,* 80–85.

Chang, H. (1996). *Daojiao yu minjianxinyang yiliao wenhua: Yi zhaojingzhenghouqun weili* [The healing culture of Taoism and folk religion: A study on fright neurosis]. In F. Lee & R. G. Chu (Eds.), *Yishi, miaohui yu shequ: Daojiao, minjianxinyang yu minjianwenhua* [Rituals, temple fairs and community: Taoism, folk religion and folk culture] (pp. 427–457). Taipei: Institute of Chinese Literature and Philosophy, Academia Sinica.

Cheng, C. M. (2008). *Minsu shengsixue* [The studies of life and death in folklore]. Taipei: Wenchin Publishing House.

Cheng, C. M. (2010). *Minjian xinyang yu yishi* [Folk religion and rituals]. Taipei: Wenchin Publishing House.

Fei, X. T. (1999). *The pluralistic integration of the Chinese nation.* Beijing: Zhong yang min zu da xue chu ban she.

Jin, Z. (2002). A preliminary study on the gathering and dispersing phenomena of folk beliefs. *Xi bei min zu yan jiu, 2,* 146–157.

Jin, Z. (2018). The form construction of contemporary Chinese folk belief. *Min su yan jiu, 4,* 7–15.

Li, J. F., & Cai. H. (2011). Traditional renaissance and cultural reconstruction: An anthropological analysis of the revival of the Tuzhu culture in Weishan. *Hei long jiang min zu cong kan, 1,* 147–151.

Li, Y. (1995). *Chuantong zhongguo jiazhiguan yu huaren jiankang xingwei tezhen* [Traditional Chinese values and the characteristic of Chinese health behaviors]. In W. S. Tseng (Ed.), *Huaren de xinli yu zhiliao* [The psychology and therapy of Chinese people] (pp. 29–52). Retrieved from https://www.ioe.sinica.edu.tw/WebTools/FilesDownload.ashx?Siteid=530167135246736660&Menuid=530167136456177050&fd=ResearcherPublication&Pname=etliy-0037b.pdf

Lin, M., & Chen, W. (2008). *Mazhu liedao de fushi limiao yanjiu: Chong Makang Tian Hou Gong tanqi* [Temple founded for "drifting corpses" in the Mazu Islands: The Makang Mazu Temple as a preliminary case study]. *Taiwan Journal of Anthropology, 6*(1), 103–131. doi: 10.7115/TJA.200806.0103

Luo, B., Ni, P., Yin, H., Gao, H., & Lee, C. (2017). Psychological exploration of "ghost possession" and other folk faiths in Chinese ghost culture. *Advances in Psychology, 7*(3), 377–387. https://doi.org/10.12677/AP.2017.73048

Wang, J. X. (2009). On methodology of ethnic religion research from the perspective of anthropology. *Min zu yan jiu, 3,* 23–31.

Wang, M. (2006). *Huaxia bianyuan: Lishi jiyi yu zuqun renting* [The edge of China: Historical memory and ethnic identity]. Beijing: Social Sciences Academic Press.

Yu, A. (2002, October 24–25). *Taiwan hanren de renguan, jibingguan yu minxuliaofa: yi shoujingweili* [Taiwan Han's people views of human, disease and folk treatments: The example of shoujin]. Paper presented at the Academic Conference of Medicine and Culture. http://proj1.sinica.edu.tw/~abyu2004/rect-event/reading8-1.doc

Zhang, K. J. (2015a). Ethnic identity and religious structural characteristics: A case study of the Nuosu Yi nationality and its native religion in Liangshan. *Shi jie zong jiao wen hua, 6,* 121–126.

Zhang, K. J. (2015b). *The structure, characteristics, and operation mechanism of ethnic religious identity.* (Doctoral dissertation.) Beijing: *Zhong yang min zu da xue.*

Zhang, K. J., Ting, R. S. K., & Luo, Y. S. (2020). Constructing a peaceable psychology paradigm in the study of indigenous religion among China's ethnic minorities. Accepted for publication in *Zong Jiao Xin Li Xue, 6,* 183–198.

Zhang, Y. (2015). Holy mountain and home of Jiarong Tibetan: Social structure generated in the holy history. In M. M. Wang & Y. Su, *Cultural complexity: Rituals, characters and exchanges in southwest China* (pp. 135–169). Beijing: *Bei jing lian he chu ban gong si.*

Zhang, Z. G. (2016). The stone of other mountains of Chinese folk belief: A case study on Ou Da nian's theory exploration. *Shi jie zong jiao wen hua, 5,* 7–12.

ENGLISH PUBLICATIONS

Adler, J. A. (2005). Chinese religion: An overview. In L. Jones (Ed.), *Encyclopedia of religion* (2nd ed.). Detroit: Macmillan Reference.

Clarke, I. (2000). Ancestor worship and identity: Ritual, interpretation, and social normalization in the Malaysian Chinese community. *Sojourn: Journal of Social Issues in Southeast Asia, 15*(2), 273–295. Retrieved from http://www.jstor.org/stable/41057042

Connor, N. (2016, May 15). "I let witch doctors steam my wife alive": Chinese villagers defy government attempts to stamp out black magic. *The Telegraph.* Retrieved from https://www.telegraph.co.uk/news/2016/05/15/i-let-witch-doctors-steam-my-wife-alive-chinese-villagers-defy-g/

Deacon, T. W. (1997). *The symbolic species.* New York: W. W. Norton.

Dueck, A. C. (1995). *Between Jerusalem and Athens: Ethical perspectives on culture, religion, and psychotherapy.* Grand Rapids, MI: Baker Publishing Group.

Dueck, A., Ansloos, J., Johnson, A., & Fort, C. (2017). Western cultural psychology of religion: Alternatives to ideology. *Pastoral Psychology, 66*(1), 397–425. https://doi:10.1007/s11089-016-0731-3

Dueck, A. C., & Han, B. (2012). Psychology of religion in China. *Pastoral Psychology, 61,* 605–622.

Granovetter, M. S. (1973). The strength of weak ties. *American Journal of Sociology, 78,* 1360–1380.

Harrell, S. (1979). The concept of soul in Chinese folk religion. *Journal of Asian Studies, 38*(3), 519–528. doi:10.2307/2053785

He, Q. (2012). Religious traditions in local communities of China. *Pastoral Psychology, 61*(5/6), 823–839. doi: 10.1007/s11089-012-0438-z

Hoopes, J. (Ed.). (1991). *Peirce on signs.* Chapel Hill: University of North Carolina Press.

Katz, R. (2017). *Indigenous healing psychology: Honoring the wisdom of the first peoples.* Rochester, VT: Healing Arts Press.

Kilcullen, M., & Day, A. (2018). Culturally informed case conceptualisation: Developing a clinical psychology approach to treatment planning for non-indigenous psychologists working with Aboriginal and Torres Strait Islander clients. *Clinical Psychologist, 22,* 280–289. Retrieved from https://aps.onlinelibrary.wiley.com/doi/pdf/10.1111/cp.12141

Kirmayer, L. J., Dandeneau, S., Marshall, E., Phillips, M. K., & Williamson, K. J.

(2011). Rethinking resilience from indigenous perspectives. *Canadian Journal of Psychiatry, 56*(2), 84–91.

Laufer, B. (1917). Origin of the word Shaman. *American Anthropologist 19*, 361–371.

Li, Y. (1988). Ancestor worship and the psychological stability of family members in Taiwan. In K. Yoshimatsu & W. S. Tseng (Eds.), *Asia family mental health* (pp. 26–33). Retrieved from https://www.ioe.sinica.edu.tw/WebTools/FilesDownload .ashx?Siteid=530167135246736660&Menuid=530167136456177050&fd=Researcher Publication&Pname=etliy-0008.pdf

Li, Y. (1992). Notions of time, space and harmony in Chinese popular culture. In C. Huang & E. Zcher (Eds). *Time and space in Chinese culture* (pp. 383–402). Retrieved from https://www.ioe.sinica.edu.tw/WebTools/FilesDownload .ashx?Siteid=530167135246736660&Menuid=530167136456177050&fd=Researcher Publication&Pname=etliy-0036b.pdf

Lin, F. (2016). *Wuzhe de shijie* [The world of wizards]. Guangzhou, China: Guangdong People's Publishing House.

Lin, W. (2000). *Renguan, kongjian shijian yu zhibing yishi: yi yige taiwai xinan nongcun weili* [The concept of the person, spatial practices, and healing cults: An ethnography of a village in southwestern Taiwan]. *Bulletin of the Department of Anthropology (National Taiwan University), 56*, 44–76.

Mou, Z. (2016) A study of Chinese traditional patriarchal religion. *Studies in Chinese Religions, 2*(4), 331–365, doi:10.1080/23729988.2017.1286899

Pargament, K. I., Koenig, H. G., & Perez, L. M. (2000). The many methods of religious coping: Development and initial validation of the RCOPE. *Journal of Clinical Psychology, 56*(4), 519–543.

Parmentier, R. J. (1994). *Signs in society: Studies in semiotic anthropology.* Bloomington: Indiana University Press.

Sue, D. W., & Sue, D. (2003). *Counseling the culturally diverse: Theory and practice* (5th ed.). New York: J. Wiley.

Sundararajan, L. (2011). Spiritual transformation and emotion: A semiotic analysis. *Journal of Spirituality in Mental Health, 13*, 78–90.

Sundararajan, L. (2015). *Understanding emotion in Chinese culture: Thinking through psychology.* New York: Springer SBM.

Ting, R. S.-K. (2016). Celebrating life and death: Resiliency among post-earthquake Tibetans' religious community. *Journal of Psychology and Theology, 44*(2), 124–132.

Ting, R. S.-K., Foo, P.-L., Tan, & N. L.-T. (In press). Mental health issues among Chinese communities in Malaysia: A cultural and historical approach. In Minas H. (Ed.), *Mental health in China and the Chinese diaspora: Historical and cultural perspectives.* New York: Springer.

Ting, R. S.-K., & Sundararajan, L. (2018). *Culture, cognition, and emotion in China's religious ethnic minorities: Voices of suffering among the Yi.* Palgrave Studies in Indigenous Psychology. New York: Palgrave Macmillan.

Ting, R.S.-K., Zhang, K. J., & Huang, Q. B. (2019). An inclusive indigenous psychology for all Chinese: Heeding the mind and spirit of ethnic minorities in China. In K. H. Yeh (Ed.), *Asian indigenous psychologies in global context* (pp. 249–276). Palgrave Studies in Indigenous Psychology. New York: Palgrave Macmillan.

Ting, S.-K. (2019). The HIV epidemic among the Yi people in Southwest China. Symposium presentation for Toward a More Equitable Global Psychology: Challenges and Promises, 127th American Psychological Association (APA) Annual Convention, Denver, CO, August 8–11.

Ting, S.-K., & Ng, L. O. (2012). Use of religious resources in psychotherapy from a tradition-sensitive approach: Cases from Chinese in Malaysia. *Pastoral Psychology: Special Issues, 61,* 941–957.

Ting, S.-K., Sundararajan, L. K. W., & Huang, Q. B. (2017). Narratives of suffering: A psycholinguistic analysis of two Yi religious communities in Southwest China. *Research in the Social Scientific Study of Religion, 28,* 232–255.

Todd, P. M., & Gigerenzer, G. (Eds.). (2012). *Ecological rationality: Intelligence in the world.* New York: Oxford University Press.

Waley, A. (1955). *The nine songs: A study of shamanism in ancient China.* London: City Lights Books.

Yang, C. K. (1961). *Religion in Chinese society: A study of contemporary social functions of religion and some of their historical factors.* Berkeley: University of California Press.

Yang, F., & Hu, A. (2012). Mapping Chinese folk religion in Mainland China and Taiwan. *Journal for the Scientific Study of Religion, 51*(3), 505–521. doi:10.1111/j.1468-5906.2012.01660.x

ENDNOTES

1. Acknowledgment: Some of the research conclusions in this chapter are supported by Monash University Malaysia, a Global Asia in the 21st Century (GA 21) internal grant, and the National Social Science Fund of China (No. 19BMZ131).

INNOCENT F. OKOZI

AFRICAN TRADITIONAL RELIGION AND PSYCHOLOGY OF RELIGION

HISTORY AND CONCEPTS OF THE PSYCHOLOGY OF AFRICAN TRADITIONAL RELIGION

African traditional religion (ATR) comprises a set of indigenous beliefs and practices of people of African origin. It includes belief in the existence of a supreme Being who supersedes all other divinities. The divinities act as intermediaries and ensure the harmony that should exist within the cosmos between humans, their ancestors, and other living beings. For example, the Yoruba Traditional Religion (in Nigeria) includes belief in the existence of a self-existent Being who is the creator and overseer of heaven and earth, people as well as the divinities and spirits, who act as functionaries of the self-existent Being in a theocratic world and as intermediaries between mankind and the self-existent Being (Awolalu, 1979).

ATR is an integral part of the life and culture of people of African descent, and is interwoven into the fabric of every aspect of the life of Africans. For example, in celebrations of new life (birth of a child) or death (funeral); of initiation (e.g., passage to adulthood), marriage, or an achievement; as well as celebrations of a rich harvest (new yam festival in Nigeria) or end of the harvest season, African people incorporate some music, dances, and animal sacrifices into their celebration of life, especially to express their gratitude to the benevolent spirits and ward off malevolent spirits, experiences, or disasters. ATR also consists of the sustained beliefs in and veneration of the forebears of the Africans, which

is practiced in various forms by a very large number of Africans, including individuals who claim to be Muslims or Christians (Awolalu, 1976). In
other words, many Africans who are Muslim or Christian proselytes are
still influenced by some ATR beliefs and practices, especially when facing some challenges in their lives that their Muslim or Christian leaders
have not satisfactorily explained to them.

There are different African traditional religions, just as there are
many African nations and peoples, with different cultures, languages,
and dialects. For example, the Yoruba traditional religions are practiced
in Nigeria, Benin Republic, Togo, and Brazil, whereas the Voodoo traditional religions are practiced in Benin Republic, South West Nigeria,
Colombia, and Cuba. Some of the common threads among these religions include system of belief in a self-existent Being and religious
practices, rituals, and symbols with some slight cultural variations and
expressiveness. In this chapter I present mostly the Yoruba traditional
religion as practiced in Nigeria and occasionally make references to other
ATRs. ATR has survived through oral transmission and spread beyond
the African continent as people of African descent migrated to or were
shipped into slavery to Europe, America, or Asia.

We can think of ATR in a similar way that we think of Christianity,
Islam, or other world religions, knowing that these comprise various religious categories or movements within each religious tradition. However,
unlike Christianity and Islam, ATR evolved without a known founder or
reformer or any resulting scriptural documents. ATR was passed from
one generation to another, and in that process may have undergone various modifications, while maintaining core religious beliefs and practices such as communication with the divinities and spirits as well as the
ancestors through designated traditional religious priests and doctors.
The priests and doctors could prescribe what type of sacrifices, including
animal sacrifices, could be offered to praise a benevolent spirit or appease
a malevolent spirit. Communication with divinities, spirits, and ancestors
is in the form of incantations or divinations and may involve some music
chants and dancing as well as trance states. The sacrifices could be animals (such as hens, goats, cows, sheep, deer, or turkeys), or fruits from
trees, including kola nuts, and local palm wine. There were even some
stories of human sacrifice. The sacrifices were believed to help cure ill-

nesses, increase fertility, gain an advantage over one's enemies (including in a battle or quarrel with one's opponents), or ward off natural disasters. In ATR, only the self-existent Being is worthy of worship. All the other divinities, spirits, and ancestors are worthy of veneration.

ATR survived and flourished in different historical, geographical, sociological, cultural, and physical environments (Mbiti, 2015). Of note is that the earliest documented histories of African culture and religion were those of ancient Egyptians.

In addition to oral transmission of cultural and religious symbols, artifacts, and practices, archaeological digs have revealed the religious systems and practices of ancient Egyptian pharaohs and their subjects. For example, analysis of the remains of the boy king known as Tutankhamun suggests that he spent much of his rule (ca. 1332–1323 BC) trying to restore Egypt's traditional religion, something that had been interrupted when his father, the Pharaoh Akhenaten (Amenhotep IV), started a revolution that emphasized the primacy of the Aten, the Sun disk (cited in Onyewuenyi, 2005; Hawass, 2004), as a state religion.

THE SUPREME BEING AND INTERMEDIARY DIVINITIES IN ATR

The African cosmology comprises the Supreme Being (God), the intermediary deities, ancestors, deceased relatives, and the living. In ATR, God is considered the Supreme Being. In different African language groups, God is designated with different names, each of which is descriptive of a Supreme Being who is unique, almighty and majestic, unchanging and faithful.

Among the Yoruba-speaking communities, the intermediary divinities are called *Orisha*. They would be similar to Christian angels. Some of the Yoruba Orisha include *Orunmila*, known for his wisdom, knowledge, and divination. *Shango* was known as a royal ancestor of the Yoruba, the third Alaafin (ruler) of the medieval Oyo Kingdom before his posthumous deification. He could be likened to the Greek deity *Thor*, due to his temperamental nature and ability to conjure up lightning.

TABLE 1. NAMES FOR THE SUPREME BEING IN WEST AFRICAN CULTURES

Language Group	Name for God
Yoruba	*Olorun* (literally meaning the "Lord or owner of heaven") and *Eleda* (the Creator of the universe)
Edo (Nigeria)	*Osanobuwa* means "God who is the Source and Sustainer of the World"
Ibos (Nigeria)	*Chukwu* (the Great Source of life and being) or *Chineke* (the Creator)
Hausa (Nigeria, Niger, Ghana)	*Ubangiji* (the Only Supreme Being)
Ewe language (Togo and Ghana)	*Nana Buluku* (the Ancient of Days or the Eternal One)
Akan (Ghana and Cote d'Ivoire)	*Onyame* (the Great and Shining One)
Fon (Benin Republic and Togo)	*Mawu* (the Creator)

EPISTEMOLOGICAL CHALLENGES OF
AN ETIC APPROACH TO ATR

Recent documentation of ATR has been facilitated by scientific, anthropological, sociological, and epistemological studies, conducted mostly within the last two centuries. As this book has highlighted, most Western studies of ATR and evaluation of its cultural beliefs and practices were often based on an etic approach (a top-down viewpoint) to ATR, rather than on an emic approach (a bottom-up viewpoint). This etic approach resulted in the creation of some negative or derogatory concepts and misunderstandings of ATR. Examples of misleading terms include *primitive, savage, fetishism* or *magic, juju, heathenism, paganism, animism, idolatry* or *ancestral worship,* and *polytheism* (Awolalu, 1976). This approach lacks scientific humility as well as fails to capture a true understanding of the tenets of ATR. Thus, it is important to explore some of these misconceptions.

COMMON MISCONCEPTIONS ABOUT ATR

ANCESTRAL WORSHIP. In African traditional culture, ancestors are regarded as the "living dead." They are departed blood relatives who are believed to exist in the spiritual world (or world of the dead) but continue to show interest in the daily lives of their relatives (Van Dyk, 2001; Mbiti, 2015). These relatives, who include, among others, departed or deceased nuclear or extended family members, are regarded as superior to the living because they continue to exist in the spirit world. They are also regarded as mediators between the living and the Supreme Being, God. It is inappropriate to refer to this belief and practice as ancestral worship. The correct term is *ancestral reverence* or *veneration* (Berg, 2003; Mbiti, 2015; Child & Child, 1993).

The ancestral veneration in ATR could be compared to veneration of the saints in the Christian context. For example, in some ATR funeral rites, a recently deceased family member is often requested by their living relatives to bring their concerns and needs to the ancestors. Similarly, the ancestors are asked to assist in restoring harmony and well-being to the surviving relatives. Likewise, in extended periods of drought or other natural disasters that threaten human life, community ancestors are implored to intervene on behalf of the community or village. Sometimes, sacrifices are offered to appease the benevolent spirits and ward off the malevolent spirits. For instance, bits of food or libations are placed on the grave of family ancestral spirits. Some shrines are dedicated to the memory of ancestor(s).

ANIMISM. The concept of animism is attributed to Sir Edward Tylor, an English anthropologist, who is regarded as the father of cultural anthropology. In his book *Primitive Culture* (1871; cited in Awolalu, 1976), Tylor describes animism as the belief in innumerable spiritual beings, capable of helping or harming human interests. Animism could be described as a system of belief and practices based on the idea that some objects and natural phenomena are inhabited by spirits or souls (Mbiti, 2015). This ATR belief is an attempt to acknowledge the interconnectedness among Africans, their community, and the "life-force" in their environment. Some examples of objects associated with animism include rivers or streams (e.g., the "Osun" River in Oshogbo, Osun State, Nigeria), trees (e.g., the "Iroko" or Oaktree), rocks (e.g., the "Olumo Rock" in Abeokuta, or Egbaland, Ogun State, South West Nigeria), and animals (e.g., the "Royal Python" in Ouidah or Abomey-Calavi, Benin Republic, or in Ogwashi-Uku, Delta State, Nigeria). Similarly, lightning and thunder are manifestations of the thunder spiritual being.

The animistic entities, such as the royal python, are held in high esteem, are unharmful to humans, and the belief is that they help to protect endangered species of animals from extinction. My mother once told me a story about a royal python that visited the home of a newborn baby; the baby's family members offered the python some food and let it go as it willed, and no harm was done to the baby.

Although some elements of animism could be found in ATR, it would be fallacious to conclude that ATR is simply animism.

PAGANISM. Paganism or heathenism is a derogatory term sometimes applied to someone who worships false gods or idols. It is also sometimes used to describe Africans who do not practice the Christian, Jewish, or Islamic religion. This type of labeling is as inappropriate as addressing as pagans Westerners who do not practice the Christian, Jewish, or Islamic religion.

IDOLATRY. Idolatry is the worshipping of false gods or emblems. A religious emblem could be a wooden carving or a stone or iron or bronze sculpture. The emblem may be symbolic and point to a meaning beyond itself. In ATR, emblems are used to aid the worshipper in understanding the divine presence. Of note is that the variety of divine beings represented by the emblems are considered servants or representatives of the Supreme Being. In ATR, there is no official representation or emblem of the Supreme Being. Hence, emblems are effective to the extent to which a spiritual meaning has been ascribed to them. Therefore, in principle, the adherents of ATR do not worship the idols per se, but venerate the spiritual beings represented by the emblems.

FETISHISM OR MAGIC. ATR has been wrongly referred to as a fetishistic religion. The word *fetish*, which is of Portuguese origin, was used to refer to the charms and amulets that the early Portuguese merchants who came to Africa saw the Africans wearing (Awolalu, 1976; Mbiti, 2015). Some dictionaries describe the word *fetish* as any object, animate or inanimate, natural or artificial, regarded by someone as having mysterious or magical powers (Merriam-Webster's Collegiate Dictionary, 2019). Fetishism could also be described as the worship of or the emotional attachment to inanimate objects. In the twentieth century, the word took on a medical meaning, such as an object or bodily part whose real or fantasized presence is psychologically necessary for sexual gratification (Merriam-Webster's Collegiate Dictionary, 2019).

Although there are some elements of magic, witchcraft, and sorcery in the African traditional culture, they do not equate to ATR, which is a world religious system, much like Christianity, Judaism, Islam, Confucianism, or Hinduism. Awolalu (1976) noted that many writers had indiscriminately used the word *fetish*; for example, the prayers said during ATR worship had been wrongly described as fetish prayers, and the ATR priests or priestesses who led those prayers had been wrongly described as fetish priests or priestesses. Similarly, the herbs used by the ATR priests, priestesses, or herbalists in treating their patients were wrongly referred to as fetish herbs. According to E. G. Parrinder (1954), the word *fetish* is most ambiguous, and the time has come for all serious writers and speakers to abandon it completely.

JUJU. The word "juju" is of French origin and is used to refer to a little doll or toy. Some English writers erroneously employed it to describe African divine entities.

POLYTHEISM. Parrinder (1954) observed that the adherents of ATR in West Africa believed in great pantheons of gods that are as diverse as the Greek or Hindu gods. Many of the gods represented forces of nature, which were either feared or appeased for a favor. Most of the gods had their own shrines or temples as well as priests or servants and adepts, or nonpriestly custodians of the knowledge and actions of the god they venerate. However, it would be a mistake to describe ATR as polytheistic, because the adherents of ATR believe in the Supreme Being as Almighty and All-Powerful, Unique and Superseding all beings. For example, in Yoruba culture, the Supreme Being, *Olodumare*, is never ranked with the divinities, *Orisha* (Awolalu, 1976). For these Africans, the various divinities are servants of the Supreme Being, and they play an intermediary role between the Supreme Being and the living.

SAVAGE OR PRIMITIVE. Both words, *savage* and *primitive*, are derogatory and are often seen as the opposite of *civilized*. The dictionary meaning of *savage* includes fierce, ferocious, cruel, or an untamed beast or a brutal, cruel, or barbarous person. The dictionary meaning of *primitive* includes belonging to a very early stage of development, for example, a people or culture that has not evolved. Hence, it is inappropriate to apply these terms to ATR. Like other world religions, ATR has been evolving alongside the evolution of African traditional cultures. Some elements of ATR have been discontinued while some still exist. From the definition of the two terms we are exploring here, we can say that some elements of savagery in varying degrees exist in each person irrespective of creed, race, ethnicity, or sex.

EPISTEMOLOGY AND PHILOSOPHY OF ATR

Africans have different means of acquiring or expressing their knowledge about their communities and the universe. Traditional forms of African epistemology include perceptive knowledge, proverbs, oral history, traditional heritage, arts (e.g., paintings and sculptures), intuitive or tacit knowledge, divination, music and poems, taboos, and social learning. Greek philosophy provided the foundation for Western philosophy. Onyewuenyi (2005) dedicated his book to exploring the African origin of Greek philosophy. He argued that some of the Greek philosophers studied in Egypt. He also stated that Aristotle's revelation on ancient Egypt as the origin of philosophy is corroborated by other documents showing that Thales, the universally acclaimed father of philosophy, studied in Egypt and borrowed his doctrine of the cosmic origin, his geometry, and his political and epistemological theories from Egypt (Onyewuenyi, 2005).

From the previous paragraph, African ways of knowing and Western ways of knowing seem to share a similar origin. However, African epistemology seems to have developed into an inductive rather than a deductive approach to knowledge. The traditional African is more concrete. The experiential knowledge of the traditional African is based on a relational or collective cultural worldview. Because of belief in the harmony in the cosmos and between the divinities, spirits, and humans, knowledge of the unknown is gained by religious priests and herbal doctors through divination and consultation of the divinities, spirits, and ancestors, in view of restoring the harmony in the community and in the world. Through these divinations and consultations, the priests or doctors may gain some special revelation that would guide their prescription or messaging to the intended recipient of their practice, including individuals, the community, or a group of persons. Similarly, the Aristotelian doctrine of the immortality of the soul was claimed by Herodotus to have originated from Egypt (Onyewuenyi, 2005). The Egyptian pharaohs were said to spend their entire life on earth preparing for their eternity or immortality by building their pyramids. Additionally, Egyptian mystery system schools produced medical doctors of repute, including the first physician of antiquity, Imhotep, who was a black Egyptian, and who lived about 2980 BC during the third dynasty (Onyewuenyi, 2005). Imhotep was purported to have cured both physical and psychological illnesses and was revered as a kind of god centuries after his death.

ATR emphasizes the immortality of the human soul. Hence, it is normal for some treasured items belonging to a dead relative to be buried with him or her. The belief is that the dead person would use the item in their world of the spirits. Additionally, belief in the reincarnation of the soul is widely held in ATR.

The traditional African believes that wisdom comes with experience or age. Hence the elderly in the community are respected and consulted for their wisdom in relation to resolving certain community or household problems. Some knowledge is also obtained through wise sayings, proverbs, or quotes, such as the Yoruba maxim, "The dog that will be lost would not hear the whistle of the hunter" (meaning: it is easy to lose one's way when one ignores visible warning signs). The traditional African seeks empirical knowledge as well as intuitive and experimental knowledge.

VIEWS OF THE PERSON/SELF AND MEANING

In African epistemology, the human person does not exist in isolation but is part of a family or community. Given that African culture is a collectivistic culture, the person or self has meaning within the context of his or her community. Where Rene Descartes defined Western philosophy with his famous quote, "I think; therefore, I am," African epistemological concept of the person or self could be defined with the quote, "We think; therefore, we are."

Adjei (2019) noted that Western thought and mainstream psychological theorizations and practices are based on the cultural background of individualism, which views a person as independent and atomistic. Hence, the concept of society generally refers to the aggregated sum of individuals who constitute it, whereas the African view of society or community refers to a thoroughly fused collective (Menkiti, 1984).

In collectivistic cultures like the African cultures, people see themselves as interdependent with their families, coworkers, communities, and other group memberships. In other words, the experience of a person is relationally connected to others and the community in an ontological experience of how things are (Adams, 2005). This implies that the community or extended family influences the person and the person can influence their community or group. Hence, there is a tendency for the person to prioritize group goals over personal goals. African cultures would emphasize the quote that "it takes a village to raise a child."

Ikuenobe (2006) identified a tripartite notion of the person/self in the African worldview, namely the ontological, cosmological, and spiritual, while normatively connected to the community. In other words, a person in the African worldview is self-conscious, communally conscious, and cosmically conscious (Adjei, 2019). The concept of the person is *Eniyan* (person or persons, people, human) in Yoruba (Nigeria), and *Onipa* (person or human) in Akan (Ghana). In both examples, a person is viewed in relation to his or her community and moral standing in the community. The connectedness experienced by a person in the African worldview helps to maintain the cosmic balance between the self, others, nature, the living dead, and God. The fundamental difference between the experience of interdependence in African thought in comparison to Western thought is in terms of duties and obligations (in African thought) as opposed to rights of the individual (in Western thought).

VALUES AND MORALS

Values and morals are an integral part of religious ideals, which are used to further or maintain people's lives in their relationship to one another and their environment. In ATR, the common values and morals include differentiating between right and wrong, truth and falsehood, good and evil; included are upholding justice, promoting love, appreciating beauty, decency, respect for people (parents and older people) and property, keeping one's promises, rightfully apportioning praise and blame, punishment for crimes, knowing one's rights and responsibilities of both the individual and his or her community, character, and integrity (Mbiti, 2015). In addition to helping people live with one another, values and morals help people settle their differences, maintain peace and harmony, make use of their belongings, and celebrate new births, funerals, and the end of the harvest season.

Adjei (2019) observed that morality in the African context has social intentionality in the sense that it is normative and rooted in what the community specifies as acceptable, in contrast to what a person individually thinks. The African notion of morality is embedded in the conception of acceptable social relations and attitudes of the members of the society, while maintaining social harmony, cooperative living, justice, and fairness (Gyekye, 2011).

MENTAL ILLNESS AND ITS CAUSE: MENTAL DISORDERS, PSYCHOLOGICAL SUFFERING, AND PSYCHOLOGICAL CHANGE WITHIN ATR

In ATR, all human suffering or illness—including natural disasters, poor harvest or environmental disasters, snake bites or accidents at work or social activities, family problems or psychosocial problems, or psychological disorders—are attributed to the breach of the natural harmony of the societal or communal laws or taboos. Quite often, misfortunes and illnesses are considered the result of negative attacks or curses placed on an unsuspecting victim by witches, wizards, sorcerers, or evil spirits. Sometimes, illness or misfortune is considered the consequence of a negative attack or curse by an ancestor or intermediary divinity for an offense or breach of the community's code of conduct or taboo. Hence, treatment would involve getting a traditional healer or priest to diagnose the cause of the disharmony. Then the healer would prescribe measures that would help to remove the curse or attenuate the attack and restore the harmony once again to the community.

To provide us with some perspective on how mental health is understood in African popular culture, Aina (2004), a psychiatrist in the Department of Psychiatry at the College of Medicine, University of Lagos, Nigeria, examined the impact that the portrayal of psychiatry and the activities of supernatural forces in indigenous movies, produced in West Africa, had in reinforcing the strong beliefs of Africans in witchcraft, sorcery, divination, and ancestral spirits as well as how the manipulation of these supernatural agents affected the well-being of their victims. In an analysis of 163 West African movies (produced for a West African audience but sold all over the world) over thirty-six months, Aina (2004) found that the movies attributed the symptoms of mental illness to those of a vagrant and psychotic disorder, resulting from affiliation with sorcery, witchcraft, and charms (fifteen movies); overwhelming psychosocial stressors (six movies); curses from enemies and offended divinities or supernatural forces (three movies); and polysubstance dependence (one movie). Furthermore, two movies showed scenes of prominent visual and auditory hallucinations.

In thirteen of the examined movies, there was no attempt to seek treatment of the mental illness, while alternative therapies of traditional and spiritual healings produced greater effectiveness in ten movies, with only two movies showing treatment in orthodox hospitals (Aina, 2004). Aina argued that these findings seem to be consistent with popular but erroneous beliefs among many Africans that most cases of psychiatric or psychological disorders have no cure, while some effective healing can take place through spiritual interventions such as prayer, fasting, and exorcism as well as traditional treatment through incantations, use of herbal potions, and sacrifices to appease the benevolent spirits or ward off the malevolent spirits or supernatural beings.

In Africa, many life mishaps or misfortunes and questionable causes of deaths are attributable to the subtle manipulation of witches, sorcerers, demons, and other beings with supernatural powers. Oftentimes, open discussions of such believed occurrences are considered taboo subjects out of fear of reprisal attacks (Morakinyo & Akiwowo, 1981; Makinde, 1985). Thus, a lot of unexpressed fear of these supernatural forces pervades the mind of many Africans, irrespective of their educational level. Hence, one should note the similarities between phobias in African and Western cultures. For example, among Africans, pathological fear of negative spiritual forces is often accompanied by functional somatic complaints (Odejide, Oyewumi, & Ohaeri, 1989; Freeman et al., 2001).

TREATMENT

Every society has its way of dealing with illnesses and diseases, their methods and remedies for the treatment of ill health or illness. Given that the worldview of Africans in the traditional society is highly spiritually connected, adherents of ATR view their illnesses or ill health through their religious or spiritual lens. Different methods are used to try to diagnose the illness or determine its treatment. One of the methods is known as divination. Divination is the practice of determining the hidden significance or cause of events by various natural, psychological, and other techniques (*Merriam-Webster's Encyclopedia of World Religion*, 1999). The techniques of divination enable humans to have insight and knowledge of the future, or about things that may be mysterious or obscured. Divination relates to the supersensible world (Abdullahi, 2011). Traditional African medicine involves divination, whereby the diviners or traditional healers use various forms of divination to unravel and diagnose their clients' maladies. Forms of divination include dreams and visions, body actions, ordeals, spirit possession or trance, animal types, necromancy, and mechanical techniques (Ajima & Ubana, 2018). The appearance of some animal types was totem to an ethnic group. For example, there were some shared belief about some deity or dead traditional ruler who seemed to have reincarnated into a leopard or inhabit a royal python.

Mental disorders or psychological suffering is considered the result of sorcery and witchcraft, which are employed mostly to hunt or harm an unsuspecting victim or enemy. For example, someone suffering from schizophrenia may be considered a victim of some form of witchcraft or sorcery. Hence, the traditional healer uses divination to discern the client's disorder or disease as well as to determine the best way to treat the client. Treatment often consists of using physical restraint to control violent clients, whereby the violence is seen as a sign of possession with demonic or malevolent spirits. Sometimes the client is flogged or beaten to submission or given some herbal sedative potion to calm them down. The family of the client is sometimes requested to offer some sacrifices to ward off the harmful spirits and free the client from the possession.

VIEW OF HEALTH AND WELL-BEING
FOR ADHERENTS OF ATR

In ATR, wellness and ill health are seen in terms of a person's ability to maintain a harmonious relationship with all the forces that impinge on the person's life and being. This may involve appeasing benevolent spirits (to maintain well-being) or keeping malevolent spirits at bay (to ward off ill health). Hence, psychological well-being would be perceived within the framework of maintaining harmony between the spiritual and the physical dimensions of the community vis-à-vis the individual. Similarly, health treatment would involve both the physical and the spiritual, as well as the psychological aspects of the human person. In other words, any medical or psychological treatment of illness is seen as the fundamental attempt to restore wholeness in an individual as well as in the community to which that individual belongs.

The World Health Organization (2000) described a traditional healer or doctor as a person who is recognized by the community where he or she lives as someone competent to provide health care by using plant, animal, and mineral substances and other methods based on social, cultural, and religious practices. The traditional healer or doctor is known in different nations by different names: *Babalawo* (in Yoruba, Nigeria), *Dibia* (in Ibo, Nigeria), and *Boka* (in Hausa, Nigeria).

It should be noted that many Africans, including Nigerians, Beninese, and other West Africans, East Africans, and South Africans, still patronize the African traditional doctor or healer for illnesses that were not successfully treated by the Western Orthodox hospital doctors. Through African traditional medicine, illness in the African context is properly treated as physical, psychological, social, and economic, in contrast with orthodox medicine, which tends to neglect some aspects of a patient's universe and focus mostly on the physical aspects of a patient's problems (Ajima & Ubana, 2018). Many traditional Africans believe that every illness has a natural, supernatural, or mystical (somatic or physical and spiritual) dimension. The collective dimension of the illness would comprise the arousal of a wide variety of feelings in the patient as well as in those close to the patient, and those close to the patient would seek to be involved in treatment. A visit to a traditional African doctor or herbalist would involve the expectation of a wholistic diagnosis and treatment (Abdullahi, 2011). For example, the diagnosis would comprise dialogue between the doctor and the patient (and patient's relatives if present), but also physical examination of the body or the ailing part of the patient's body (use of physical touch to feel the body part). The traditional doctor may also engage in some divination or consultation with the world of the spirits and divinities with some special chants or songs in order to determine what exactly may have led to the illness. Then the doctor would proceed to describe the patient's illness and how the pain is caused. The prescribed treatment would include some physical activities and practices that would help the patient restore the balance they seek in life or the harmony with oneself, one's community, or one's family (Hillenbrand, 2006).

In recent years, there is an increasing interest in giving more consideration to a patient's spiritual affiliation and psychological aspects, especially in the medical field but in the psychological field too. This is particularly important in the treatment of patients of African descent who may be hesitant in seeking psychological help, especially if they had prior negative experience with a counselor or psychologist who was dismissive of their ATR as occultic or superstitious. The disappointment felt by the patient would be proportional to the underlying fear of not finding help for one's ailment. In this respect, Onu (1999), a Nigerian social anthropologist at the Department of Sociology and Anthropology, University of Nigeria, Nsukka, highlighted the social dimension of illness and argued that a serious illness induces the fear of death or permanent disability in the ill person and constitutes a crisis that requires the cooperative efforts from family members and health-care providers (physical or spiritual). In other words, it is helpful for family members to be included in the initial diagnosis of the patient in order to explore how the patient's illness affects the patient's family as well as what role or roles the patient's family could play in the treatment. Also, during the diagnosis of a patient's illness, it is important not to dismiss outright a patient's statement about considering his or her illness as the result of a possible curse or witchcraft. The patient's statement provides a window into the patient's salient and underlying fears and anxieties. Without arguing with the patient, the clinician is able to acknowledge the patient's emotional distress based on the patient's perception of probable cause of the illness or disorder. This brings one to acknowledge the worldview of the patient.

In the African worldview, there is harmony in the world between human beings and the spirits, plants, animals, the elements, and the dead. Sickness would be considered a consequence of the disharmony that is caused by humans in the world. Therefore, treatment would entail a conscious effort by humans to restore the harmonious relationship with all the forces that affect their life and being. For example, at its best, medicine would aim to reestablish harmony by addressing everything from power to health, from fertility to personality[1] (Ajima & Ubana, 2018). Ikenga-Metuh (1981) defined African medicine to include herbal as well as psychotherapeutic and spiritual technique (herbal mixtures, ritual objects, incantations and rites capable of changing the human condition for better or for worse). Hence, the African view of health and well-being is a complex combination of medical and psychological applications as well as a combination of the physical and spiritual aspects of the human person.

CLINICAL APPLICATIONS OF ATR IN DIAGNOSIS AND TREATMENT OF CLIENTS OF AFRICAN DESCENT

Many adherents of ATR view their illnesses through the lens of spiritual or supernatural causes, which include more challenging situations that are scientifically or medically unexplainable. Similarly, spiritual beliefs influence the diagnosis and the choice of treatment modalities for illnesses, including psychological illnesses (see Danquah, 1982).

Asare and Danquah (2017), a clinical health psychologist and a clinical psychologist, respectively, in the Psychology Department, Methodist University College, Ghana, presented a new health model in the African culture, which takes into cognizance the spiritual component of the treatment of illness, namely the biopsychosocial(s) model, with the "s" representing the spiritual component, in comparison to the orthodox biopsychosocial model in Western culture. Asare and Danquah noted that the causes of psychological disorders or illnesses seem challenging for many Africans and are more easily attributed to spiritual or supernatural powers or beings. For example, the health-seeking behaviors of clients in Ghana were mostly focused on the Charismatic and Orthodox churches, followed by consultation at ATR shrines, where the traditional herbal doctors combine divinization and herbal treatment approaches (Osei, 2004; Danquah, 1982).

Using a case study of a patient with dissociative amnesia, Asare and Danquah (2017) demonstrated how some Africans accept readily the spiritual causes of illness, especially when a diagnosis of an illness by orthodox hospital physicians seems very challenging. The case study is about a thirty-six-year-old female patient, with above-average intelligence and from a wealthy family, who had a very traumatic experience and presented with severe depression with psychotic features, following a breakup in her love relationship about two weeks before her wedding. Upon receiving the news of her fiancé's marriage to another woman, she collapsed, and on revival, was not oriented to place, day, or time, and could not recall any self-identifying information. She had also lost concentration at work. Her family had taken her to a regular hospital for diagnosis and treatment. The result of her magnetic resonance imaging (MRI) did not show any brain injury. However, the client's family was not satisfied with the results from the hospital and thought that their daughter's illness was the result of bad actors, witchcraft, or spiritual attacks. Subsequently, the client's family consulted with a charismatic evangelical church for healing without much success. However, the hospital physician had referred the client to a clinical health psychologist, who successfully diagnosed and treated the client.

The authors argued that in contrast to the great need for greater education on mental illness and the need for psychological interventions, the belief in spiritual or supernatural causes of illness is very strong (Asare & Danquah, 2017). Given that the last treatment of choice for mental illness in Ghana, for example, or other African nations is psychiatry or psychology, Krause (2010) highlighted some of the benefits of incorporating spirituality in the treatment of mental illness, such as hope and the ability to cope with a wide variety of illnesses and stressful situations. This may take the form of praying with the patient and encouraging the patient to visit with their religious leader or religious community for prayers and fellowship.

RECOMMENDATIONS FOR CLINICAL PRACTICE

In this chapter I presented some understandings of ATR practices and observances, with special focus on some historical, epistemological, and philosophical perspectives. I also presented some misconceptions of ATR resulting from an etic approach to the study of ATR. Furthermore, I presented some African understanding of the concept of mental illness or disease, based on ATR. This includes some treatment modalities that are more popularly sought by many Africans, especially when some orthodox medical or health-care treatment appears to be ineffective in treating their psychological illness.

Given the strong belief system of adherents of ATR in the spiritual or supernatural causes of psychological disorders, clinicians are encouraged to take into consideration the belief system or religion of their client. An acknowledgment and exploration of a client's belief system during the initial intake and diagnostic assessment could enable the client to be more trusting of the practitioner as well as facilitate adherence and compliance with potential psychological treatment. Sometimes, the client's spiritual beliefs could be incorporated into the treatment modalities, to help the client adopt a more positive attitude toward his or her recovery from psychological disorder or trauma. Given that there is a tendency to gravitate toward a spiritual explanation of psychological illness, efforts at providing a psychological explanation, with possible somatic or physical manifestations or symptoms of the illness, are highly encouraged.

Granted that the stigmatization of mental illness and erroneous portrayal of psychological or psychiatric illness in many African movies is of grave concern, the use of bibliotherapy and cinematherapy can be instrumental in psychoeducational efforts in shining positive light on mental illness and correcting the erroneous beliefs among this population on the primary causes of mental illness. Hence, there is a great need to engage in public psychoeducational programs and sessions in communities with high density of people of African descent to reduce or eliminate the stigma attached to mental illness and facilitate a better understanding of the causes of mental illness, without completely disparaging their ATR. Many traditional Africans are attuned to some bibliotherapy (e.g., storytelling and poetry) and/or cinematherapy (e.g., art, music, and dance), and some find them effective in the treatment of depression or anxiety. Hence, some clinicians may consider exploring these options in their treatment and work with their African clients.

It is equally important to correct the misconception among many Africans with regard to seeking psychological treatment in orthodox hospitals or mental health centers, or hospital-affiliated psychological departments, which are effective in the treatment of psychological illnesses. Hence, some health promotional videos or other media (e.g., podcasts) could be produced or used for psychoeducational purposes to educate the public on mental health and psychological illnesses. Some videos or podcasts could also be produced to promote various positive and successful treatment outcomes. This may require some collaboration with some playwrights of African movies or short films with the specific intent of educating the public on positive understanding or portrayal of some psychological illnesses and treatment. This suggestion may be viewed as outside the scope of this book.

Therapists in clinical practice should avoid the use of derogative terms to wrongly describe ATR. Hence, clinicians should familiarize themselves with these terms to avoid mistakenly using them in their work with African clients.

African concept of self or person is fundamentally connected to the community to which the person belongs. Hence, work with Africans should take into consideration the community of the client and explore the possible influences and challenges the client may be experiencing from his or her community. For example, explore with the client what is socially acceptable in their community concerning social norms and psychological behavior.

REFERENCES

Abdullahi, A. A. (2011). Trends and challenges of traditional medicine in Africa. *African Journal of Traditional, Complementary, and Alternative Medicines: AJTCAM*, 8(5 Suppl), 115–123. https://doi.org/10.4314/ajtcam.v8i5S.5

Adams, G. (2005). The cultural grounding of personal relationship: Enemyship in North American and West African worlds. *Journal of Personality and Social Psychology, 88*(6), 948–968.

Adjei, S. B. (2019). Conceptualising personhood, agency, and morality for African psychology. *Theory & Psychology, 29*(4), 484–505. https://doi.org/10.1177/0959354319857473

Aina, O. F. (2004). Mental illness and cultural issues in West African films: Implications for orthodox psychiatric practice. *Medical Humanities, 30*(1), 23–26. https://doi.org/10.1136/jmh.2003.000152

Ajima, O. M., & Ubana, E. U. (2018). The concept of health and wholeness in traditional African religion and social medicine. *Arts and Social Sciences Journal, 9*(4), Article 388. https://doi.org/10.4172/2151-6200.1000388

Asare, M., & Danquah, S. A. (2017). The African belief system and the patient's choice of treatment from existing health models: The case of Ghana. *Acta Psychopathologica, 3*(4), Article 49. https://doi.org/10.4172/2469-6676.100121.

Awolalu, O. (1979). *Yoruba beliefs and sacrificial rites*. White Plains, NY: Longman Group.

Awolalu, J. O. (1976). What is African traditional religion? *Studies in Comparative Religion, 10*(2), 1–10. Retrieved September 15, 2019, from http://www.studiesin comparativereligion.com/uploads/ArticlePDFs/268.pdf

Berg, A. (2003). Ancestor reverence and mental health in South Africa. *Transcultural Psychiatry, 40*(2), 194–207.

Child, A. B., & Child, I. L. (1993). *Religion and magic in the life of traditional peoples*. Englewood Cliffs, NJ: Prentice Hall.

Danquah, S. A. (1982). The practice of behavior therapy in West Africa: The case of Ghana. *Journal of Behavior Therapy and Experimental Psychiatry, 13*(1), 5–13. https://doi.org/10.1016/0005-7916(82)90029-5

Freeman, H., Wahl, O., Jakab, I., Linden, T. R., Guimón, J., & Bollorino, F. (2001). Forum: Mass media and psychiatry: Commentaries. *Current Opinion in Psychiatry, 14*(6), 529–535.

Gyekye, K. (2011). African ethics. In E. N. Zalta (Ed.), *The Stanford encyclopedia of philosophy*. https://plato.stanford.edu/archives/fall2011/entries/african-ethics/

Hawass, Z. (2004). *The golden age of Tutankhamun*. Cairo: American University in Cairo Press.

Hillenbrand, E. (2006). Improving traditional-conventional medicine collaboration: Perspectives from Cameroonian traditional practitioners. *Nordic Journal of African Studies, 15*(1), 1–15.

Ikenga-Metuh, E. (1981). *God and man in African religion*. London: Geoffrey Chapman.

Ikuenobe, P. (2006). *Philosophical perspectives on communalism and morality in African traditions*. Lanham, MD: Lexington Books.

Krause, N. (2010). God-mediated control and change in self-rated health. *International Journal of Psychology of Religion, 20*, 267–287.

Makinde, M. A. (1985). Cultural and philosophical dimensions of neuromedical sciences. *Nigerian Journal of Psychiatry, 1*, 85–100.

Mbiti, J. (2015). *African religions and philosophy*. London: Heinemann.

Menkiti, I. (1984). Person and community in African traditional thought. In R. A. Wright (Ed.), *African philosophy: An introduction* (pp. 171–181). New York: University Press of America.

Merriam-Webster's collegiate dictionary (11th ed.). (2019). Springfield, MA: Merriam-Webster.

Merriam-Webster's encyclopedia of world religion. (1999). Springfield, MA: Merriam-Webster.

Morakinyo, O., & Akiwowo, A. (1981). The Yoruba ontology of personality and motivation. A multidisciplinary study. *Journal of Social Biology and Structure, 4*, 19–38.

Odejide, A. O., Oyewumi, L. K., & Ohaeri, J. U. (1989). Psychiatry in Africa: An overview. *American Journal of Psychiatry, 146*, 708–716.

Onu, A. O. (1999). Social basis of illness: A search for therapeutic meaning. In A. I. Okpoko (Ed.), *Africa's indigenous technology*. Ibadan, Nigeria: Wisdom Publishers.

Onyewuenyi, I. C. (2005). *The African origin of Greek philosophy: An exercise in Afrocentrism*. Nsukka: University of Nigeria Press.

Osei, A. O. (2004). Types of psychiatric illnesses at traditional healing centers in Ghana. *Ghana Medical Journal, 35*, 106–110.

Parrinder, E. G. (1954). *African traditional religion*. London: Hutchinson House.

Tylor, E. B. (1871). *Primitive cultures*. Vols. I and II. Cambridge: Cambridge University Press.

Van Dyk, A. C. (2001). Traditional African beliefs and customs: Implications for AIDS education and prevention in Africa. *South African Journal of Psychology, 31*(2), 60–66.

World Health Organization (WHO). (2000). African traditional medicine. African Technical Report Series 1. Congo Brazzaville: WHO Regional Office for Africa.

ENDNOTES

1. Traditional medicine can also be used to cause disharmony as well—for good or bad effects. For example, in a case involving jealousy, envy, or anger toward another person, the traditional doctor, after divination or incantation, may provide a remedy or prescription that would help the client protect himself or herself and possibly cause some physical or spiritual harm to the client's perceived enemy. Sometimes, this may be seen as the result of a curse or witchcraft.

JOSHUA J. KNABB AND

TIMOTHY A. SISEMORE

———————

CONCLUSION

We opened this book with a metaphor about navigation systems that help us get where we want to go, but do not help us determine where to go. Scientific methods are useful and adaptable, but as we have seen in the previous pages, there is more than one destination. This poses a considerable problem for Western psychology.

In this concluding chapter, we briefly survey the past, present, and future of the discipline of psychology, focusing on the place of religion and spirituality in the scientific psychology literature and how to improve it and make it more relevant. Given the vast terrain we have covered in this book, a clear perspective on where we have come from and where we are going only seems fitting. In doing so, we are aiming to better understand how the burgeoning discipline of psychology—still in its infancy at about 150 years old—can improve and grow in the twenty-first century, making room for additional ways of knowing that include those who hold to a transcendent view of reality. We begin by discussing the tension that seemed to develop at the turn of the twentieth century between the new discipline of psychology and the surrounding culture, with the latter often wanting psychologists to investigate spiritual phenomena, which many psychologists steadily resisted. Next, we use the metaphor of a family tree to make sense of the historic relationship between Western psychology and the religions and spiritualities of the world. Then we explore the importance of transparency, acknowledging the "comprehensive view of life" or "worldview" that guides psychologists' investigation of thoughts, feelings, and behaviors, whether wearing the "hat" of a psychologist pursuing scientific knowledge within a nonreligious framework or a member (or invited guest) of a cohesive religious community. By recognizing its heritage and improving its ability to engage in a fruitful dialogue with its overlapping disciplines—philosophy, theology, the hard sciences, and so forth—psychology as a science can maintain a healthy balance between closeness and distance as it continues to mature in its early years of existence.

Following this discussion, we argue that an understanding of the relationship between the discipline of Western psychology and religion and spirituality can be enhanced by viewing the past, present, and future through the lens of the acculturation process, wherein a minority group interacts with a dominant culture, before offering our thoughts on the importance of recognizing the paradigm shift that needs to take place in the discipline of psychology in the twenty-first century. We conclude the chapter by offering recommendations for future research and practice in order for religion and spirituality to have a more prominent place at the proverbial table that is the discipline of psychology.

THE DILEMMA OF WESTERN PSYCHOLOGICAL SCIENCE

Entering the twentieth century, American experimental psychologists were faced with a dilemma. How were they, after the formal founding of their discipline just a few decades prior, going to advocate for psychology as a science when the American public seemed more interested in research on seemingly "pseudoscientific" areas of investigation (Coons, 1992). As religion in the West was on the decline in academic and other intellectual circles, Western psychologists frequently argued for an alternative, more "scientific" worldview, resembling some of the other sciences (e.g., physics, chemistry) in attempting to carefully measure phenomena and establish causal relationships (Coons, 1992). Yet, as the story goes, many psychologists felt the need to distance themselves from any semblance of interest in spiritual and paranormal research (e.g., the transcendent, telepathy, communicating with spirits, demonology, the activities of psychics and mediums), the very areas of inquiry the public seemed most fascinated by, for risk of taking away from the distinctiveness and scientific prestige of their newfound branch of science (Coons, 1992).[1] Certainly, psychologists needed to ameliorate the "fuzzy boundaries" that failed to fully separate them from the overlapping disciplines (e.g., philosophy, theology) that lurked in the shadows of their past (Coons, 1992), as well as protect against the label of "soft science."

Ultimately, these initial "fuzzy boundaries" between psychological science and religion and spirituality may have led, at least in part, to some of the identity problems and reactivity in present-day Western psychology, with the discipline often overcorrecting itself by severing many of its ties to its ancestors. In distancing itself from some of the seemingly "nonscientific" disciplines (e.g., philosophy, theology), attempting to be something it is not (e.g., physics, chemistry), and being unwilling to investigate some of the interests of the wider public (e.g., spirituality), Western psychology, we argue, may have some "soul searching" to do of its own, especially in a rapidly changing world that has access to a marketplace of diverse perspectives. In other words, given that both Western psychology and religion and spirituality attempt to answer similar questions about life (e.g., "Who are we?" "Where are we?" "What is wrong" "What is the solution") (see Wright, 1992), we wonder why there is not more engaging dialogue with, and appreciation for, psychology's ancestors in this contemporary, global amalgam of differing cultures and disciplines.

WESTERN PSYCHOLOGY, RELIGION AND SPIRITUALITY, AND THE "FAMILY TREE"

To offer a fitting metaphor, Western psychology at times functions like an adolescent in its relationship with the various disciplines that have existed for thousands of years, prioritizing independence and self-sufficiency in its youth and struggling to distance itself from its family tree. In this effort to be autonomous, Western psychology may sometimes fail to recognize the wisdom and life perspectives of its ancestors, including the richness and astute psychological insights of the world religions that have been striving to understand and ameliorate suffering for millennia. Certainly, these other disciplines in the family tree have been passing on well-developed frameworks for generations, offering a "comprehensive view of life" that captures a unique perspective on reality, knowledge, human functioning, health and well-being, dysfunction and suffering, and the change process, on both an individual and communal level.

To take the metaphor further, a family systems framework may help to conceptualize the patterns that have emerged within this family tree dynamic, elucidating a tenuous relationship between Western psychology and religion and spirituality in contemporary society. A "genogram," within a family systems conceptualization, is a tool used by clinicians working with families to illuminate the complex multigenerational history and interconnectedness of an extended family, which can help to capture the meta-perspective that is often missing when we simply examine each individual, or immediate family, in isolation (McGoldrick et al., 1999). Within the genogram, patterns of "differentiation" and "emotional cutoff" may be revealed between the self and larger system, with this "self" in a family system only being understood in relationship to others, given there is a continuum from "sameness" and "togetherness" to "independence" and "individuality" (Titelman, 1998, 2014). In an effort for each person in this family tree to negotiate closeness and distance, "emotional cutoff" may take place, which involves attempting to resolve the unhealthy fusion among generations of a family (e.g., the relationship between parents and young adult offspring) by severing the relationship with distance and disconnection (Titelman, 2014). This strategy, of course, may end up repeating itself from generation to generation, continuing on until family members decide to directly resolve the source of tension (Titelman, 1998). What is more, there can be heightened anxiety and emotional reactivity when family members struggle to fully understand and balance the need for closeness and distance (Titelman, 2014). Still, when a healthy sense of differentiation actually does occur, a solid sense of self and the ability to maintain a certain level of independence and awareness of personal values in the face of uncertainty can be maintained (Titelman, 2014).

To apply this conceptualization to the relationship between Western psychology and religion and spirituality, because psychology as a science has been actively striving to be its own person, it sometimes forgets about its family tree. In an effort to lead rather than follow in the footsteps of seemingly "nonscientific" disciplines (e.g., theology, philosophy) or the hard sciences (e.g., chemistry, physics), modern psychology may engage in "emotional cutoff," which, in the short term, appears to protect against the "fuzzy boundaries" (Coons, 1992) and fusion that leads to a loss of self. Yet, in the long run, Western psychology may never fully heal its relationships of the past, given a lack of dialogue with the world religions and philosophical systems that serve as the proverbial head of the family tree. To differentiate, however, is to maintain a healthy balance between closeness and distance—with psychology recognizing its overlap with other disciplines, yet simultaneously maintaining some of its distinctive features—not severing its ties to the family tree.

With the above said, we believe the present book has made a strong case for the need to repair this "emotional cutoff," starting a more authentic conversation on the ways in which Western psychology can (a) acknowledge its roots, which come from the world religions and philosophical systems from the previous millennia; (b) maintain an awareness of its "comprehensive view of life," which parallels the religious systems of the world (e.g., Buddhism, Christianity, Hinduism, Judaism) in its effort to better understand reality, knowledge, the self, health, dysfunction, and healing; (c) recognize when "emotional cutoff" has taken place because of the tenuous history between psychology and religion and spirituality; and (d) begin a more fruitful dialogue that balances the closeness that can enrich each of the various disciplines of the world (e.g., psychology, philosophy, theology, the hard sciences) with the appropriate distance that is necessary in setting healthy boundaries and carving out a unique path.

To summarize, we believe differentiation involves a more collaborative dialogue, with the discipline of psychology more actively engaging with local cultures to better understand a variety of perspectives from the inside out. Rather than assuming its parents have little to teach, we suggest that Western psychology can learn from the various world religions, given these religious frameworks have been elucidating psychological knowledge for thousands of years. To be certain, the formal discipline of psychology—with nonreligious roots that date back to the Enlightenment—by no means has the monopoly on the scientific method or what constitutes psychological "science."

WHOSE SCIENCE IS IT ANYWAY?
PSYCHOLOGICAL INQUIRY AS A COMPREHENSIVE
VIEW OF LIFE

In this book, we have attempted to shine a spotlight on the inner psychological workings of the various faith systems from around the world. These efforts, in turn, beg a fundamental question as we press forward in the twenty-first century: "Whose science is it anyway?" We argue that, since its founding, Western psychology has by no means had the monopoly on the scientific method when attempting to understand the mind and behavior, given that the various religions of the world ask similar questions about the human condition in their efforts to capture reality, knowledge, the self, health, dysfunction, and healing. In other words, from an indigenous perspective, each culture has the ability to develop its own version of psychology, with American psychology emerging in the last few centuries as one of *many* psychological frameworks for investigating cognition, affect, behavior, and other mental processes.

When American psychology can more confidently acknowledge its family tree, made up of philosophers, theologians, and other pursuers of knowledge who are embedded in local cultures and have cultivated a process for understanding a meta-perspective on the human condition, a deeper appreciation for the various disciplines that have paved the way may start to emerge. Western psychology, therefore, may need to work toward being more transparent about its assumptions, modeled by the chapters we have presented in this book, acknowledging its "comprehensive view of life" in the process. This transparent meta-view, as we see it, is vital to enriching psychology as a science, with psychologists learning to better engage with a more global society that demands contributing "voices" from a variety of local cultures.

To acknowledge this "comprehensive view of life," Western psychology must begin to see itself as one of many "worldviews," rather than as a sort of "pure science" that objectively examines the other frameworks of the world from a neutral, safe distance. To "see the forest for the trees," certainly, means first understanding that Western psychology operates based on a variety of untested assumptions, all emanating from this "life-view," which inform the very theory, hypotheses, and conclusions that hold together its empirical data (Kuyper, 1931). For example, a Western, nonreligious psychologist and leader from a religious community (e.g., pastor, rabbi, imam) may each view the exact same data—derived from carefully controlled empirical observation—much differently, given their distinct worldview assumptions. As a result, psychologists' worldview assumptions should be acknowledged when employing the hypothetico-deductive method of scientific inquiry, since the very theories that precede both the hypothesis and data may be based on the lived experiences and "life-view" of the researcher, not the "science" on its own.

Fortunately, in the last two decades, psychologists have started to advocate for a dialogue shift, based on the importance of acknowledging this "comprehensive view of life" among both religious and nonreligious communities (Johnson & Watson, 2012). Undoubtedly, we need a big-tent approach, consistent with the aspirations of the present book, inviting a more diverse group of cultures to make sense of the world from various vantage points. Quite often, though, only religious communities are seen as holding a particular worldview. In contrast, nonreligious communities (which we believe includes Western psychology as a formal discipline) may fail to see this proverbial "lens" through which the world is understood (Taves et al., 2018). To move psychology as a discipline in this direction, then, studying the big questions in life is necessary; these questions commonly emanate from several overarching categories (e.g., ontology [a view of reality and the self], epistemology [a view of knowledge], axiology [a view of values, ethics, what is considered good or evil, and change processes], teleology [a view of goals, purpose, and design]) (Johnson et al., 2011; Taves et al., 2018). With this "shared conceptual foundation" (Taves et al., 2018) in mind, psychologists can increasingly recognize their assumptions as such, given that many of the building blocks of "a comprehensive view of life" are untested and emanate from culture, religion, lived experiences, and so on. Conversely, when Western psychology struggles to recognize its own worldview assumptions—even denying they actually exist in the first place—biases can quickly seep into scientific investigations in a variety of ways.

All of this may require a structural revolution in the concept made famous by Thomas Kuhn. After noting how science trains persons to see certain patterns in keeping with the current paradigm, Kuhn (1976) argued that the gestalt must change. He stated further:

Therefore, at times of revolution, when the normal-scientific tradition changes, the scientist's perception of his environment must be re-educated—in some familiar situations he must learn to see a new gestalt. After he has done so the world of his research will seem, here and there, incommensurable with the one he had inhabited before. (p. 134)

In sum, by acknowledging these overarching categories for explaining life, we are advocating for the amelioration of Western psychology's position of neutrality (Slife & Whoolery, 2006), given that Western psychology as a discipline emanates from naturalism, which is in contrast with the religious frameworks elucidated in this book. With naturalism, a distinct set of worldview assumptions may include determinism (a lack of free will), materialism (only matter exists), hedonism (pursuing pleasure is prioritized), and positivism (data are only derived in the natural world and based on sensory experience) (Slife & Whoolery, 2006). With more transparency, Western psychology can make more room for the world religions and spiritualities in this book—which we have explored from the "inside out"—as well as recognize that (a) many perspectives in Western psychology emanate from unacknowledged worldview assumptions, which should not be conflated with empirical observation in and of itself, and (b) worldviews, whether nonreligious or religious, "have powerful effects on cognition and behavior" (Koltko-Rivera, 2004). When examining these sometimes conflicting worldviews more closely, we can see that we are often talking about differing cultures, including how such cultures negotiate their boundaries when living in shared communities. Making sense of how these cultures interact with one another, therefore, may be helpful for us to better understand the path ahead in the twenty-first century.

WESTERN PSYCHOLOGY, RELIGION AND SPIRITUALITY, AND ACCULTURATION

Acculturation typically refers to the ways in which a minority culture adjusts to the surrounding dominant culture. As one model to explain this interaction, Berry and colleagues (2011) offered several ways that people tend to orient themselves to the cultural surround, presented along two continua—the ability to maintain the culture of origin and the ability to relate to the surrounding culture. With "separation," an individual prioritizes his or her culture of origin and remains separated from the surrounding culture, whereas "marginalization" captures the individual's desire to neither hold on to the culture of origin nor interact with the dominant culture. "Assimilation" leads to the individual adopting the cultural identity of the surrounding culture, but at the expense of his or her culture of origin, with "integration" revealing the individual's efforts to remain connected to his or her cultural heritage, while, at the same time, attempting to relate to the dominant culture. As Berry revealed, these four different approaches can lead to very different outcomes.

In the context of our current conversation, it appears as though Western psychology has attempted to separate itself from its surrounding religious cultures, traced back to its formal founding and corresponding "fuzzy boundaries" (Coons, 1992) with other disciplines. As a way to carve out their own path, therefore, we believe many Western psychologists have mistakenly attempted to completely isolate themselves from other disciplines in the academy, along with the worldview assumptions of their surrounding religious communities. This approach seems to become even more apparent when Western psychologists have attempted to study religion and spirituality, given their emphasis on developing etic perspectives that are divorced from the very religious groups they are trying to understand, consistent with a separation strategy that leads to segregation (Berry et al., 2011). On the other hand, as we move further into the twenty-first century, we suggest that integration is an acculturation strategy that is most fitting for Western psychology, which leads to multiculturalism, a more indigenous approach to psychological inquiry, and a plurality of worldview perspectives (Berry et al., 2011). Ultimately, throughout this book, we are arguing for nothing short of a paradigm shift in how the discipline of psychology engages with religious and spiritual communities.

WESTERN PSYCHOLOGY, RELIGION AND SPIRITUALITY, AND PARADIGM SHIFTS

As we conclude this book, we are advocating for a paradigm shift in both the general psychology and psychology of religion literatures, with the discipline of psychology—which is only in its adolescence, in terms of the maturation process that has been slowly taking place for such a new discipline—acknowledging the wisdom of its ancestors and recognizing the need to interact with its family tree in a more balanced manner. If the scientific method is about careful observation, no one discipline has the monopoly on "science," and using the hypothetico-deductive approach means different cultures should be able to generate their own theories, hypotheses, and conclusions, given that much of theory is based on worldview assumptions, not "pure science." This shift can begin to occur when psychologists strive to be more transparent about the differences between science as merely empirical observation and the worldview assumptions that add the color, shape, and texture to such observations.

Thomas Kuhn in 1962 wrote *The Structure of Scientific Revolutions*, a groundbreaking work in which he presented several phases that take place when a discipline in the sciences changes its views and methods of investigation. With the first phase, scientists have certain ideas and methods of inquiry that are relatively fixed, with the second phase involving the accumulation of evidence to suggest the current paradigm needs to be questioned. In the third phase, a new paradigm emerges to replace the existing paradigm, with some scientists reluctant to embrace this change.

As we enter the third decade of the twenty-first century, we argue for a paradigm shift, with the discipline of psychology (a) recognizing its historic tension with religion and spirituality, based in part on its desire to be a unique and separate discipline; (b) acknowledging its naturalistic worldview assumptions, which influence its theories, hypotheses, and conclusions; (c) gaining more insight into the notion that communities with differing worldviews may interpret psychological data in much different ways, given that theories emanate from untested worldview assumptions; (d) balancing etic and emic strategies for understanding and intervening with local communities; (e) making more room for religious psychologists to influence the field, given their inside-out perspective when engaging with local religious and spiritual communities; and (f) attempting to more genuinely meet the needs of the surrounding culture by recognizing the importance that religion and spirituality play in the lives of many faith communities. Before concluding the chapter and book, though, we would like to offer recommendations for the future for both general psychology and the psychology of religion and spirituality.

WESTERN PSYCHOLOGY, THE PSYCHOLOGY OF RELIGION AND SPIRITUALITY, AND THE PATH AHEAD

Although by no means exhaustive, we believe the following recommendations can help shift the conversation in the psychology literature as we continue to evolve in the twenty-first century:

1. The Western psychology literature should acknowledge its most common worldview assumptions (e.g., ontology, epistemology, axiology, teleology) (Johnson, 2019), such as determinism, hedonism, materialism, and positivism (Slife & Whoolery, 2006), including the impact these assumptions have on the development of theory, study hypotheses, and conclusions. Although, within the scientific method, data should be collected in a careful manner within controlled conditions, worldview assumptions invariably impact the ways in which psychologists develop and refine theory.

2. Scholars in the field of Western psychology should recognize that psychology as a discipline, broadly defined, is not innately secular and nonreligious (Kuyper, 1931). Rather, philosophers, theologians, and other careful thinkers throughout the ages have also been attempting to understand the human condition. Certainly, Western psychology does not have the monopoly on science and the

scientific method. Instead, indigenous groups—including religious and spiritual communities—can also use the scientific method to better understand psychological functioning from the inside out.

3. The Western psychology literature should be more transparent in acknowledging its occasional biases toward religion and spirituality (Gorsuch, 1988), which may potentially be traced back to its formal founding as an alternative, "scientific" worldview and early tension with the surrounding culture. At times, Western psychologists may not view religion as a vital part of life, leading to psychology as a discipline relying purely on secular, nonreligious perspectives (Gorsuch, 1988). Because of this, a more fruitful dialogue with religious and spiritual communities can help to make room for theistic perspectives and a more transcendent view of reality.

4. The psychology of religion and spirituality literature should make more efforts to understand the differences between, and unique features within, specific religious communities, rather than mostly pursuing an etic, global strategy for understanding the similarities between religious groups, simply combining them all together (e.g., we might develop measures flowing from a tradition, rather than imposing our current measures onto a tradition).

5. The psychology of religion and spirituality literature should pursue more emic, qualitative studies in order to emphasize an inductive approach, developing theories based on the lived experiences of local religious groups, rather than mainly focusing on quantitative research that starts with an etic theory and hypotheses, which are disconnected from the very communities that researchers are trying to understand. Rather, like an anthropologist who enters into a local group to capture an "insider" perspective, inductive research can help to start with psychological data so as to build theory that is anchored to religious culture.

6. The psychology of religion and spirituality literature should emphasize more emic scale development projects to illuminate the constructs that are both particular and familiar to local religious groups (Knabb & Wang, 2019; Hill, 2013; Zinnbauer & Pargament, 2005), rather than mostly etic scales that combine religious groups together to elucidate global functioning.

7. The psychology of religion and spirituality literature should focus on more emic interventions (Knabb & Vazquez, 2018; Knabb, Frederick, & Cumming, 2017; Knabb et al., 2019), rather than mostly emphasizing accommodative approaches that start with nonreligious, secular theory and merely add on a religious perspective, post hoc. In doing so, researchers can appropriately respond to the local needs of religious groups by developing interventions that are worldview-consistent, not anachronistic in attempting to find, after the fact, consistencies on well-being, suffering, and psychological change between an already-developed secular, nonreligious approach and a particular religious community.

8. The psychology of religion and spirituality literature should attempt to balance basic and applied research by interacting more closely with religious communities in order to develop and evaluate intervention programs that are responsive to local groups' actual needs. In doing so, psychologists who study religion and spirituality will hold the best interests of religious groups in mind. By attempting to actually improve the lives of real people in real religious and spiritual communities, psychologists will ameliorate the tendency to observe religious groups at a distance in an abstract manner. To be sure, because religion and spirituality are experienced by many people throughout the world as a foundational part of daily life, devoutly lived out in the real world, understanding these beliefs and practices can best occur by a joining process to impact change.

9. The psychology of religion and spirituality literature should make greater efforts to study, understand, and operationalize the constructs and "comprehensive views of life" that naturally emanate from the actual sacred texts of religious communities. Since theology is intertwined with psychology (after all, religious communities have carefully documented their beliefs and practices, which offer a psychological framework that has been passed on from generation to generation), rich psychological knowledge is available in local communities' sacred texts and doctrines (Pankalla & Kosnik, 2018).

CONCLUSION

Since its formal founding in the nineteenth century, psychology as a discipline has helped humans to capture and understand the mind and behavior through careful observation in controlled settings. As labs began to form in American psychology, psychologists increasingly employed the scientific method and a mechanical understanding of psychological functioning to carefully observe and document cause-and-effect relationships. In doing so, like physics, psychologists emphasized the importance of elucidating *how* psychological processes work, which is a tremendous benefit to contemporary society, but not *why* they are there (Perlman, 2004).

In the study of religion and spirituality, psychologists have commonly kept their distance when studying religious and spiritual functioning among faith communities, pursuing an etic, "outsider" understanding of the beliefs and practices of religious groups by developing their own theories that precede, and conclusions that emanate from, the collection of data on religious and spiritual variables. Yet, in doing so, like a navigation system that is limited in its ability to only reveal the how of travel, Western psychologists have yet to fully understand the most salient beliefs and practices that are at the core of religious and spiritual functioning. To be certain, like a navigation system that is only meant to offer the how of human travel, imperfectly captured with mere pixels and graphics on a computer screen, such a system by no means reveals the actual lived experience of traveling to one place or another, nor does it offer an understanding of the why, who, where, and what of traveling from here to there. The intentions and why of travel, of course, can only come from the traveler.

By dually surveying the history of the indigenous psychology movement and the limitations of Western psychological science, this book has sought to offer a path forward that captures the real-life experience of travel. What is more, in providing an insider understanding of religious and spiritual life within the well-developed faith communities of the world, our hope is that a paradigm shift will begin to take place in both general psychology and the psychology of religion and spirituality.

Culture, from our perspective, is foundational to understanding psychological life, rather than something that is simply added on post hoc to secular, nonreligious theory and research. As Western psychologists increasingly interact with diverse communities on a more intimate level, developing theories and research agendas that start with these local perspectives in mind, our hope is that the psychology literature will begin to prioritize the documentation of unmediated experiences that go to the actual source, rather than solely viewing psychological life through a navigation screen that lacks the sights, sounds, smells, touches, and tastes of a direct encounter. These unmediated experiences, to be sure, take place when researchers shift from an etic, distant observation method to a closer emic strategy that honors the richness of religion and spirituality. Ultimately, Western psychology is one of many ways to understand reality, knowledge, goals and purpose, values, and so forth. Thus, we conclude with a plea for a more fruitful dialogue, wherein psychologists recognize the difference between the theories they develop, conclusions they draw, and data they collect, as well as the notion that the scientific method has its limitations in fully capturing the human condition.

REFERENCES

Berry, J., Poortinga, Y., Breugelmans, S., Chasiotis, A., & Sam, D. (2011). *Cross-cultural psychology: Research and applications.* (3rd ed.). New York: Cambridge University Press.

Coons, D. (1992). Testing the limits of sense and science: American experimental psychologists combat spiritualism, 1880–1920. *American Psychologist, 47*, 143–151.

Gorsuch, R. (1988). Psychology of religion. *Annual Review of Psychology, 39*, 201–221.

Hill, P. (2013). Measurement assessment and issues in the psychology of religion and spirituality. In R. Paloutzian & C. Park (Eds.), *Handbook of the psychology of religion and spirituality* (2nd ed., pp. 48–74). New York: Guilford.

Johnson, E. (Chair). (2019, August). *Worldviews and human development.* Symposium conducted at the meeting of the American Psychological Association, Chicago, Illinois.

Johnson, E., & Watson, P. (2012). Worldview communities and the science of psychology. *Research in the Social Scientific Study of Religion, 23*, 269–283.

Johnson, K., Hill, E., & Cohen, A. (2011). Integrating the study of culture and religion: Toward a psychology of worldview. *Social and Personality Psychology Compass, 5*, 137–152.

Knabb, J., Frederick, T., & Cumming, G. (2017). Surrendering to God's providence: A three-part study on providence-focused therapy for recurrent worry (PFT-RW). *Psychology of Religion and Spirituality, 9*, 180–196.

Knabb, J., & Vazquez, V. (2018). A randomized controlled trial of a two-week Internet-based contemplative prayer program for Christians with daily stress. *Spirituality in Clinical Practice, 5*, 37–53.

Knabb, J., Vazquez, V., Garzon, F., Ford, K., Wang, K., Conner, K., ... & Weston, D. (2019). Christian meditation for repetitive negative thinking: A multi-site randomized trial examining the effects of a four-week preventative program. *Spirituality in Clinical Practice*. Advance online publication.

Knabb, J., & Wang, K. (2019). The Communion with God Scale: Shifting from an etic to emic perspective to assess fellowshipping with the Triune God. *Psychology of Religion and Spirituality*. Advance online publication.

Koltko-Rivera, M. (2004). The psychology of worldviews. *Review of General Psychology, 8*, 3–58.

Kuhn, T. (1962). *The structure of scientific revolutions*. Chicago: University of Chicago Press.

Kuhn, T. (1976). Scientific revolutions as changes of worldview. In S. G. Harding (Ed.), *Can theories be refuted: Essays on the Duhem-Quine thesis* (pp. 133–154). Boston: D. Reidel Publishing.

Kuyper, A. (1931). *Lectures on Calvinism: Six lectures delivered at Princeton University*. Grand Rapids, MI: Wm. B. Eerdmans Publishing Company.

McGoldrick, M., Gerson, R., & Shellenberger, S. (1999). *Genograms: Assessment and intervention*. New York: W. W. Norton & Company.

Pankalla, A., & Kosnik, K. (2018). Religion as an invaluable source of psychological knowledge: Indigenous Slavic psychology of religion. *Journal of Theoretical and Philosophical Psychology, 38*, 154–164.

Perlman, M. (2004). The modern philosophical resurrection of teleology. *The Monist, 87*, 3–51.

Slife, B., & Whoolery, M. (2006). Biased against the worldview of many religious people? *Journal of Psychology and Theology, 34*, 217–231.

Taves, A., Asprem, E., & Ihm, E. (2018). Psychology, meaning making, and the study of worldviews: Beyond religion and non-religion. *Psychology of Religion and Spirituality, 10*, 207–217.

Titelman, P. (Ed.). (1998). *Clinical applications of Bowen family systems theory*. New York: Routledge.

Titelman, P. (Ed.). (2014). *Differentiation of self: Bowen family systems theory perspectives*. New York: Routledge.

White, C. (2008). A measured faith: Edwin Starbuck, William James, and the scientific reform of religious experience. *Harvard Theological Review, 101*, 431–450.

Wright, N. (1992). *The New Testament and the people of God*. Minneapolis: Fortress Press.

Zinnbauer, B., & Pargament, K. (2005). Religiousness and spirituality. In R. Paloutzian & C. Park (Eds.), *Handbook of the psychology of religion and spirituality* (pp.
21–42). New York: Guilford.

ENDNOTES

1. Here, though, we wish to acknowledge that there was an active group of psychologists around this time researching the psychology of religion (e.g., William
James, Edwin Starbuck, G. Stanley Hall) (see White, 2008).

ACKNOWLEDGMENTS

I am overwhelmed by the graciousness so many people have shown in helping bring this book into print. Thanks to Louise Sundararajan for her leadership in the area of indigenous psychology, and to Ralph Hood who was instrumental in connecting us to some of the authors. I am grateful to Carrie York Al-Karam for working with me in the initial visioning of this book. A heartfelt thanks to Josh Knabb, whose keen eye and clear thinking have improved the project, and to all of the contributors who have worked so tirelessly with us. Finally, and most importantly, thank you to my wife, Ruthie, who consistently is the wind beneath my wings. —*TAS*

I would like to thank my wife, Adrienne, and children, Emory and Rowan, who regularly help me to see the foundational role of spiritual health in daily life. Also, thanks to my coeditor, Tim Sisemore, and each of the chapter authors from around the world, who have generously contributed their "insider" knowledge to this important conversation on an emic approach to the psychology of religion and spirituality. Finally, I would like to thank the staff at Templeton Press, including Angelina Horst, who has offered helpful comments each step of the way in order to strengthen this writing project.—*JJK*

ABOUT THE EDITORS

JOSHUA KNABB, PSYD, ABPP, is a board-certified clinical psychologist and the director of the Doctor of Psychology (PsyD) in Clinical Psychology Program in the College of Behavioral and Social Sciences at California Baptist University. He is the incoming editor for the *Journal of Psychology and Christianity* and author of several books with Routledge, including *Faith-Based ACT for Christian Clients: An Integrative Treatment Approach* and *The Compassion-Based Workbook for Christian Clients: Finding Freedom from Shame and Negative Self-Judgments.*

TIMOTHY SISEMORE, PHD, is a clinical psychologist and professor at California Baptist University. He is also past president of the Society for the Psychology of Religion and Spirituality (APA Division 36).

ABOUT THE
CONTRIBUTORS

M. TODD BATES, PHD, is a professor of theology and dean of the School of Christian Thought at Houston Baptist University. Dr. Bates has written broadly in the areas of philosophy, theology, rhetoric, and education. He received his MDiv from Beeson Divinity School, Samford University, and as an ordained minister has pastored churches in Alabama, Florida, and Texas. Research interests include phenomenology, philosophical anthropology, and cultural studies.

AL DUECK, PHD, is Distinguished Professor of Cultural Psychologies at Fuller Theological Seminary's Graduate School of Psychology. He has encouraged research in indigenous spiritualities in Guatemala, Kenya, and China. His work in China was funded through grants from the John Templeton Foundation.

SAYYED MOHSEN FATEMI, PHD, is presently an associate professor of psychology and the chair of the Desk of North America at Ferdowsi University of Mashhad. Dr. Fatemi is also an adjunct faculty member in the Graduate Program in Psychology in the Department of Psychology at York University, Canada. He completed his postdoctoral studies at Harvard University in the Department of Psychology, where he has also served as a teaching fellow, an associate, and a fellow. He has published with Oxford University Press, Cambridge University Press, Wiley, Springer, Routledge, Lexington, Palgrave McMillan, American Psychological Association (APA), and the American Psychiatric Association.

JACQUELINE S. GRAY, PHD, is associate director of the Center for Rural Health at the School of Medicine and Health Sciences at the University of North Dakota. She oversees indigenous programs through the center including the National Indigenous Elder Justice Initiative and the National Resource Center on Native American Aging. Dr. Gray has served as president of the Society of Indian Psychologists (2011–2013) and president of Division 45 of APA: The Society for the Psychological Study of Culture, Ethnicity and Race.

KIN CHEUNG (GEORGE) LEE, PHD, is a faculty member of the Master of Buddhist Counseling program at the Centre of Buddhist Studies, the University of Hong Kong. His areas of research interest include the explication of Buddhism as a theoretical orientation, Buddhist counseling, applied Buddhism, Buddhist meditation, and Buddhist-derived interventions.

SIEW-CHUNG MAH, MS, is a registered clinical psychologist with the Singapore Register of Psychologists. He practices primary care psychology at National Healthcare Group Polyclinics, Singapore, and is pursuing a doctorate in clinical neuropsychology.

CHUN FAI (JEFFREY) NG is currently studying in the Master of Buddhist Counseling program at the Centre of Buddhist Studies, The University of Hong Kong. He is also a certified teacher with the Search Inside Yourself Leadership Institute. His academic areas of interest include Buddhist counseling, mindfulness and Buddhist meditation, contemporary Buddhist practice, transpersonal psychology and comparative spirituality.

INNOCENT OKOZI, PHD, is a priest psychologist with the Southdown Institute, Holland Landing, Ontario, Canada. Prior to the Southdown Institute, he worked with the Roman Catholic Diocese of Portland, Maine. He graduated from Seton Hall University in 2010 with his PhD in counseling psychology and he has taught there as adjunct faculty. Although a citizen of the United States, who was born and raised in Nigeria, Okozi observed some of the traditional religious practices in some of the local towns in Yorubaland (Western Nigeria) and in midwestern Ibo cultures. He also traveled to and worked in some Catholic missions in East, West, and Central African countries, where he encountered other African traditional religious practices, including the Voodoo religion in Abomey-Calavi and Ouidah (Southern Benin Republic).

DOUG OMAN, PHD, is professor of public health, University of California, Berkeley, where he has been teaching since 2001. His more than ninety published journal articles and chapters have emphasized spirituality and religion, especially in relation to health. He has led two randomized controlled trials of a nonsectarian, spiritually based method of meditation developed by a Hindu spiritual teacher, and recently coedited a special issue on spirituality in *Psychological Studies*, the official journal of the National Academy of Psychology, India. He is a former president of the Society for the Psychology of Religion and Spirituality (Division 36 of the American Psychological Association).

ANAND C. PARANJPE, PHD, is Emeritus Professor of Psychology and Humanities, Simon Fraser University, Canada, where he began teaching in 1967. After completing his doctorate at Pune University in India, he did postdoctoral research under the direction of Professor Erik H. Erikson at Harvard University. His publications have emphasized theoretical and Indian psychology. He was born and raised in a Hindu household in India, in which his father taught him how to recite chapters in the *Bhagavad-Gītā*

STEVEN PIRUTINSKY, PHD, is a clinical psychologist whose practice and research focus on the Orthodox Jewish community. He holds a PhD in clinical psychology from Columbia University, is an assistant professor at the Graduate School of Social Work at Touro College, and frequently publishes research in journals such as *Clinical Psychological Science*, *Journal of Affective Disorders*, *Psychology of Religion and Spirituality*, and *Mental Health Religion and Culture*.

LOUISE SUNDARARAJAN, PHD, is founder and chair of the Task Force on Indigenous Psychology, joined by over two hundred researchers around the globe. She is a Fellow of the American Psychological Association, and recipient of the Abraham Maslow Award for 2014, from Division 32. She is the editor in chief of *Palgrave Studies in Indigenous Psychology*.

RACHEL SING-KIAT TING, PHD, holds the bachelor of science in psychology degree from National Chung Cheng University, Taiwan; the master of arts in clinical psychology degree from Wheaton College (APA accredited); the master of arts in theology from Fuller Theological Seminary; and the doctor of philosophy in clinical psychology from Fuller Graduate School of Psychology (APA accredited). She has taught in various countries, including China, Malaysia, and the United States since 2006, and is currently employed as senior lecturer at Monash University, Malaysia. She is an active international affiliate of APA and a licensed psychologist in California.

KEJIA ZHANG, PHD, graduated from Minzu University of China, School of Philosophy and Religious Studies. She is currently working as an associate researcher at Southwest Minzu University, Chengdu, China.

INDEX

Aboriginal communities, 38
acceptance and commitment therapy
  (ACT), 141
acculturation, 286
  integration in, 293–94
  Western psychology, religion and
    spirituality and, 293–94
ACEs. *See* Adverse Childhood Experiences
ACT. *See* acceptance and commitment
  therapy
addictions
  alcoholism, 216
  Buddhism and Hinduism on, 196n3
Adverse Childhood Experiences (ACEs),
  216
Africa
  collectivistic culture in, 272
  neoliberalism and dilemma tale
    of, 47
African traditional religion (ATR)
  ancestral worship in, 267
  animism in, 267–68
  clinical applications of, 278–80
  clinical practice recommendations,
    280–82
  diversity in, 264
  epistemology of, 266, 270–76
  etic approach epistemological
    challenges of, 266
  fetishism or witchcraft in, 268–69
  Greek philosophy and, 270
  health and well-being view of,
    276–78
  history of, 263–70
  idolatry in, 268
  juju in, 269

on mental illness, 273–75
on morality, 273
paganism in, 268
person view in, 271–72, 281–82
polytheism in, 269
sacrifices in, 264–65
savage or primitive in, 269–70
Supreme Being and intermediary
  divinities in, 265–66
treatment in, 275–76
values in, 273
agnosticism
  of science, 19
  in Western psychology, 4
AIRFA. *See* American Indian Religious
  Freedom Act
Akiva (Rabbi), 68
Alaska Native, 198, 236n6
alcoholism, 216
Ali (Imam), 121–22
American Indian Religious Freedom
  Act (AIRFA) (1978), 200
American Indians, 236n7. *See also* North
  American Indigenous spirituality
  Chennai, 46
  Choctaw, 230–31
  federally recognized tribe, 198,
    235n1
  Hopi, 212, 222
  Inuit, 198, 236n5
  Lakota, 202–5, 210, 212, 222–25
  Pan-Indian, 211, 236n9
  state-recognized tribes, 198, 235n2
American Psychological Association
  (APA)
  on communities, 218
  MCC guidelines of, 18

Amish
　culture of, 22
　forgiveness discourse of, 30
ancestral worship, in ATR, 267
Andersson, G., 79–80
animism
　in ATR, 267–68
　on cosmic unity, xii
　of Yi-Bimo, 41–42
APA. *See* American Psychological Association
Arab communities, Mizrachi Jews expulsion by, 61
Aristotle, 31, 271
ARSH higher realm, in Islam, 118
asceticism, in Jewish psychology, 77–78
Ashkenazi Jews, 60
assimilation, 214–15, 293
ATR. *See* African traditional religion
attachment research, 33
attunement, in Buddhist psychology, 156
Atwood, George, 13
awareness
　Hinduism, Buddhism on, xii
　Western psychology on social location, 31–32
Āyurveda, Hinduism and, 182–83, 189

Babcock, Maltbie, 109–10
bechira (choice), in Jewish psychology on free will, 67–68
beliefs
　North American Indigenous forced religious, 198
　North American Indigenous spirituality persecution for, 200–201
　transcendent, 4, 7
believers, methodological atheism study of, 14
Bhagavad-Gita, 35–36, 167, 186
　psychology in, 31, 38–39
　on yoga, 182

bias
　in colonization, 16
　microaggressions and, 17–18
Bible, 7, 36, 103
Black Elk, 200
　on medicine men, 202–3
Black Elk Speaks, 200
Black Hills, Lakota Indians on, 203–5
Blackfeet Tribe, Maslow time with, 212
Body-Mind-Consciousness Trident model, Hinduism and, 178
Bradford, William, 198
Buddhism, 161–62
　on addiction, 196n3
　on awareness, xii
　brief history of, 137–39
　dependent origination in, 142–46
　dukkha as psychopathological symptom, 150–52
　five aggregates in, 146–50, 159–60
　Four Noble Truths of, 139–41
　letting go of desire discourse of, 30
　mental health and, 139–40, 153–59
　on mindfulness, 35, 101, 141, 196n3
　nature of self in, 146–52
　path to liberation in, 152–53
　theoretical assumptions in, 142
Buddhist psychology
　attunement in, 156
　concentration building interventions, 156–57
　counseling case example, 159–62
　Dalal and Misra on, 38–39
　knowledge fostering interventions, 157–59
　Note, Know, Choose Model in, 154
　self-cultivation of counselors in, 155–56
Burroughs, Jeremiah, 103–4

Calvin, John, 114n3
Canada
    First Nations in, 198, 235n3
    Métis in, 198, 236n4
caste system, in India, 174–75
causality, scientific psychology focus
    of, 86
CBT. *See* cognitive behavioral
    therapy
CCS. *See* Christian Contentment
    Scale
CGS. *See* Communion with God
    Scale
Chakkarath, P., 38–39
Chan, J., 16
character traits. *See middos*
Chennai Indians, hearing God's voice
    of, 46
China
    Fei on nationality in, 239
    global religious diversity in, 238
    institutionalized and diffused
        religions in, 237–38
    moral language of, 36
Chinese folk religions, of Han majori-
    ties, 240
    clinical applications and treatment
        view, 244
    on dietary treatment, 244
    on divination and fortune-telling,
        245
    on external and internal forces,
        244
    health and illness view, 242
    person view, 241
    Ren system or individual organ-
        isms, 243
    She Hui system or society, 243
    Tian system or heavenly order, 242
    on witchcraft, 244–45
Chinese native religions, of ethnic
    minorities, 245

clinical application and treatment
        view of, 249–50
    health and illness view, 248–49
    person view, 246–48
    on suffering, 248–49
Chinese Taiwan psychology, of Yang
    and Hwang, 32
Chinese traditional religions
    clinical applications of,
        254–58
    communal space in, 257
    conflicts addressed in, 256–57
    ecological rationality theory, 42–44,
        239, 250–52
    epistemology of, 250–54
    on ethnic identification, 255
    external orientation of, 237
    major types of, 239–45
    mental health, 237–58
    patriarchal, 240
    religious healing in, 256
    semiotic analysis, 252–54
    on suffering and cultural diagnosis,
        255
Chinese Yi
    cognitive styles and emotional
        expression of, 42
    culture and psychological process-
        es study of, 41–42
    ecological rationality model for
        study of, 42–44
    shaman and religious coping, 42
    spirit possession discourse of, 30
    Yi-Bimo of, 41–43, 252, 257
    Yi-Christian, 41–43, 252
Choctaw Indians, creation story,
    230–31
choice
    in institutionalized religions, x
    Jewish psychology *bechira* or, 67–68
    of religion, x
Christian Contentment Scale (CCS), 104

Christian psychology, 24, 85–88, 109–10
    Christian mental health and com-
        munion, 99–100
    clinical applications of, 104–8
    on communion lost, 94–95
    on contentment, 103–4
    creation as communion event, 92
    distinctive lens of, 89
    earthly mindfulness and dysfunc-
        tion in, 100–101
    on God as personal and relational,
        91–92
    health, dysfunction and healing in,
        98–108
    heavenly-mindedness and healing,
        100–101, 106, 107
    history of, 90–91
    on *hupomone* and acceptance, 101–3
    indigenous Christian model of, 97
    knowledge as communion act,
        92–93
    meditation in, 105–8
    on redemption and restoration,
        95–98
    in Western culture, ix
Christianity
    Bible of, 7, 36, 103
    daily practices of, 87, 96, 98
    God as center in, 87
    grace of God in, 16
    humility, meekness, and self-
        esteem values of, 4
    surrounding culture and, 22
    syncretism and, 87–88
    teleology of, 85–87, 89–90
    transcendent God in, 7
    Trinitarian relationship in, 91–92,
        114n1
    worship in, 89–90
Circular 1665 (1922), 199
*The Clash of Civilizations and the Remaking
    of the World Order* (Huntington), 122

clinical applications. *See also* North
    American Indigenous clinical appli-
    cations; treatments
    ACEs and, 216
    ACT as, 141
    of ATR, 278–82
    CBT as, 101
    of Chinese ethnic minority native
        religions, 249–50
    for Chinese Han majorities folk
        religions, 244
    of Chinese traditional religions,
        254–58
    of Christian psychology, 104–8
    DBT as, 141
    EFT as, 115n4
    of Hinduism, 185–89
    for IP solutions, 23–24
    for Islam-based psychology,
        129–33
    MBCT and MBSR as, 141
    of psychotherapy, 23–24, 188
cognitive behavioral therapy (CBT),
    101
cognitive dissonance, 71
    Festinger theory of, 80
cognitive processing, of Yi-Bimo, 43
cognitive styles, of Chinese Yi, 42
Cohen, D., 32–33
collectivism
    in Africa cultures, 272
    communal well-being and, 45–46
    hearing God's voice in, 46
    individuation in, 46
    of Jewish culture, 61
Colombiere, C., 103
colonialism, 49
colonization
    bias in, 16
    decolonization, 49
    neoliberalism and worldviews,
        35–36

North American Indigenous spirituality and, 197–98
science overreach in, 16
scientism and, 16
commandments, of G-d, 70–71
primacy of behavior and, 72
communal space, in Chinese traditional religions, 257
communal well-being, 45–46
communion
creation as event of, 92
examples of, 100
knowledge as act of, 92–93
lost, in Christian psychology, 94–95
Communion with God Scale (CGS), 99
communities. *See also* indigenous communities
Aboriginal, 38
APA on, 218
Granovetter on strong- and weak-tie, 42
hunter-gatherer, 29
independence in WEIRD, 48
Mizrachi Jews expulsion by Arab, 61
normative discourse of, 30
compassion, Islam-based psychology on mercy and, 121–22
concentration building interventions, in Buddhist psychology, 156–57
conflicts, Chinese traditional religions on, 256–57
Confucianism, as diffused religion, 238
Confucius, moral language influence by, 36
consciousness
in Buddhism five aggregates, 147, 149, 160
Hinduism on, 179
contentment, 103–4
context-sensitive thinking, 33
conversion, x

neoliberalism and, 47
cosmic unity, animism and, xii
cosmology, North American Indigenous spirituality and, 203
counseling
Buddhist psychology case example for, 159–62
North American Indigenous methods of, 215–16
relationship issues, in North American Indigenous clinical applications, 214
creation. *See also* North American Indigenous creation stories
Christian psychology on communion event of, 92
Oden on, 92
creatures of earth terms, of Lakota Indians, 202
cultural humility, 22
APA MCC guidelines and, 18
as IP solution, 18–19
cultural psychology, 32–33
cultural-historical psychology, Wundt model of, 40
cultures, 299
Amish and, 22
Chinese Yi study on psychological processes and, 41–42
Christianity and surrounding, 22
collectivism, in Africa, 272
Jewish collectivism in, 61
Jewish tight, 60–61
Judaism and surrounding, 22
language of moral development and, 36
local, 29
psychology scientific study of, 4
Sapir on, 50
Ting and Sundararajan on psychological processes and, 31, 41–42
Western, ix, 13–14

daily practices, of Christianity, 87, 96, 98
Dalal, A. K., 31
David, *middos* of, 69–70
DBT. *See* dialectical behavioral therapy
decolonization, 49
dependent origination, in Buddhism, 142
 metaphor for, 143
 therapeutic models for, 145–46
Descartes, Rene, 271–72
dialectical behavioral therapy (DBT), 141
dietary treatment, Chinese Han folk religions on, 244
diffused religions, x
 in China, 237–38
 of Confucianism and Taoism, 238
 native and folk religion in, 238, 240
dilemma tale, neoliberalism and Africa, 47
discourse
 Amish forgiveness, 30
 Buddhism letting go of desire, 30
 Chinese Yi spirit possession, 30
 communities normative, 30
 Pentecostalism hearing of God's voice, 30, 46
 of serpent-handling groups, 30
diversity
 in ATR, 264
 China global religious, 238
divinations
 in ATR, 264–66
 in Chinese Han folk religions, 245
divine justice, 73
dukkha as psychopathological symptom, in Buddhism, 150–52
Duran, B., 201
Duran, E., 201

ecological rationality model, 239, 250–52
 of Chinese Yi study, 42–44
economy, neoliberalism and, 35

EFT. *See* emotionally focused couple therapy
El Salvador psychology, of Martín-Baró, 32
emic approach, 5–6, 299
 of first-person perspective, 21
 to internal point of view, 87
 of IP, 18, 34
 psychology of religion and spirituality literature on, 296, 297
emotional cutoffs, in family systems, 288, 289
emotional expression
 of Chinese Yi, 42
 of Yi-Christian, 43
emotionally focused couple therapy (EFT), 115n4
emotions, cultural psychology and, 33
empirical science
 hypothetico-deductive method and, 12–13
 personal knowledge and, 11–12
 privileged epistemology and, 13–15
 social isolation and, 10–11
empiricism
 science priority of, 9
 social rationality and, 21
 in Western culture, 14
enchanted world
 religion as knowledge source in, 8
 transcendent believe and, 7
Enlightenment
 knowledge and, 7
 Kohlberg on terms of morality, 36
 science and, 7
Enriquez, Virgilio, 32
epistemology, 9–10
 of ATR, 266, 270–76
 of Chinese traditional religions, 250–54
 empirical science and privileged, 13–15

of Islam-based psychology,
    127–29
multiple, as IP solution, 21
openness, as IP solution, 19
privileged, 13–15
Erickson, Erik, 212
Esav, *middos* of, 69–70
eternal life, Islam-based psychology
    and, 120
ethics
    persons of faith treatment and, 23
    research, 22
    Salanter ethical system, 59
ethnic identification, Chinese tradition-
    al religions on, 255
ethnic minorities, Chinese native reli-
    gions of, 245–50
etic approach, 3, 298–99
    of ATR, 266
    in psychology of religion and spiri-
        tuality literature, 296
experience
    Buddhism five aggregates on mo-
        ment of, 149–50
    James on religious, 9, 12
    language interpretation problem
        on, 11
    personal knowledge and interpre-
        tation of, 11
    psychology of human, 5–6
    science and religious lived, 10
external forces, Chinese Han folk reli-
    gions on, 244
external orientation
    of Chinese traditional religions, 237

Faces in a Cloud (Atwood and Stolorow),
    13
faith
    health benefits of, x–xi
    persons of, ethics and treatment
        of, 23

family systems, emotional cutoff in,
    288, 289
family tree metaphor, in Western
    psychology, religion and spirituality,
    287–89
federally recognized tribe, 198, 235n1
Fei, X. T., 239
Festinger, L., 80
fetishism, in ATR, 268–69
financial aid experiment, neoliberalism
    and, 47–48
First Nations, in Canada, 198, 236n3
first-person perspective, 21
five aggregates, in Buddhism
    consciousness, 147, 149, 160
    moment of experience and,
        149–50
    perception, 147, 148, 159
    physical process, 147, 148, 159
    sensation, 147, 148, 159
    volition, 147, 149, 159–60
Florentine Codex (Sahagún), 37
folk psychology, 29
    mythic spiritualities and, 38–41
    neoliberal psychology distortion
        of, 36
folk religion. *See also* Chinese folk
    religions
    Chinese examples of, 240–41
    in diffused religion, 238, 240
forgiveness, Amish discourse of, 30
fortune-telling. *See* divinations
Four Noble Truths, of Buddhism,
    141
    cause of suffering, 140
    suffering, 139–40
free will
    Akiva on, 68
    bechira, in Jewish psychology on,
        67–68
    middos and, 70
Freud, Sigmund, 80, 84n1

Fuller, Christopher, 171
fundamentalists, Hill on psychology
and, 17

G-d, Jewish
commandments of, 70–71
Torah given by, 62
Torah on names of, 69
trust in, 78–80
The Geography of Thought (Nisbett), 33
global neoliberalism, 36, 48
goals and pathways, in Hinduism,
168–69
God
Chennai Indians on hearing of
voice of, 46
Christianity center of, 87
collectivism and hearing voice of,
46
grace of, 16
love for, xi
Pentecostalism discourse of hearing God's voice, 30, 46
as personal and relational, 91–92
as religion ultimate standard, 20
as transcendent, 7
good and evil inclinations, in Jewish
psychology, 65–67
government, Islam and nature and laws
of, 22
grace of God, 16
Granovetter, M., 42
Greek philosophy, ATR and, 270
guru, in Hinduism, 171–72

habituation, Mishna on, 71
Haidt, J., 80
Hakimi, M. R., 122–23
Handbook of Cultural Psychology (Kitaya-
ma and Cohen), 32–33
happiness. See meaning and happiness
Haudenosaunee creation story, 219–22

healing
Chinese traditional religions on
religious, 256
in Christian psychology, 98–108
heavenly-mindedness in Christian
psychology and, 100–101, 106, 107
rituals, in Chinese traditional
religions, 239
by shamans, 30
WHO on, 276
health. See also well-being
ATR view of, 276–78
Chinese ethnic minorities native
religions view of, 248–49
Chinese Han folk religions view
of, 242
in Christian psychology, 98–108
faith benefits for, x–xi
Hinduism views of, 182–83
in Islam, 118–24
in North American Indigenous
spirituality, 207–11
WHO on healing and, 276
heart as central construct, in Islam-based psychology, xii, 120–21
heavenly. See Malakoot
heavenly-mindedness and healing, in
Christian psychology, 100–101, 106, 107
Hill, Peter, 17
Hillel's aphorism, Jewish psychology
and, 72–73
Hinduism
on addiction, 196n3
on awareness, xii
Āyurveda and, 182–83, 189
Body-Mind-Consciousness Trident
model and, 178
Chakkarath on, 38–39
clinical applications, 185–89
on consciousness, 179
Fuller on fluid polytheism of, 171
future directions on, 189–91

goals and pathways in, 168–69
guru in, 171–72
health, well-being views, 182–83
human nature views, 179–81
Jesus Christ in, 196n1
on karma, 173–74
knowledge and science views of,
175–77
on mental health, 183–85
mindfulness meditation in, 187–88,
196n3
personal and impersonal in, 169–72
philosophical systems in, 172–75
psychological concepts, 177–79
psychotherapy and, 188
pūjā in, 166–67
on reincarnation, 173
self-realization in, 169
stages of life in, 175
statistics on, 165
suffering, change, mental illness
views, 183–85
texts of, 166, 167
tradition of, 166–75
Vedas in, 166, 175–77
yoga in, 168–69, 172–73, 182, 188,
191–92
historical trauma (HT), 216
Holman Illustrated Bible Dictionary, 103
Holocaust, 61
Hood, R., 15, 31, 41, 50
Hopi Indians
Jung with, 212
migration story, 222
HT. *See* historical trauma
hubris, science overreach in, 16–17
human development, Slavic spirituality
on, 41
human experience, psychology of, 5–6
human nature views, in Hinduism,
179–81
humanism, as morality basis, 15

humility
Christianity value of, 4
cultural, 18–19, 22
hunter-gatherer communities, 29
Huntington, Samuel P., 122
hupomone and acceptance, in Christian
psychology, 101–3
Hwang, K. K., 32
hypothetico-deductive method, 12–13
personality psychology and, 13

icon, in semiotic analysis, 253
Ideological Surround Model (ISM), 5
on science as social rationality, 20
idolatry, in ATR, 268
IHS. *See* Indian Health Service
illness social dimension, ATR and,
277–78
The Imitation of Christ (Kempis), 103
impassioned science, 12
impersonal. *See* personal and impersonal
imprecision, of language, 12
independence, in WEIRD communities,
48
index, in semiotic analysis, 253
India
caste system in, 174–75
IP Oriya research, 33–34
on knowledge, 176
on science, 177
Indian Civilization Fund Act (1819), 199
Indian Health Service (IHS), 214, 217
Indian National Academy of Psychology,
Psychological Studies of, 178
Indian Religious Crimes Code (1883),
199
Indian Reorganization Act (1934). *See*
Wheeler Howard Act
indigenization from without, 28n2
indigenous Christian model, of Christian psychology, 97

indigenous communities
  interviews in, 50
  moral witness and, 49
  Narvaez on, 50
  neocolonialism impact on, 49
indigenous knowledge, 4
  morality and, 14–15
indigenous psychology (IP), ix
  Aboriginal communities and, 38
  emic approach of, 18, 34
  of Enriquez, 32
  historical context for, 31–34
  Hood and Williamsons on serpent-
    handling groups, 15, 31, 41, 50
  individuation in, 44–50
  local language of, 31
  of Martín-Baró, 32
  neoliberal psychology and, 34–36
  Oriya of India research, 33–34
  response to Western psychology
    by, 4
  studies on, 41–44
  of Yang and Hwang, 32
indigenous psychology pioneers, 36
  on folk psychology and mythic
    spiritualities, 38–41
  Ricci as, 37
  Sahagún as, 37
indigenous psychology solutions
  clinical applications for, 23–24
  cultural humility, 18–19
  epistemologies openness, 19
  first-person perspective, 21
  future for, 24–25
  innovative research methods, 21–22
  ISM and, 20
  multiple epistemologies, 21
individualism
  individuation in, 45–46
  well-being and, 45–46
individuation, in IP, 44, 49–50
  in collectivism, 46

in individualism, 45–46
  in language, 45
  in neoliberalism, 46–48
insanity, Talmud on, 68, 74
Institutes of the Christian Religion (Calvin), 114n3
institutionalized religions
  in China, 237–38
  choice in, x
integration, in acculturation, 293–94
interdependence, neoliberalism on, 48
internal forces, Chinese Han folk religions on, 244
internal point of view, emic approach
  to, 87
internal spirituality, of Yi-Christian, 43
interpersonal language, problem of, 12
interviews, on indigenous communities,
  50
Inuit, 198, 236n5
IP. *See* indigenous psychology
Islam
  ARSH higher realm in, 118
  government nature and laws, 22
  health and, 118–24
  Malakoot heavenly element in,
    117–18
  transcendent God in, 7
  well-being and, 118–19
Islam-based psychology, 24, 134
  clinical implications for, 129–33
  on compassion and mercy, 121–22
  epistemology of, 127–29
  eternal life and, 120
  heart as central construct in, xii,
    120–21
  Imam Ali on, 121–22
  introduction to, 117–18
  love and, 123–24
  mental illness from self fragmenta-
    tion, 124–27
  mindfulness and, 120

monotheism in, 126
peace and, 122–23
power right relationship with,
    118–19
spirituality as kindness journey,
    119–20
taqwa in, 125
ISM. *See* Ideological Surround Model

Jafari, M. T., 121–22
James, William
    on language passion, 12
    on religious experience, 9, 12
Jesus Christ, in Hinduism, 196n1
Jewish history, 62
    Ashkenazi Jews in, 60
    collectivist culture of, 61
    Mizrachi Jews in, 60, 61
    Second Temple era in, 60
    tight culture in, 60–61
Jewish identity, 61
Jewish psychology, 59, 84n1
    asceticism and, 77–78
    bechira or choice in, 67–68
    good and evil inclinations in, 65–67
    Hillel's aphorism and, 72–73
    Jewish history and, 60–62
    Jewish identity and, 61
    Judaism described, 62–63
    knowledge in, 63–65
    on meaning and happiness, 76–78
    mental illness and emotional
        health in, 74–76
    middos or character traits in, 68–70,
        75
    primacy of behavior in, 70–72
    principles of, 81
    reward and punishment in, 72–73
    Skinnerian behaviorism and, 73
    trust in G-d in, 78–80
    in Western culture, ix
Judaism. *See also* G-d, Jewish

Jewish psychology description of,
    62–63
    of Lurianic Kabbalah, 59
    Maimonides philosophy in, 59
    Mishna and, 62–63
    on morality, 76
    on omnipresence, 78
    Rabbinic or Orthodox, 61
    religious laws of, 63
    of Salanter ethical system, 59
    of Spero, 59
    spirituality focus of, 62
    surrounding culture and, 22
    Torah and, 62
    transcendent God in, 7
juju, in ATR, 269
Jung, Carl, 212

karma, Hinduism on, 173–74
Kempis, Thomas à, 103
Kidwell, C. S., 201
kindness
    Islam-based psychology on spiritu-
        ality as journey of, 119–20
    Prophet Muhammad on, 120
    Zahra on, 119
kinship-based relations, xii
Kitayama, S., 32–33
knowledge. *See also* personal knowledge
    as communion act, in Christian
        psychology, 92–93
    Enlightenment and, 7
    fostering interventions, in Buddhist
        psychology, 157–59
    Hinduism on, 175–77
    India on, 176
    indigenous, 4, 14–15
    in Jewish psychology, 63–65
    religion in enchanted world as
        source of, 8
    science and, 7
Kohlberg, L., 36

Kośnik, K., 39–40
Krumrei, E. J., 79–80
Kuhn, Thomas, 291–92, 294

Lakota Indians
    on Black Hills, 203–5
    creation story, 222–25
    creatures of earth terms of, 202
    Erickson with, 212
    Medicine Wheel and, 210
language
    China and Confucius moral, 36
    experience interpretation problem
        with, 11
    imprecision of, 12
    interpersonal problem of, 12
    IP individuation in, 45
    local, in IP, 31
    of moral development, culture
        and, 36
    passion of, 12
    Polanyi on problem of, 12
    de Sahagún study of Nahuatl, 37
Lawrence (Brother), 106–7
letting go of desire discourse, of Bud-
    dhism, 30
life view, psychological inquiry and,
    290–92
local categories, of religion, x
local culture, 29
love
    for God, xi
    Islam-based psychology and, 123–24
Lurianic Kabbalah Judaism, 59

Maimonides
    on mental illness, 75
    philosophical approach of, 59
Malakoot (heavenly) element, in Islam,
    117–18
Manifest Destiny, 204
Manifesto on Indian Psychology, 177–78

Martín-Baró, Ignatio, 32
Maslow, Abraham, 212
material domain of life, 117
materialism, as scientism, 86
MBCT. See mindfulness-based cognitive
    therapy
MBSR. See mindfulness-based stress
    reduction
MCC. See multicultural competencies
McKenney, Thomas L., 199
meaning and happiness, Jewish psy-
    chology on, 76–78
medicine men, 217
    Black Elk on, 202–3
Medicine Wheel, in North American
    Indigenous spirituality, 209–11
meditation
    in Christian psychology, 105–8
    Hinduism mindfulness, 187–88,
        196n3
meekness, Christianity value of, 4
mental health
    Buddhism and, 139–40, 153–59
    Chinese traditional religions on,
        237–58
    communion with God and Chris-
        tian, 99–100
    Hinduism on, 183–85
    Jewish psychology on, 74–76
    microaggressions and, 17
mental illness
    ATR on, 273–75
    Hinduism views on, 183–85
    Islam-based psychology on self
        fragmentation and, 124–27
    in Jewish psychology, 74–76
    Maimonides on, 75
    middos and, 75
    North American Indigenous spiri-
        tuality view on, 211–12
    Orthodox Jews on, 75–76
    of Saul, 74–75

mercy, Islam-based psychology on compassion and, 121–22
metaphors
for Buddhism dependent origination, 143
family tree, in Western psychology,
religion and spirituality, 287–89
of life, 33–34
methodological atheism, believers
studied by, 14
methodological pluralism, in psychotherapy research, 23
Métis, in Canada, 198, 236n4
microaggressions
bias and, 17–18
mental health and, 17
middos (character traits), in Jewish
psychology
of David and Esav, 69–70
free will and, 70
mental illness and, 75
Talmud on, 68–69
Torah on, 69
mindfulness
Buddhist, 35, 101, 141, 196n3
Christian psychology dysfunction
and earthly, 100–101
Islam-based psychology and, 120
meditation, in Hinduism, 187–88,
196n3
neoliberal psychology and Buddhism, 35
mindfulness-based cognitive therapy
(MBCT), 141
mindfulness-based stress reduction
(MBSR), 141
mind-over-body telos, 258
Mishna
on good and evil inclinations, 66, 67
on habituation, 71
Judaism and, 62–63
on meaning and happiness, 77

religious laws in, 63
on reward and punishment, 73
Talmud and rulings of, 64
on trust in G-d, 79
Misra, G., 31
Mizrachi Jews, 60
Arab communities expulsion
of, 61
monotheism, xii. *See also tawhid*
Monroe, James, 199
moral development, culture and language of, 36
moral language, of China and Confucius, 36
moral psychology, of Haidt, 80
moral witness, indigenous communities
and, 49
morality
ATR on, 273
humanism as basis of, 15
indigenous knowledge and, 14–15
Judaism on, 76
Kohlberg Enlightenment terms
of, 36
as science basis, 14
scientific basis for, 14
Muhammad (Prophet), 127
on heart, 121
instruction of, 129
on kindness, 120
story of, 122–23
multicultural competencies (MCC), APA
guidelines for, 18
mythic spiritualities, folk psychology
and, 38–41

Nachmanides, on rainbows, 63–64
Narvaez, Darcia, 50
Native American Post-Colonial Psychology
(Duran, B., and Duran, E.), 201
A Native American Theology (Kidwell,
Noley, and Tinker), 201

native religion. *See also* Chinese native
   religions
   by Chinese ethnic minorities,
      245–50
   in diffused religion, 238, 240
naturalism, 14
   methodology, 7
nature
   as science ultimate standard, 20
   of self, in Buddhism, 146–52
neocolonialism, indigenous communities impacted by, 49
neoliberal psychology, 34
   on Buddhism and mindfulness, 35
   folk psychology distortion by, 36
   on religion as superstition, 36
neoliberalism, 49–50
   African dilemma tale on, 47
   conversion and, 47
   economy and, 35
   financial aid experiment, 47–48
   global, 36, 48
   on interdependence, 48
   in IP individuation, 46–48
   WEIRD and, 47
   worldviews and colonization,
      35–36
New Agers, 201, 236n8
Nisbett, R., 33
Noley, H., 201
normative discourse, of communities, 30
North American Indigenous clinical
   applications
   ACEs and, 216
   on alcoholism, 216
   on assimilation or traditional cul-
      tures, 214–15
   counseling methods, 215–16
   counseling relationship issues, 214
   for HT, 216
   IHS providers and, 214, 217
   on suicide, 216–17

therapeutic relationships and, 213
   tribal-specific treatments, 217
   White Bison program, 217
North American Indigenous creation
   stories
   characteristics of, 209
   Choctaw creation story, 230–31
   Haudenosaunee creation story,
      219–22
   Hopi migration story, 222
   Lakota creation story, 222–25
   of Yup'ik People, xi, xii, 225–30
North American Indigenous spirituality,
   212–31
   beliefs persecution in, 200–201
   colonization and, 197–98
   commonalities of, 204–5
   cosmology in, 203
   forced religious beliefs of, 198
   health and well-being in, 207–11
   holy people and medicine men in,
      202–3
   Medicine Wheel, 209–11
   mental illness view, 211–12
   person view in, 205–6
   psychology concepts of, 201–4
   reservations and, 199–200
   sacred meaning in, 205–6
   The Sacred Pipe in, 200
   The Sacred Tree in, 200–201, 208–9
   symbolism, 205
   values comparisons, 207–8
Note, Know, Choose Model, in
   Buddhist psychology, 154

objective observation, of religion, 9
objectivity
   described, 17
   Polanyi on, 11
   in Western psychology, 4
Oden, Thomas, 92
omnipresence, Judaism on, 78

Oriya of India study, 33–34
Orthodox Jews, on mental illness, 75–76

paganism, in ATR, 268
Pan-Indian, 211, 236n9
Pankalla, A., 39–40
paradigm shifts, in Western psychology, religion and spirituality, 294–95
participants, researcher relationship with, 22
passion, of language, 12
path
    Hinduism goals and pathways, 168–69
    to liberation, in Buddhism, 152–53
    to suffering cessation, 141
patriarchal Chinese traditional religions, 240
peace, Islam-based psychology and, 122–23
Peirce, Charles Sander, 239, 252–54
Pentecostalism
    first-person perspective on, 21
    hearing God's voice discourse of, 30, 46
perceptions, in Buddhism five aggregates, 147, 148, 159
person view
    of ATR, 271–72, 281–82
    of Chinese ethnic minorities, 246–48
    of Chinese Han folk religion, 241
    in North American Indigenous spirituality, 205–6
personal and impersonal, in Hinduism, 169–72
personal knowledge
    empirical science and, 11–12
    experience interpretation and, 11
    Polanyi on, 21
personality psychology, hypothetico-deductive method and, 13

persons of faith, ethics and, 23
Philippines psychology, of Enriquez, 32
philosophical approach, of Maimonides, 59
philosophical systems, in Hinduism, 172–75
physical impact, of science, 7–8
physical process, in Buddhism five aggregates, 147, 148, 159
Polanyi, Michal
    on language problem, 12
    on objectivity, 11
    on personal knowledge, 21
polytheism, xii
    in ATR, 269
    Fuller on Hinduism fluid, 171
    of Slavic spirituality, 40
power right relationship, in Islam-based psychology, 118–19
The Practice of the Presence of God (Brother Lawrence), 106–7
Pratt, Richard H., 199, 205
primacy of behavior, in Jewish psychology, 70
    commandments and, 72
    Rabbi Elazar and Reb Yehuda story, 71–72
primitive. See savage or primitive
Primitive Culture (Tylor), 267
privileged epistemology, 13, 15
    morality scientific basis in, 14
    science as, 14
Psychological Bulletin, 178
psychological concepts, in Hinduism, 177–79
psychological inquiry, view of life and, 290–92
psychological processes, Ting and Sundararajan on culture and, 31, 41–42
psychological science, Western, 286–87
Psychological Studies, of Indian National Academy of Psychology, 178

psychology. *See also* Buddhist psychology; Christian psychology; indigenous psychology; Islam-based psychology; Jewish psychology; Western psychology
  Aristotle and, 31
  in *Bhagavad-Gita*, 31, 38–39
  cultural, 32–33
  cultural-historical, Wundt model of, 40
  cultures scientific study and, 4
  El Salvador, 32
  folk, 29, 36, 38–41
  Hill on fundamentalists and, 17
  of human experience, 5–6
  improvement of, 285
  moral, of Haidt, 80
  neoliberal, 34–36
  North American Indigenous spirituality concepts of, 201–4
  personality, 13
  Philippines, of Enriquez, 32
  science limitations in, 3
  scientific, 30, 86
  in *Vedas*, 31, 38–39
  Wundt on, 8
psychology of religion and spirituality literature
  on basic and applied research, 297
  on emic interventions, 297
  emic scale development projects, 296
  etic approach and, 296
  on views of life, 297
psychotherapy
  Hinduism and, 188
  research, 23
  teleology for, 23–24
pūjā (worship), in Hinduism, 166–67

queen of sciences, theology as, 7

Rabbi Elazar and Reb Yehuda story, 71–72
Rabbinic or Orthodox Judaism, 61
rainbows, Nachmanides on, 63–64
redemption and restoration, in Christian psychology, 95–98
reincarnation, Hinduism on, 173
religion. *See also specific religion*
  as choice, x
  diffused, x, 237–38, 240
  as enchanted world knowledge source, 8
  on God as ultimate standard, 20
  institutionalized, x, 237–38
  local categories of, x
  neoliberal psychology on superstition of, 36
  objective observation of, 9
religious and spiritual behavior, science on, 3–4
religious coping, by Chinese Yi, 42
religious experience, James on, 9, 12
religious gloss, science overreach in, 15–16
religious laws, in Judaism, 63
religious lived experience, science inadequacy on, 10
Ren system, of Chinese Han folk religions, 243
research
  attachment, 33
  ethics, 22
  hypothetico-deductive method of, 12–13
  innovative methods of, as IP solution, 21–22
  psychology of religion and spirituality literature on, 297
  psychotherapy, 23
researchers, participants relationship with, 22

reservations, North American Indigenous spirituality and, 199–200
restoration. *See* redemption and restoration
reward and punishment, in Jewish psychology, 72–73
Ricci, Mateo, 37
Rosmarin, D. H., 79–80
Rules for the Court of Indian Offenses (1882), 199

sacred meaning, in North American Indigenous spirituality, 205–6
The Sacred Pipe, 200
The Sacred Tree, 200–201, 208–9
sacrifices, in ATR, 264–65
Sadra, Mulla, 129
Sadrolmotaaleheen, 128
de Sahagún, Bernardo, 37
Salanter (Rabbi), 59
Sapir, Edward, x
    on cultures, 50
Saul, mental illness of, 74–75
savage or primitive, in ATR, 269–70
science. *See also* empirical science
    agnosticism of, 19
    empiricism priority of, 9
    Enlightenment and, 7
    history of rise of, 7–9
    impassioned, 12
    India on, 177
    ISM on social rationality of, 20
    knowledge and, 7
    Kuhn on, 291–92
    morality as basis of, 14
    on nature as ultimate standard, 20
    physical impact of, 7–8
    as privileged epistemology, 14
    psychology limitations of, 3
    on religious and spiritual behavior, 3–4
    religious lived experience inadequacy, 10
    theology as queen of, 7
    transcendent beliefs and, 4
science overreach
    in colonization, 16
    in hubris, 16–17
    in microaggressions, 17–18
    in religious gloss, 15–16
scientific method, Western psychology and, 295–96
scientific psychology, 30, 86
scientism
    colonization and, 16
    described, 8
    inadequacies of, 5
    materialism as, 86
    psychotherapy research and, 23
Second Temple era, in Jewish history, 60
secularization, Western culture increased, 13–14
self
    Buddhism on nature of, 146–52
    -cultivation of counselors, in Buddhist psychology, 155–56
    -esteem, Christianity and value of, 4
    fragmentation, Islam-based psychology on mental illness from, 124–27
    -realization, in Hinduism, 169
semiotic analysis, in Chinese traditional religions, 239, 252–54
sensation, in Buddhism five aggregates, 147, 148, 159
serpent-handling groups
    discourse of, 30
    Hood and Williamson on, 15, 31, 41, 50
shamans
    Chinese Yi assistance of, 42
    healing by, 30
    Yi-Bimo use of, 43

She Hui system, of Chinese Han folk
religions, 243
Skinnerian behaviorism, 80
   Jewish psychology and, 73
Slavic spirituality
   on human development, 41
   Pankalla and Kośnik on, 39–40
   polytheistic, 40
   soul in, 40–41
sleep paralysis, Thai Buddhists on, 45
snake handling groups. *See* serpent-
handling groups
social isolation, empirical science and,
10–11
social location, Western psychology
awareness of, 31–32
social rationality
   empiricism and, 21
   ISM on science as, 20
Society of Indian Psychologists, 217–18
Sohrevardee, Shahabeddin, 128
soul
   permutations of, x
   in Slavic psychology, 40–41
Spero, Moshe Halevi, 50
spirit possession discourse, of Chinese
Yi, 30
spirituality. *See also* North American
Indigenous spirituality; Slavic spirituality
   Judaism focus on, 62
   as kindness journey, in Islam-based
psychology, 119–20
   Yi-Christian internal, 43
stages of life, in Hinduism, 175
state-recognized tribes, 198, 235n2
statisticism, 8
Stolorow, Robert, 13
strong-tie culture, 42
   of Yi-Bimo, 43, 252
The Structure of Scientific Revolutions
(Kuhn), 294

suffering
   in Buddhism Four Noble Truths,
139–40
   cause of, Buddhism Four Noble
Truths on, 140
   Chinese native religions on,
248–49
   Chinese traditional religions on,
255
   path to cessation of, 141
suicide, North American Indigenous
clinical applications on, 216–17
Sundararajan, Louise, xiii, 31, 41–42
superstition, neoliberal psychology on
religion as, 36
Supreme Being and intermediary divinities, in ATR, 264–66
symbol, in semiotic analysis, 253
symbolism, in North American Indigenous spirituality, 205
syncretism, Christianity and, 87–88

Talmud
   on *bechira* or choice, 68
   on good and evil inclinations, 66–67
   on insanity, 68, 74
   on meaning and happiness, 76–78
   on *middos*, 68–69
   Mishna rulings and, 64
   on primacy of behavior, 70–72
   on reward and punishment, 73
   on trust in G-d, 78–79
Taoism, as diffused religion, 238
taqwa, in Islam-based psychology, 125
tawhid (monotheism), 126
teleology
   of Christianity, 85–87, 89–90
   of mind-over-body, 258
   for psychotherapy, 23–24
texts, of Hinduism, 166, 167
Thai Buddhists, on sleep paralysis, 45
Thanksgiving Day, 198

theology, as queen of sciences, 7
theory
  Buddhism assumptions in, 142
  Chinese ecological rationality,
    42–44, 239, 250–52
  Christian meditation model, 106
  of cognitive dissonance, of Festing-
    er, 80
  tripartite theory of mind, of Freud,
    80, 84n1
therapeutic models, for Buddhism
  dependent origination, 145–46
"This Is My Father's World" (Babcock),
  109–10
Tian system, of Chinese Han majorities,
  242
Ting, R. S.-K., 31, 41–42
Tinker, G. E., 201
Toosee, Khaje Nasseereddine, 128
Torah
  authority of, 64
  on good and evil inclinations, 66
  Jewish G-d giving of, 62
  Judaism and, 62
  on meaning and happiness, 77
  on middos, 69
  on names of Jewish G-d, 69
traditions. See also African traditional
  religion; Chinese traditional religions;
  Yoruba Traditional Religion
  of Hinduism, 166–75
  Yi-Bimo animist, 41–42
transcendent belief
  enchanted world and, 7
  science and, 4
transcendent God, 7
treatments. See also counseling
  in ATR, 275–76
  Chinese ethnic minorities native
    religions view of, 249–50
  Chinese Han folk religions view
    of, 244

dietary, Chinese Han folk religions
  on, 244
ethics and persons of faith, 23
North American Indigenous tribal-specific, 217
tribes
  federally recognized, 198, 235n1
  state-recognized, 198, 235n2
Trinitarian relationship, in Christianity,
  91–92, 114n1
tripartite theory of mind, of Freud, 80,
  84n1
trust in G-d
  in Jewish psychology, 78–80
  Mishna on, 79
  Talmud on, 78–79
Trustful Surrender to Divine Providence
  (Colombiere), 103
Turtle Island, 197, 204
Tylor, E. B., 267

ultimate standard
  religion on God as, 20
  science on nature as, 20
Upanishads, 167

values
  in ATR, 273
  of Christianity humility, meekness
    and self-esteem, 4
  North American Indigenous spiri-
    tuality comparisons of, 207–8
Vedas
  in Hinduism, 166, 175–77
  psychology in, 31, 38–39
Vespucci, Amerigo, 197
volition, in Buddhism five aggregates,
  147, 149, 159–60

Watson, P. J., 20
We Have No Idea (Chan and Whiteson),
  16

weak-tie culture, 42
  of Yi-Christians, 43, 252
WEIRD. *See* Western, educated, industrial, rich, and democratic
well-being
  ATR view of, 276–78
  Chinese native religions on, 248
  collectivism and communal, 45–46
  Hinduism views of, 182–83
  individualism and, 45–46
  Islam and, 118–19
  in North American Indigenous
    spirituality, 207–11
Western, educated, industrial, rich, and
  democratic (WEIRD)
  independence in, 48
  neoliberalism and, 47
Western culture
  Christian and Jewish psychology
    in, ix
  empiricism in, 14
  increased secularization in, 13–14
Western psychological science, 286–87
Western psychology, 285
  literature transparency in, 296
  objectivity and agnosticism in, 4
  scientific method and, 295–96
  social location awareness, 31–32
  worldview assumptions in, 295
Western psychology, religion and spirituality
  acculturation and, 293–94
  family tree metaphor, 287–89
  future for, 295–97
  paradigm shifts in, 294–95
Wheeler Howard Act (1934), 200
White Bison program, 217

Whiteson, D., 16
WHO. *See* World Health Organization
Williamson, W. P., 15, 31, 41, 50
witchcraft
  in ATR, 268–69
  in Chinese Han folk religions,
    244–45
World Health Organization (WHO), on
  healing, 276
worldviews, neoliberalism and colonization, 35–36
worship. *See also* *pūjā*
  in Christianity, 89–90
Wundt, Wilhelm
  cultural-historical psychology of,
    40
  on psychology, 8

Yang, K. S., 32
Yi-Bimo, 257
  animist tradition of, 41–42
  cognitive processing of, 43
  shaman use by, 43
  strong-tie culture of, 43, 252
Yi-Christian, 41–42
  emotional expression of, 43
  internal spirituality of, 43
  weak-tie culture of, 43, 252
yoga
  Bhagavad-Gita on, 182
  in Hinduism, 168–69, 172–73, 182,
    188, 191–92
Yoruba Traditional Religion, 263, 264
Yup'ik People, creation story of, xi, xii,
  225–30

Zahra, Hazrat, 119